# The Dream of Reason

ANTHONY GOTTLIEB

# The Dream of Reason

A History of Western Philosophy from
the Greeks to the Renaissance

W. W. Norton & Company
New York • London

For information about permission to reproduce selections from this book, write to
Permissions, W. W. Norton & Company, Inc., 500 Fifth Avenue,
New York, NY 10110

Manufacturing by Maple-Vail Manufacturing Group

Library of Congress Cataloging-in-Publication Data

Gottlieb, Anthony.
The dream of reason : a history of western philosophy from the
Greeks to the Renaissance / Anthony Gottlieb.
p. cm.
Includes bibliographical references and index.
**ISBN 0-393-04951-5**
1. Philosophy—History. I. Title.

B72.G68 2000
180—dc21                                                              00-049012

W. W. Norton & Company, Inc. 500 Fifth Avenue, New York, N.Y. 10110
www.wwnorton.com

W. W. Norton & Company Ltd., 10 Coptic Street, London WC1A 1PU

1 2 3 4 5 6 7 8 9 0

# Contents

# Introduction

The last thing I expected to find when I began work on this book, more than ten years ago, is that there is no such thing as philosophy. Yet that, more or less, is what I did find, and it explained a lot. Determined to forget what I thought I knew, I set out to look at the writings of those from the past 2,600 years who are regarded as the great philosophers of the West. My aim (politely described by friends as 'ambitious' when they often meant 'mad') was to approach the story of philosophy as a journalist ought to: to rely only on primary sources, wherever they still existed; to question everything that had become conventional wisdom; and, above all, to try and explain it all as clearly as I could.

As I ploughed through the diverse cast of characters from the fifth and sixth centuries BC who are traditionally lumped together as philosophers, through Socrates, Plato, Aristotle (often bracketed as a trio, but were there ever three more different men?), on to the intellectual therapists of Hellenistic times, through the mystics and occultists of late antiquity, to the first Christian thinkers, the logic-obsessed monks of the early Middle Ages, medieval scientists and theologians, Renaissance magicians, visionaries, grammarians and engineers and on to the beginnings of modern times, the fabric of 'philosophy' – supposedly the oldest of subjects – unravelled before my eyes. Traditional histories, which seek to distinguish it from the physical, mathematical and social sciences, and from the humanities, had drastically over-simplified, I concluded. It was just not possible to confine what is usually referred to as 'philosophy' to a single subject that can be placed neatly on the academic map.

One reason for this is that the place-names on such maps tend to change. In the Middle Ages, for instance, 'philosophy' covered practically every branch of theoretical knowledge that did not come under theology. Newton's subject was 'natural philosophy', a term that was still widely used in the first half of the nineteenth century to cover most of what we now regard as science and some of what we now think of as philosophy. What has been called philosophical thinking is naturally inclined to stray across conventional boundaries. Its wanderlust and insatiable curiosity have often given birth to new areas of thought, which again complicates the task of map-drawing. As we shall see in the first chapter, Western science was created when a few Greek thinkers – those who are known as the first 'philosophers' – were perverse enough to ignore the usual talk of gods and to look instead for natural causes of events. Much later on, psychology, sociology and economics came about largely from the work of people who at the time were called philosophers. And the same process of creation continues today. Computer languages, for example, stem from what was long regarded as the most tedious invention of philosophers, namely formal logic. A small but typical example of how 'philosophy' sends out new shoots is to be found in the case of Georg Cantor, a nineteenth-century German mathematician. His research on the subject of infinity was at first written off by his scientific colleagues as mere 'philosophy' because it seemed so bizarre, abstract and pointless. Now it is taught in schools under the name of set-theory.

The fact is that the history of philosophy is more the history of a sharply inquisitive cast of mind than the history of a sharply defined discipline. The traditional image of it as a sort of meditative science of pure thought, strangely cut off from other subjects, is largely a trick of the historical light. The illusion is created by the way we look at the past, and in particular by the way in which knowledge tends to be labelled, chopped up and re-labelled. Philosophical work is regularly spirited away and adopted by other disciplines. Yesterday's moral philosophy becomes tomorrow's jurisprudence or welfare economics; yesterday's philosophy of mind becomes tomorrow's cognitive science. And the road runs in both directions: new inquiries in other disciplines prompt new questions for the philosophically curious. Tomorrow's economics will be meat for the moral philosophers of the day after. One effect of these shifting boundaries is that philosophical thinking can easily seem to be unusually useless, even for an intellectual enterprise. This is largely because any corner of it that comes generally to be regarded as useful soon ceases to be called philosophy. Hence the illusory appearance that philosophers never make progress.

The psychologist William James once described philosophy as 'a peculiarly stubborn effort to think clearly'. This is a rather dry definition, but is more nearly right than any other I know. True, clarity is not exactly the first thing that comes to mind when most people think of philosophy. There is no denying that philosophers' attempts to think clearly have often rudely backfired. (Any subject that is responsible for producing Heidegger, for example, owes the world an apology.) Still, William James was right to describe philosophy as he did. Even the darkest of its practitioners are struggling to make sense of things, and it is this effort that makes them philosophers. Sometimes the effort does not pay off, but often it does.

To call philosophical thinking 'stubborn' was particularly apt. Bertrand Russell once described it as 'unusually obstinate'. For the one thing that marks it off from other sorts of thinking is its unwillingness to accept conventional answers, even when it seems perverse not to do so from a practical point of view. That is why philosophers often make such excellent figures of fun. The earliest Greek historians of philosophy understood this better than we do today, for their books were peppered with ludicrous anecdotes, some of which may actually have been true and most of which are very much to the point even if they were made up. To disapprove of such lampoons of the eminently lampoonable is to miss the joke at the heart of philosophy. Philosophers have regularly cocked an eyebrow at what passes for the common sense of the time; the punch line comes later, when it is 'common sense' that turns out to have been uncommonly confused. Sometimes the joke goes wrong, of course, and it is the philosopher who ends up looking foolish, but that risk comes with the job.

The attempt to push rational inquiry obstinately to its limits is bound often to fail, and then the dream of reason which motivates philosophical thinking seems merely a mirage. At other times, though, it succeeds magnificently, and the dream is revealed as a fruitful inspiration. This book tries to show both sides of the story of this dream of reason, from the sixth century BC to the Renaissance. A second volume will continue the tale from Descartes to the present day.

# Acknowledgements

Many scholars helped me by making comments, suggestions and criticisms, or by answering my questions: I am most grateful to Jonathan Barnes, Walter Burkert, Brian Copenhaver, the late Father Copleston, John Dillon, Sir Kenneth Dover, Anthony Grayling, Jim Hankinson, Edward Hussey, John Marenbon, W. V. Quine, John Vallance and Martin West. For other help and encouragement, I am grateful to Oliver Black, Daniel Boorstin, Ray Monk, Andrew Rashbass, Matt Ridley, Ileene Smith (whose idea this was), Sir Peter Strawson, and my wife, Miranda Seymour. Two successive editors of *The Economist*, Rupert Pennant-Rea and Bill Emmott, deserve thanks for allowing me long leaves of absence to work on the book.

# PART ONE

# I

# The Archetypes:
## *the Milesians*

Nobody will ever be sure who started it. It could be that some poor genius invented philosophy and then fell into the abyss of unwritten history before he could announce himself to posterity. There is no reason to think that there was such a person, but then there wouldn't be. Happily, there are at least records of one start to philosophy, even if one cannot be certain that it was not preceded by other false starts.

Nowadays they are soberly studied in libraries and universities, but many of the earliest known philosophers made their first reputations in what could be regarded as a branch of show business. They appeared in public, often in resplendent clothes, and held discourses or recited poems. Such performances attracted passing audiences, devoted followers and sometimes ridicule. Some of these men were more outgoing than others. At one extreme is an itinerant poet, Xenophanes, who – purporting to be ninety-two at the time – apparently claimed to have spent 'seven and sixty years . . . tossing my cares up and down the land of Greece'. At the other is a contemptuous aristocrat, Heraclitus of Ephesus (variously known in antiquity as 'the dark', 'the weeping' and 'the obscure'), who on his own proud admission loathed all sages and the mobs who listened to them, and presumably kept himself to himself. Most of the early philosophers fell somewhere between these two extremes. This was in the sixth and fifth centuries BC, in parts of what are now Greece, Turkey and Italy.

Today these people are generally called the 'Presocratics', which marks the fact that nearly all of them had what some historians in the nineteenth century regarded as the misfortune of being born before Socrates (469–399 BC). One might as well leave this label around their necks; but in fact they were far from being a mere overture to the Socratic opera. As Nietzsche said, they invented the archetypes of all later philosophy. They also invented science, which in those days came to much the same thing.

The first of these miracle-men did not suddenly drop from the sky. Sixth-century Greece was not the dawn of time, and perhaps a case can be made for beginning even earlier, with rudimentary Babylonian geometry or early Greek religion. It may be said that the Presocratics, although fine thinkers, did not invent thinking itself, and that looking at some earlier efforts will help to clarify their ideas. But this is a history of philosophy, not of everything, and we have to start somewhere.

The place to begin is Miletus, one of the Ionian city-states on the coast of Asia Minor (now in Turkey). In the sixth century BC, when Thales, Anaximander and Anaximenes flourished there, it was a rich sea power with many colonies to the north in Thrace and around the Black Sea, and commercial links with parts of southern Italy, the east and Egypt. It was a cultivated place, giving some people the leisure which Aristotle was later fond of claiming to be a prerequisite for philosophy. Writing two centuries afterwards, Aristotle discussed these three men from Miletus several times. He divided early Greek thinkers into *theologi*, who saw the world as controlled by impetuous supernatural beings, and *physici* (naturalists), who tried instead to explain an apparently disordered world in terms of simpler and impersonal principles. He said that the Milesians were the first *physici*.

Many of the Presocratics wrote down their thoughts as well as holding forth in public, but you would hardly know it from what is left today. Their writings have been shattered by time and survive, if at all, only in tiny fragments. For some 2,000 years scholars have been poring over passages of little more than a few sentences, picking at a few words here and there, and depending heavily on secondary sources. Some ancient commentaries on these shards can be relied on at least to attempt accuracy. But even the best of them were written generations, or even many hundreds of years, after the Presocratics lived. Other second- and third-hand sources, such as the writings of the often unreliable but most enjoyable biographer, Diogenes Laertius (who lived in the third century AD), need to be read with at least one eyebrow raised. Diogenes was an undiscerning whale of a historian who swallowed every story that floated by.

4

With these caveats in mind, consider Thales of Miletus. He was famed in ancient Greece for many things, the most famous of which he did not in fact do, namely predict an eclipse of the sun in 585 BC. The eclipse came during a battle between the Milesians' two neighbours to the east – the Lydians and the Medes – which added to its dramatic impact. It made Thales' intellectual fortune. The combatants were so impressed by the fact that there was an eclipse while they were fighting that they laid down their weapons and made peace. The Greeks in general were so impressed by the fact that Thales seemed to have predicted it that they later attributed to him an implausible number of wise words, wise deeds and discoveries, from the proofs of various geometrical theorems to the ability to make vast amounts of money. More importantly, they developed a deep respect for his way of thinking.

THALES.

But Thales did not make a genuine prediction, just a lucky informed guess. In all likelihood he was so far from understanding the true nature of solar eclipses that he would not even have known that the moon had anything to do with it. Fortunately for him he was a well-travelled man and this explains his guess. From the painstaking records of observant Babylonian star-gazers, he would have learned of a cycle that seemed to be characteristic of eclipses in the past. There were certain years in which eclipses might happen and other years in which they could not. The most that he could reasonably have inferred from this record is that there was a fair chance that an eclipse would be seen from somewhere at some time during 585 BC. If Thales claimed anything more precise than that, he was bluffing.

The eclipse was a lucky break for the naturalists' view of the world. Clearly they were thinkers to be reckoned with. This may seem odd when one considers the surviving details of their views, because the theories most reliably attributed to Thales are that magnets are alive

5

and that the world is made of water. He probably also said many other less speculative things, which earned him the respect of his peers as a man of practical knowledge. But even these two apparently outrageous ideas deserve some respect when seen in their proper contexts.

Take water first. One distinguishing feature of what we now call a scientific account of things is that it should aim to be as simple as possible. Thales rather overshot this mark and tried to reduce everything to just one thing, namely water. It seems that he did not actually manage to come up with any watery explanations; these were, after all, early days. But in seeking a natural substance to unify and thus simplify the phenomena of the observable world, instead of making things more complicated by invoking lots of gods, he was at least looking for knowledge in what we now regard as the right sort of place.

It is not clear whether he really meant to say that everything consisted of water in some sense, or merely that it originally came from water. He may well have meant to say both. It is anachronistic but not necessarily too misleading to interpret him, as Aristotle did, as holding that water was the *arche*, a term used by some slightly later thinkers to mean not only the origin of things but also the fundamental substance of which everything somehow consists and to which it will ultimately return.

Either way, water was not a bad candidate for Thales to choose. Unlike the other common elements, such as earth or fire, water can easily be seen to take on different forms, such as that of ice or of steam. It is thus versatile and apparently active. Aristotle, when suggesting reasons why Thales might have favoured water, also noted its intimate connection with life. Food, blood and semen all contain water; plants and animals are nourished by water. Living things tend to be moist, to some extent, and they dry up when they die. Many mythological accounts of the universe also gave water a leading role. The Babylonians and Egyptians both had creation myths in which water played a pre-eminent part. This is hardly surprising since both cultures depended on the rivers around which their people settled. In Homer (eighth century BC), Okeanos, the personified body of water surrounding the circular surface of the earth, is the begetter of all life and possibly of all gods. According to Plutarch (AD *c.*46–*c.*120), Egyptian

6

priests liked to claim that both Homer and Thales got their ideas about water from Egypt.

Thales presumably knew of the Egyptian and Babylonian myths. But this does not mean that he was merely echoing them or even that he first got his ideas from them. It is just as likely that both the myths and his own speculations stemmed in part from an awareness that water is evidently active, many-sided and involved in the processes of life. Besides, Thales made an entirely different use of this awareness. His water is not, like Homer's Okeanos, the brother (and husband) of the goddess, Tethys. Nor is it an amalgam of the three personified types of water in Babylonian cosmology, Apsu, Ti'amat and Mummu, who gave rise to the gods. Nor is it Nun, the primordial water which was father to the sun-god of the morning in Egyptian myth. It is perfectly ordinary water, such as one might swim in or drink. And it is not related to any personified gods, either by birth or by marriage.

Another difference between Thales and his myth-making precursors is that he seems to have felt the need to give reasons for at least some of what he said. He held that the earth rests upon water, and apparently said this 'because it floated like wood and other similar substances, which are so constituted as to rest upon water but not upon air'. The question of what holds up the earth is one that most of the naturalists tried to answer. Instead of dogmatically asserting a solution, Thales thus seems to have tried to reason it out. Water is capable of supporting some things, such as logs; so maybe it supports the earth itself. This reasoning did not impress Aristotle, who pointed out that if the earth needs something to rest on, then so too does the water which allegedly supports it; thus Thales had not really answered the question. And there is another, fatal, objection to Thales' argument: logs may float, but some other things do not. Why assume that the earth would float like a log rather than sink like a stone? Yet even this defeat is a sort of victory for Thales. In order to refute him we have to reason with him, a compliment we would not think of paying the Egyptian priests.

Thales probably deserves the same compliment for his claim that magnets and amber are alive (or have a soul, *psuche*, which in those days meant much the same thing). He noticed that they can cause some other objects to move and can move themselves towards them, and he was trying to account for this mystery by proposing that they have a type of animation. Spontaneous motion is, after all, often a sign of life. We would object to Thales that the power to cause motion is not quite enough on its own to justify calling a stone alive; but this does not mean we can dismiss his ruminations as mere crankiness. Today there is still no precise definition of life, and in the seventh century BC there was barely even a vague one. Thales' apparently outlandish idea may therefore be seen as the natural result of having an inquiring mind at a time when precious little was understood.

Before leaving Thales to examine the other Milesians, there is one anecdote about him that is worth retelling, even if it is by Diogenes Laertius:

It is said that once, when he was taken out of doors by an old woman in order that he might observe the stars, he fell into a ditch, and his cry for help drew from the old woman the retort, 'How can you expect to know all about the heavens, Thales, when you cannot even see what is just before your feet?'

If the story is true, Thales has a claim not only to the title of first philosopher but also to that of first absent-minded professor. At any rate, the story attests to the fact that the connection between philosophy and unworldliness is one that people have long enjoyed making. Socrates tells a version of the same story against Thales in one of Plato's dialogues. And in his play, *Clouds*, Aristophanes tells a similar but coarser version of it against Socrates himself.

The Greeks appreciated intellectual order and liked to establish it wherever it seemed to be lacking. That is one reason why people study them. One facet of this desire to lay things out neatly can be found in the way they wrote their own history: in the ancient sources which tell the story of early philosophy, we find a stately procession of teachers and pupils, each one passing the torch of knowledge to an appointed successor. Thus Anaximander (*c*.610–*c*.546 BC), a slightly younger fellow-citizen of Miletus, was commonly said to be the 'pupil and successor' of Thales, though he may not have studied under him at all. Like Thales, Anaximander was a polymath, and although only a part of one sentence of his *On Nature* survives, there is enough evidence left to say that he definitely wrote a book, with approximately that title (in Greek), and that it covered practically everything. He even drew the first recognized map of the known parts of the earth. What he did not know about nature – which was, of course, plenty – he made up.

This is not to say that he lied, but that he tried to think things out for himself. He speculated about the origin and fate of the universe, the principles that govern natural processes, the composition of the sun, moon and stars, the development of life, the weather and much else. He employed similar images and ideas to explain all the things he saw. Yet in one sense what he did not see is even more important than what he did see. He realized that the best accounts of nature could not always rely on what was directly observable but sometimes had to dig deeper. Instead of Thales' water, he postulated something invisible as the *arche*, or basic stuff, of the world. If the philosophy of Thales demonstrated one essential facet of scientific thinking, namely the urge to simplify and reduce observable phenomena, Anaximander's work exemplified an additional and equally fundamental one: science says there is more to the world than meets the eye.

Anaximander called his basic stuff *to apeiron*, 'the indefinite', primarily in the sense of 'indeterminate'. His term is often translated as 'the infinite', but that makes Anaximander sound more mysterious than necessary. No doubt he did think of the raw material of the world as unbounded, in the sense of 'vast', just as Homer had described the ocean as *apeiron*. But what mattered most to Anaximander was that the basic stuff, whatever it was, should be something with no observable qualities of its own, so that all observable phenomena could be explained in terms of it.

Observable things, Anaximander noticed, tend to come in opposites – hot and cold, wet and dry, for example – and these elements, as he calls them, tend to be in a state of war. They 'pay penalty and retribution to each other for their injustice according to the assessment of Time', as it says in his only surviving words. His idea seems to have been that things encroach on one another (committing their 'injustice') and take turns alternately as victim and avenging aggressor while Time plays the role of referee. Time ordains, for example, that darkness and light should have roughly equal cracks of the whip. We see the outcome

9

of this particular struggle in the orderly sequence of days and nights. Other struggles are going on all the time in a cosmic game of paper-scissors-stone: sometimes fire will attack water by evaporating it; sometimes water will retort by quenching fire.

The notion of elements in conflict, which makes its first appearance in Anaximander, recurs frequently in Western literature. Thus Milton:

> Hot, Cold, Moist, and Dry, four champions fierce
> Strive here for mastery

and countless others. But how do hot, cold, moist and dry come forth out of the indeterminate *apeiron*? Anaximander could say no more than that some sort of process of 'separating out' is involved. His theory may leave several questions unanswered, but it is at least an attempt to deal with some other ones. For Anaximander, the virtue of supposing that everything somehow developed out of an inchoate and indeterminate mass is that it addresses a puzzle which should have troubled Thales, or anybody else who thinks that one of the ordinary elements is the 'principle' of existing things. The puzzle is this: if everything was once water, how did fire ever manage to come about? Would it not have been extinguished at birth? Anaximander's solution is to say that the fundamental opposites were born together out of the indeterminate, so that none of the battling substances had an unfair head start on its opponent.

In more detail, Anaximander's story of the birth of the cosmos went as follows. Some sort of egg, germ or seed containing the fundamental opposites of hot and cold separated off from the indeterminate *apeiron*. This seed grew into a cold, damp mass surrounded by a ring of fire, and the shock of hot against cold gave rise to a dark mist between the two. The cold became the earth and the fire formed the stars. The earth is a flat disc, or perhaps a cylinder, but certainly not a sphere. And, rather oddly, not only are the sun, moon and stars not spheres either, they are instead wheels of fire rotating around the earth, each one enclosed in a hollow ring of mist. These rings have breathing holes out of which the fire peeps. Thus each ring of mist is like the punctured inner tube of a bicycle tyre pumped full of fire. What we see when we look at the lights in the sky are in fact the punctures. And an eclipse is what we see when one of the punctures becomes blocked up for a while.

On this account, as promised, there is certainly more to the cosmos than meets the eye. Anaximander's picture of the heavenly bodies appears a little less bizarre if we try to reconstruct how he came to draw it. It was perhaps the image of a tree growing and shedding its bark that led him to form the idea of stars as rings. Anaximander apparently used such an image to illustrate how a shell of flame formed around the earth in the original separation of the hot from the cold. With this picture in his mind it is easier to see how he could think of the heavenly bodies as wheel-shaped: the earth had sloughed them off like a skin, which at least explains where they came from. All he then needed to account for was why they appear to us as points or spheres of light. This the theory of breathing-holes, or punctures, did for him.

There is another imaginative idea in Anaximander's cosmology which is remarkable more for its sophistication than for its apparent eccentricity. He did not think that the earth needed any sort of cushion – either of water or of anything else – to support it. He held that it rested at the centre of a spherical universe, with everything else circling around it, and that it is this pivotal position which explains why it does not fall through space. It is kept in place by equilibrium, as Aristotle explained (describing Anaximander's view, not his own):

For it behoves that which is established at the centre, and is equally related to the extremes, not to be borne one whit more either up or down or to the sides; and it is impossible for it to move simultaneously in opposite directions, so that it stays fixed by necessity.

Thus the earth is like Buridan's proverbial ass, which, placed exactly the same distance between two bales of hay, could not decide which one to eat and so starved to death in the middle. This idea of Anaximander's is an advanced one in several respects (for our purposes it does not matter that it is also quite wrong, not least in its premise that the earth is at the centre of things). First of all, it is pleasingly mathematical. Like a trapeze artist who jumps into empty space, confident that his partner will swing over to catch him, Anaximander bravely stepped beyond the realm of material support and trusted in a mathematical idea to catch the earth. We do not yet have here laws of motion in the style of Galileo or Newton, which keep objects on their steady courses in a way that can be the subject of detailed calculation. But we do have a universal principle, mathematical insofar as it cites the equal distance from the earth to the edges of the universe, which is used to explain something fundamental. Like his indeterminate *apeiron*, Anaximander's principle of equilibrium is invisible and impersonal, and yet it is as powerful as one of the gods. This idea was a bit too novel for other naturalists, who quickly gave back the earth its material cushion to sit on.

The consistency of Anaximander's story is impressive. Animal life on earth is described by him, in characteristically unmythological terms, as being brought about by the same process of 'separating out' that accounts for the birth of the cosmos. Just as the primeval mist which enfolds the heavenly bodies was formed by the action of hot against cold, so life sprang forth out of the moist because of the stimulus of the sun's warmth. The idea that living things can be generated spontaneously out of warm, moist matter was almost universal until the seventeenth century, when microscopes began to suggest a different story; it even survived into the nineteenth century. Anaximander is also supposed to have held that the first creatures were cocooned in prickly skins, using the same word for this skin or bark that he used in his account of the shell of flame which became the stars. The whole story was designed to be as uniform and therefore as simple as possible.

Anaximander's explanation for the arrival of man himself was ingenious, though not quite as prescient as has been supposed. There is a myth that he anticipated the theory of evolution, which is fuelled by remarks such as one in an influential source from the second century AD that attributes to him the idea that man originated from creatures of a different species. Alas, Anaximander was no Darwin. Fuller accounts suggest that what he had in mind was that the first men were carried inside fishes, or fish-like creatures, which acted as surrogate mothers. He did not mean that one species, man, gradually developed from another species, fish. He seems to have been led to his theory by the observation that man needs an unusually long period of suckling, during which he cannot fend for himself, and by the thought that the very first men would therefore never have survived on their own. Once they had been nursed by fish and were capable of looking after themselves, this first generation of water-babies emerged on to land, where they could then presumably bring up their own young.

Anaximander's own offspring, in the traditional genealogy of Milesian philosophers, is Anaximenes, the last of the line. He was about twenty-five years younger than Anaximander, and the end of his career coincides with the destruction of Miletus by the Persians in 494 BC. The city was refounded fifteen years later, but thereafter was renowned more for its wool than for its philosophy.

Ancient historians of philosophy regarded Anaximenes as the greatest of the three Milesians. In their tidy minds, the fact that he was the last of his line led naturally to the thought that he was also its culmination. But to modern eyes he has often seemed the least important of the three. He is not so delightfully imaginative as Anaximander, after whose leaps of speculation he seems not only to be plodding but to be plodding backwards. For example, Anaximenes discarded Anaximander's sophisticated, if misguided, idea about equilibrium and went back to the view that something material props up the earth. He said it was supported by air, drawing the analogy of a leaf borne up by the wind, just as Thales before him had plumped for water and drawn the analogy of a floating log. Anaximenes also looked backwards for his choice of *arche*, the fundamental stuff of the world. Like Thales, he picked one of the everyday elements rather than Anaximander's mysterious *apeiron*. But once more he substituted air for Thales' water.

Why was Anaximenes so interested in air, the most insubstantial of elements? The answer has much to do with breath, which was connected in the Greek mind with life and the soul. Anaximenes apparently suggested a parallel between the soul of man and the *arche* of the world: both, he said, were air. At first this seems to be not so much an illuminating parallel as a double puzzle. How can air be the soul? And even if it were, what could that have to do with the question of what rocks and trees are made of? But Anaximenes was not being quite so obscure as it seems; the word for soul, *psuche*, had rather different connotations in those days. No clear distinction had yet been made between mind and matter, and the soul was understood to be simply the stuff that made living things alive. If there were such a stuff, then air, in the form of breath, would be a reasonable candidate. Anaximenes was not the first to elect it. Already in Homer, *psuche* was, among other things, the breath of life which escaped through a hero's mouth as he died. In the *Iliad*, the wind could impregnate and fertilize females, at least in the case of horses.

If we think of air as some sort of life-giving force, then Anaximenes' main idea comes into focus. All early Greek thinkers shared the view that the world somehow grew or developed on its own rather than being created out of nothing by gods. The gods of traditional myth may have fashioned things, but they did so out of pre-existing materials of which they themselves were also made. Thus it was natural for the Greeks to think that the fundamental stuff of the world itself had the power to grow and change – that is, that it was connected with life in some way. Thales, we may reasonably assume, now noted a connection between water and life: he was struck by the fact that plants and animals need water. Anaximenes, on the other hand, noted a connection between air and life: he was more struck by the fact that people breathe and corpses do not.

In the case of Thales, as we saw, one cannot be sure whether he believed that everything is made of water or just that water had existed first and somehow gave rise to everything else. Of Anaximenes, one can be more certain: he definitely held that everything is made of air and he even tried to explain how. It is the manner of this attempted explanation which has impressed some of his successors to the present day. It has even led some of them to credit him with the discovery of a fundamental form of scientific explanation. This may seem a strange honour to give a man who is apparently committed to the view that trees, boulders and everything else are made of thin air.

In fact, for Anaximenes the crucial point about the air out of which trees and boulders are made is that it is anything but thin. Air takes on various forms, he thinks, depending on how rarefied or condensed it is. The most rarefied of all is fire; then comes ordinary air; condense this and you get wind; denser still are clouds; then water, earth and stones, in that order. The atmospheric air we breathe is in some sense the natural state of the substance, to which all the other forms will return. But it is disturbed by being constantly in motion, which is why there is more of it in some places than in others, making the air denser in those places. Thus condensation and rarefaction caused by motion of the air are the engines of change in Anaximenes' world. They account for the warm and the cold, the wet and the dry, the solid and the insubstantial. This is an improvement on the inexplicable 'separating out' which Anaximander uses to account for the appearance of different elements out of the indeterminate *apeiron*.

The important novelty in this story is that Anaximenes makes differences of quality or kind depend on differences of quantity or number: the variety of elements is explained by the varying amounts of air packed into them. The practice of reducing the colourful diversity of the world to such quantitative notions is one that runs more or less continuously from Anaximenes to the scientists of today. But the idea behind it, that the book of nature is written in the language of mathematics, did not reach full expression until Galileo and Newton in the seventeenth century. (There are further and more impressive anticipations of it in the Pythagoreans – our next subject – who saw numbers in nature because they saw numbers in everything.)

The rest of Anaximenes' story does not sound at all like Galileo or Newton. According to Hippolytus, a Christian apologist of third-century Rome:

He says that the heavenly bodies do not move under the earth, as others have supposed, but round it, just as if a felt cap turns round our head; and that the sun is hidden not by being under the earth, but through being covered by the higher parts of the earth and through its increased distance from us.

Anaximenes saw the world as if it were a modern planetarium, where we sit looking up at a domed ceiling (his 'felt cap') with models of the stars moving above us. Like the earth, the sun and stars are flat, which enables them to float like leaves in the wind. They are said to be fiery bodies which rose in the form of moisture that evaporated from the earth and became progressively more rarefied until it burst into flame. The darkness of night comes when the sun – the biggest flaming leaf – disappears behind northerly mountains.

Anaximenes also tried to use his new tools of rarefaction and condensation to describe the weather, a popular subject with the seafaring Milesians. But he ended up saying much the same sort of thing as Anaximander. He took over Anaximander's account of thunder and lightning as the violent escape of wind that has become trapped in cloud. This idea was satirized during the late fifth century BC in Aristophanes' *Clouds*:

*Strepsiades*: . . . Then what *is* the thunderbolt?
*Socrates*: Whenever a dry wind is raised aloft and gets shut up into these clouds, it puffs them up inside like a bladder; then by necessity it bursts them and goes rapidly outside because of its density, and by its rushing and impetus it itself kindles itself.
*Strepsiades*: Yes, by Zeus! At any rate, this is just what happened to me once . . . I was roasting a thick sausage for my kinfolk, and I carelessly failed to slit it; it got puffed up and, suddenly breaking open, it spattered my eyes with crap and burned my face.

Thunder and earthquakes, though not the bursting of sausages, are just the sort of thing which the mythologists explained by invoking the actions of gods. In the works of the Ionian poets, Homer and Hesiod, earthquakes were caused by Poseidon, the 'loud-crashing Earth-Shaker'. But for Anaximenes they were caused (according to Aristotle) when

the earth, through being drenched and dried off, breaks asunder, and is shaken by the peaks that are thus broken off and fall in. Therefore earthquakes happen in periods both of drought and again of excessive rains; for in droughts . . . it dries up and cracks, and being made over-moist by the waters it crumbles apart.

Thus naturalism, the world-view of the *physici*, has made Poseidon redundant. It may be wondered in what sense the Greeks had ever really believed in him. The question is intriguing – presumably there was as wide a range of attitudes to religious belief as there is today – but it is irrelevant here. Even if those who believed in Poseidon and the other gods also entertained the possibility that there were natural explanations for earthquakes and such things, the fact is that we do not know of anybody before the Milesians who actually came up with any such explanations.

With the decline of Miletus, the focus of philosophical activity moved westward for a while to the Greek colonies of southern Italy. In so doing, it underwent a sea-change: dispassionate discussions of the weather were supplemented by ruminations on the destiny of the soul and on the proper way to live. Some readers will be comforted to hear it; such subjects fit more easily into the popular conception of philosophy. But before passing on to Pythagoras and his followers in the West, it is worth weighing up the Milesians and explaining why they too are entitled to be called philosophers.

When compared with the Hippocratic doctors just 100 years later, let alone Archimedes and Euclid in the third century BC, the methods of the Milesians were horribly crude. That, paradoxically, is why they count as philosophers. Scientific thinking had barely been born, yet still they dared to look for the natural causes of things. Thus they tried to delve deeper than the conventional world-picture suggested was possible. The fact that they did this, and that they used reason as their spade, makes them philosophers.

The use of reason was an act of faith. There is little point in trying to describe the impersonal laws that govern the cosmos if there aren't any, or if they are beyond the bounds of understanding. The Milesians simply assumed that there were such laws and that the mind was capable of comprehending them. This faith in an intelligible pattern in nature was rewarded when they came up with what seemed to them to be good explanations of such things as life, eclipses and thunder. Anaximander's talk – albeit in somewhat poetical terms – of 'necessity' and of the elements paying 'penalty and retribution to each other for their injustice according to the assessment of Time' illustrates the Milesians' new-found belief in a world governed by comprehensible law.

It was not until later that such beliefs were explicitly stated. The medical men who gathered around Hippocrates of Cos (c. 460–c. 370 BC), positively flaunted the new naturalism. They had this to say of epilepsy, which was commonly called 'the sacred disease':

This disease styled sacred comes from the same causes as others, from the things that come to and go from the body, from cold, sun, and from the changing restlessness of winds ... there is no need to put the disease in a special class and to consider it more divine than the others; they are all divine and all human. Each has a nature and power of its own; none is hopeless or incapable of treatment.

They did not divide the world into the divinely mysterious on the one hand and the naturally explicable on the other. Like the Milesians, they seem to have assumed that everything can be explained.

The Hippocratic doctors were relatively careful observers of fact and suspicious of the unverifiable. It is sometimes said that the Milesians were, by contrast and to their discredit, uninterested in verifying their speculations. There is some truth in this, though there is also evidence that Anaximenes for one did conduct a sort of experiment. He got it utterly wrong but that is beside the point. He said (to paraphrase a plausible account) that if you purse your lips to make your mouth into a small hole and blow on your hand, the breath will be cold, but that if you exhale through a wide-open mouth the breath will be hot. This fact apparently supports his theory of rarefaction and condensation, which says that compressed air is cooler and rarefied air is hotter. (In fact, compressed air is hotter, but since it passes over the hand more quickly in this 'experiment', it makes the hand feel cooler.)

Anaximenes' attempt to support his theory of the universe by warming his hands is the exception that proves the rule: in general the Milesians did not bother themselves with experiments. This is hardly surprising since their favourite areas of inquiry – the heavens, the weather and the origin of things – do not exactly lend themselves to it. Thunderstorms and the setting sun cannot easily be manipulated or dissected. Faced with such mysteries, the Milesians did what they were best at: they tried to reason them out, with whatever analogies and observations lay closest to hand. Given their interests, it is hard to believe that they would have got much further if only they could have thought of a few more experiments to do.

A more serious criticism, which can be made both of the Milesians and of the Hippocratic doctors, is that their claims to possess superior

knowledge were largely a sham. For example, the author of the Hippocratic work quoted above believed that epilepsy was caused by phlegm
from the head flowing into the veins and interrupting the passage of
air. Thus although he scorned the charlatans who use magic in their
attempts to cure epilepsy, he can hardly have had much better luck
himself. On the whole, the first exponents of naturalism are notable
more for the firmness of their rejection of mythological accounts of
nature than for the details of their own alternatives.

Not many later Ionians can have managed to stick to the new way
of looking at the world. There were too many things that evidently
could not yet be explained. Take Herodotus (*c.*485–*c.*430 BC), for
example. He is usually dubbed the father of history, and sometimes,
less kindly, of lies, and is rightly cited as a matter-of-fact inquirer in
the spirit of the Milesians. But alongside his more naturalistic passages,
such as an attempt to account for the flooding of the Nile, and his
robust scepticism towards some supernatural tales, there are regular
lapses into the ways of the myth-making *theologi*. For instance, he
says that an earthquake on Delos was sent as a warning by the gods.
It is not the mere mention of divinity that marks his deviation from
the narrow and sceptical path of the *physici*. Anaximander and Anaximenes are said to have referred to their respective *archai* as divine, but
the modern reader should not read too much into such pronouncements. In order for something to qualify as divine in those days, little
more was necessary than that it should be alive, in the sense of being
able to cause motion, and yet never die. As one modern commentator
has put it: 'Any power, any force we see at work in the world, which
is not born with us and will continue after we have gone could thus be
called a god, and most of them were.' The sin of Herodotus was not
that talk of divinity slipped from his lips, but that he introduced
personal beings, shrouded in the mystery appropriate to objects of
religious devotion, as the whole cause of a natural event. This is what
Thales, Anaximander and Anaximenes resolutely refused to do.

What made the Milesians and the Hippocratic doctors look at nature
in this new fashion, unencumbered by mythology and by superstitions
about sacred diseases? Nobody knows exactly. Aristotle thought that
the important thing about the first philosophers was that they had
spare time on their hands, but this can hardly have been the whole

story, if indeed it is any of it. Three other facts about them are probably more pertinent. First, the Ionians (and particularly the Milesians) were practical men, keen on developing their skills as astronomers, geographers, sailors and land-surveyors. They had little time for fanciful myths. Second, as industrious traders many of them were well-travelled and had met plenty of foreigners, or at least heard about them. Foreigners tended to have different myths and superstitions, which encouraged some Ionians to reflect sceptically on their own beliefs. Third comes their relatively free-thinking attitude to religion. The Ionians had their orthodox gods, namely the Olympian ones found in Homer, and temples dedicated to them; but on the whole it seems that they were not particularly enthusiastic believers. Compared with the adherents of the many mystery cults and folk religions which had developed to the north in Thrace and to the west, the Milesians seem to have been an almost agnostic lot. It can hardly be coincidence that it was in such a setting that naturalism first sprang up.

Perhaps the prevalence of competitive public debate also helps to explain how naturalism, and thus philosophy, arose in Greece. The citizens of the Greek city-states were famously argumentative; indeed, the Greeks seem to have regarded advocacy and criticism as the noblest uses of speech. Aristotle wrote that 'the power of speech is intended to set forth the expedient and the inexpedient, and therefore likewise the just and the unjust'. It is no miracle that in at least some of the city-states, the tools of disputation should eventually have been turned on the study of nature. It is also worth noting that when the first philosophers declaimed and expostulated, it was to the ears of an increasingly literate audience. Alphabetic writing first arose in Greece in around the eighth century and was becoming widespread by the sixth. This allowed everything that could be said to be written down easily, a novelty that is hard for us to appreciate. By crystallizing beliefs, myths, theories and stories of all kinds, it made them available for examination and criticism in a way that was unthought-of in tale-telling, pre-literate cultures. For all their shortcomings, the Milesians seem to have been the first to try to exploit this opportunity.

# 2

# The Harmony of the World: *the Pythagoreans*

Tales about Pythagoras flew to him and stuck like iron filings to a magnet. He was said, for example, to have appeared in several places at once and to have been reincarnated many times. Taken literally, this idea can be consigned to the same over-flowing bin which contains the story that he had a golden thigh; but taken figuratively, it is an understatement. Pythagoras – or at least Pythagoreanism – was every-where and still is.

Even schoolchildren are likely to have met his name at least twice: in geometry (for the famous theorem about the lengths of the sides of right-angled triangles), and in Shakespeare:

*Clown*: What is the opinion of Pythagoras concerning wild-fowl?
*Malvolio*: That the soul of our grandam might haply inhabit a bird.
*Clown*: What thinkest thou of his opinion?
*Malvolio*: I think nobly of the soul, and no way approve of his opinion.
*Clown*: Fare thee well; remain thou still in darkness: thou shalt hold the opinion of Pythagoras ere I will allow of thy wits; and fear to kill a woodcock lest thou dispossess the soul of thy grandam.

As if triangles and the transmigration of souls were not variety enough, it could also be said that we meet Pythagoras whenever we use arith-metical expressions such as 'squares' or 'cubes' of numbers; or come across the poetic image of the 'music of the spheres'; or use the term 'philosopher' in its popular sense of a lover of wisdom who tries to transcend mundane worries. What is more, Plato fashioned some of his most influential doctrines around Pythagorean ideas.

When he quotes the above exchange from *Twelfth Night* in his chapter on Pythagoras in the *History of Western Philosophy*, Bertrand

Russell says facetiously that Pythagoras founded a religion 'of which the main tenets were the transmigration of souls and the sinfulness of eating beans'. Russell excusably exaggerates the significance of beans,

but he did not in general belittle Pythagoras. Quite the reverse: he wrote that Pythagoras was 'intellectually one of the most important men that ever lived'. For a time, Russell himself was a passionate Pythagorean in certain respects, which perhaps explains his overestimate.

If Pythagoras is everywhere, from school exercise books to the mind of Bertrand Russell, he is also nowhere. Nothing that he may have said or written has survived (at least, not with his name on it: some sixth-century poems ascribed to the mythical singer Orpheus may in fact be by him). In the ancient accounts of the Pythagoreans, it is impossible to distinguish Pythagoras' own thoughts

PYTHAGORAS.

from those of his followers. This is largely because the members of the religious cults or brotherhoods inspired by Pythagoras regarded it as only proper to attribute anything they came up with to the master himself. It is also because the Pythagoreans prided themselves on guarding their doctrines as secrets, to be revealed only to initiates. Their secrecy succeeded to some extent, but only indirectly: it provoked so much uninformed tattle about the Pythagoreans that it is almost impossible to hear the real Pythagoras amidst the buzzing cloud of gossips.

Here is a typical example of the contradictory trivia that was written in ancient times about the life of Pythagoras:

Above all, he forbade as food red mullet and blacktail, and he enjoined abstinence from the hearts of animals and from beans, and sometimes, according to Aristotle, even from paunch and gurnard. Some say that he contented himself with just some honey or a honeycomb or bread, never touching wine in the daytime, and with greens boiled or raw for dainties, and fish but rarely

... The offerings he made were always inanimate; though some say that he would offer cocks, sucking goats and porkers, as they are called, but lambs never. However, Aristoxenus has it that he consented to the eating of all other animals, and only abstained from ploughing oxen and rams.

He had, it is safe to say, the most discussed diet in antiquity. The best-attested theory about it is that he was a vegetarian, and that this was a consequence of his belief that people were sometimes reincarnated in the form of animals (or, as Malvolio put it, that the soul of our grandam might haply inhabit a bird).

Although there is no connection between Pythagoras' diet and his geometry, the scientific and the mystical sides of Pythagoreanism do on the whole fit neatly together. Before giving an account of them, I shall briefly say what is known of the circumstances of Pythagoras' life and school. There is precious little of it.

He was born in about 570 BC and died some seventy years later, making him a contemporary of Anaximenes. Although, like Anaximenes, he was an Ionian, born on the island of Samos just north-west of Miletus, he left for the Greek colonies of southern Italy when he was about forty and spent the rest of his life there. At the time of his migration he had already established a reputation as an ascetic sage. Although there is no evidence that the rather serious-minded Pythagoras and his followers were driven out of Samos, it is hardly surprising that they left a city whose prosperity was turning towards decadence under its dissolute and tyrannical ruler, Polycrates. Some real persecution certainly came later, though, when he had settled and founded his school at Croton in southern Italy. Here Pythagoras and his followers took a leading part in the politics of the city, though exactly what he got up to, and why after two decades of prominence there should have been a violent revolt against him, is unclear. Many of the foremost Pythagoreans in Croton and neighbouring cities were rounded up and killed around the turn of the sixth and fifth centuries BC. Pythagoras himself was banished. One historian suggests that the evident hostility towards Pythagoras must have been partly fostered by 'the irritation felt by the plain man of those days at having his legislation done for him by a set of incomparable pedants, who made a point of abstaining from beans, and would not let him beat his own dog because they recognized in its howls the voice of a departed friend'.

After the revolt, Pythagoras drifted, ending up probably at Metapontum in the Gulf of Tarentum. Pythagorean societies soon flourished again and spread further through southern Italy. But around the middle of the fifth century BC there was another, worse, purge of Pythagoreans, many of whom then scattered and left Italy for Greece. These transplanted cuttings of Pythagoreanism took on divergent forms in their new soils, and also began to weaken. By the beginning of the fourth century BC practically all of the Pythagorean societies had left their native Italy, and in the course of that century they more or less died out everywhere.

The influence of their ideas, though, continued to grow, mainly through Plato, who had a close friend who was a Pythagorean, Archytas of Tarentum. This man was a statesman as well as a thinker and

ARCHYTAS.

mathematician, and is likely to have been one of the inspirations for Plato's famous 'philosopher-kings'. Aristotle wrote – exaggerating, but not ridiculously – that Plato's philosophy 'in most respects followed' the Pythagoreans. It is certainly true that Pythagorean ideas were swallowed up by Platonism, to such an extent that it is now often hard to tell the two philosophies apart. Pythagoras ought, presumably, to have been pleased to have such an eminent reincarnation.

The picture of Pythagoreanism that follows is a composite one. Little attempt will be made to separate its earlier from its later forms, let alone the views of the man himself from those of his followers. Of Pythagoras himself it is safe to say that he believed in reincarnation and that he was at least fairly interested in numbers; but more or less everything else about him is speculation. Also, I shall pretend that the Pythagoreans were all much of a muchness, though in fact some were primarily interested in scientific and intellectual questions while others wallowed in the taboos, obscure sayings and superstitious guides to life that made up the religious side of the Pythagorean curriculum. Even in the twentieth century there were still two quite different sorts of interest in Pythagoras. On the one hand, one finds scientists and philosophers of science, such as Werner Heisenberg and Sir Karl Popper, arguing that modern physics is reminiscent of Pythagoras. On the other hand one finds books about him published in a series that also includes works on alchemy, Druids and astrology. It took an exceptionally audacious mind like Pythagoras' to marry these two aspects.

The join between the two can most easily be seen in the Pythagoreans' novel conception of spiritual salvation. This might be parodied as: if you want to live forever, study mathematics. To understand that conception more seriously it is necessary first to know something about the religious ideas of the cult of Orpheus.

It is not, however, necessary to know anything about Orpheus himself or about the history of Orphism. This is just as well since nobody knows anything much about either. When ancient sources refer to Orphics or Orphism they are usually alluding to beliefs, originating in Thrace, about reincarnation, and to the idea that the soul needs purification in order to have a satisfactory afterlife. Some people think that there was a detailed official doctrine of Orphism already written down by the time of Pythagoras. Others think that Orphic ideas were then much more fluid and did not solidify until several hundred years later. Either way, the notions that interest us here are all expressed in a version of the myth of Dionysus, which the various forms of Orphism united in admiring.

Dionysus, according to the relevant myth, was the product of a twice-incestuous union between Zeus and Persephone (twice-incestuous because Persephone herself was the product of a union between Zeus and his own mother). Zeus made Dionysus ruler of the world, but the unfortunate child was killed and eaten by the Titans, whom Zeus then struck with lightning. From the ashes of the Titans sprang forth man, who is therefore a curate's egg: in part he is good – in fact, divine – because the digested remains of Dionysus were in the ashes. But he is also bad in part, because these ashes come from the

Titans, and man is therefore polluted by their evil deed. The two elements, defiled and divine, correspond to man's mortal, impure body on the one hand and his immortal soul on the other. Only rigorous purification can help him to rise above his polluted legacy. And death provides the only hope of complete liberation from the body, which is seen as a tomb imprisoning the soul. Sometimes, though, death is a case of out of the frying pan and into the fire, because unpurified souls are punished horribly after death.

This myth provides the main gist and imagery of Orphic poems and inscriptions. It is, as it were, the sacred text of the religion of which Orpheus was regarded as the prophet. Just as Orphism can be seen as a more intellectualized revival of the religion of the Dionysian or Bacchic cults – it was more ascetic than they were, which is not hard – so Pythagoreanism can be seen as a more intellectualized version of Orphism.

In the worship of Dionysus, the main duty of religious observance was to achieve some sort of union with the god by initiations and other rites that were renowned for their indulgence (in sex, wine, violence or any combination of the three). In Orphism, the rituals were more ceremonial, decorous and concerned with self-denial rather than self-indulgence. But they were still largely mumbo-jumbo. A rare picture of Orphic followers, or at least of how some people saw them, is to be found in Euripides' play *Hippolytus*, which was first produced some seventy years after the death of Pythagoras. When Theseus turns in anger on his bastard son, Hippolytus, he ridicules him thus:

So, now flaunt your purity! Play the quack with your fleshless diets! Take Orpheus for your lord and prophet and wallow in frenzied adoration of his wordy vapourings! Yes, you are exposed!

In the Pythagorean variant of Orphism, there is a new twist: purity, and thus reunion with the divine, are to be achieved by living a life of contemplation (*theoria*) and inquiry. According to the philosopher Heraclitus (*c.*540–*c.*480 BC), Pythagoras 'practised inquiry beyond all other men'. This comprised many things, but mathematics was held to be particularly valuable. The good Pythagorean was above all supposed to study numbers, geometry, astronomy and music, because each revealed some aspect of the principles of order in the universe.

The Pythagoreans held that nature should be investigated purely for the sake of disinterested knowledge and not for any practical reward. They seem to have been the first to use the term *philosophia* to mean the love of wisdom for its own sake, as the following story from Cicero illustrates:

Leon [*the ruler of Phlius, a centre of Pythagoreanism in south-east Greece*] . . . asked him to name the art in which he put most reliance; but Pythagoras said that for his part he had no acquaintance with any art, but was a philosopher. Leon was astonished at the novelty of the term and asked who philosophers were . . . Pythagoras . . . replied that the life of man seemed to him to resemble the festival which was celebrated with most magnificent games . . . for at this festival some men . . . sought to win the glorious distinction of a crown, others were attracted by the prospect of making gain by buying or selling, whilst there was on the other hand a certain class, and that quite the best type of free-born men, who looked neither for applause nor gain, but came for the sake of the spectacle and closely watched what was done and how it was done. So also we, as though we had come from some city to a kind of crowded spectacle . . . entered upon this life, and some were slaves of ambition, some of money; there were a special few who, counting all else as nothing, closely scanned the nature of things; these men gave themselves the name of lovers of wisdom (for that is the meaning of the word philosopher); and just as at the games the men of truest breeding looked on without any self-seeking, so in life the contemplation and discovery of nature far surpassed all other pursuits.

One unmistakably Orphic theme that pervades Pythagorean accounts of inquiry (especially those of Plato in his more Pythagorean moments) is a contrast between, on the one hand, the defiled mortal body and what can be learned of the world through its sense organs, and, on the other hand, the higher, purer knowledge which can be attained by the soul. This can be seen in one description, from the fifth century AD, of Pythagoras' interest in geometry:

Herein I emulate the Pythagoreans who even had a conventional phrase to express what I mean, 'a figure and a platform, not a figure and sixpence', by which they implied that the geometry which is deserving of study is that which, at each new theorem, sets up a platform to ascend by, and lifts the soul on high instead of allowing it to go down among [*physical objects perceived by the senses*] and so become subservient to the common needs of this mortal life.

In other words: if you use geometry only for mundane purposes, as, for example, the ancient Egyptians did for calculating areas of land, your soul remains locked up in the prison of your earthly body. But geometry can also provide a means of escape for the soul, if it is used as a subject of disinterested and abstract study – that is, if it is pursued primarily in order to find out which theorems are true. That is a worthy pastime for a pure soul. Although the mathematical inquiries of the Pythagoreans eventually paid off in all sorts of practical ways, their motives for undertaking them were largely moral or spiritual. An understanding of the orderly arrangement and beauty of the universe was thought to bring with it some form of participation in that order and beauty. In short, some of the grandeur of the universe rubbed off on the man who studied it.

This idea, which has come to be regarded as quintessentially Pythagorean, is expressed by Socrates in Plato's *Republic*:

For surely, Adeimantus, the man whose mind is truly fixed on external realities has no leisure to turn his eyes downward upon the petty affairs of man . . . but he fixes his gaze upon the things of the eternal and unchanging order, and seeing that they neither wrong nor are wronged by one another, but all abide in harmony as reason bids, he will endeavour to imitate them and, as far as may be, to fashion himself in their likeness and assimilate himself to them . . . Then the lover of wisdom associating with the divine order will himself become orderly and divine.

Some 2,300 years later, Bertrand Russell wrote something strikingly similar in the final chapter of one of his first books, *The Problems of Philosophy*. According to him, philosophy is worth studying 'above all because, through the greatness of the universe which philosophy contemplates, the mind also is rendered great, and becomes capable of that union with the universe which constitutes its highest good'.

This all sounds most elevating; but what exactly is it on which the philosopher is supposed to fix his gaze? For the Pythagoreans, it was apparently the heavenly bodies, wheeling in their orderly and harmonious paths through the sky. For Plato, it became something more abstract, which the heavenly bodies symbolized: the ideal Forms, of which earthly things are inferior copies (I shall say more about these Forms when we come to Plato himself). Russell seems simply to have been singing the praises of the intellectual life while being less definite about what precisely that life might involve. What unites these accounts is the idea that by contemplating something one can acquire some of its desirable characteristics, presumably by becoming impressed by it and trying to emulate it. For example, Plato held that the philosophical study of the immortal universe gave one a sort of immortality:

he who has been earnest in the love of knowledge and of true wisdom ... must have thoughts immortal and divine, if he attain truth, and in so far as human nature is capable of sharing in immortality, he must altogether be immortal.

This is from Plato's *Timaeus*, his most Pythagorean dialogue. Again Bertrand Russell echoes: 'through the infinity of the universe the mind which contemplates it achieves some share in infinity'.

Having a 'share' of immortality or infinity is a cloudy enough idea to be regarded as a harmlessly euphuistic tribute to philosophy. Russell, for one, certainly intended no more than such a tribute, though his choice of language gestures backwards towards Pythagoras. It is not immediately clear how one can become literally immortal, as Pythagoras is said to have believed, merely by contemplating something immortal (i.e., the universe). The main idea, insofar as it can be explained at all, seems to have been something like the following. The soul is weighed down by earthly or practical concerns, and so, if it remains unpurified, will never escape from the realm of the body. At death it will merely pass on to another body, either human or animal. But if a man follows the right programme of purification – a sort of spiritual work-out: soul-building, as opposed to body-building – then the soul will be cut free and will be capable of ascending to the immortal and immaterial realm that is its real home. This purgative programme has two parts: observing the right superstitious taboos (e.g., not eating beans, or whatever); and living a life of rigorous philosophical exercise – a life of *theoria*, or pure inquiry.

We have seen that, for the Pythagoreans, mathematics is the key to the order and beauty of the universe, which it is the task of philosophy to unlock. According to tradition, they began to turn the key when they made a momentous discovery about the relation between numbers and musical sounds. It is a measure of our debt to the Pythagoreans that most educated people today would find the discovery totally unsurprising.

What they found is that there is a direct relationship between the three musical intervals that the Greeks regarded as consonant or pleasant-sounding – the octave, fourth and major fifth – and three numerical ratios. This relationship can be expressed in terms of the lengths of strings that are plucked to produce musical notes. Consider the monochord, a single-stringed instrument on which the discovery may first have been made. By holding down the string in different places along its length and plucking it, varying notes can be sounded, as with a guitar. If the string is held down exactly halfway along its length, the resulting note is one octave higher than it would be if the string could vibrate freely (i.e., if it were not held down at all). The musical interval of an octave, then, corresponds to the ratio 2:1 – the lower note is produced by a string that is in effect twice the length of the string that produces the note one octave higher. Similarly, the pleasant-sounding musical intervals known as the fourth and major fifth correspond to the ratios 4:3 and 3:2 respectively.

This was excellent news. It showed that phenomena (in this instance, musical sounds) had a hidden structure that could be laid bare. Here was concrete proof that numbers could unlock the secrets of how the world worked. Also, the three ratios (2:1, 4:3, 3:2) involve just the numbers one, two, three and four, which add up to ten. This, too, was good news. The number ten was regarded by the Pythagoreans as the perfect number, having great mystical import. It was especially pleasing for them to notice that the consonant intervals, which had a special significance in Greek music, corresponded to numbers that also had a special significance.

With the benefit of scientifically informed hindsight, we can say that the explanation for what the Pythagoreans found lies in three facts: that the pitch of a musical sound is a matter of the rate of vibration of air; that this rate of vibration is, in the case of a stringed instrument, determined by the rate of vibration of a string; and that the rate of vibration of the string is in turn a function of the length of the string. (The magic number ten is a complete red herring.) The Pythagoreans were in no position to offer any such explanation. But, armed with this striking discovery, they seem to have felt themselves in an excellent position to jump to a rather large conclusion: numbers are fundamental to all of the order that exists in apparently chaotic nature. So, in a sense, they are – insofar as numbers (or, more generally, quantitative notions) play an indispensable role in the explanation of natural phenomena. Try to imagine a textbook of physics or chemistry with no numbers in it. It cannot be done. The Pythagoreans, unsurprisingly, did not quite know how to put all this. They fell back on the vocabulary they had inherited from the Milesians and thus said that numbers were the *arche* of all things.

In our discussion of Thales and his successors we have already noted the haziness of the concept of *arche*. Would saying that numbers are *archai* mean that they were the first things to exist, or that they are what everything is made of, or that numbers somehow cause everything? Aristotle explored several suggestions about what the Pythagoreans may have meant, and was unsympathetic to most of them. His tone when speaking of his distant predecessors was often that of a kindergarten teacher recounting the charmingly silly things he has heard the children say in school today, especially when he reports the Pythagoreans and their babblings about number. To 'the Pythagoreans ... who make all nature out of numbers' he curtly objects that this cannot be right because 'natural bodies are manifestly endowed with weight and lightness, but an assemblage of units [*i.e., of numbers*] can neither be composed to form a body nor possess weight'. But surely Aristotle is being too literal-minded here. Can the Pythagoreans really have supposed that, for example, the number six had a certain weight, or that if you smashed a rock you would be left with a pile of numbers? Presumably not. Certainly the Pythagoreans had come to the conclusion that nature was fundamentally mathematical, and, given the times, it would have been only natural for them to sum up this rather vague thought by pronouncing numbers to be *archai* – the principles of all things. But this does not necessarily mean that they believed physical objects to be made of numbers in exactly the way that houses are made of bricks.

However, it does seem that the Pythagoreans believed that physical objects were constructed out of numbers in a certain rather special sense. This special sense derives from their approach to geometry. Consider the following procedure: draw a pattern of four dots like the shape on the face of a die; join up the dots into lines and thus form a square; then draw in more points and lines to make a cube. In this simple exercise, points have formed lines, lines have formed a plane figure and planes have formed a solid. That is more or less how the geometrically minded Pythagoreans liked to think of physical objects: as constructed out of points, lines and so on. Aristotle took them to be offering a wildly implausible answer to the old Milesian question of what sort of material stuff things are made of. But in fact they were shifting to a new question. They found it an exciting novelty to focus on the mathematical aspect of things, and chose to discuss that instead. That is why they may have said that physical things were in some sense made of numbers. Although we distinguish clearly between numbers and geometrical points, the Pythagoreans spoke more loosely of units, which can be understood as sometimes meaning the one and sometimes the other. This ambiguity was no doubt fostered by their practice of representing numbers by geometrical patterns of dots or pebbles, like the shapes on dominoes or dice.

Unfortunately, even the most charitable interpreters of the Pythagoreans cannot rescue them from some of the extremes that their number-worship led to. It seems that they went so far as to identify particular numbers with various abstractions. According to one ancient commentator, they held that mind was one, maleness was two, femaleness three, justice four, marriage five and opportunity seven (other sources give different numbers for several of these). In some instances one can faintly see what might have inspired such numerological ramblings. Justice as four is the simplest example: the number four was represented as a square figure in which all sides are equal – it is thus, one might say, an even-handed figure – and we still sometimes use 'square' to mean 'fair', for example when we speak of 'squaring' debts. But although there may sometimes be method in the madness, it seems to be madness none the less. No doubt something made them say this sort of thing, and it would be intriguing to know what, but there are other more consequential Pythagorean ideas to look at.

The last part of the Pythagoreans' general philosophical doctrine to be examined here is the one which they would have put first: the part that deals with the ultimate origins and principles of the universe. Although they thought that numbers were in some sense constituents of all things, they did not believe that numbers were the ultimate constituents. They thought it was possible to dig even deeper. Numbers themselves were generated out of something else. This something was Anaximander's indefinite or unlimited *apeiron*, or something like it.

The two basic concepts in Pythagorean thought are the limited and the unlimited: according to the Pythagoreans, whenever you look for an account of the order or beauty in any phenomenon, these two are sure to be at the bottom of it. Plato later dug up a doctrine that must have belonged to the Pythagoreans:

The men of old, who were better than ourselves and dwelt nearer the gods, passed on this gift in the form of a saying. All things, so it ran, that are ever said to be consist of a one and a many, and have in their nature a conjunction of limit and unlimitedness.

The idea behind this talk of a conjunction of limit and unlimited seems to have been something like the following. Order and beauty are created when some form of limit, or definition, is imposed on the unlimited raw material of the universe. A mundane example of this might be the way that a baking ring can be used to press a recognizable shape out of a formless lump of pastry. Similarly, as the Pythagoreans would have seen it, the musical ratios mark the attractive results of the imposition of order on formless sound. Just as the ratios carve musical harmony out of cacophonous noise, so the Pythagoreans regarded many other sorts of desirable things as being in effect instances of harmony or attunement. A healthy body, a virtuous soul and a just society were all thought of as essentially matters of having the right ratio or mixture of elements. In each case, the harmonious ratio or mixture counted as an instance of the establishment of order or limit. The twin notions of limit and unlimited come to have a bearing on numbers via the arithmetical concepts of even and odd. The unlimited somehow corresponds to (or possibly gives rise to) the even, and the limited stands in the same relation to the odd. Odd and even combine to form the number one, and all the other numbers are generated from one.

That gives us the recipe for numbers, and thereby for all the other things of which numbers are somehow themselves supposed to be the ingredients. But how was it all first cooked? The Pythagoreans offered an account of the beginning of the cosmos. In Anaximander's version of this story, a sort of egg or seed somehow separated off from the indefinite *apeiron* and grew into the world we know (see page 10). The Pythagoreans' version also starts with a seed: their seed grows by sucking in the unlimited and thereby giving some of it form or limit. Everything in the world – planets, rocks, music and, presumably, people – are the result of this growth, which is fed by the formless placenta of *apeiron*. The sucking seems to have been meant more or less literally: the unlimited was apparently also spoken of in this context as *pneuma*, that is, air or breath (which also came to mean 'soul'). Thus we have an account of the development of the cosmos which is dominated by the image of a growing organism breathing in and drawing sustenance from its environment.

But how is this pseudo-biological account supposed to sit alongside the Pythagoreans' more abstract and sophisticated-sounding reflections on geometry and number? It is one thing to say that all the numbers can be generated from one (for example, by repeatedly adding one) or that a cube can be thought of as constructed out of points and lines. But are we now to suppose that the number one literally begat the other numbers – which begat lines, which begat plane figures, and so on – at a particular moment in the development of the cosmos? It is as if a few pages from the beginning of the Book of Genesis had gone missing and got muddled up with pages from an elementary mathematics text.

This is the point at which it would be wise to stop supposing. The sources for all this speculation about the Pythagoreans are sketchy and possibly corrupt; at some stage one is forced to admit that no more enlightenment can be squeezed out of them. More importantly, it is worth remembering that the Pythagoreans were not supermen who with one bound leapt free of the more primitive ideas of their predecessors. They still had one foot in the camp of the first *physici*, who, as we have seen, focussed on crude stories of how it all began. The Pythagoreans were straining to move on to other sorts of questions, particularly mathematical ones, but they did not yet see how to make a clean break with the old ways of talking.

We saw earlier that the good Pythagorean was meant to devote himself to his studies of nature, particularly astronomy, mathematics and music. That is what was supposed to purify his soul. Good intentions are easy enough to announce at the beginning of term, but how much did the Pythagoreans actually achieve?

What we know of their contribution to music (or, strictly speaking, harmonics) is short but sweet. It consists of the observations discussed above which revealed the connection between ratios and the pleasant-sounding harmonic intervals. That is all. Modern historians of science have nevertheless been impressed: one says that the Pythagoreans' tinkerings with acoustics are 'the one major case where we have evidence of philosophers engaging in empirical research' before the time of Plato. However, the Pythagoreans' most famous musical idea – their doctrine of the 'harmony' or 'music of the spheres' – had little to do with empirical research. It is best thought of as an image that powerfully encapsulated their picture of the cosmos, and which was believed largely because it seemed such an attractive idea. Its suggestiveness is attested by its appearance in Plato, Cicero, Chaucer, Shakespeare, Milton, Pope, Dryden and in many other places. Aristotle describes it well, but Lorenzo, in *The Merchant of Venice*, puts it even better:

> Sit, Jessica. Look how the floor of heaven
> Is thick inlaid with patines of bright gold;
> There's not the smallest orb which thou behold'st
> But in his motion like an angel sings,
> Still quiring to the young-eyed cherubins:
> Such harmony is in immortal souls;
> But, whilst this muddy vesture of decay
> Doth grossly close it in, we cannot hear it.

In fact, Lorenzo puts it so well that he seems to have improved on the Pythagoreans. The original doctrine appears to have been that the heavenly bodies make sounds because they hurtle through space at various speeds; that the ratios between these different speeds are just the right ones to ensure that the sounds are harmonious; and that we do not notice this music because we have heard it since birth and so are used to it. As Aristotle put it in his exposition (he did not himself accept the idea): 'What happens to men, then, is just what happens to coppersmiths, who are so accustomed to the noise of the smithy that it makes no difference to them.' Although there was one Pythagorean tradition which said that Pythagoras himself could hear the harmony of spheres because he was really a god and not a man, there is not much evidence anywhere before Shakespeare of the idea that it is because we are mortal that we cannot hear it. Yet, in a way, Shakespeare's idea is more Pythagorean than the Pythagoreans. The notion of the soul temporarily locked up in a 'muddy vesture of decay' during mortal life, and thereby kept from fully appreciating the harmonious order and beauty of the universe, is pure Orphism. Pythagoras would have loved it, but seems never to have thought of applying the idea to the question of why we do not hear the harmony of the spheres.

Aristotle's own attitude to the subject was less picturesque:

melodious and poetical as the theory is, it cannot be a true account of the facts . . . Excessive noises, we know, shatter the solid bodies even of inanimate things . . . But if the moving bodies are so great, and the sound which penetrates to us is proportionate to their size, that sound must needs reach us in an intensity many times that of thunder, and the force of its action must be immense. Indeed the reason why we do not hear, and show in our bodies none of the effects of violent force, is easily given: it is that there is no noise.

For the Pythagoreans, though, the theory was simply too good not to be true. It bound together three things which it was the essence of Pythagorean philosophy to connect: the orderliness of nature (in the form of the regular motions of the heavenly bodies), its beauty (in the form of the harmony these motions created) and the pervasiveness of numbers (in the form of the ratios which explained this harmony).

Just as this theory suffered the embarrassment of postulating a sound that nobody had actually heard, so the Pythagoreans' other astronomical doctrines were dependent on suspiciously invisible objects. At least, that is true of the later and most influential Pythagorean astronomical theories, which come from fifth-century writers. These theories say that the earth and the heavenly bodies all circle around an unseen central fire, a 'central hearth' like the fire at the heart of a home, and that there is a 'counter-earth', also unseen, in an orbit between the earth and the central fire. It has been suggested that the Pythagoreans' explanation for the fact that we see neither of these things is that we live on a side of the earth which is permanently turned away from them.

The most significant fact about this theory is that it displaced the earth from the centre of things and made it move around the central fire just like all the other heavenly bodies. This novel idea seems to have had no connection with any other part of Pythagorean thought, but it is no small matter. In the dedication to his *De revolutionibus*, which was published in 1543, Copernicus says that it was the consideration of just this ancient system which gave him the courage to explore the then-unorthodox hypothesis that the earth moves around the sun rather than sitting in the centre of the universe (which is what everyone believed in the Middle Ages): 'Taking this as a starting point, I began to consider the mobility of the earth . . .' Thus Pythagoreanism was, albeit accidentally, the starting point for modern astronomy.

Whatever reasons the ancient Pythagoreans may have had for advancing their astronomical views, there is scant evidence of any detailed observations of the heavenly bodies on their part, or, surprisingly, of any application of their beloved mathematics to astronomy. But the first man to make a serious attempt to apply mathematics to find laws of celestial motion, namely Johannes Kepler (1571–1630), was a confirmed (if rather belated) Pythagorean. His faith that the heavens must be arranged in a harmonious pattern that reveals itself in simple mathematical relationships led him to formulate several generalizations about the planets. Some of them are misguided fantasies that are now conveniently forgotten, especially by those who wish to distance the modern men of science from the odium of association with demented ancient philosophers. But others are now regarded as landmarks of physics. Kepler's three laws of planetary

37

motion are often cited as the turnstile from which medieval cosmology emerged transformed into modern astronomy. Yet he was still so much a Pythagorean that his treatise on *The Harmony of the World* (1619), in which several of his most famous discoveries were announced, not only analysed planetary motion in terms of major and minor harmonic scales but even specified the different tunes played inaudibly by the orbits of Saturn, Jupiter, Mars, Venus, Mercury, the moon and the earth.

Inspiring though they were to later generations, it is hard to say what credit the original Pythagoreans deserve for advancing the nascent science of astronomy in their own times. Pure mathematics was another matter: even the sceptical Aristotle was forced to admit that 'they were the first to advance this study'. It seems that the most consequential of the mathematical advances which have been credited to Pythagoreans, including the famous theorem itself, belong to the middle of the fifth century BC or later, long after the death of Pythagoras. But some other parts of mathematical doctrine may well date back to him. The classification of numbers such as four and nine as 'square' was probably around from the earliest days (the Pythagoreans represented these numbers as squares of dots, which is why the terminology occurred to them). The same probably goes for various theorems about number which lend themselves easily to such geometrical representation. And the division of numbers into odd and even may also be an early Pythagorean invention. But the idea that Pythagoras himself was the first to produce rigorous mathematical proofs or demonstrations, rather than just miscellaneous observations about numbers, triangles and so on, seems to be wishful thinking on the behalf of some of his champions.

Of these champions, Russell was the boldest in modern times. His claim that Pythagoras was the most influential of all thinkers rests on the idea that Pythagoras alone was responsible for the impact of mathematics on other areas of thought. Russell appears to have had two such sorts of impact in mind, though he did not explicitly distinguish them. One has to do with the method of mathematical proof found in Euclid's *Elements*, which was written in around 300 BC and remained the bible of geometry until several New Testaments were added in the nineteenth century. Euclidian proofs proceed by careful steps of deduction from simple axioms, which are assumed to be self-evident, towards substantial and often complex conclusions. This plodding style of logical bricklaying has been deeply influential outside mathematics as well as within it, not just as a model of the way to organize scientific results (Newton, for example, laid out his *Principia* in this fashion), but also in law and theology. Without Pythagoras, wrote Russell, 'theologians would not have sought logical *proofs* of God and immortality'. However, although we can safely say that the notion of mathematical proof was developed by the Greeks, and at some time before Euclid (who flourished in the fourth century BC), there is no reason to think that it is Pythagoras or his followers who deserve all or even any of the credit for inventing it. Rigorous deduction is more clearly seen in the work of Parmenides, who comes in a later chapter. What they do deserve credit for is something related but more subtle. The early Pythagoreans seem to have been the first to stress that mathematics can be pursued for the sake of intellectual satisfaction and not just because it is useful for working things out. Jonathan Swift probably had a caricature of the Pythagoreans in mind when he described the absent-minded mathematicians of Laputa in *Gulliver's Travels*:

Their houses are very ill built . . . without one right angle in any apartment, and this defect ariseth from the contempt they bear for practical geometry . . . I have not seen a more clumsy, awkward, and unhandy people, nor so slow and perplexed in their conceptions upon all other subjects, except those of mathematics and music.

Taking a resolutely theoretical approach to mathematics, as the real Pythagoreans undoubtedly did, would have helped at least to pave the way for the notion of mathematical proof, which more practically minded Greeks of the time would have had little use for. With his concern for contemplative *theoria* and his desire to uncover the mathematical basis of things, a Pythagorean would be interested in mathematical objects, such as triangles and numbers, in their own right and not just as proxies for bits of land or amounts of money. He would try to reason about these things in the abstract, to see how mathematical truths and concepts are related to one another. And this would bring him to the doorstep of Euclidian-style proofs, whether or not he crossed the threshold himself.

The other sort of impact of mathematics which Russell credited to Pythagoras is more nebulous. It comes from the idea that mathematics provides knowledge about a realm of perfect objects (such as perfect circles and perfectly straight lines) which is somehow superior to what we learn through our senses about the jagged and imperfect physical world. Mathematical knowledge is supposed to be not only more exact but also more uplifting and more revealing, precisely because it is more abstract, and thus to set an example for all other sorts of knowledge. When Russell later wrote of his own eventual 'retreat from Pythagoras', what he says he abandoned was 'the feeling that intellect is superior to sense [*meaning sensory perception, such as sight*]'. It is easy to see this feeling as a natural outgrowth of Orphism: the body and what it tells us are seen as tainted; the mind, or soul, and what it tells us are better. The most influential champion of this attitude was Plato, and Russell was right to regard the Pythagoreans – though probably not Pythagoras himself – as part of Plato's inspiration in the matter. Where Russell goes too far is in assuming that because the Pythagoreans apparently got there first, they deserve the credit for all later attempts to tread the same path. But in fact it seems to be a perennially tempting route that many people have found for themselves. Nevertheless, if mystically minded mathematicians want a patron saint, Pythagoras is their man. He may not in fact have performed the miracles with which he is credited, but that is true of most or all saints.

# 3

## The Man Who
## Searched for Himself:
### *Heraclitus*

The popular idea of the philosopher as absent-minded professor goes back as far as Thales, as we have seen. It was Heraclitus (*c.*540–*c.*480 BC) who first exemplified another aspect of the traditional caricature: that of rank obscurity. His reputation as 'the riddler' was well-earned. When Euripides asked Socrates what he thought of Heraclitus' writings, Socrates is supposed to have replied that 'the part I understand is excellent, and so too is, I dare say, the part I do not understand; but it needs a Delian diver to get to the bottom of it.' This was not just Socrates' little joke. Here are two examples of the memorable impenetrability of what Heraclitus had to say:

Death is all things we see awake; all we see asleep is sleep.

Lifetime is a child at play, moving pieces in a game. Kingship belongs to the child.

Not all of his epigrammatic sayings are quite as baffling as that, but there is some degree of paradox in nearly all 130 or so surviving fragments of his book. One commentator on Heraclitus said of an apparently straightforward fragment that 'the absence of anything enigmatic in this text might almost cast doubt on its authenticity'.

Yet Heraclitus was no concocter of aimless puzzles. On the whole, his work is tantalizing rather than merely annoying, because there is usually something new that he is struggling to say. There is also a point to his paradoxical style. 'Nature', as he put it, 'loves to hide.' That is to say, things are not what they seem. In fact, for Heraclitus they are often the opposite of what they seem, and some of his apparently contradictory puzzles are just his idiosyncratic way of expressing that

41

fact. In Aristotle's treatise on rhetoric, he drily complained about Heraclitus' ambiguous syntax. If Heraclitus had had the opportunity to reply, he might well have responded that it was the world itself which was ambiguous. Thus the form and the content of Heraclitus' thought are intimately connected: nature is a nest of riddles, a fact which he used his own riddles both to illustrate and to explain.

Heraclitus was unlike anybody who had come before. His interests and his situation set him apart from the Milesians and from Pythagoras. Unlike Pythagoras, whom he called 'the prince of impostors', he

HERACLITVS.

seems not to have inspired any sort of school in his own lifetime and he certainly did not follow one himself. The best-attested fact about him is that he was haughty and disdainful of other people, which may help to explain his inaccessible style. He probably liked to think of himself as manifesting his wisdom like the Delphic oracle, which, as he put it, 'neither declares nor conceals, but gives a sign'. He is said to have deposited the only copy of his book in a temple so that the rabble could not get at it. This would have been at some time in the beginning of the fifth century BC, shortly after the death of Pythagoras, and probably in Ephesus (some thirty miles north of Miletus), where Heraclitus was a member of the extended royal family.

Despite his proximity to the home of the first *physici*, the motives of Heraclitus were quite different from those of Thales, Anaximander and Anaximenes. True, he adopted much of their way of talking about the physical elements, which he agreed were transformed into one another by everyday processes. In this respect he was closer to the Milesians than to the Pythagoreans, since he seems to have been uninterested in numbers and their role in explaining nature. But the blundering physics and astronomy of the Milesians were not enough for him, and he made no worthwhile contribution to these subjects or to any other science. Moreover, he seems not to have shared the Milesians' belief that the universe grew out of one sort of stuff at a particular moment of creation; he held that it had always existed. Thus he did not look for the origin of things, since he did not believe that there was one. Instead, he says, 'I went in search of myself.'

None of the Milesians would have said such a thing. They were too busy with the world outside to look for one within. Heraclitus was interested in both, and, since he thought that the same principles governed man and nature, he believed that one way in which he could find out about the latter was by examining the former. It is in Heraclitus that some have claimed to see the first stirrings of psychology: he may have been the first thinker to regard the soul not only in the traditional way, as a heavenly breath which animates the body, but also as something that does man's thinking and perceiving for him. He was keenly aware of the enigmas of this thinking self: 'You will not find out the limits of the soul by going, even if you travel over every way.' So his voyage of discovery sailed inwards. He turned to introspection to describe some of the action on the inner stage, discussing dreams, the emotions and character ('Man's character', he reflected, 'is his fate').

This introspective turn does not mean that he abandoned the sort of objective inquiry which distinguished the *physici* from the myth-making *theologi*. For one thing, he did not look only within. He also stressed the importance of the evidence of the senses ('Whatever comes from sight, hearing, learning from experience: this I prefer'). And his use of supporting examples and illustrative descriptions puts him firmly in the camp of the reasoners rather than the inventive poets. In fact, he explicitly warns against trusting the testimony of poets when it comes to 'things unknown'.

Careful observation of the inner and outer worlds was not the whole story, though. According to Heraclitus, neither the evidence of the senses, nor indeed any sort of learning, amount to much unless you have a proper understanding of the ruling principle of nature, which he referred to as the *logos* (the 'principle', 'theory' or 'formula' of things). Pythagoras was one of many whose learning got nowhere because it was not guided by the correct *logos*: 'much learning, artful knavery'. Everyone except Heraclitus, it seems, was gravely misguided:

'Men are deceived in the recognition of what is obvious, like Homer who was wisest of all the Greeks.' Elsewhere Heraclitus compares men to beasts, to drunkards, to deep sleepers and to children (saying that their opinions are like toys) – all because they do not grasp the true *logos*, which, he says, 'men ever fail to comprehend, both before hearing it and once they have heard'.

So what was it that Heraclitus saw and everybody else missed? After all this bluster, it may come as a disappointment to discover that he did not have one big secret that can be summed up easily in a single slogan. Instead, he had a mixed bag of related secrets, most of which can be encapsulated in two slogans. The first slogan is that everything is strife and turmoil. As he puts it, 'All things come to pass according to conflict.' What this means is that beneath the apparent harmony and stability of things, everything is in a state of flux, a battleground of conflicting opposites. But – and this is his second main secret – these opposites are yet somehow the same: 'All things are one.' This double truth is what he discovered when he went in search of himself. No wonder he found it impossible to express his revelation simply.

For Heraclitus, these ideas about conflict, change and the oneness of things are all part of a single picture, derived partly from what struck him on his introspective journey and partly from his observation of nature. To make sense of the scene he depicts, it is easiest to cut the picture into segments and view them separately. I shall look first at his notion of flux; then at his ideas about conflict (and the special role played in it by fire); then at what he says about opposites and how they are really the same. Lastly I shall suggest how the pieces of the picture might be put together.

Heraclitus illustrated one aspect of his notion of flux with a simple analogy, the point of which will not be obvious at first: 'Even the potion separates unless it is stirred.' The potion which Heraclitus is referring to consists of barley and grated cheese stirred into wine. The stirring is crucial. Unless the barley and cheese are swirling when you drink it, they will sit at the bottom of the beaker and you might as well be drinking ordinary wine. The potion thus depends on the motion. This example can serve to symbolize what for Heraclitus is a well-disguised truth about nature as a whole, namely that its properties depend on underlying motion or change. Another example is rivers:

'As they step into the same rivers, other and still other waters flow upon them.' Here he is drawing attention to the fact that each river really consists of perpetually changing waters. Thus if I step into the Thames at one place today and at the same place again tomorrow, I shall be stepping into different water each time. Heraclitus seems to have thought that what is true of rivers is true in some respect of everything we see, and of the soul too. As one ancient slogan put it, *panta rhei* – all things flow.

But they do not flow peacefully. 'War is father of all and king of all,' as Heraclitus melodramatically put it. Why does he gloss his theory of flux and change with the fanciful notion of strife? Since nature loves to hide, we cannot expect all of Heraclitus' discoveries to be immediately evident to common sense; but part of the answer seems to lie in the way he talks about opposites:

Homer was wrong when he said: 'Would that conflict might vanish from among gods and men!' For there would be no attunement without high and low notes nor any animals without male and female, both of which are opposites.

For Heraclitus, to be an opposite is always to be an opponent. Thus music involves conflict because it uses both high and low notes, which are at opposite ends of the musical scale. The fact that he tripped so lightly from 'opposite' to 'opponent' to 'conflict' to 'war' -- as if it were obvious that every opposite was somehow in a state of war – may reflect the picture of a perpetual battle between physical elements as described by Anaximander with his talk of penalty, retribution and injustice. While the Milesians saw war in the interaction of elements, which was the sort of change they were mostly concerned with, Heraclitus reflected on a greater variety of change or difference, and so exported their metaphor of strife into his wider domain. As for rivers, which are by no means always violent or obstreperous, perhaps it is unwise to look too hard for evidence of conflict or strife within individual things, for fear of missing the wood for the trees. From Heraclitus' point of view, flowing rivers are part of a larger tableau of striving elements: 'The death of fire is birth for air, and the death of air is birth for water.'

Heraclitus gave one of the elements pride of place. He was an intellectual pyromaniac: fire fascinated him. The universe is 'fire ever-living, kindled in measures and in measures going out'. He also says that 'all things are requital for fire, and fire for all things, as goods for gold and gold for goods', thus drawing a parallel between the role of gold as a medium of economic exchange and the role of fire as a medium of physical change. This seems exaggerated. It is plain to see that fire (at least in the ordinary sense) is not involved in every physical process. So what is so special about it? Heraclitus may have held a cyclical theory of the universe, according to which everything period-ically turns to fire in a recurring series of cosmic conflagrations. If so, then there is indeed a sense in which the shadow of fire flickers over everything. Be that as it may, fire fits his turbulent picture of nature particularly well, even if there are no regular universal bonfires, because consuming flames symbolize the strife at the heart of things. A steadily burning flame (of a candle, say) demonstrates the flux hidden behind apparent stability, since it can exist in its seemingly constant state only because it is perpetually consuming some fuel. Like a river, it needs an incessant flow of new material. Fire is also the element which can most easily be observed to transform one thing into another (wood into ash, for example), thus doing the essential work of change. All in all, it is perfect for Heraclitus' picture of perpetual turbulence.

He also sometimes identified fire with the soul, with divinity and with the guiding principle or *logos* of the world. At first these seem unlikely bedfellows. But there are two sorts of fire for Heraclitus. The divine and soulful fire is not the same as its lowly relation, the visible flame that we see burning things in a hearth. It is the heavenly *aether*, rarefied, hot, dry air that comes from the upper realms, which earlier thinkers too had identified as the stuff of which souls are made. Heraclitus, as we saw, regarded the soul as a rational, thinking thing. So for him it is a short step from the traditional ethereal soul-stuff to the guiding *logos* of nature: just as a person's soul can be regarded as the motive force behind his actions, so the world-soul is the guiding principle behind the events of the world. And for a Greek it was natural to describe such an 'ever-living' world-soul as divine. We usually think of fire as randomly destructive. But Heraclitus saw it as a force for order that somehow maintained the balance between elements. It was involved in some leading way in the alternations between hot and cold, and wet and dry, in which the Milesians were so interested ('Cold warms up, warm cools off, moist parches, dry dampens').

Heraclitus also frequently referred to the alternation between sleep and waking and between life and death, and he linked these changes in the living world to the ebb and flow of the physical elements. For example, he says that death comes when a soul becomes too moist, but that this moisture also eventually becomes life again: 'For souls it is death to become water, for water it is death to become earth; out of earth water arises, out of water soul.' This cyclical process, in which water leads to life and also to death, depending on the stage of the cycle, shows how two opposites can be linked together.

This leads to the final component of Heraclitus' picture: the unity of things – that is, the way in which opposites are somehow the same. Failure to appreciate this truth is one of the shortcomings for which Heraclitus berates earlier wise men. Hesiod, he said, is revered as having been the wisest of all, but he did not even realize the truth about day and night, which is that 'they are one'. Hesiod thought of night as a sort of dark force that temporarily blotted out the day, rather like the comic novelist Flann O'Brien's fictitious philosopher who regarded night as an insanitary condition of the atmosphere caused by accretions of black air. Hesiod does not seem to have recognized that day and night are two sides of the same spinning coin. Heraclitus thought that Hesiod was thereby missing something crucial about the world, of which there were many other sorts of instances. For example:

The way up and down are one and the same.

The same . . . living and dead, and the waking and the sleeping, and young and old.

It is disease that makes health sweet and good, hunger satiety, weariness rest.

The sea is the purest and foulest water: for fish drinkable and life-sustaining; for men undrinkable and deadly.

These are four of Heraclitus' examples of the unifying connections between apparently opposite things. The first is straightforward: a path going up a hill is also a path going down the hill, just as an entrance is also usually an exit. The second one is not so straightforward, for a living man is not a dead man, a young girl is not an old girl and a sleeper is not awake. But in the Heraclitean cosmic-recycling programme, these pairs of opposites do come to the same thing in the end, because sleeping things wake up, waking things drop off, the living becomes dead and the dead becomes living (and thus, in a sense, the old becomes young). As for health and disease and the other pairs in the third fragment quoted above, perhaps what Heraclitus had in mind is that weariness gives rest its significance and vice versa, disease gives health its significance, and so on. In the fourth fragment we have yet another sort of connection between opposites: an example of one and the same substance having opposite effects on different creatures.

What all this added up to for Heraclitus is that each pair of opposites is really not two things but one, just as night and day are one. To us this seems like a confused over-generalization with little serious point. We can spell out the respects in which sleep, for example, is not the same thing as waking even though the two are linked. We can draw distinctions between various senses of the terms 'opposite' and 'the same' and so we fail to be convinced by Heraclitus' efforts to yoke them all together. But just as it seems worthwhile to us to draw these distinctions, so it seemed worthwhile to Heraclitus to highlight the connections between youth and age, health and sickness, the ways up and down, and so on. He presumably thought that this helped him to understand these things. Just as Pythagoras was struck by the connection between musical harmonies and numbers, and jumped to the conclusion that numbers somehow explained everything, so Heraclitus was struck by some of the connections between opposites, and jumped to the conclusion that 'all things are one'.

One of the many things which at first sight appear not to be 'all one' is Heraclitus' own thought: it seems to be self-contradictory, as we are now in a position to see. On the one hand, he finds flux, change and strife wherever he looks. On the other hand, this strife seems to be in some respects a mock battle, since the warring opposites – be they the elements, or night and day, or youth and age – are all really on the same side in the end. So do flux and strife really exist according to Heraclitus or not? The answer is that they do, but that flux and stability, unity and diversity are themselves two sides of the same coin, like night and day. Consider his example of the river once more. Although it is just one river, yet it consists of many waters. And although it consists of many waters, still it is only one river. In this way Heraclitus' ideas about strife and unity can be drawn together into one harmonious whole. Although he never quite spells it out, this dual account of flux-in-unity and unity-in-flux seems to be the *logos* which he believed that earlier thinkers had failed to comprehend.

Some later thinkers still failed to comprehend what was going on even after Heraclitus had tried to explain it. Plato did Heraclitus a big disservice by disseminating a distortion of his views. Plato knew a philosopher called Cratylus who apparently seized on one aspect of Heraclitus' thought and blew it up out of all proportion. Plato, and then his pupil, Aristotle, repeated Cratylus' ideas, and most subsequent thinkers saw Heraclitus only through their eyes.

Cratylus' idea seems to have been that everything suffers from severe flux all the time. As a result, one cannot say anything true about anything, since it is all changing so fast. Thus Aristotle referred to 'the views . . . of the professed Heracliteans, such as . . . Cratylus, who finally did not think it right to say anything but only moved his finger'. In one of Plato's dialogues, Socrates diagnosed this extreme view as resulting from a bad case of flux in the head:

many of our modern philosophers . . . in their search for the nature of things, are always getting dizzy from constantly going round and round, and then they imagine that the world is going round and round and moving in all directions. And this appearance, which arises out of their own internal condition, they suppose to be a reality of nature; they think that there is nothing stable or permanent, but only flux and motion.

Once he had attributed this nonsense to Heraclitus, it was easy for Plato to ridicule Heraclitus' alleged followers (of whom Cratylus is the only recorded example):

there is no discussing these principles of Heraclitus ... with the Ephesians themselves, who profess to be familiar with them; you might as well talk to a maniac. Faithful to their own treatises they are literally in perpetual motion ... When you put a question, they pluck from their quiver little oracular aphorisms to let fly at you, and if you try to obtain some account of their meaning, you will be instantly transfixed by another, barbed with some newly forged metaphor. You will never get anywhere with any of them; for that matter they cannot get anywhere with one another, but they take very good care to leave nothing settled either in discourse or in their own minds.

One remark of Heraclitus' which seems to support Plato's and Aristotle's extremist interpretation has become the best-known of his sayings: 'One cannot step twice into the same river.' The idea behind this proverb is fairly plain. Since the waters that compose a river are forever changing as it flows past, it is a different river each time you step into it. But how seriously are we supposed to take this? According to the extreme view of Cratylus, we are to take it absolutely literally: rivers, as we ordinarily conceive them, simply do not exist. If there is a river Thames at all, it exists only for a fleeting instant before it becomes a different river. And similar considerations – on Cratylus' interpretation – show that the same is true of everything else. The matter of which they consist is forever changing. As Socrates put it when describing this view, 'there is nothing stable or permanent, but only flux and motion'.

Yet, if you look at it closely, Heraclitus' other saying about rivers, quoted above on page 45, directly contradicts this: 'As they step into the same rivers, other and still other waters flow upon them.' This speaks explicitly of different waters flowing in the *same* rivers: in other words, different waters do not necessarily make different rivers. So you can step into the same river twice after all. What Cratylus, Plato and Aristotle seem to have done is to take just one half of Heraclitus' double-edged philosophy and simply ignore the other. It is impossible to make sense of Heraclitus if you assume, as they did, that he meant 'you cannot step into the same river twice' to be taken literally.

What Heraclitus was proud to have discovered, and was trying to draw attention to, is the fact that rivers, and everything else, are full of change and flux even when they appear not to be. But he did not think that they are so utterly chaotic that you cannot speak of them at all, and are reduced, like Cratylus, to wagging your finger. After all, that crude exaggeration defeats the point of what he was trying to say. If there were no rivers, then obviously they could not be full of flux, or indeed full of anything.

At least Plato put his misinterpretation to fruitful use. Although he ridiculed what he took to be Heraclitus' theory, he thought there was a grain of truth in it. According to Aristotle, Plato was

persuaded of the truth of the Heraclitean doctrine that all sensible things [ie, *things perceived by the senses*] are ever passing away, so that if knowledge or thought is to have an object, there must be some other and permanent entities, apart from those which are sensible; for there can be no knowledge of things which are in a state of flux.

Thus Plato's exaggeration of Heraclitus served to raise a genuine question: how is it possible to have certain knowledge of a changing world?

The fascination of this question has eclipsed the more elusive things which Heraclitus himself said. His own ideas were never really developed by anybody else; maybe they would not have led anywhere if they had been. But a parallel and independent treatment of one of his themes did constitute the next major stage in philosophy. The work of Parmenides, whom we turn to next, can be seen as a development of the Heraclitean theme of the connectedness of things. Both men criticized the earlier, piecemeal accounts of the development of the cosmos and the workings of everyday phenomena. Both tried to substitute a vision in which 'all is one'. But they were very different visions. In Parmenides' version, nothing ever changes, whereas in Heraclitus' everything always does (though not so drastically as Cratylus seems to have believed). It was the thought of Parmenides which had a far greater impact. The ideas of Heraclitus survived only in Plato's misappropriation of them.

So, thanks to Plato, the real Heraclitus has been all but blotted out for much of the history of philosophy. This tradition of misunderstanding and over-simplification serves Heraclitus right for being intentionally obscure and paradoxical. He is said to have wanted to keep his doctrines secret, so in a way he got what he wanted in the end.

# 4

# The Truth About Nothing:
## *Parmenides*

With the arrival of Parmenides, it has been said, a serpent slithered into the Eden of Greek philosophy. Unlike the biblical serpent, however, this one did not offer knowledge; he threatened to take it away. The arguments of Parmenides undermined all the accounts of nature that had come before. Most earlier thinkers tried to explain how the cosmos had developed, but Parmenides seemed to show that it could not have developed at all. Earlier thinkers tried to account for the events in a changing world of varied phenomena, but Parmenides seemed to prove that there was no such thing as change or variety. Reality, according to him, consisted of one complete, unchanging and eternal thing. After Parmenides and his pupils, the edifice of knowledge had to be rebuilt from the rubble that their puzzling proofs left behind.

Yet Parmenides did not see himself as a destroyer. He thought he was lighting the way out of a forest of delusion and towards what he called the *Way of Truth*. To emphasize this, he cast his reasoning in the form of a revelation, which he pretends to have received from a goddess whilst on a celestial journey:

And the goddess greeted me kindly, and took my right hand in hers, and addressed me with these words: 'Young man, you who come to my house in the company of immortal charioteers with the mares which bear you, greetings. No ill fate has sent you to travel this road – far indeed does it lie from the steps of men – but right and justice. It is proper that you should learn all things.'

Little is known of the man who wrote these words. While the rumbustious Heraclitus still appears larger than life, Parmenides is barely there at all. We have the dry bones of his ideas but no flesh of the man. A description by Plato of a supposed meeting between Socrates and Parmenides suggests that he was born in around 515 BC. He was certainly younger than Heraclitus and older than Socrates. But beyond that one can say only that he and his famous pupil Zeno lived in Elea, an Ionian colony on the west coast of Italy, and that like most of the early philosophers he seems to have been relatively wealthy and prominent.

His ideas seem to come from nowhere, as if they had indeed been spoken to him from above. The fact that Parmenides came from Italy led some to call him a dissident Pythagorean; but there is no real reason to think he was that, except for the fact that he used the sort of deductive proofs which Pythagoreans are presumed to have used in mathematics at around the same time. He is also said to have once been a pupil of the wandering poet and theologian Xenophanes. But this is unenlightening, even if true, since the thought of Parmenides is highly original and seems to owe little to anybody.

As we shall see, Parmenides toyed with the concept of 'nothing' in ways that recall the punning jokes about 'Nobody' which Lewis Carroll found so hard to resist:

'Who did you pass on the road?' the King went on, holding out his hand to the Messenger for some more hay.

'Nobody,' said the Messenger.

'Quite right,' said the King: 'this young lady saw him too. So of course Nobody walks slower than you.'

'I do my best,' the Messenger said in a sullen tone. 'I'm sure nobody walks much faster than I do!'

'He can't do that,' said the King, 'or else he'd have been here first . . .'

Similar jokes were known to the Greeks, from Homer. In the *Odyssey*, an awesome but stupid cyclops called Polyphemus captures Odysseus and asks him what his name is. Odysseus, who was famous for his tricks, identifies himself as 'Nobody'. Odysseus later manages to poke out the giant's solitary eye, and the roars of pain rouse Polyphemus' neighbours, who come out into the night to see if their fellow-cyclops needs help. Polyphemus calls out that 'Nobody' is harming him, which the neighbours naturally misunderstand and so go back to bed. It can be argued that this tale contains the germ of Parmenides' philosophy. But the use that Parmenides made of such wordplay was entirely novel.

The form in which he chose to write was unusual too, at least for a philosopher. He used hexameter verse, the metrical form which was familiar from the work of Homer, Hesiod and many lesser poets. Of the Presocratic philosophers, the only other ones to write in verse were Xenophanes and (later) Empedocles. Unlike Xenophanes, though, Parmenides echoes the style and imagery of the heroic poets, at least in the introductory section of his verse. His journey, for example, is reminiscent of Odysseus' journey to Hades. And the goddess who greets him recalls the muses who inspired more conventional poetic visions. Thus the muses on Mount Helicon who appear at the beginning of Hesiod's *Theogony* tell the poet, 'We know how to speak many false things as though they were true; but we know, when we will, [*how*] to utter true things.' Likewise, Parmenides' goddess says that she will inform him about true things and also about false ones – 'both the unshaken heart of well-rounded truth, and the opinions of mortals, in which there is no true reliance'.

Fortunately for Parmenides, or rather for his readers, the goddess's true words are kept separate from her false ones. His poem, of which some 150 lines survive, is in three parts: the heroic prologue quoted above; the dense and obscure *Way of Truth*, in which Parmenides argues that the world is unchanging and eternal; and the avowedly delusive *Way of Seeming*, of which there are only a few fragments. The surviving lines of this final part of the poem are relatively easy to follow: they give a naturalistic account of a changing physical world. The puzzle is why they are there at all. Why should the goddess give an account of things which she admits to be misleading and which contradicts the earlier *Way of Truth*? I shall suggest an answer to that question later on. The important part of the poem is the *Way of Truth*, and we must look at that first. (To make this account easier to follow, I shall draw on some ideas from his loyal and simpler pupil, Melissus, and fill out Parmenides' line of reasoning in ways that fit his overall argument.)

\*

Parmenides started with a simple idea about thought and language and turned it into a whole philosophy. He held that one cannot meaningfully think or say anything about 'what is not'. In his view, this would amount to speaking of nothing, and a man who speaks or thinks of nothing does not succeed in speaking or thinking intelligibly at all. So we must try to eliminate 'what is not' and 'nothing' from our thoughts. This is surprisingly hard to do, because such negative notions are involved in all sorts of things. It turns out, for example, that we cannot meaningfully speak of anything coming into existence, because this would imply that there was a time when it did *not* exist. And this, for Parmenides, is impossible, since we cannot speak of what is *not*. Similarly, we cannot speak of anything ceasing to exist, because that too involves the impossible idea that there is a time at which it does *not* exist. Thus it is never true to say that anything comes into existence or passes away. So everything is eternal.

This alone would be surprising enough: after all, we seem to see things being born and dying, coming into existence and ceasing to exist. But there is worse to come. Another consequence of the principle that one cannot think or speak of what is *not* is that nothing can ever change. For if something changes, this means that at one time it is one way and at another time it is *not*. But we cannot speak of what is *not*, so we cannot speak of change. It also follows that nothing moves: if something moves, then at one time it is in one place and at another time it is *not* in that place. But we cannot say that something is not in a certain place, so we cannot say that it moves. If Parmenides is right, then Heraclitus with his perpetually turbulent universe could not be more wrong.

Parmenides also argues that whatever exists must always have been complete. To say that it lacks something, or once did so, would be to say that there is or was something which it is *not*, and such a thing cannot be said or thought. The accounts of the universe given by Anaximander and Anaximenes must therefore be utterly mistaken if Parmenides is right. The universe could not have developed in the way they said, or in any other way, because it must always have been fully developed. In the course of arguing that the universe cannot have developed over time, Parmenides offers an extra reason for thinking that it cannot have sprung into existence out of nothing. He asks, 'what need would have driven it later rather than earlier, beginning from the nothing, to grow?' That is to say, if the universe came from nothing, why did it do so at the precise moment when it did and not at some other time? This is a question which nobody before Parmenides seems to have addressed.

Just as the universe – or 'what is', as Parmenides prefers to call it – is the same at all times, so it is the same in all places. There is no part of the universe which is empty, for that would imply that there is nothing in this part, which is clearly impossible for Parmenides. The whole thing must be full. Lastly, since Parmenides believes that 'what is' is uniform and undifferentiated, he maintains that it is a single and unique thing. That is to say, he holds that only one thing exists. At one point he says that 'what is' is 'whole and of a single kind and unshaken and perfect'. Because it is perfect (and also for more complicated reasons, which I omit), Parmenides ends the *Way of Truth* by cryptically comparing the one existing thing to a sphere, which was commonly regarded by the Greeks as the perfect shape. It is, he says, 'equally balanced in every direction from the centre'. So now we know the Truth, or rather Parmenides' incredible version of it. There is no birth, death, change, motion or diversity. There is just one eternal, immovable thing, which is complete, indivisible and not unlike a sphere.

One remarkable thing about this train of thought is its consistency. Again and again Parmenides comes back to the impossibility of thinking about 'what is not'. That is the beauty of it: from this one alleged impossibility, he spins a web that captures and lets him devour change, motion, birth, death, diversity and imperfection. But something has gone very wrong somewhere. As Aristotle put it, 'although these opinions appear to follow logically, yet to believe them seems next door to madness when one considers the facts'.

It is not just that Parmenides' opinions clash violently with common sense. They also clash with each other, and in a particularly blatant way. He frequently denies things – for example, he denies that motion or birth or death exist – and in so doing he is speaking and thinking of what is not, which by his own lights ought to be impossible. It is odd to do so much denying when you profess to shun all negative thoughts.

Yet this objection does not get to the heart of the matter. It proves that something is wrong with what Parmenides is saying, which we surely knew anyway, but does not show where he went wrong, or why. What we need is a post-mortem, not a death certificate. Fortunately, we do not have to look far to find where the trouble started. It was right at the beginning, in his principle that you cannot think or speak of what is not. Plainly we can do this, whatever Parmenides says. We can meaningfully say and think, for example, that unicorns are not anywhere to be found, that Christopher Columbus is not alive today, that chalk is not cheese, that I have nothing in the bank, and a great many other things, all of which could be described as 'speaking of what is not'. And if there is nothing wrong with speaking or thinking of what is not, then we can resist Parmenides' bizarre conclusions.

Parmenides would not have been impressed with this diagnosis. Of course, he would say, people believe they can think and speak of what is not, but they are mistaken. According to him, all we are doing, when we appear to be thinking or speaking of what is not, is making 'meaningless sound'. As his goddess puts it:

you must hold back your thought from this way of inquiry, nor let habit, born of much experience, force you down this way, by making you use an aimless eye or an ear and a tongue full of meaningless sound: judge by reason the much-disputed refutation spoken by me.

Never mind the appearances, she seems to be saying, just consider what reason tells you. Look at my argument with an open mind, forget your commonsense prejudices, and then you will see the truth.

This advice would be easier to follow if the goddess had said more to Parmenides and he had said more to us. The parts of the poem which explain the principle that you cannot think or speak of what is not are tangled, dark and possibly not all there. Besides, Parmenides was not a good poet and frequently got knotted in his own hexameters. And even if he had written in straightforward prose, he might have been unable to spell out why he found this principle so compelling, so perhaps nobody can now do it for him. (Lewis Carroll's King would presumably add that Nobody is, therefore, cleverer than Parmenides.) Still, it is possible to reconstruct part of the story. It emerges that

Parmenides did not merely make some stupid mistake about what you can think and say and what you cannot. Instead, it seems, he made a rather clever mistake.

Parmenides apparently came to the conclusion that the act of thinking involves a sort of direct contact with whatever is being thought about. In effect, he regarded thinking as rather like touching, though he did not put it like that. Since you cannot touch something which is not there, so, according to Parmenides, you cannot speak or think about it either. Trying to think about what is *not* is like trying to touch a ghost. That seems to be why he set out to exorcize negative notions such as 'nothing' and 'what is not' from his account of the world.

What was clever about this idea that the mind must be in contact with what it thinks about is that it was part of an answer to a question that nobody else had even thought of asking. The question is: how do words and thoughts in your head come to refer to and describe things outside? Or, to put it another way, how are language and thought connected to the world? The only answer that Parmenides could come up with was that the mind must somehow almost literally touch the world. This is not very enlightening, but it is at least a start.

Nowadays we can make more sense of the subject than Parmenides did, but there are many questions about thought and meaning that remain unresolved. They occupy psychologists, theoretical linguists, philosophers and cognitive scientists. Ever since Parmenides, thinkers have asked precisely what sort of contact between the mind and the world makes thought and language possible. Several philosophers focussed on such questions at the beginning of the last century, and some of their earliest answers had faint echoes of Parmenides about them. Still, it has been a long time since anyone has gone so far as to maintain that whenever you speak about what is not, you are in fact saying nothing. Indeed, it seems that nobody except Parmenides and his pupils ever quite swallowed that.

It was Plato who began to untangle Parmenides' web, by pressing the question of what exactly Parmenides meant by 'speaking of what is not'. Plato distinguished several different ways in which 'is not' can be used, and thereby demonstrated how crude it is to lump them all together as Parmenides apparently did. It turns out that once the notions of 'what is' and 'what is not' have been sorted and elucidated, there is less cause to be puzzled by the possibility of speaking of 'what is not'. It becomes easy to see that using negative terms or making denials is not the same as saying nothing. Plato did not offer a complete treatment of the matter, but his analysis was enough to make his pupil, Aristotle, dismiss Parmenides with the remark: 'His assumption that "is" is used in a single way only is false, because it is used in several.'

However, before we write off Parmenides as a man who not only produced poor poetry but could not even understand his own native language, there is something worth bearing in mind. The tools of grammatical analysis that Plato used to clarify the notion of 'speaking of what is not' had only just been developed, apparently by the itinerant 'Sophist' teachers who congregated in Athens at the time of Socrates (see page 109). Such grammatical terms and distinctions were not yet common currency in Parmenides' youth and it may never have occurred to him to think about such matters systematically. Indeed, it might never have occurred to Plato or Aristotle to think about them either, if the enigmatic statements of Parmenides and other early thinkers had not prompted them to do so. Parmenides was certainly not alone in being unable to appreciate some facts about language that we now regard as so obvious as to be almost trivial. In his defence, it is also worth noting that the analogy between thinking and touching which seems to have appealed to him probably appeared less far-fetched in his day than it does in ours. The Greek verb in the *Way of Truth* which is translated as 'think' (*noein*) had different connotations from our word 'think'. It suggested a sort of recognition of real objects in the world, usually through the senses, so that it sometimes meant little more than 'perceive'. Indeed, Aristotle once noted that the people of Parmenides' time and earlier 'look upon thinking as a bodily process like perceiving'.

Although Plato dissected the *Way of Truth* with a merciless linguistic scalpel, he spoke of the man himself with reverence. In one of his dialogues, Plato had his hero Socrates say: 'there is one being whom I respect above all. Parmenides himself is in my eyes, as Homer says, a "reverend and awful" figure. I met him when I was quite young and he quite elderly, and I thought there was a sort of depth in him that was altogether noble.' Indeed, Parmenides turns out to have been a formative influence on Plato. One notion that Plato admiringly took over from him is the idea that whatever is ultimately real must be unchanging, uncreated and immortal, though the arguments which Plato offered for this conclusion had nothing to do with the alleged impossibility of 'thinking of what is not'. Plato also echoed Parmenides' sharp contrast between reason and the senses, together with the Pythagorean (and ultimately Orphic) idea that the intellect is somehow superior. The Pythagoreans had, as we have seen, already vaguely espoused such 'rationalism'. But Parmenides was the first to put it to work.

On the foundation of this contrast between the intellect and the senses, Plato built a theory according to which the world is divided into two realms: one that is eternal and unchanging and which we come to know about through the exercise of reason; and another, shifting and changing one, which we learn about through the senses. Unlike Parmenides, Plato was prepared to accept that the inferior world that we see, hear and touch is still real, albeit in a lesser sense. Parmenides had condemned it as an impossible illusion, and would not have said that we learn about it through the senses but rather that the senses somehow trick us into mistakenly believing in it. Another difference between the two men is that although Plato held that the superior realm was eternal and unchanging, he maintained that it contained many things; the ultimate reality was not, as Parmenides had said, 'One'. It consisted of pure, immutable Forms, or Ideas (which will be described more fully when we come to Plato himself). Thus Plato kept some parts of Parmenides' picture and rubbed out others. He was attracted by the idea of an ultimate reality which is not born, and does not change or die. But this was not enough for him, and he was not impressed by Parmenides' reasons for believing that the ordinary world could not exist as well. So he tried to find room for that too.

He was not the first to do so. Four notable thinkers of the fifth century BC, writing mostly before Plato, struggled to reinstate the everyday world while hanging on to at least some of Parmenides' ideas. Thus Empedocles (c. 495–c. 435 BC) said that there were four elements – fire, air, water and earth – and that they were eternal and unchanging, just like Parmenides' One. But although each element itself does not ever change its properties or come into existence or pass away, Empe-docles held that the four can move about and combine with one another to make the everyday phenomena we see. Anaxagoras (*c.* 500–*c.* 428 BC) agreed that no fundamental substance is ever created or extinguished. But instead of having just four elements, like Empedocles, he promoted all natural substances to eternal and unchangeable status. Ordinary objects consist of a mixture of these immortal substances. As with Empedocles, a diverse and changing world is thus cooked up out of ingredients that are themselves eternal and unchanging.

The last and most influential variation on this menu was 'atomism'. Leucippus (*c.* 460–*c.* 390 BC) and Democritus (*c.* 460–*c.* 357 BC) proposed a theory of tiny, moving 'atoms' that had the usual Parmenid-ean qualities of being eternal and unchanging, and which differed from one another only in respect of their shapes and their positions in space. Everything else is explained in terms of them: all natural substances and objects, including people and animals, consist of atoms, which career around in the 'void' (i.e., empty space) until they collide with others to form a tree, a man, a lump of silver, and so on. This busy world is a long way from the one Parmenides envisaged: it contains motion, diversity, and (in some places) empty space.

We have now seen how some of Parmenides' successors tried to cope with what he had argued. How did he himself cope? He had got himself in an impossible position. If there is only one thing (as he thought), then where does that leave him as a man? According to his argument, either he must be as fictitious as the moving, changing commonsense world which he rejected, or else he must be identical with the unchang-ing, sphere-like One. And, leaving that choice of absurdities aside for a moment, how is one supposed to behave in his sort of world? There would be no point in trying to do anything, because motion and change are impossible. Consider the dilemma of Parmenides' loyal follower Melissus. As well as being a part-time philosopher, he was an admiral of the Samian fleet who won a famous battle against the Athenian navy in 441 BC. Yet he accepted virtually all of his master's views. So what did he think he was up to? Ships cannot move, he cannot move, battles cannot take place, and besides there is nobody to fight.

One can only assume that Parmenides and Melissus regarded ordinary life as some sort of illusion, or at least a mystifying puzzle, which one might as well play along with. They never said so, but it is hard to see what else they can have thought. They both led normal lives and thus failed to act – or rather, not act – according to their professed philosophical beliefs.

Perhaps the difficulties of squaring what they believed with the necessities of everyday life barely occurred to them. We cannot tell. And there is no help to be had in the *Way of Seeming*, the second part of Parmenides' poem, in which the goddess gives her account of the false beliefs of men. In fact those fragments just add to the puzzle. As Plutarch (AD *c.* 46–*c.* 120) put it: in the *Way of Seeming*, Parmenides 'said much about the earth and about the heavens and sun and moon, and he recounts the coming into being of men . . .' But Parmenides does not explain how such a story is to be reconciled with the arguments of the austere *Way of Truth*, according to which there is only one thing, and nothing new ever comes into being.

Yet if the *Way of Seeming* does not give Parmenides' own considered views, neither is it presented as merely an historical record of what other people had said. It is an original account, in the style of the *physici* but more sophisticated in parts, which the goddess says she is providing so that 'no thought of mortal men shall ever outstrip you'. This suggests that he included the *Way of Seeming* in his poem in order to show that he had a firm grasp of the conventional wisdom. He exploited the tradition of having muses speak both the truth and also falsehood – as in Hesiod – in order to demonstrate that he too could play the game of devising a naturalistic explanation of the everyday world. Anybody can do that, he seems to be saying, and I can do it better than most.

Be that as it may, not just anybody could have written the *Way of Truth*, which is a marvellous achievement when considered in its place and time. Parmenides' abstract argument may be reason run riot, but at least it is reason running, and apparently for the first time. By its attempt to spin a web of ideas out of one principle – that of avoiding all thought of 'what is not' – in a logically rigorous way, it inaugurated the systematic use of deduction outside of mathematics. It also began the form of thinking in which an extended argument about general principles is used to derive shocking conclusions about the world and man's knowledge of it. We have already met other philosophers who held that the world is not as it appears to be. What is new in Parmenides is his use of detailed proof in an attempt to demonstrate this, and to work out what the true features of reality are. This aspect of his teaching marks the start of a seam that comes to the surface at several places in the history of thought; the most extreme examples of it are the writings of Hegel and his followers. In his lectures on the history of philosophy, Hegel said that 'Parmenides began Philosophy proper', by which he seems to have meant that Parmenides was the first thinker wise enough to anticipate Hegel.

The rest of what Hegel says about Parmenides is obscure, but it seems that what most appealed to him is the view that 'the transient has no truth' – which means, roughly, that anything that changes cannot be real. This is indeed Parmenides' leading idea and it can easily be made to sound like a religious or mystical one, even though his use of closely reasoned argument sets him far apart from more conventional and romantic mystics. (Nietzsche aptly wrote of Parmenides' 'cold bath of . . . awe-inspiring abstractions'.) There are certainly strong similarities between Parmenides' conception of ultimate reality as timeless, unified and unchanging, and Xenophanes' conception of a single, unchanging God – which was at that point an unusual idea for a Greek. But there is no point in speculating whether Parmenides was influenced by Xenophanes, or whether, as Nietzsche thought, the similarities between them are a remarkable coincidence. The vision of a realm of heavenly permanence and rest beyond the turbulence of the everyday world, which is reflected in both the poetry of Xenophanes and in the arguments of Parmenides, lies too deep to be any one writer's property.

Despite its originality and historical significance, one cannot escape the fact that Parmenides' reasoning was more than a little absurd. Is it not utterly fatuous to concoct arguments which, from the comfort of an armchair – or, in the case of Parmenides, supposedly from a chariot in the sky – blithely contradict what we can find out by more direct and reliable means? What is the point of trying to prove that only one thing exists when you can see that this is nonsense simply by looking around you?

Yet Parmenides' strikingly unconvincing start should not be allowed to cast too long a shadow over such projects. Even when it directly conflicts with what is taken to be the common sense of the time, abstract logical argument can reveal important truths. This is because 'common sense' is sometimes wrong and always incomplete. The first and perhaps still one of the most valuable attempts to follow in Parmenides' footsteps is to be found in the work of his pupil, Zeno, who comes next.

# 5

## The Ways of Paradox:
## *Zeno*

It did not take the world some two and a half thousand years to realize that the conclusions of Parmenides' *Way of Truth* are absurd. This was obvious enough in his own time, and it did not deter his loyal pupil Zeno at all. Zeno (who was born in around 490 BC) remained a convinced Parmenidean because he thought he could turn the tables on the rival views of 'common sense'.

There is an account, in what purport to be Zeno's own words, of how he tried to do this. Plato tells how Parmenides and Zeno once went from their native Elea to Athens for the Great Panathenaea, a four-yearly festival of music, poetry and sport dedicated to the goddess Athena. While they were there they met the young Socrates, and Zeno read out a treatise he had written. Socrates questioned him about the book and Zeno replied that it 'is in fact a sort of defence of Parmenides' argument against those who try to make fun of it. It pays them back in their own coin with something to spare.' Zeno had wisely concluded that attack was the best form of defence. His troops consisted of a series of ingenious paradoxes that try to discredit commonsense views by demonstrating that they lead to unacceptable consequences. The intended result of these puzzles is to cast Parmenides in a better light by showing that his opponents are at least as absurd as he is.

Consider, for example, one of Zeno's infamous paradoxes of motion. Suppose for the sake of argument that motion is indeed possible, as common sense says it is and Parmenides denies. And suppose, for the sake of illustration, that the famously fast Achilles intends to run a race at the Great Panathenaea. Zeno points out to Achilles that before he can reach the finishing post, he must get halfway there. And before he can get halfway, he must get a quarter of the way.

And before he can get a quarter of the way, he must get one-eighth of the way. Achilles begins to realize that he is in trouble, for this line of reasoning can evidently be continued indefinitely. Zeno persuades him that he therefore cannot run any distance at all, because before he can cover that distance he will have to cover half of it, and so on *ad infinitum*. Thus the race can never start. This, Zeno seems to imply, is the sort of mess you get into if you start talking about motion. Better to admit that Parmenides was right and say that nothing moves.

There are plenty more puzzles where that came from. Nine of Zeno's paradoxes survive: four about motion; three aimed at 'plurality' – that is, the idea that there are many things rather than just Parmenides' One; one directed against the notion of space; and one which attempts to show that the senses cannot be trusted. There may originally have been many more, for Zeno was evidently a genius at inventing puzzles for use in debate. Plutarch, in his biography of the Athenian statesman and orator Pericles, says that Pericles was once 'a pupil of Zeno the Eleatic, who . . . perfected a species of refutative catch which was sure to bring an opponent to grief'.

Aristotle, who had an answer to almost everything, was not brought to grief by Zeno's paradoxes. He thought he could see how to escape from them – though in fact some of his solutions do not work. But he did acknowledge Zeno as the 'inventor of dialectic'. By 'dialectic', Aristotle seems to have meant the sort of method for getting at the truth that Socrates is seen to use in Plato's early dialogues. Socrates liked to interrogate people about their opinions, gently drawing out consequences they had not thought of by his incisive questions. Thus, inch by inch, he undermined their opinions and made them realize that they needed to look further in order to get a good answer to the question at hand. This practice does indeed seem to be an extension of Zeno's 'refutative' technique. In the above paradox, Zeno takes the commonsense view that it is possible to move (in particular, to run a race), and tries to show that this idea soon leads to problems. Zeno apparently specialized in quick, knock-down arguments, while Socrates slowly wrestled his opponents to the ground, and always gave the impression that it was for their own good. But both used the outwardly negative tactic of deducing unwelcome consequences from what others said or believed.

Plato rightly regarded the sort of dialectic practised by Socrates as ultimately positive, as a necessary preliminary to knowledge. Its object was not so much to refute opponents in debate as to eliminate error in the mutual enterprise of attaining wisdom. Socrates himself saw his own interrogations in this way.

Zeno's aims seem to have been less elevated. Unlike Socrates, he does not seem to have had any constructive intentions, except for a desire to defend the grand implausibilities of his master, Parmenides. Zeno is thus left looking rather mischievous – a pure trouble-maker, albeit an ingenious one. But history has vindicated him, not by unearthing anything charitable about him, and certainly not by showing that his conclusions were right after all, but rather by finding so much that is perennially provocative in his paradoxes. As the philosopher and mathematician Alfred Whitehead wrote in 1932, 'To be refuted in every century after you have written is the acme of triumph ... No one ever touched Zeno without refuting him, and every century thinks it worth while to refute him.'

Zeno's paradoxes, particularly those about motion, have outlived the other main arguments in Presocratic thought. They have been discussed in detail by mathematicians, physicists and philosophers from his day to this. Bertrand Russell's treatment at the beginning of this century breathed a new life into them that has not yet expired. They have also cropped up in some unlikely places, from Tolstoy's *War and Peace* (in which they serve to prompt a tenuous analogy between the perception of motion and the understanding of history) to a twentieth-century farce (in which a tangled form of one of them serves to provide light relief).

Not only do they continue to fascinate, it is sometimes said that even now they have not been laid to rest, and that we still have lessons to learn from them. This surprising claim has some truth in it, but it is also a little misleading. The longevity of Zeno's paradoxes owes quite a lot to the fact that we do not know exactly what they were. In the case of his best-known ones we have to rely almost entirely on compressed, obscure and possibly inaccurate summaries of them by Aristotle. This leaves room for plenty of dispute, and means that commentators can play an endless game of interpretation and reinterpretation in which their own ideas get written into Zeno's missing text. Also, most of the paradoxes involve the notion of infinity in one way or another, and the fact that there always seems to be more to be said about them reflects the fact that there always seems to be more to be said about infinity (which is rather fitting). The scientists and philosophers of each age tend to use Zeno's paradoxes as a peg on which to hang their thoughts about subjects that are tangled up with infinity, such as the divisibility of space and matter, and the concepts of time and motion. By prompting thinkers to open the Pandora's Box of infinity, Zeno let loose a swarm of difficulties which still plagued Newton more than 2,000 years afterwards. The paradoxes have even been dragged into disputes in contemporary physics.

Thus one fruitful feature of Zeno's paradoxes is that they raise more questions than are strictly relevant to their resolution. For example, the solution to the paradox about Achilles' race may be put like this. It is true that if Achilles is to traverse any distance, he must thereby also traverse half that distance, and so on *ad infinitum*. And it follows from this that there is, in a sense, an infinite number of distances he must cross. But it does not follow that he must cross them one at a time, traversing each of the segments before he can proceed to the next. This is the crucial flaw. An analogy from a modern commentator on the paradoxes may help. The fact that an egg can in theory be divided into infinitely many parts does not mean that in order to eat it you have to eat each part one after the other. If you did have to do this, then either you would have to be able to eat infinitely fast, or else you would have to keep eating breakfast until the stars went out. Happily, neither is necessary. Just as it is possible to eat the infinitely many parts of an egg in a few mouthfuls, since each mouthful will dispose of an infinity of tiny parts, so it is possible to run infinitely many distances in manageably few steps, since each step will take you infinitely many tiny distances forward. This point alone is enough to rebut the version of the race paradox given above. But it prompts further questions. How can an ordinary racetrack – of, say, 100 metres – have infinitely many distances packed into it? Why does this not make it infinitely long? If an egg has infinitely many parts, why does that not make it an infinitely large egg?

In effect, Zeno asked this question himself in another one of his paradoxes. The answer to it lies in the fact that, as you subdivide them into halves, halves of halves, and so on, the parts of the egg and the parts of the racetrack get smaller and smaller without limit. (Such a series of diminutions is said by mathematicians to 'converge' on a limit without ever reaching it.) Although Zeno seems not to have realized it, the fact that there is no ultimate limit of smallness in such cases means that there is always room to pack in more parts. So there is no contradiction involved in supposing that a normal-sized egg has infinitely many parts, nor in supposing that a 100-metre racetrack contains infinitely many distances.

Any reader who is still puzzled by such nests of infinities may take heart from the fact that he is far from the first to feel uneasy. The notion of a series of divisions that keep diminishing without ever quite disappearing was not satisfactorily explained until the nineteenth century. By that time, Newton and Leibniz had made some progress on related questions with their invention of the calculus. But although their work let scientists perform various calculations about motion and change that had been impossible before, it involved some confused ideas that were not made clear until the further work of Dedekind, Weierstrass, Cantor and other nineteenth-century mathematicians. Newton's ill-formed idea of infinitesimal quantities, a feature of the calculus with which he himself was unhappy, was rightly attacked by the eighteenth-century philosopher, Bishop Berkeley, among others. Berkeley derided such 'infinitesimals' as 'the ghosts of departed quantities'. It took the genius of Cantor and the others to exorcize these ghosts, so one need hardly feel embarrassed to be a little haunted by them still.

Another of Zeno's paradoxes of motion is less obviously mathematical but equally ingenious. It seeks to show that an arrow which is apparently in flight is in fact motionless, since at any given moment of its flight it occupies a space that is exactly equal to itself. For example, a 'moving' 12-inch arrow would occupy a series of spaces each of which is 12 inches long. Zeno seems to have taken this to imply that it is always at rest in each 12-inch space. We can put his point in a different way by asking when exactly the arrow is supposed to move. If we consider its alleged flight, we find that now it is in one place, then it is in another, and at each intermediate instant it is in an intermediate place. So it seems that it is always at rest in some place or other. When does it then move from one place to the next? There appears to be no time for it to do so.

It is as if Zeno had frozen the fluid motion of an arrow into a series of still photographs by considering each instant of its flight separately. In a way he was right to do so: the truth that he had dimly grasped is the fact that motion consists of a series of immobilities. Zeno's error was to conclude from this that nothing ever moves. For to say that an object is in motion is merely to say that it occupies a succession of different places at successive times. Zeno was therefore right to deny that an arrow can be said to move during an instant of time – not because the arrow is at rest during each instant, but because the distinction between motion and rest does not make sense when applied to individual instants. It makes sense only when you consider an extended period of time. Thus if an arrow is in one and the same place for all of the times in a period, then it can be said to be at rest; if it is in different places, it has moved. Motion is nothing more nor less than that.

This account is known as the static theory of motion, and Zeno's paradox of the arrow unintentionally provides a powerful reason for accepting it. Another of his paradoxes, which will not be examined here, unintentionally demonstrates the fact that the motion of an object can be determined only relatively to the motion of other objects; that is, nothing can be said to move in itself, but only with respect to other things. Thus instead of banishing the idea of motion, which was his explicit aim, Zeno's paradoxes in fact put it on a firmer footing by pointing us towards a more accurate understanding of what it consists in.

We are now in a position to say something about Zeno's overall achievement. We have seen that his paradoxes raised questions which the thinkers of his day, and indeed of some much later days, did not know how to answer in full. As with Parmenides, it can be claimed on Zeno's behalf that one reason why we can make more sense than he did – on such matters as the paradox of the racetrack, for example, or the definition of motion – is that his enigmas led later thinkers to refine their ideas in order to deal with them. Ideas evolve, and ingenious problems such as Zeno's help them to do so.

It seems that Zeno went too far in his enthusiasm for hunting down puzzles and ended up throwing out the proverbial baby with the bath-water. Instead of taking the extreme step of denying that anything moves, would it not have been more reasonable to say merely that motion and infinity call for some further investigation? With hindsight we can say that the answer is yes, Zeno went too far, which at least ensured him plenty of attention. But we should recognize just how much hindsight is packed into that verdict. It has proved possible to improve and reconstruct the ideas of motion and of infinite divisibility in order to take account of his objections; but Zeno himself could not foresee how this was to be done. As far as he could see, the ideas of motion and of infinite divisibility just made no sense.

One thing that Zeno's paradoxes successfully show is how much can be achieved by well-informed armchair reflection. They serve to clarify and stimulate ideas, which is essential to the progress of knowledge. Abstract argument and reflection about concepts play a greater role in finding out about the world than one might at first think. The idea that scientists merely wander around making careful observations and gathering facts embodies a naively incomplete picture of what they are up to. They also try to find new ways to describe what they observe, to fit their facts into neat explanatory theories, and to reflect and speculate on the evidence they have harvested. In other words, they try to rebuild and reshuffle our ideas or concepts. This is where the arguments of Zeno and similar thinkers come in. What such arguments provide may best be described as conceptual criticism. Such criticism is not, by any means, uniquely the province of people calling themselves philosophers. It is not uniquely the province of anybody. It does not matter where ideas such as those expressed in Zeno's paradoxes come from, nor whether they conflict with what is taken to be the common sense of the day, so long as they are found to be stimulating and useful lessons can be extracted from them.

The immediate effect of the ideas of Parmenides and Zeno was to stimulate some of the work of fifth-century thinkers such as Empedocles, Anaxagoras, Leucippus and Democritus (especially the latter two). These men constitute the final stage of Presocratic thought, a period of compromise in which attempts were made to sneak back into the Eden of naturalistic inquiry that had been enjoyed by the thinkers before Parmenides. To 'judge by reason', as Parmenides' goddess urged, is excellent advice, so long as it is taken not as a recommendation to ignore the evidence but as a recommendation to try and make better sense of it. That is how these last Presocratics seem to have taken her words. As I shall show, the interest of these diverse thinkers also goes far beyond their role as rebellious heirs to Parmenides and Zeno.

# 6

## Love and Strife:
### *Empedocles*

Empedocles of Acragas (now Agrigento) in southern Sicily invented a theory of matter which was so simple and apparently convincing that nearly everybody believed a version of it until the Renaissance. The fact that Aristotle endorsed it, with some modifications, helped no end. With Aristotle's authority behind it, the theory even survived in some backward work until as late as the eighteenth century, by which time it ought to have succumbed to the enlightened criticisms of chemists such as Boyle. The theory says that everything is made of a mixture of four elements – earth, air, fire and water – none of which has primacy over the others and which are combined in differing proportions in different things. Thus, to cite one of the only two recipes to survive from Empedocles, bone is said to consist of two parts water to two parts earth and four parts fire. It is tempting to give a similar formula for Empedocles himself: he was two parts proto-scientist to two parts Pythagorean preacher and one part miracle-worker, with a dash of Heraclitean arrogance mixed in.

Empedocles has been compared to Faust, for he claimed that the knowledge he had acquired made him god-like and enabled him to perform magic, such as raising the dead and controlling the weather (or 'the elements', as we still sometimes call it). This recalls what the Evil Angel says to Marlowe's Dr Faustus:

> Go forward, Faustus, in that famous art
> Wherein all Nature's treasure is contain'd.
> Be thou on earth as Jove is in the sky,
> Lord and commander of these elements.

Legend even awarded Empedocles an appropriately Faustian end. After dining with some followers, he is said to have leapt into the flames of Etna and disappeared, just as Faustus was dragged down to the fires of hell at midnight. The story has stuck, thanks to Diogenes Laertius, Milton and Matthew Arnold. In fact Empedocles died while exiled from Sicily for political reasons, probably in the Peloponnese. It was his life not his death that was colourful and extraordinary.

He was born in around 492 BC of prominent parents and was not exactly inconspicuous himself. He wore a purple robe with a golden

Empedocles.

girdle, bronze shoes and a Delphic wreath, all of which seems to have had the desired effect:

I go about honoured by all, as is fitting, crowned with ribbons and fresh garlands; and by all whom I come upon as I enter their prospering towns, by men and women, I am revered. They follow me in their thousands . . .

Just before this boast, Empedocles confesses that he is an 'immortal god, mortal no more'. People who do not appreciate his teachings are, simply, 'Fools!' Given this arrogance, it may come as a surprise that his political activity in Acragas consisted of a brave defence of democracy against tyranny; the grateful citizens even offered him the kingship for his successful egalitarian efforts. Actually, his writings were in harmony with his politics even if his personality seems not to have been. He wrote fondly of a past golden age when all men lived happily together, and his religious teaching implies that all men, and not just the fortunate Empedocles, can regain the divine status they once had. Thus he was a spiritual egalitarian. In fact, he took this to extremes and held that all living things are spiritually akin. He shared the Pythagorean belief that souls transmigrated after death and could be reincarnated as plants or animals as well as people. He himself had 'already been once a boy and a girl, a bush and a bird and a leaping journeying fish'.

How do such Pythagorean ravings fit in with the sober chemical theory of the elements which earned him his place in history? As in the case of the Pythagoreans, Empedocles' scientific activities and his religious views are related. For the Pythagoreans, a link between spiritual matters and the knowledge of nature was provided by their conception of *theoria*, the form of disinterested contemplation that purifies the soul. With Empedocles the connection is more direct. The Orphic or Pythagorean ideas about the soul and its salvation, of which Empedocles gives his own version in a poem (or part of a poem) known as *Purifications*, can be seen as an application to the human sphere of ideas in his 'scientific' poem (or it may have been part of the same poem), *On Nature*. The human drama is just one act in the universal play of elements, and the cast is much the same in both *Purifications* and *On Nature*. Thus the force of Love, which attracts the chemical elements to one another and causes them to combine, is the same force that people feel in their hearts and which explains sexual attraction. The force of Strife, which drives elements apart, is also responsible for the spiritual fall of man.

The remains of Empedocles consist of some 450 scattered lines of verse that fell from his two poems and were preserved, in quotation, pressed in the pages of other writers. This is more than survives from any other thinker of the time and presumably reflects the fact that he was generally found to be the most quotable of them. He was the last of the Greek philosophers to write in verse and perhaps the most skilful to do so; Aristotle called him the father of rhetoric. He is certainly easier to follow than Parmenides, but perhaps this is not saying much.

Empedocles agreed with Parmenides that nothing is ever created or destroyed, but he found a more acceptable way to put it: 'of all mortal things none has birth, nor any end in accursed death, but only mingling and interchange of what is mixed – birth is the name given to these by men'. This amounts to a compromise between Parmenides and common sense. Empedocles is prepared to 'comply with custom' and speak of birth and death, so long as it is remembered that birth or creation is really just the formation of something out of pre-existing ingredients, and that death or destruction is really just the dispersal of those ingredients, which may then go on to form something else. The ingredients themselves are uncreated and indestructible, so Parmenides was right in a way. He also agrees with Parmenides about the impossibility of empty space, but little is heard about the impossibility of motion or about there being only one thing. On the whole, Empedocles seems to have just ignored these inconvenient parts of Parmenides' doctrine, and likewise Zeno's arguments in favour of them.

Empedocles' 'mingling and interchange' refers to the combination of his four elements. He draws an analogy between the way nature mixes the elements to fashion natural things and the way artists mix their paints:

men . . . seize pigments of many colours in their hands, mixing in harmony more of some and less of others, they produce from them forms resembling all things, creating trees and men and women, beasts and birds and water-bred fish, and long-lived gods, too, highest in honour.

Empedocles' earth, air, fire and water – the pigments of which the real world is mixed – were not quite the same as what we mean by those words. 'Air' covered all gases, and 'water' all liquids, and metal counted as a liquid because it melts and mingles with other metals. He also gave each element the name of a deity (sometimes two) and this was not just poetic licence. Since the elements were eternal, they qualified as gods in the loose and generous theology of the time. The same goes for his two basic forces, Love and Strife, which are also sometimes called by the names of gods. Love pulls the elements together and Strife drives them apart. The result of this tug of war is the changing world we perceive.

There was, according to Empedocles, once a time when Love ruled completely and all the elements were united in a single, divine sphere (perhaps like Parmenides' sphere-like One). But Strife gradually gained in power and succeeded in separating the elements. Then Love fought back and managed to assemble the world of mountains, sea, stars and so on. In our present stage of the world, Love and Strife are still competing all around us, like Lewis Carroll's lion and unicorn fighting for the crown. Love manages briefly to throw some elements together into a creature, then Strife dissolves it into ashes, and so it goes on.

One day Strife will triumph (though not forever) and everything will be broken down into fragmented elements once more. But then Love will launch a huge counter-attack and draw them together into another giant Sphere, and the whole business will start all over again. Rough parallels can be drawn between this account and the 'big bang' and 'big crunch' of today's cosmology. According to current wisdom, all matter and energy was at one time compressed in one place, whereupon it exploded and separated in a 'big bang'. If conditions are right, this will then be followed in the distant future by a 'big crunch' in which everything will be sucked back together again into a single point by the force of gravity. This final cosmological clinch corresponds to Empedocles' triumph of Love. Thus Empedocles' account of the cosmos can be made to seem a mixture of the physics of Stephen Hawking and the romantic novels of Barbara Cartland.

Some of Empedocles' story may sound suspiciously similar to earlier accounts as well as eerily anticipatory of later ones. We have already seen the Milesians make use of the four 'opposites' – hot, cold, wet and dry – which sound rather like Empedocles' quartet of elements. And his Strife seems a little like Heraclitus' War, and perhaps Anaximander's process of 'separating out'. So how original was this self-confessed god? It is true that in his fundamental ideas Empedocles was not as revolutionary a thinker as Heraclitus or Parmenides, which is perhaps why his theory of the elements was more easily assimilated into conventional wisdom than was any doctrine of theirs. His ingenuity lies more in the detail of his explanations and speculations, particularly in biology, which we shall come to shortly. Still, his refinements of earlier ideas about substances and forces, though subtle and sometimes apparently slight, do go quite a long way.

For example, the important thing about his elements is that they are equal partners: none of them came first, so none of them is the original *arche* of the world in the Milesian sense. There is no one fundamental stuff for Empedocles, so he does not have to explain how the variety of existing things mysteriously derives from it. What he expressed more clearly than any of his predecessors is the idea that the infinite variety of life and matter is to be explained by reference to the proportions which objects contain of a relatively small number of pure substances that cannot be reduced to anything else. When seventeenth-century chemists concluded that four elements were not enough to do the job (at the time of writing, 115 of them are recognized), and that Empedocles' four were not pure substances anyway, they were still closer to him than they were to any earlier Greek. As for Love and Strife, despite their fanciful names they come nearer than any earlier thinker managed to get to the conception of forces enshrined in classical physics. Before Empedocles, the material elements or opposites had somehow themselves to do all the work of making the world. No real distinction was drawn between material stuff and the forces which act on it. But Empedocles' Love and Strife plainly were independent forces, like our gravity or electromagnetism.

If Empedocles had merely said that Love somehow draws the elements together, and had left it at that, we could write him off as some sort of misty-eyed romantic who happened to anticipate some modern science, and move on to somebody more informative. But he did not leave it at that. The actions of Love and Strife in making the world were held by Empedocles to be embodied in more familiar natural processes, which he took pains to describe consistently and coherently. As in all the best early Greek thinkers, these accounts are a mixture of astute observation and imaginative extrapolation; the extrapolation is anchored to experience not by being put to the test of any sort of artificial experiment but by the persuasive use of metaphors and practical analogies.

Thus Empedocles describes the action of Love in making the first living creatures as a version of pottery: clods of earth are moistened by water and then hardened into shape by the fire of the sun. He also uses the image of baking flour and water. It is presumably because bone is brittle and bleached in colour, and has thus apparently been baked in a particularly fierce heat, that Empedocles makes it consist of fire in as much as four parts out of eight. (One might wonder why he evidently never attempted to verify this recipe by trying to make some bone. Perhaps he thought it impossible, even sacrilegious, to try and call down the sun's fire himself.) In general, natural objects are said to be produced by the hardening action of fire on earth and also on water. The prominence he gives to the effect of the sun's fire on the element of earth is hardly surprising when one considers that he lived in the scorching heat of Sicily. The fact that he was a Sicilian also helps to explain his otherwise puzzling notion that solids may be produced by heating water as well as by heating earth: rocks are said to come out of water – an apparently groundless idea. But in the Sicily of his day, salt crystals were extracted from the sea by evaporation on a commercial scale. So that may have seemed to him to be a case of getting rocks out of water. Also, the lava of Etna evidently spewed forth rock, and since lava is liquid it counts as water for Empedocles. If Empedocles had been an Eskimo rather than a Sicilian, he would presumably have reached different conclusions about the basic processes of nature. He might, for example, have put more weight on the way the sun can melt solids into liquids if he had seen his igloo melt into a puddle.

Empedocles made more headway with his accounts of living things. For one thing, he realized that apparently dissimilar features of different organisms can serve the same function and have analogous workings – a fundamental principle of biology. Thus he describes the olives of an olive tree as its eggs, and he says that hair, feathers and scales are all the same thing. The most detailed of his biological explanations to survive is an account of respiration in animals and man. According to this theory, the regularity of breathing is caused by the movement of blood past little holes in blood-carrying tubes at the back of the nostrils. This motion sucks in the air. The tiny perforations are big enough to let in the air, but not big enough to let blood escape (air is thus assumed to be more fine-grained than blood). He cleverly illustrates the mechanical principle involved by drawing an analogy with a simple and then-familiar vacuum-based device for carrying water. The theory is wide of the mark, but not bad for someone who was also capable of believing himself to have been a reincarnated bush.

On the central question of biology, Empedocles hit the mark with surprising accuracy. He said that creatures owe their useful and fortunate features to the fact that there were originally many sorts of creatures and that the strange, deformed ones failed to survive because they were unsuited to do so, leaving only the well-suited creatures to reproduce their kind and populate the earth. His account has fantastical elements and includes a bestiary that would be more at home in a traditional mythology ('Here sprang up many faces without necks, arms wandered without shoulders, unattached, and eyes strayed alone,

79

in need of foreheads'). But he seems thus to have had a grasp of the principle of natural selection some 2,300 years before Darwin and Wallace became famous for offering real evidence in favour of it. As Aristotle put the theory: 'Most of the parts of animals came to be by chance,' having been randomly thrown together in the mêlée of the battle between Love and Strife; and when those parts were useful the creatures which were lucky enough to have them 'survived, being organized spontaneously in a fitting way; whereas those which grew otherwise perished and continue to perish'. As Darwin said of this passage, 'We here see the principle of natural selection shadowed forth.'

Aristotle described this prescient story of Empedocles in order to refute it. He could not accept an account of nature that left out the notion of purpose and replaced it with chance. For Aristotle – and, even more so, for Plato before him – nature was full of purposeful design and could not be explained in purely mechanical terms. Plato and Aristotle won that battle: Empedocles' explanation of biological adaptation was effectively stamped out until Darwin came along. Although Aristotle gratefully accepted Empedocles' theory of the elements, he had many criticisms of almost everything else he wrote, at one point even intemperately implying that Empedocles had 'nothing to say'.

One of Empedocles' most-used tools in his kit-box of mechanical explanations was his theory of pores and effluences. He held that all matter is porous, having tiny passages or holes of various sizes, and that it also somehow gives off microscopic particles. Objects continuously exchange these effluences through their pores, but they do so selectively. Some pores admit certain sorts of particles, others admit others. This mechanism was held to explain how elements combine and why some substances mingle and others do not – why, for example, water mixes with wine but not with oil. Empedocles used it to account for all sorts of phenomena, including magnetism and decay (things waste away when they give off more effluences than they absorb). His most ingenious use of it is in an attempt to explain perception. He says that each of the sense-organs has its own sort of pores and admits a corresponding sort of particle. Thus, for example, 'colour is an effluence from shapes commensurate with sight and perceptible by it', as

Plato later put it, and smell, taste and hearing are explained along similar lines.

There are two distinct ideas involved in Empedocles' picture of perception, one of which blends into a general theory of the nature of thought. There is the crude mechanical thesis that perception takes place by physical contact between our sense-organs and external objects, via the effluences that pass between them. And there is a vaguer and more general principle at work, namely the principle that 'like is known by like'. This was a piece of proverbial wisdom for the ancient Greeks, related to the nebulous idea that like attracts like. For example, it was held that we manage to see bright things because the material of which our eyes are made itself contains bright things: this was thought to be somehow relevant, though to modern minds it is not clear how.

If the account of pores and effluences is an attempt to describe the physiological mechanisms of the eyes, ears and nose, then the idea that like is known by like can be seen as a stumbling attempt to say something about the general nature of consciousness. For Empedocles, perception and thought are special instances of the affinity between man and the rest of nature. We can see and be aware of the elements because we too are made of them. The forces of Love and Strife are also to be found in man, and it is by virtue of this that he can perceive and comprehend these forces at work in the world. Sadly, Strife has become too powerful in man's life, or so Empedocles thought, and much of man's troubled existence reflects this fact. That sentiment opens the way to the Orphic and Pythagorean ideas in his religious poetry, *Purifications*.

Empedocles' audience would have recognized *Katharmoi* (Purifications) as referring to the rites of cleansing, both literal and figurative, which were necessary for those who had offended against the gods or broken some sacred rule. This part of his writings is about the moral forms of Love and Strife, and describes how the power of Strife divorced man from his divine nature by tempting him to sin, with the result that he was cast out from heavenly bliss:

for thrice ten thousand years he wanders apart from the blessed, being born throughout that time in all manner of forms of mortal things, exchanging one hard part of life for another. The force of the air pursues him into the sea, the sea spews him out on to the floor of the earth, the earth casts him into the rays of the blazing sun, and the sun into the eddies of the air; one takes him from the other, but all abhor him. Of these I too am now one, an exile from the gods and a wanderer, having put my trust in raving Strife.

In Hesiod, an Olympian god could be banished for a fixed period if he misbehaved: 'For nine years he is cut off from the eternal gods and never joins their councils or their feasts. But in the tenth year he comes again to join the deathless gods who live in the house of Olympus.' Empedocles married this idea from orthodox mythology with elements of Orphism and other mystery-cults. Thus the punishment for erring is not just exile but a cycle of reincarnations. And it is not just delinquent Olympian gods but everyone who is punished in this way. Everyone has, or had, a divine spark and every man is thus 'an exile from the gods and a wanderer'. It seems that the sin which brought about this demeaning fate of lowly rebirth is the sacrifice and eating of animals ('Alas that the pitiless day did not destroy me first, before I contrived the wretched deed of eating flesh'). As in Pythagorean belief, the way to atone for this dreadful mistake is to become a vegetarian.

The basic moral of his tale is that one should live in the ways of Love, not Strife. He speaks of a golden age when *daimones* (which may roughly be translated as 'spirits') lived happily before they were clothed 'in an alien garment of flesh' for punishment: 'Among them was no war-god . . . worshipped . . . but Cypris [i.e., Love] was queen' . . . 'All things were tame and gentle to men, both beasts and birds, and their friendship burned bright.' Killing animals for food or sacrifice is thus presumably wrong primarily because one should live in peace with them, as with all things.

Man's fall from this paradise, to be tossed among the elements in a cycle of rebirth, echoes the dissolution of the earlier empire of Love when Strife destroyed the cosmic Sphere and separated the elements. Just as the elements will eventually recombine by the force of Love, so too will the *daimones* which are presently clothed in flesh of various kinds be restored to their divine state. They work their way upwards through a series of incarnations:

But at the end they come among men on earth as prophets, bards, doctors and princes; and thence they arise as gods highest in honour, sharing with the other immortals their hearth and their table, without part in human sorrows or weariness.

It just so happens that prophet, bard and doctor is exactly what Empedocles was, and he also rejoiced in being treated like the prince that he apparently was. Medicine, or at least crude physiology, seems to have been his main scientific interest, just as mathematics was the favourite of the Pythagoreans. The Pythagoreans exalted mathematics as the study most likely to bring salvation, and Empedocles seems to have promoted medicine to a similar status. It was at least more likely than geometry to bring admiration from ordinary people.

He was credited with being the founder of one of the three main schools of ancient medicine, known as the 'empirical' school, to mark his supposed method of acquiring knowledge through careful observation. He was certainly far removed from Parmenides' view that the senses were merely a source of utter delusion. Empedocles urged his audience:

Come now, observe with all your powers how each thing is clear, neither holding sight in greater trust compared with hearing, nor noisy hearing above the passage of the tongue, nor withhold trust from any of the other organs, by whatever way there is a channel to understanding, but grasp each thing in the way in which it is clear.

For all his admiration of Parmenides, Empedocles abandoned the earlier thinker's reliance on pure reason as the sole guide to truth and refused to 'withhold trust' from the organs of perception. Our next subject, Anaxagoras of Clazomenae, shared Empedocles' desire to make sense of the everyday world rather than dismiss it. But Anaxagoras had no trace of the prophet or bard about him. Like the Milesians, he was an inquirer into nature, pure and simple. Any mystery-cult ideas of reincarnation in the form of a bush, beast, fish or bird had flown away.

# 7

## Mind and Matter:
## *Anaxagoras*

Anaxagoras (*c.* 500–*c.* 428 BC) was born in Clazomenae, near Smyrna, but fortunately he did not stay there. He was the man who brought Ionian naturalism westwards to Athens. When he arrived there in around 460 BC, Socrates was a young boy, Plato had not yet been born and the city had apparently never seen a philosopher or man of science before. The Athenians tolerated him for some thirty years, giving him the faintly derisive nickname 'Mind' (*Nous*) and revelling in stories of his ironic wit and unworldliness. But their indulgence went only so far, and eventually he was convicted of impiety. He escaped back east, to Lampascus, having left quite a mark on the Athenians.

Officially his crime was to have believed that the heavenly bodies are not gods to be worshipped but red-hot rocks to be avoided. Several ancient writers said that the reason why he was prosecuted was his friendship with the great Athenian leader, Pericles, whose enemies found the unworldly Anaxagoras an easier target. This is all too plausible: other friends of Pericles were similarly accused, and politically motivated trials for unorthodoxy were common towards the end of the fifth century BC in Athens. Still, such trials could not have served their political purposes if heresy and disbelief in the super-natural had not aroused genuine displeasure among the Athenians, or at least some of them.

Anaxagoras is mentioned in Plato's account of Socrates' own trial for impiety some thirty years later. Socrates asked one of his accusers, Meletus, whether the allegation against him was that 'I do not believe that the sun and moon are gods, as is the general belief of mankind.' Meletus concurred: 'He certainly does not, gentlemen of the jury, since he says that the sun is a stone and the moon a mass of earth.' This reply let Socrates have some fun at Meletus' expense: 'Do you imagine that you are prosecuting Anaxagoras, my dear Meletus? Have you so poor an opinion of these gentlemen, and do you assume them to be so illiterate as not to know that the writings of Anaxagoras of Clazomenae are full of theories like these?'

Anaxagoras certainly had a robust Ionian interest in astronomy. He was said to have predicted a meteorite that fell in Aegospotami in Thrace in 467 BC. This is even more implausible than the prediction of an eclipse that was credited to Thales more than a century earlier. Nevertheless the story has a point: hearing of a rock that fell from the sky probably confirmed Anaxagoras' view of what the stars were made of. Such a conjecture about the nature of the heavenly bodies was all very well in free-thinking Ionia, but it evidently did not go down well in conservative Athens.

Anaxagoras was opposed to superstition in general, not only when it concerned the stars. There is a story in Plutarch's *Life of Pericles* according to which Pericles was once brought the head of a ram that had only one horn, sticking out of the middle of its head. A seer called Lampon declared that the finding of this unusual object on Pericles' land meant that Pericles would become the leading figure in Athens (which he did). But Anaxagoras, so the story goes, simply had the head dissected and showed how the unicorn-like horn had come to grow as it did because the ram's brain was deformed. Plutarch implies that as far as Anaxagoras was concerned, there was no need to look for any further meaning in the matter once this physiological fact had been discovered.

Having such a sceptical and inquiring mentor on hand seems to have done Pericles good. According to Plutarch, he was 'filled full of the so-called higher philosophy and elevated speculation' by his association with Anaxagoras, and was 'lifted by him above superstition', which 'affects those who are ignorant of the causes of . . . things, and are crazed about divine intervention . . .' Plutarch attributed much of Pericles' dignity and good humour to his exposure to the philosophizing of Anaxagoras. And Socrates said that it accounted for Pericles' great skill in argument and rhetoric. But whatever he may have thought of its happy effects on Pericles, Socrates did not swallow Anaxagoras' world-view whole. He thought it was too narrowly scientific: it paid, in his view, too much attention to the mechanical causes of things and not enough to their meanings and purposes.

This rejection by Socrates of Anaxagoras' outlook has been hailed as a turning-point in the history of philosophy. It is sometimes said to mark the crux at which the subject transformed itself from the speculative study of nature into the serious moral study of man. As Cicero put it some three centuries later:

from the ancient days down to the time of Socrates . . . philosophy dealt with numbers and movements, with the problem whence all things came, or whither they returned, and zealously inquired into the size of the stars, the spaces that divided them, their courses and all celestial phenomena; Socrates on the other hand was the first to call philosophy down from the heavens and set her in the cities of men . . . and compel her to ask questions about life and morality and things good and evil.

There is some truth in this version of events, but not much. It is not true that philosophy was solely concerned with scientific questions until Socrates came along. Several philosophers, including Pythagoras and Heraclitus, discussed 'questions about life and morality and things good and evil' long before he did. Their dark, sixth-century pronouncements were admittedly less sophisticated than what Socrates had to say. But there were other subtle and argumentative treatments of ethics at around Socrates' own time in Athens that were independent of his influence (see pages 107–8). Also, philosophy continued to deal with astronomical and other scientific questions, both in Athens and elsewhere in Greece, long after Socrates had allegedly called it down from the heavens.

The reason why Socrates himself was uninterested in the scientific side of philosophy is partly that he found it too controversial. He did not know which of the many rival schools to believe. But it was mainly because he was more interested in man and his behaviour, about which science then had little to say. There was something else wrong with philosophers like Anaxagoras, as far as Plato and Aristotle were concerned. Scientific philosophy such as his made too little of the role of reason and purpose in nature. It is not clear to what extent Socrates shared this attitude, but Plato makes out that he did. Plato's Socrates wanted to hear explanations of nature that cited the intelligent operations of a mind. He would have liked an account of the behaviour of nature that somehow made it analogous to the behaviour of man, explaining its operations in terms of the goals it was trying to achieve.

This is why, according to Plato, Socrates was at first intrigued by what he had heard of Anaxagoras. Anaxagoras had obscurely said that some sort of universal 'Mind' – *Nous*, which may also be translated as 'reason' – permeates the world and somehow controls all natural processes. But Socrates' interest in this idea soon turned to disappointment because Anaxagoras never really made anything of it:

When I was young . . . I had an extraordinary passion for that branch of learning which is called natural science. I thought it would be marvellous to know the causes for which each thing comes and ceases and continues to be . . . Is it when heat and cold produce fermentation, as some have said, that living creatures are bred? Is it with the blood that we think, or with the air of the fire that is in us? . . . at last I came to the conclusion that I was uniquely unfitted for this form of inquiry . . . I was so befogged by these speculations that I unlearned even what I had thought I knew . . .

However, I once heard someone reading from a book, as he said, by Anaxagoras, and asserting that it is mind that produces order and is the cause of everything. This explanation pleased me. Somehow it seemed right that mind should be the cause of everything, and I reflected that if this is so, mind . . . sets everything in order and arranges each individual thing in the way that is best for it. Therefore if anyone wished to discover the reason why any given thing came or ceased or continued to be, he must find out how it was best for that thing to be . . .

These reflections made me suppose to my delight that in Anaxagoras I had found an authority on causation who was after my own heart. I assumed he would begin by informing us whether the earth is flat or round, and would then proceed to explain in detail the reason and logical necessity for this by stating how and why it was better that it should be so . . . It never entered my head that a man who asserted that the ordering of things is due to mind would offer any other explanation for them than that it is best for them to be as they are . . . [*Socrates says he then bought a copy of Anaxagoras' works:*]

. . . As I read on I discovered that the fellow made no use of mind and assigned to it no causality [*i.e. explanation*] for the order of the world, but adduced causes like air and aether and water and many other absurdities.

In other words, it was the same old stuff. Later on I shall return to this idea that things ought to be explained by reference to mind or reason and to how it is 'best for them to be'. Plato and (to a lesser extent) Aristotle championed such an approach, and for 2,000 years their influence eclipsed the more materialist and mechanical type of scientific thinking that Anaxagoras and the *physici* before him had been developing. Materialist science was later reborn and flowered in the age of Galileo and Newton. But before temporarily sinking behind the figures of Plato and Aristotle, it reached its high point in the ancient world with the so-called 'atomists', Leucippus and Democritus, who can in some respects be seen as seventeenth-century thinkers ahead of their time.

Like the atomists after him and Empedocles before, Anaxagoras' account of nature grew under the shadow of Parmenides. He needed to find a way to reconstitute the changing, material world that Parmenides had attacked. Although Anaxagoras said too little about mind to please Plato, he did say quite a lot about matter. And it is mainly for what he said on this subject, rather than for his attacks on superstition, that he is remembered in the history of philosophy.

Anaxagoras started out from the same point as Empedocles but ended up somewhere completely different. Whereas Empedocles quadrupled the eternal and indestructible One of Parmenides and came up with an eternal and indestructible Four, Anaxagoras performed a more ambitious metaphysical multiplication. He made all substances eternal, uncreated and indestructible. To see why he did so, consider an odd question that struck him: 'How could hair come from what is not hair . . . ?'

In this question, Anaxagoras is alluding to the fact that the food we eat, which seems (on the whole) not to contain any hair, is transformed into our growing bodies, which do have hair. Thus hair comes from what is not hair. Why should he find this puzzling? Because, as a good Parmenidean, he held that it is impossible for anything to come into existence, either out of nothing or out of anything else, and this led him to try to explain away all apparent cases of coming into existence such as the growth of hair. Empedocles' theory of the four elements had tried to explain away such changes by saying that they merely consist in a reshuffling of the elements. Shuffle water, earth and fire in the right way, for example, and you get bone. It would follow from this that nothing new comes into being when bone develops, because it is just one of the many possible rearrangements of the world's pre-existing constituents. But Anaxagoras was not impressed by this idea. And so he offered his own more radical theory.

His key idea is that every substance contains small portions of many others. This solves the problem of how one thing can apparently turn into another, because it says that the 'new' substance was present in the old one all along, so nothing new is created after all. Thus when our food nourishes us and becomes hair, bone and so on, this is because it had hair in it from the start. Anaxagoras seems to have thought that absolutely anything can develop into absolutely anything else (perhaps via many intermediate stages), and so he maintained that every substance contains portions of not just many but in fact every other substance. Thus what we call bread also contains flesh, water, earth, flour, gold and everything else, but in such tiny amounts that we perceive only the predominating bread. As Aristotle described this idea (which he did not agree with):

things ... appear different from one another and receive different names according to what is numerically predominant among the innumerable constituents of the mixture. For nothing ... is purely and entirely white or black or sweet, or bone or flesh, but the nature of a thing is held to be that of which it contains the most.

This was, to put it mildly, an imaginative solution. The Roman philosopher Lucretius (c.98–c.55 BC), in his poem *On the Nature of Things*, found it easy to ridicule. He claimed that according to Anaxagoras' theory, 'corn also, when it is being ground by the crushing strength of the millstone, should show often a sign of blood or something of those substances which are nourished in our bodies'. Lucretius took this consequence to be absurd; but Anaxagoras would have had an answer ready for him. He would have said that corn does indeed contain blood and that the only reason why it does not appear to bleed is that millstones cannot grind it small enough for the minute particles of blood to become visible. Just looking at corn is not enough to get to the bottom of what it is really like.

Thus Anaxagoras held that the senses do not provide a comprehensive and accurate guide to the world. Referring to the invisible portions of everything that are allegedly to be found in, say, bread or water, Anaxagoras says that these substances have 'parts which only reason can apprehend'. What he means is that it is reasoned argument, not the senses, which tells us that bread must contain tiny bits of other things. The argument in question is that otherwise we could not explain how bread turns into other substances in our bodies and nourishes us. By thinking along these lines, Anaxagoras was following the injunction of Parmenides' goddess to 'judge by reason' and not be misled by what we merely perceive. But he is not as extreme as Parmenides. For Anaxagoras, judging by reason is not a matter of ignoring the evidence completely but of trying to make better sense of it. As he cryptically puts it, 'Appearances are a glimpse of the obscure': that is, the senses provide us with blurred outlines of the world, which reason then brings into focus.

Anaxagoras argued that matter had to be infinitely divisible. However small you grind up a piece of, for example, gold (which, for Anaxagoras, means a piece of matter that is predominantly gold), each particle will still contain portions of gold, and so on *ad infinitum*. Otherwise it would be possible to destroy a piece of gold by grinding it so small that none of it survived, and the idea of such absolute destruction would never do for a neo-Parmenidean like Anaxagoras. As he put it: 'Neither is there a smallest part of what is small, but there is always a smaller (for it is impossible that what is should cease to be through being cut).'

So the world according to Anaxagoras is crowded with infinitely intricate Chinese boxes of matter packed inside one another. How did it get like that? Empedocles explained the way in which matter was arranged throughout the universe by invoking his forces of Love and Strife, which made the four original elements alternately combine and separate to take on the varied and changing forms we see. Anaxagoras invoked a force that was less picturesque but a more imaginative choice, namely mind. In the beginning, he said, there was a motionless and undifferentiated mass of stuff that consisted of all substances packed together. Mind then somehow started things moving:

And it began to rotate first from a small area, but it now rotates over a wider and will rotate over a wider area still . . . And all things that were to be . . . Mind arranged them all, including this rotation in which are now rotating the stars, the sun and moon, the air and the aither that are being separated off. And this rotation caused the separating off. And the dense is separated off from the rare, the hot from the cold, the bright from the dark and the dry from the moist.

Some of this may sound familiar. Anaxagoras borrowed Milesian ideas about the original separating-off of opposite qualities and updated them, in two main ways. First, to accommodate the Parmenidean principle that nothing can come from something else, we find the new idea that all types of matter were present in the original mixture. Secondly, an external force, in the shape of mind, is introduced in order to account for motion. Anaxagoras evidently did not go so far with Parmenides as to agree that motion was impossible; but he does seem to have been sufficiently unsettled by Parmenides' attack to feel the need for some sort of explanation of it. Unlike the Milesians, Anaxagoras could not just take motion for granted.

Admittedly, his explanation of motion does not amount to much. He merely gestured at his mysterious 'mind' and accused it of starting it all. As to why he chose mind for the role, his line of reasoning probably went something like this. He elsewhere says that, as well as impelling the original rotation of primordial matter, mind continues to control all living things; and that in addition to the fact that each piece of matter contains all other types of matter, 'there are some things [*by which he means living things*] in which there is mind as well'. Now, to a Greek the main difference between living and non-living things is that only the former can move themselves. Anaxagoras presumably inferred that it was the presence of mind which enabled them to do so (maybe plants had rudimentary minds that enabled them to grow). And from there it would be a short step to the conclusion that mind animated the early cosmos and caused it to move, just as it continues to animate living creatures.

Because Anaxagoras spoke of his mind as an entity having 'all knowledge about everything and the greatest power', and as 'infinite and self-ruled, and . . . all alone by itself', separate from ordinary matter, it is tempting to conclude that here at last we have an ancient Greek who has managed to throw off crude materialism and to credit him with a 'dualist' view of the world, according to which reality is divided into distinct realms of incorporeal, intelligent mind on the one hand and brute, solid matter on the other. But this would be premature; in fact Anaxagoras thought of mind as a special form of matter, not as something completely different. He describes it in clearly material terms, as a thin and pure substance, and as somehow occupying space rather than being wholly immaterial. Thus although Anaxagoras was indeed straining against the limits of crude materialism, he did not escape it.

After its brief appearance at the birth of the cosmos, mind soon disappears from the scene, as Socrates later noted with disappointment. As far as inanimate matter is concerned, it seems to have had nothing left to do once it started off the original rotation. Impersonal, natural causes soon took over, and only they are mentioned in Anaxagoras' accounts of how the cosmos evolved after it had started spinning. The stars are said to be stones that were flung off the spinning earth and made to glow with heat because of the speed with which they moved. Anaxagoras proceeded to explain as many natural phenomena as he could in a similarly mechanical manner, citing centrifugal and centripetal forces and the old Greek principle of the attraction of like by like. Thus the role of mind is simply to launch the ball in a cosmic pinball-machine. Once launched, matter careered off on its own noisy and colourful path.

It is fortunate for Anaxagoras that he quickly pushed mind into the background, because this is what saved him from relegation to the ranks of the old *theologi* with their stories of the unpredictable whims of the gods. By leaving the explanation of most processes to natural and impersonal forces, he re-establishes his credentials as a latter-day member of *physici*, one of the early natural scientists.

Among the things he speculated about were the weather, a little biology, and perception, as well as cosmology and astronomy. He seems to have realized that the moon gets its light from the sun and to have understood that the earth's shadow is responsible for eclipses of the moon. In all this one can see the Milesian inheritance at work. Unlike Thales, however, Anaxagoras was not a practical man. He was born rich but abandoned his estates to concentrate on philosophy, showing no interest in politics or money. According to one story, his stoical indifference to worldly matters extended even to his own children. When news was brought to him that his sons were dead, he is reputed to have said, 'I knew that my children were born to die.' And when someone – perhaps an Athenian, wishing Anaxagoras had stayed in Clazomenae – allegedly rebuked him with the words, 'Have you no concern in your native land?' he is said to have replied, 'I am greatly concerned with my fatherland,' and to have pointed to the sky.

# 8

## He Who Laughs Last:
### *Democritus*

The final and most remarkable of the early Greek theories to surface in the wake of Parmenides was atomism. It seems to have been invented by Leucippus, about whom virtually nothing is known, and to have been developed by Democritus (*c*.460–*c*.370 BC), who seems to have known virtually everything, or at least to have thought he did. The historian Diogenes Laertius makes him sound like a cross between Sherlock Holmes and the Delphic Oracle: on tasting some milk he is said to have deduced that it must have come from a black she-goat who had just produced her first kid, which is about as plausible as the story that at the age of more than 100 years old he postponed his own death at will by inhaling the aroma of freshly baked bread. After his eventual death, Democritus was remembered as 'the laughing philosopher', apparently because he scoffed at the folly of mankind. You would hardly guess from his surviving writings that he was such a gay dog. Their earnestness makes it difficult to imagine him laughing at anything: 'Do not be suspicious of everybody; but be canny, and on the safe side'; 'Repentance for wrongdoing is the saving grace of life'; 'Those whose demeanour is well-ordered have a well-ordered life.'

Hindsight suggests that a more fitting rationale for his nickname is that he turned out to have the last laugh. For most of the 2,400 years that separate us from Democritus, his doctrines lay submerged under the disapproving weight of Plato, Aristotle and the Christian Church. But his fortunes revived in the scientific revolution of the seventeenth century and have stayed high ever since, while the physical theories of Plato and Aristotle have been discarded. The modern world-picture has more in common with the ideas of Democritus and his followers than with those of any other Greeks. As we shall see, some apparently revolutionary ideas that were credited to Galileo (1564–1642) were in fact largely restatements of the words of Democritus. Even more impressively, a daisy-chain of influence extends from the ancient atomists to the triumph of the modern atomic theory of matter in the nineteenth century. Admittedly, Galileo and the modern atomists worked hard to establish and test their conclusions, whereas Democritus simply made it all up and luckily turned out to be right. Nevertheless, ancient atomism has aptly been described as the crowning achievement of Greek philosophy before Plato.

Perhaps the most striking thing about it is that this seemingly scientific philosophy grew straight from the dark and incredible notions of Parmenides. It took just one tweak of Parmenides' premises to turn his motionless, unchanging One into Democritus' buzzing profusion of atoms. How that came about will be explained shortly.

Although atomism made it to the seventeenth century, and beyond, it had a hard time getting there. Aristotle devoted considerable effort to proving that it was mostly nonsense. Plato found it so distasteful that he apparently could not bring himself even to mention Democritus, let alone refute him. It is said that he wanted to have all of his books burned, which would have been quite a task since Democritus may have written more than all his predecessors put together. Unfortunately, Plato got what he wanted anyway because nearly all of Democritus' writings disappeared through neglect. Early Christian thinkers seized every opportunity to condemn atomism and to discourage the study of it. Their hostility had nothing to do with the fact that atomism says that all matter consists of indivisible particles, a subject on which neither Jesus nor the Old Testament prophets ever expressed an opinion. Early Christians abhorred atomism for two main reasons. First because it tried to explain everything in terms of mechanics, not the activities of a deity (whom it renders redundant). Secondly because it held that there is no life after death, since all things – including souls and, if there happen to be any lurking in the background, gods – are purely temporary configurations of atoms that will eventually dissolve back into chaos.

Atomism also suffered from keeping what was held to be bad company. The fact that it was championed and developed by Epicurus (341–270 BC), who was later regarded as having glorified the vices of sensual pleasure and over-eating, did not help its reputation among the virtuous-minded. Even worse, the best-known and most influential version of atomism was that propounded in an openly anti-religious poem, *De rerum natura*, by Lucretius. Lucretius made it plain that his poem was designed to liberate man from superstition, the fear of death and the tyranny of priests:

When man's life lay for all to see foully grovelling upon the ground, crushed beneath the weight of Superstition, which displayed her head from the regions of heaven, lowering over mortals with horrible aspect, a man of Greece was the first that dared to uplift mortal eyes against her, the first to make stand against her; for neither fables of the gods could quell him, nor thunderbolts, nor heaven with menacing roar, but all the more they goaded the eager courage of his soul, so that he should desire, first of all men, to shatter the confining bars of nature's gates.

Lucretius's heroic 'man of Greece' was Epicurus; but it was really Democritus and Leucippus who first rattled the bars of nature's gates in the name of atomism.

Democritus once said that he would rather find a single genuine explanation than become the king of Persia. His curiosity led him far afield: to Babylon, Egypt, Persia and perhaps India and Ethiopia. His wide experience and interests produced some fifty treatises on such diverse subjects as magnetism, farming, music, painting, physiology, and possibly one on how to fight in armour, as well as books on purely philosophical subjects. One of his main passions was biology, but relatively few of his own words survive on this or indeed most other topics. There are 299 remaining catalogued fragments of Democritus, more than of any other philosopher before Plato; but almost all are from his rather pedestrian ethical writings, and some are just single words that he is thought to have used. Still, there is enough left, mainly from passages of later criticisms, to piece together the outlines of the atomist system.

According to Aristotle, these outlines were first sketched by Leucippus, who was born in around 460 BC in either Elea or Miletus, two of the most productive well-springs of philosophy. Democritus was born in about the same year in Abdera, an Ionian city on the coast of Thrace, which somehow became proverbial for the stupidity of its inhabitants. Democritus studied with Leucippus and took over the one idea for which the latter is remembered: that innumerable tiny atoms career around in empty space (called 'the void') until they collide and adhere to one another, thus creating all the familiar objects of the world, both living and inanimate. As a later commentator put it:

DEMOCRITVS.

these atoms move in the infinite void, separate one from the other and differing in shapes, size, position and arrangement; overtaking each other they collide, and some are shaken away in any chance direction, while others, becoming intertwined one with another according to the congruity of their shapes, sizes, positions and arrangements, stay together and so effect the coming into being of compound bodies.

The word 'atom' comes from *atomos*, meaning 'uncuttable', and the atoms of Democritus and Leucippus were held to be absolutely solid, indivisible and indestructible. Ordinary things die or fall apart when the atoms of which they consist are dispersed. Thus the atomist system, like the systems of Empedocles and Anaxagoras, tries to account for the change and destruction which Parmenides held to be impossible by proposing a compromise. All three compromises say that ordinary, changing things consist of components that do not change in themselves except insofar as their configurations alter when they come together or fly apart. Such reconfiguration produces the changing world we see.

The force that brings atoms together is the old Greek principle that like attracts like. As Democritus put it: 'Creatures . . . flock together with their kind, doves with doves, cranes with cranes and so on. And the same happens even with inanimate things, as can be seen with seeds in a sieve and pebbles on the seashore.' Similarly shaped atoms tend to stick to one another; some were even held to have little hooks to hang on by. Democritus tried to explain as much as possible about the perceived qualities of everyday things in terms of the different shapes, sizes and configurations of their atoms. Sweet things are made of round and large atoms; sharp-tasting things have small, angular, unrounded (and thus literally sharp) ones; salty things consist of large, angular, crooked atoms with equal sides; bitterness corresponds to round, smooth but irregular atoms. Oily things have fine, round and small ones (and are thus like ball-bearings that easily slip past one another, which Democritus presumably thought explained why oil is viscous).

According to Democritus, we are constantly rained on by a shower of these minute building-blocks. Since everything must ultimately be a matter of atoms in motion, perception itself is crudely explained as the result of small numbers of atoms emanating from objects and entering the body through the sense-organs. What actually happens inside the body when something is perceived is left rather vague. The mind is said to be a collection of spherical atoms somewhere in the body, and thought somehow consists in the motion of these mind-atoms when they have been agitated by the influx of the atomic rain. Democritus' explanations of larger-scale phenomena, such as the weather, borrow freely from the familiar accounts of the day. For example, he held that thunder is caused by an uneven combination of atoms forcing down the cloud which encloses it.

Democritus appropriated all the conventional ideas that suited him and reworked them just in so far as was required to fit atoms into the picture. What was powerful and original in the physical theory of the atomists was their idea of the atoms themselves, and their determination to account for all of nature – and indeed human awareness of nature – on an extremely economical basis. By insisting that only the size, shape and arrangement of atoms be allowed to figure in genuine explanations, Democritus succeeded in digging deeper than Empedocles or Anaxagoras, even if he did not quite manage to strike gold. Empedocles and Anaxagoras had both been content to stop digging as soon as they came up with everyday qualities or stuffs in one form or another ('elements' of earth, air, fire and water in the case of Empedocles, or tiny quantities of all the everyday substances in the case of Anaxagoras).

Where did the idea of atoms come from? And where was the evidence for what Democritus said about their shapes, in sweet or salty things for instance? There is no hint of any experiments or testing of these ideas. Democritus may have been struck by the notion of minute particles while looking at some floating dust, for he once compared atoms to 'the motes in the air which we see in shafts of light coming through windows'. As for the shapes of atoms, it seems that his sort of account has some intuitive plausibility to untutored common sense. More than 2,000 years later, in the late seventeenth century, a French chemist could still write in a textbook:

The hidden nature of a thing cannot be better explained than by attributing to its parts shapes corresponding to all the effects it produces. No one will deny that the acidity of a liquid consists in pointed particles. All experience confirms this. You have only to taste it to feel a pricking of the tongue like that caused by some material cut into very fine points.

This chemist had no more evidence for what he said than Democritus had; it just seemed to feel somehow right.

Leucippus and Democritus seem to have been led to atoms not by any evidence but primarily by Zeno. They came to the conclusion that what was wrong with Zeno's paradoxes, or at least some of them, was that he assumed that physical stuff could be divided *ad infinitum*. Zeno did indeed suppose that if everyday matter existed, it would have to be infinitely divisible; this idea, he argued, led eventually to absurdities, which is one reason why he rejected the world of common sense. But perhaps, thought Leucippus and Democritus, infinite divisibility is the Achilles heel of the paradoxes. After all, Zeno never offered any proof of the idea; he simply assumed it, and let his paradoxes proceed from that point. If one supposed instead that matter is not infinitely divisible – i.e., that there is a smallest scale of matter beyond which further cutting or division is impossible – then Zeno could be stopped in his tracks, or so Democritus and Leucippus believed. And so they proposed their *atoma* as this smallest scale of matter.

Having dealt with Zeno, the next step for the atomists was to cope with Parmenides. One of Parmenides' objections to the idea of motion was that it required empty space, otherwise there would be no room for anything to move. But since empty space was 'nothing', it could not exist for Parmenides, and because empty space was therefore impossible, motion was impossible too. Without actually saying what they thought was wrong with this refutation of empty space, the atomists begged to disagree. They held that there could in fact be such a thing as 'void', and as soon as this vacuum was established, their world of moving atoms rushed in. The atomists' argument went roughly like this. Once a void is allowed, it follows that so too is the idea that are many things, not just Parmenides' One, because there is now empty space to come between different things and keep them distinct. But there is no empty space inside the atoms themselves. If there were, the atoms would not be solid, and so would be divisible into smaller parts – which, by definition, they are not. Since they have no parts, they are not subject to change or decay, and so they are eternal.

Thus by carefully removing one cog from Parmenides' logical machinery (namely the alleged impossibility of empty space), the atomists converted it to their own purposes. Apart from the difference that atoms move and that there are lots of them, a Democritean atom has much in common with Parmenides' mysterious One. Both last forever, never change, do not have parts and have no empty space inside them. In fact, Parmenides' follower Melissus seems to have dimly anticipated that such a development of his master's views was possible. He once said that if there were many things, each would turn out to be very like the Parmenidean One.

The atomist system has a slightly Pythagorean flavour as well as a strongly Parmenidean one. In the Pythagorean universe, everything is built up out of combinations of 'units' that are held to be somehow more real than anything else. For the Pythagoreans, these units were, mysteriously, numbers; for Democritus and Leucippus, they were solid, physical objects instead. There is no talk of numbers, or even of any desire to measure any quantities, in accounts of ancient atomism (though Democritus is supposed to have written a dozen books on mathematical topics). This fact marks the division between ancient and modern atomism: the doctrine blossomed into a mature scientific enterprise only when chemists and physicists developed sophisticated ways to measure material phenomena.

Still, if the features of Democritus' atoms could not actually be quantified in his own day, it is significant that they were the sorts of things which could in theory be measured precisely. They were the right stuff for mathematics and physics to get to work on. Atoms moved, they had sizes, they had positions, they had weights and they had geometric shapes. And that was the whole truth about them. They definitely did not have, as intrinsic properties, any of the qualities that are particularly associated with the human senses, such as colour, smell or taste. According to Democritus, the colours and flavours of everyday things were not objective properties of the outside world at all. It seems that instead they were states of the human body, caused by the influx of atoms. So when he says, for example, that the atoms of sweet-tasting things are round and large, he does not mean that such atoms are themselves literally sweet, but that their roundness and largeness causes us to have a sensation of sweetness.

One thing that apparently prompted him to say this was the fact that sensations sometimes vary from person to person even while the object perceived remains the same. In Aristotle's words: 'The same thing is thought sweet by some who taste it, and bitter by others and even to the senses of each individual, things do not always seem the same.' As Democritus put it: 'By convention sweet, by convention bitter, by convention hot, by convention cold, by convention colour: but in reality atoms and void.'

In other words, what the senses tell us about warmth, taste, colour and so on is purely subjective. It is just a common convention that we ascribe such qualities to physical objects themselves and usually agree about which ones they have. For in fact there is nothing out there but combinations of atoms in space, with their sizes, weights and so on. This once more recalls Parmenides, who said that such things as colour, which people believe in because they naively trust their senses, are mere 'names'. Like Parmenides, Democritus distrusted the senses, though he did not follow him in going so far as to discount them entirely. Democritus distinguished between knowledge obtained through the intellect (or reason), and knowledge obtained through the senses:

He expressly declares – 'of knowledge there are two forms, the genuine and the bastard; and to the bastard belong all these – sight, hearing, smell, taste, touch; but the other form is distinct from this and genuine.' Then – he proceeds: 'Whenever the bastard kind is unable any longer to see what has become too small, or to hear or smell or taste or perceive it by touch, one must have recourse to another and finer instrument.' Thus reason is the criterion [*by which to judge truth and falsehood*].

According to the atomists, the 'bastard' senses are just about reliable enough to confirm the existence of a world of moving, everyday objects. Parmenides was wrong to deny such a world. But only reason is trustworthy enough and powerful enough to reveal the deeper truth about it, namely that it ultimately consists of colourless atoms. Reason is led to this truth by reflecting on, qualifying and building on arguments such as those of Zeno and Parmenides.

The picture that emerges from all this is strikingly similar to Galileo's. In a passage that is often quoted for its supposedly novel scientific world-picture, Galileo says:

Whenever I conceive any material . . . substance, I immediately feel the need to think of it as . . . having this or that shape; as being large or small in relation to other things, and in some specific place at any given time; as being in motion or at rest; as touching or not touching some other body; and as being one in number, or few, or many . . . But that it must be white or red, bitter or sweet, noisy or silent, and of sweet or foul odour, my mind does not feel compelled to bring in as necessary accompaniments. Without the senses as our guides, reason or imagination unaided would probably never arrive at qualities like these. Hence I think that tastes, odours, colours and so on are no more than mere names so far as the object in which we place them is concerned, and that they reside only in the consciousness. Hence if the living creature were removed, all these qualities would be wiped away and annihilated.

Democritus would have thoroughly approved of all this (unless he had been inclined to see it as plagiarism). In the seventeenth century, it was an idea whose time had at last come. Robert Boyle (1627–91), an Irish physicist and chemist who espoused 'an atomical philosophy, corrected and purged from the wild fancies and extravagancies of the first inventors of it', expressed the matter in terms of what he called the 'primary' and 'secondary' qualities of things. The primary qualities were the size, shape, order, texture, solidity and motion of particles: these were all that a scientist needed in his toolbox to explain the phenomena of nature. Thus Boyle tried, with considerably more success than Democritus, to account for heat, cohesion, fluidity, firmness, colour and much else in terms of his primary qualities. The philosopher John Locke (1632–1704) developed a detailed and influential theory on this basis. He recognized five primary qualities – size, shape, number, solidity and state of motion or rest – and said that the secondary, sensory qualities – such as colour or smell – were 'nothing in the Objects themselves, but Powers to produce various Sensations in us by their primary Qualities'. Modern science has kept the idea of a basic set of precisely measurable properties in terms of which everything else is to be explained (though today's list differs from that of Boyle or Locke). But it is less quick to assert, with Galileo, that sensory qualities such as colour are 'mere names' and that they would not exist if there were nobody to perceive them. People still disagree about whether or not that is a misleading thing to say.

One thing that today's scientists do not follow Democritus in saying – and neither did Galileo, Boyle nor Locke say it – is that the 'bastard' senses have no real part to play in the business of finding out about the world. On the contrary, the senses are involved to a greater or lesser degree in the accumulation and testing of evidence for all respectable physical theories. To avoid exaggerating the extent to which ideas of later physics resemble those of Democritus, it is worth saying how far experimental evidence has driven modern atomism away from its ancient forebears. Our atoms are not the same as the atoms of Leucippus and Democritus, though they are descended from them. First of all, modern atoms are not eternal, indestructible, solid or indivisible. They are created by natural processes, they decay, they consist mostly of empty space (they are clouds of electrons around a tiny, dense nucleus) and they can be 'split' into their components. Democritus had no inkling of most of the important properties and forces used to describe their behaviour. For example, he knew nothing of electric charge – which, to make matters worse, behaves in exactly the opposite way to what an ancient Greek might expect. In the world of electromagnetism, like does not attract like – it repels it.

The list of differences between ancient and modern atomism could go on, but it can also be misleading. One must beware of being led to false contrasts by accidents of terminology. For example, it is regularly pointed out by historians of science that whereas the atoms of Leucippus and Democritus were by definition unsplittable, what we now call 'atoms' have famously been split and are no longer regarded as the basic building-blocks of matter. In their place we now have our even smaller elementary particles, which are divided into the two classes of quarks and leptons. But this is a red herring. It does not mean that the central thesis of ancient atomism turned out to be false. The fact that what we call 'atoms' turned out after all not to be the fundamental constituents of matter shows only that modern physicists were too hasty in dignifying these particular particles with the name of 'atoms'. Nineteenth-century scientists called the particles that they investigated 'atoms' because they believed – falsely, as it turned out – that these particles could not be split. The atomism of Democritus and Leucippus will not be refuted until it is shown that there are no unsplittable basic particles, whatever you wish to call them. Whether or not there are remains an open question. It is, however, an increasingly irrelevant one. In modern physics, the very notion of a particle, considered in itself, is an outmoded one. Particles are ever more intimately involved with forces and fields, and in some cases are considered as little more than a *façon de parler*. As one contemporary account puts it: 'elementary particles of various types appear as bundles of the energy and momentum of corresponding types of fields'.

The premature modernity of Leucippus and Democritus is more easily apparent if we look at their conception of the cosmos as a whole, and of man's place in it, rather than at the details of what they said about the small-scale structure of matter. They saw a vast, unlimited and impersonal universe, quite unlike the almost homely and human one that Plato and Aristotle bequeathed to the first seventeen centuries of the Christian era. Because they had somehow to account for the emergence of order and life out of the chaos of careering atoms, the atomists proposed an infinite universe, vast enough for it to seem reasonable to suppose that every sort of world cropped up somewhere:

In some worlds there is no sun and moon, in others they are larger than in our world, and in others more numerous. The intervals between the worlds are unequal; in some parts there are more worlds, in others fewer; some are increasing, some at their height, some decreasing; in some parts they are arising, in others failing. They are destroyed by collision one with another. There are some worlds devoid of living creatures or plants or any moisture.

Our world is thus merely one of the many possibilities, one in which the conditions are right for life (a 'world' here means, roughly, a planet or group of planets). For the atoms, as Lucretius later put it,

from infinite time up to the present, have been accustomed to move and to meet in all manner of ways, and to try all combinations, whatsoever they could produce by coming together; for this reason it comes to pass that being spread abroad through a vast time, by attempting every sort of combination and motion, at length these come together which often become the beginnings of great things, of earth and sea and sky and the generation of living creatures.

Compare that with some words from a recent science book, *The Selfish Gene* by Richard Dawkins. Dawkins begins with a thoroughly Lucretian declaration: 'We no longer have to resort to superstition when faced with the deep problems: Is there a meaning to life? What are we for?' He describes how science 'shows us a way in which simplicity could change into complexity, how unordered atoms could group themselves into ever more complex patterns until they ended up manufacturing people'. Thus 'there is no need to think of design or purpose or directedness. If a group of atoms . . . falls into a stable pattern it will tend to stay that way.'

Modern science has thus put flesh on the bare bones of Democritus, Epicurus and Lucretius. It is rapidly filling in the details of how atomic chaos can turn into order and life naturally and without a Designer, thus fulfilling their hope. The largest single piece of the part of the puzzle that concerns life was slotted into place by Darwin's account of evolution by natural selection, the most general principles of which we have seen to be dimly anticipated by Empedocles. It is no surprise that the atomists' story of the creation of man met with the same incredulous disapproval that later greeted Darwin in the nineteenth century. The atomists, said a puzzled Christian in the fourth century, thought that people 'emerged from the ground like worms, without a maker and for no reason'.

Democritus did not end his story with what Tennyson, in a poem about Lucretius, called 'those blind beginnings that have made me man'. He went on to offer an account of the development of human culture, a theory of human happiness and indeed a whole system of ethics. The first people, he says, battled alone for survival in a hostile world and began to co-operate when faced by the common enemy of wild beasts. Soon they started to refine their grunting noises and to communicate by agreeing on meanings for some of the more recogniz-able of the sounds they produced. Gradually experience taught them to survive more effectively by sheltering in caves and storing some food. They learnt much by copying other creatures: in the most important matters, says Democritus, men are pupils of the animals. For example, spinning and mending were first copied from spiders; singing was copied from the nightingale; house-building comes from swallows. But man's most valuable gift is his own natural intelligence, which enables him to learn from experience how the world works. Thus the 'bastard' knowledge provided by the senses does have its uses after all.

When man had learnt enough to provide a regular supply of basic necessities, he could afford to turn to more leisurely pastimes, starting with music. He could also devote himself to the pursuit of happiness. For Democritus, happiness was produced by moderation, equanimity and the absence of disruptive desires for the unobtainable or the ephem-eral. When the mind or soul is shaken by such disturbing passions, its atoms are disordered and unsettled. This idea reflects traditional notions of Greek medicine, according to which physical health is an equable balance of elements in the body. Because the mind, like the body, consists of physical atoms, according to Democritus, mental health and happi-ness have the same ingredients as bodily health. Balance, and the absence of the sort of disturbance caused by conflict, are essential.

The same ingredients of stability, moderation and order are needed for a healthy society, too. Civilization, which for Democritus meant the city, is a precarious human creation that could easily slip back into barbarism. If the harmony and restraint on which it depends were to be upset, the arts, philosophy and happiness itself would soon disappear.

Democritus evidently took this danger seriously, since he urged the death penalty for anyone who threatened to disrupt the stability of the city. In order for society to continue to flourish, care had to be taken to pass on wisdom and responsible conduct to the next generation. Many of Democritus' surviving fragments deal with education, which he took to be a stern responsibility: he wrote that the worst thing of all is indulgence in the schooling of the young. It is not known whether he had children himself; one suspects not, or that if he did then he later regretted it:

A man who wants children would, I think, do better to get one from friends. The child will then be the sort that he wants – in this way it is possible to choose according to one's mind from many, whereas, if one begets his own children, there are many dangers involved; for he must live with whomever he begets.

Given his harsh insistence on the inculcation of virtue, he must have been a little trying to live with himself. The morality he wanted to teach – justice, contentment with one's lot, and prudence – was nothing revolutionary. It reflected the traditional ideals of his time, adapted to incorporate an atomist account of the mind. The novelty in his preaching lay largely in the fact that he urged virtuous behaviour on his fellows not because it would please or placate the gods, or ensure a satisfactory afterlife, but because such virtues paved the one reliable path to individual happiness here on earth. In other words, virtue is really a matter of self-interest. It was this non-religious morality that was later developed by Epicurus and Lucretius, to the consternation of early Christians.

Such a man-made morality prompted some troublesome questions for the more thoughtful of Democritus' contemporaries. How does one stop prudent self-interest from degenerating into amoral selfishness? Consider the position of someone who is powerful enough to do whatever he wants and to get away with it, and who can therefore afford to ignore conventional moral rules. If such a miscreant does not go so far as to destroy the stability of the city, and if such behaviour makes him personally content, on what basis could Democritus condemn him?

The discussion of such questions flourished in the latter half of the fifth century among an intellectual movement in Athens known as the Sophists. Plato was later extremely hostile towards the Sophists and represented them as having been cynical tricksters who abused the art of intellectual argument. He was not the only one to do so: it is largely a reflection of the success of such propaganda that the word 'sophistry' and its cognates have ever since been used simply to mean fallacious reasoning, quibbling or verbal trickery. It is in this spirit that Disraeli referred to his political rival, Gladstone, as 'a sophistical rhetorician, inebriated with the exuberance of his own verbosity'.

Whatever may have been true of Gladstone, the original Sophists deserve better than that. Among other things they fuelled the engine of Athenian intellectual life and steered it in the direction of what we would now call the humanities. While some of the philosophers we have so far examined transformed speculation about nature with their search for rational explanations, the more philosophically minded of the Sophists tried to reason about the conflicts between nature and man-made convention or law. This clash between convention and nature had several sides to it. The Sophists had something of interest to say not only about the opposing demands of man's selfish instincts on the one hand and the requirements of justice on the other, but also about the problems posed for the notion of objective knowledge by the Democritean idea that much of what man professes to know is merely a matter of human convention. Remember Democritus' atomist dictum: 'By convention sweet, by convention bitter, by convention hot, by convention cold, by convention colour: but in reality atoms and void'. The best-known Sophists would not have put it like that, for they reached a different conclusion about the extent of knowledge. But they would have recognized all too well the problem with which Democritus was wrestling, namely the contrast between objective reality and individual perception.

Democritus almost belongs in the Sophists' world, but not quite. It is not time that separates him from them: the earliest Sophists were already teaching when Democritus was still young. It was different professional and intellectual interests that divided them. Although Democritus' thoughts turned to many of the issues that they set off to explore – indeed, he discusses some of their ideas – it seems that he never quite made it on the same expedition himself.

# 9

# Opening Pandora's Box:
## *the Sophists*

Ambassador, tutor, public-relations consultant, lecturer, stage entertainer, speech-writer, philosopher, after-dinner speaker, psychotherapist: the so-called 'Sophists' of Athens in the second half of the fifth century were in some cases all of these things and in most cases at least several of them. To see how anybody, let alone a whole class of people, could end up combining such roles, it is worth standing back from philosophical controversies to look at the Athenians and their city.

By the middle of the fifth century, what had begun as a loose anti-Persian alliance of Greek states was evolving into an empire with Athens at its heart, thanks largely to the successes of the Athenian navy. This made Athens rich. The other members of the alliance paid it tributes, and some of the money was spent on things that can still be seen today, including the Parthenon. Much of this glorification was instigated by Pericles, the leading citizen of Athens, who has already been mentioned in the intellectual company of Anaxagoras. 'Mighty indeed are the marks and monuments of our empire which we have left. Future ages will wonder at us, as the present age wonders at us now.' So predicted Pericles, correctly, in a memorial oration for the city's war-heroes.

In the same speech, Pericles praises the feature of Athenian life which, together with the city's wealth, best explains the rise of the Sophists:

Our constitution is called a democracy because power is in the hands not of a minority but of the whole people. When it is a question of settling private disputes, everyone is equal before the law; when it is a question of putting one person before another in positions of public responsibility, what counts is not membership of a particular class, but the actual ability which the man possesses.

One particular ability counted for more than most: the ability to speak and debate persuasively before the political assembly or the juries. Pericles' own power lay to a considerable extent in his ability to carry the assembly with him. His praise of Athens continues with the words:

We Athenians, in our own persons, take our decisions on policy or submit them to proper discussions: for we do not think that there is an incompatibility between words and deeds; the worst thing is to rush into action before the consequences have been properly debated.

The Athenians loved a good argument, or even a bad one provided the debate was entertaining. They were famously litigious and occasionally made fun of themselves for it. In a comedy of the time by Aristophanes, a student is guiding a simple farmer called Strepsiades around his school and showing off its educational equipment:

*Student*: And here we have a map of the world. This is Athens.
*Strepsiades*: Come off it. I don't believe you. Where are the juries?

It happens that Strepsiades is interested in this school because he wants his son to learn how to speak well enough to fight off creditors in the bankruptcy court. Not only rogues were eager for some training in debate. How was a citizen to seize the opportunities presented by democracy if he was not a born orator? The everyday educational system, such as it was, would not have been much help. Athenian boys learned reading and writing, music, sport, gymnastics, perhaps some mathematics and a great deal of epic poetry. They started at the age of seven and most would have finished their schooling by the age of fourteen. Girls were simply taught a few manual tasks. It is hardly surprising that there was a demand for some form of higher education among those who could afford to pay for it. The Sophists were the men who came from all over the Greek world to meet the demand for intellectual self-improvement.

Any gifted and educated Greek-speaker would naturally feel drawn to Athens. If such a man were not an Athenian citizen, he could not argue in the assembly and advance himself that way. But he could earn

a good living and enjoy generous hospitality by preparing Athenians
to do so and by teaching their children, entertaining and edifying their
dinner-parties and performing at their festivals and offering advice.
One of the first to come from abroad and earn money by teaching was
Protagoras, a contemporary of Anaxagoras and Empedocles, who
became a friend of Pericles and who appears by name or in person
in several of Plato's dialogues. He originally came to Athens as an
ambassador from his native Abdera; other famous Sophists came as
ambassadors too, including Gorgias from Leontini in Sicily and Hippias from Elis.

Before the time of these men, the term *sophistes* was applied to all
sorts of sages and wise men. Confusingly, even after that time some
fourth-century writers continued to use it to refer to every philosopher
all the way back to Thales. But in their own day the term was reserved
mainly for people who taught for money, especially those who offered
instruction in rhetoric, political skills and how to excel in moral and
legal discourse (this is how I shall continue to use the term 'Sophist').
In one of Plato's dialogues, Socrates, who narrates, asks Protagoras
precisely what it is that he proposes to teach a prospective pupil.
Protagoras answers:

The proper care of his personal affairs, so that he may best manage his own
household, and also of the state's affairs, so as to become a real power in the
city, both as speaker and as man of action.

Do I follow you? said I. I take you to be describing the art of politics, and
promising to make good citizens.

That, said he, is exactly what I profess to do.

But Plato is making Protagoras oversimplify. Although Plato usually
refers to the more famous Sophists with respect, he nearly always
disagrees with their doctrines, and he was particularly opposed to the
idea that it was proper or even possible to buy instruction in such
virtues as those of the good citizen or the skilled politician. It was,
therefore, the Sophists' claim to teach practical success on which Plato
focussed, in order to attack it. In fact, this was far from being the
whole of their curriculum. Among the subjects taught and discussed by
the Sophists are grammar, linguistic theory, rhetoric, literary criticism,

music, law, the nature of religion, ethics and politics, the origins of
man and of society, mathematics and some natural science. Between
them they offered a complete course of higher education. In so doing,
they began to replace the traditional poets, rhapsodes and the odd
unpaid philosopher, like Anaxagoras, as purveyors of wisdom.

No doubt some of them specialized in a few subjects while others
offered a broader training. Take Protagoras himself. He wrote a treatise on the nature of the gods, which is said to have had its first public
reading at the house of the tragedian Euripides. He must have taken a
keen interest in law and government too, since Pericles let him write
the laws for a new city in southern Italy. He and Pericles are said to
have once whiled away a whole day discussing the legal question of
who was liable for an accidental death in a javelin contest. He also
expounded on the meanings of poems. He taught and wrote about
language and is sometimes described as the first grammarian (linguistic
distinctions such as his turned out to be useful for Plato, who built on
them to unravel Parmenides' tangled statements about 'nothing'). As
for more narrowly philosophical topics, in Plato's dialogues, Protagoras is heard discussing various moral questions and the nature of
knowledge. Protagoras also wrote a philosophical treatise on truth
containing the famous and obscure saying that man is the measure of
all things; this idea will be examined later.

All this makes Protagoras sound an impressive polymath, which he
was. He even wrote a treatise on wrestling. But his range is nothing
when compared to that of a younger Sophist called Hippias. Hippias
was prepared to teach about practically anything at all, and his talents
were not limited to teaching. According to Plato, he once boasted that
when he appeared at the Olympian Games to recite some of his poems,
he had made his own shoes, cloak, tunic, girdle and rings, as well as a
brush and oil-flask that he happened to have with him. In public
appearances, from which he claimed to earn a great deal of money, he
was prepared both to deliver prepared orations and to take questions
from all comers. In his time off from making clothes and knick-knacks,
he compiled histories of mathematics and of philosophy. And he wrote
plays. Plato poked fun at him, which is hardly surprising. Hippias'
learning was much less deep than it was wide and he does not seem to
have made significant contributions to any of the many subjects he

taught, except perhaps to have discovered one reasonably important curve in geometry. History has not endorsed the estimate of himself that Plato puts in Hippias mouth: 'I have never found any man who was my superior in anything.'

A less bumptious fellow-Sophist was Antiphon, whose surviving words sometimes express a weary pessimism: 'The whole of life is wonderfully open to complaint, my friend; it has nothing remarkable, great, or noble, but all is petty, feeble, brief-lasting, and mingled with sorrows.' 'Life', he also wrote, 'is like a day-long watch, and the length of life is like one day, as it were, on which having seen the light we pass on our trust to the next generation.' The more significant of his remaining writings are about ethics, particularly the nature of justice, and this is probably what he especially taught. He also offered more intimate goods for sale. He was particularly interested in dreams and their interpretation and seems to have set up a sort of psychotherapy service.

One of the more specialized of the Sophists was Gorgias, a renowned orator who wrote several handbooks on rhetoric. Among other things, Gorgias left a number of orations that were intended to be studied and emulated as models of persuasive argument, the longest of them being a powerful defence of Helen of Troy. It was this side of the Sophists that Plato made the biggest fuss about. He claimed that they could not care less about truth in debates and were only concerned to teach their patrons the tricks of winning. It did not matter whether you had justice or the stronger argument on your side: the Sophists would happily coach you in all sorts of ruses to help you in any verbal joust. Plato's most eminent pupil, Aristotle, followed up his master's line of attack, saying that 'the art of the sophist is the semblance of wisdom without the reality, and the sophist is one who makes money from an apparent but unreal wisdom'.

The mud that Plato and his sympathizers flung at the Sophists has stuck, as any dictionary definition of sophistry will attest. Was it deserved? Why exactly did they fling it? It is not as if the Sophists' detractors thought that argument and persuasion should not be developed as skills or taught at all. After all, Aristotle himself wrote the most influential treatise on rhetoric and happily incorporated in it what he had learned from Gorgias ('Gorgias said that you should kill your opponents' earnestness with jesting and their jesting with earnestness; in which he was right'). Nor can Plato and Aristotle really have thought that it was immoral to teach pupils how to see both sides of a question, a charge that was frequently brought against the Sophists as if this were the heart of their villainy. For as Aristotle himself says in one place:

we must be able to employ persuasion . . . on opposite sides of a question, not in order that we may in practice employ it in both ways (for we must not make people believe what is wrong), but in order that we may see clearly what the facts are, and that, if another man argues unfairly, we on our part may be able to confute him.

Nor, again, was it that Plato and Aristotle held the leading Sophists to be unprincipled and worthless men. Most of them were treated respectfully – even praised – when discussed by name. The curious fact is that the 'bad' Sophists, whoever they were, always seem to be somewhere off-stage, unnamed fraudsters who rarely suffered the brunt of Plato's insults in person. This is largely because the real motives for the attacks ran too deep for Plato to express them clearly or for him to confront any major Sophist with them openly.

There are several strands to the story. One may well be a kind of snobbery. Plato was an aristocrat who (unlike his fellow member of the nobility, Pericles) was sceptical of the virtues of democracy and probably objected to the egalitarian presupposition of the Sophist profession, namely that anyone could be made wise, virtuous and fit to play a part in government provided only that he had the money to pay for a Sophist tutor. One associate of Socrates has him comparing Sophists to prostitutes because they are prepared to sell their services to any paying client. But there was also something more personally distressing for Plato. Most (perhaps all) of his works were written after the trial and death of his hero, Socrates, in 399 BC, a tragedy for which Plato seems to have held the Sophists indirectly responsible. The offences with which Socrates was commonly charged – particularly an allegation that he corrupted the young because he 'makes the weaker argument defeat the stronger, and teaches others to follow his example'

– were, in Plato's view, prompted by the reputations of some of the Sophists. The main accuser of Socrates at his trial was a democrat called Anytus, whom Plato suggests had an extreme dislike for Sophists and yet was rather vague about exactly who or what they were. In a dialogue which is set in happier days long before the trial, Plato shows Anytus in friendly discussion with Socrates. Anytus has just launched a tirade against unnamed Sophists:

*Socrates*: Has one of the Sophists done you a personal injury, or why are you so hard on them?
*Anytus*: Heavens, no! I've never in my life had anything to do with a single one of them, nor would I hear of any of my family doing so.
*Socrates*: So you've had no experience of them at all?
*Anytus*: And don't want any either.

The average Athenian would have had no time for fine distinctions between the ways of the famous Socrates and those of other intellectuals. He would have heard of Socrates as a fiendishly clever chap who sat around all day discussing with young men who wanted to learn from him. In the plain man's eyes, then, Socrates would have been just another Sophist. As Plato saw it, the condemnation that Athenians should have aimed at the bad Sophists fell on Socrates' head by mistake, like the rogue javelin discussed by Pericles and Protagoras.

It is certainly true that many Athenians lumped all sorts of intellectuals together. Thus Euripides was sometimes regarded as a Sophist largely because his plays were disturbingly modern-minded (he sometimes showed slaves as noble and heroes as less than virtuous). A rumour went about that Socrates helped Euripides write these plays, probably on the slim basis that both men were allegedly somewhat rum characters. And Socrates himself appears in a play, shown as a hilariously foolish, immoral and sacrilegious Sophist in Aristophanes' *Clouds*, which was first performed in Athens in 423 BC. He also figured in several other comedies, perhaps equally scurrilous, which are now lost ('I loathe that poverty-stricken windbag Socrates,' says a surviving fragment of one of them). In Plato's account of Socrates' trial some years later, Socrates observes glumly of the popular misconceptions about himself: 'You have seen it for yourselves in the play by

Aristophanes, where Socrates goes whirling round, proclaiming that he is walking on air, and uttering a great deal of other nonsense.' 'I must try,' he says, 'in the short time that I have, to rid your minds of a false impression which is the work of many years.'

Aristophanes did not trouble his audience with subtle shades of difference between the early scientists, the Sophists, Socrates and immoral tricksters. That would have ruined the jokes, which had a serious point for many Athenians. Anybody who conducted scientific inquiries into nature was undermining traditional religion, and thereby undermining traditional morality. Equally, anybody who inquired into traditional morality was undermining traditional religion, and probably spouting a great deal of nonsense about thunderbolts and atoms to boot. The intellectuals were all in it together and they deserved what they had coming to them. In *Clouds*, Socrates' 'logic factory' is burned to the ground by an angry citizen (namely Strepsiades, the debt-laden farmer mentioned earlier). In real life, twenty-four years later, Socrates was condemned to death by men who may well have been in the audience of *Clouds*.

Even if they were not all as bad as the sophistical machinists in Aristophanes' logic-factory, there must inevitably have been a few genuinely bad types among the real Sophists. And even the most honourable teachers could not be responsible for the actions of their pupils. At least one of the many young men who sought Socrates' company subsequently became a murderous tyrant; in vain did Socrates protest that 'I have never countenanced any action that was incompatible with justice on the part of any person, including those whom some people maliciously call my pupils.' With no control over your colleagues or your followers, the Sophist's trade was a dangerous business to be in if you valued your reputation. Plato was well aware of the problems:

lads when they first get a taste of disputation, misuse it as a form of sport, always employing it contentiously . . . And when they have themselves confuted many and been confuted by many, they quickly fall into a violent distrust of all that they formerly held true, and the outcome is that they themselves and the whole business of philosophy are discredited.

To rescue the reputation of philosophy in general and Socrates in particular, Plato needed to distance Socrates from the Sophist movement, which he did by exaggerating the differences between the two. Socrates was virtuous and the Sophists were immoral, or at least harmful. Socrates pursued true intellectual inquiry and the Sophists did not. Plato would have acknowledged that men such as Protagoras and Gorgias were sincere, but would have said that even they were misguided in some respects and that their teaching was therefore ultimately a bad thing. He succeeded in showing up the weaknesses of some of what they said, yet he was blind to their strengths, and, apparently, to the fact that the major Sophists were searching for the truth just as he himself was. They were just looking for it in a different place.

As one might expect from their professional situation, many of the Sophists had a more down-to-earth approach to intellectual matters than other thinkers. They had little time for what they took to be ingenious but unconvincing theories and fruitless speculations. Who can tell whether the world is really a mass of water, a school of numbers, an outbreak of fire, a cocktail of elements or a storm of atoms? None of these theories was incontrovertibly better than any of the others and the choice between them made no difference to everyday life. As for everyday life itself, did not many philosophers seem to deny its very existence? Who could believe Parmenidean arguments to the effect that nothing changes, when each event of every passing day refutes the idea? The philosophy of atomism was hardly any better, for it too dismissed the world of everyday experience as a distorting veil drawn over the fundamental reality of 'atoms and the void'.

Plainly, to the Sophist turn of mind, something had gone wrong with the world of learning. Reason, argument and language itself seemed to have been hijacked, and common sense had been spirited away. There is an ingenious passage by Gorgias – a puzzle masquerading as an argument – that is probably best seen as an attempt to show up the absurdity of it all. It pretends to prove three things. First, that nothing whatsoever exists; secondly, that even if something did exist, it would be impossible to comprehend what it was; and thirdly, that even if it were possible to comprehend what it was, it would be impossible to communicate this to anybody else.

Gorgias may well have been somewhat puzzled by his own puzzle. If he was not, he certainly ought to have been. He would not have been able to explain exactly where its fallacies lay, since the critical vocabulary of the time was not sophisticated enough to do so. But he certainly did not take this logical monstrosity at its face value. He may have intended it to embarrass any philosophy unwise enough to dismiss the everyday world, by showing that such things soon went too far. Or he may have meant it to show that any so-called 'truth', however apparently certain it was, could be undermined by a skilled rhetorician such as himself. Or, again, he may just have been entertaining himself and his audience, for the Greeks enjoyed verbal puzzles. Either way the upshot is the same. The puzzle was a reminder that there was something suspect about the way most philosophers spoke and argued about ultimate truth. Such speech could evidently be made to snowball into an avalanche of utter absurdity.

There is no need to follow the twists of Gorgias' puzzle, but its rhetorical self-awareness is worth noting. In the third part of it, where he deals with communication, Gorgias draws a sharp contrast between 'speech' on the one hand and 'that which exists outside us' on the other. He was conscious of a gulf between the two, and of language's ability to mould a person's view of the world. He wrote elsewhere that 'the power of speech over the constitution of the soul can be compared with the effect of drugs on the bodily state'. And 'persuasion, when added to speech, can make any impression it wishes on the soul'. As Gorgias and others of the Sophists saw it, many earlier philosophers had used language to make useless and incredible pictures of the world. The task now was to make useful ones instead.

What these Sophists wanted was a philosophy that embraced everyday experience. This desire puts them in the opposite corner of the philosophical ring to Plato. As we have seen, Plato had a view of knowledge that was bulging with veins of Orphism and Pythagoreanism. For him, and for many of his intellectual ancestors, the task of philosophy was to lead the way beyond the world of everyday experience to the purified truths of reason. The Sophists wanted to travel in the opposite direction. For them, the task was to reinstate human experience in all its messy complexity as the best guide to life. But this was easier said than done. For just whose experience is it that is to be the guide? The world presents different and conflicting appearances to different people. This fact of varying perceptions is precisely the problem that Democritus sought to answer when he dismissed subjective judgements of sweetness, bitterness, heat, cold and so on as mere 'convention' and posited instead his objective 'atoms and void'. Protagoras answered the problem on behalf of the Sophists with a different and apparently shocking idea: instead of dismissing subjectivity, he positively embraced it. What I perceive is true for me, and what you perceive is true for you. He held that there is no universal truth about the everyday world of experience, but that this does not mean that there is no truth about it at all. Quite the reverse: there is, if anything, an abundance of truth. For what each person perceives is the truth for him. That is what Protagoras meant when he famously said that 'Man is the measure of all things.'

This sort of view is known as relativism, because it holds that truth is relative to each believer, or, more often nowadays, relative to each group or community of believers. It is one way of trying to bring knowledge back down to earth. Instead of being hidden and hard to find, truth is held to be scattered all around like manna from heaven; everybody gets a piece. Relativism seems to have been first stated clearly by Protagoras and to have been first discussed in detail between some of the Sophists and their opponents, most notably Plato. Various forms of it have cropped up now and then ever since. Much of the impetus for modern relativism can be traced to Kant (1724–1804), which would not have pleased Kant himself. He held that there are absolute and universal truths, but he accidentally left the door open to relativism because of the way in which he explained these truths. Kant argued that many features of our picture of the world are imposed by the human mind and that since all human minds are the same in crucial respects, these truths are the same for everybody. Many later thinkers kept Kant's idea that truth is partly determined by the human mind but dropped his assumption that all minds are alike. The result was a flowering of relativism: all pictures of the world reflect the conceptual equipment of those who paint them, and none is more true than any other.

Relativism itself comes in many flavours, some more wide-ranging than others. Some people hold that moral values are relative, so that what is morally right or wrong depends on the society or the period in question. Others hold that relativism does not apply to moral values, or does not only apply to moral values, but applies to scientific theories or perhaps all 'truths'. In general, strains of relativist thinking are nowadays more often found in the writings of anthropologists, sociologists and literary critics than in the pages of professional philosophers. While a working knowledge of the diversity of human beliefs and customs seems often to encourage a sympathy for relativism, philosophers tend to be more wary of the confusions and paradoxes that lie beneath the surface of many forms of it. Take moral relativism, for example. One apparently straightforward version of it says that it is wrong to condemn the morals of another culture, because whatever each culture believes is indeed right for it. But this seemingly benign and tolerant thesis is in fact self-contradictory. By whose moral standards is it 'wrong' to condemn the morals of others? If one culture believes that it is morally superior to others, then moral relativism itself entails that it is 'right' for this culture to condemn them.

Relativism, in all its forms, tends to come unstuck when applied to itself, and it has many other difficulties and obscurities too. Some of its problems were perceptively brought out by Socrates in a dialogue of Plato's called the *Theaetetus*, where the views of Protagoras are discussed, developed and in the end rejected. Early in the dialogue, Socrates quotes Protagoras' statement that man is the measure of all things, and interprets it as meaning that any given thing 'is to me such as it appears to me, and is to you such as it appears to you'. To take a favourable example where this sort of thing sounds reasonable, Socrates considers the wind.

'Sometimes, when the same wind is blowing, one of us feels chilly, the other does not, or one may feel slightly chilly, the other quite cold.' In such a case it seems plausible to say that what is the case for one man (i.e., that the wind is chilly) is not so for another. Democritus would have said that since the wind appears both chilly and not chilly, it must in itself really be neither. Protagoras concluded from the same conflicting appearances that it must be both: each man is the ultimate authority (or 'measure') of how such things appear or feel to him, so what he says about them is true.

But in saying that things really are however they appear to each person to be, Protagoras has already gone too far, because this implies that there are no false perceptions. This is an implausible thesis, on which Socrates pounces:

There remains the question of dreams and disorders, especially madness and all the mistakes madness is said to make in seeing or hearing or otherwise misperceiving – in these conditions we certainly have false perceptions, and . . . so far from its being true that what appears to any man also is, on the contrary none of these appearances is real.

That is quite true, Socrates.

What argument, then, is left for one who maintains that . . . what appears to each man also 'is' for him to whom it appears?

. . . Really, I cannot undertake to deny that madmen and dreamers believe what is false, when madmen imagine they are gods or dreamers think they have wings and are flying in their sleep.

Scenting blood, Socrates soon moves in for more. Even if Protagoras can make some sort of special case for madmen and dreamers, not to mention all the other less dramatic instances of misperception, what can he say to the objection that if relativism is true, then he has argued himself out of a job? As Socrates puts it on another occasion:

if Protagoras is right, and the truth is that things are as they appear to anyone, how can some of us be wise and some of us foolish? – For if what appears to each man is true to him, one man cannot in reality be wiser than another.

In other words, how can Protagoras teach wisdom when there isn't any?

Socrates wants to be fair to Protagoras, so he points out how Protagoras would answer the objection. This answer leads to the heart of Sophist thinking and practice. Socrates envisages Protagoras replying that a wise Sophist does not offer to teach beliefs that are in any sense more true than those which a pupil already has – that would, indeed, be impossible if his version of relativism were correct. Rather he offers to teach beliefs that are better in the sense of being more useful. The Sophist is like a doctor who treats people's minds instead of their stomachs and teaches others to do so as well. It is more useful and pleasant to have certain thoughts rather than others, and these are what a Sophist offers to produce.

At the end of the nineteenth century, a group of American philosophers calling themselves Pragmatists tried to develop the idea that the important thing about beliefs is their general usefulness and the role they play in life. The leading Pragmatist, William James (brother of Henry James), put it in a way that is strikingly reminiscent of the words Socrates put in Protagoras' mouth. Although James did not draw the conclusion that truth was relative, he thought that the most fruitful way to regard it was in terms of usefulness in a broad sense:

The true is the name of whatever proves itself to be good in the way of belief – in this world, just as certain foods are not only agreeable to our taste, but good for our teeth, our stomach and our tissues; so certain ideas are not only agreeable to think about, or agreeable as supporting other ideas that we are fond of, but they are also helpful in life's practical struggles. If there be any life that it is really better we should lead, and if there be any idea which, if believed in, would help us to lead that life, then it would really be *better for us* to believe in that idea, *unless, indeed, belief in it incidentally clashed with other greater vital benefits*.

The sort of beliefs of which such a pragmatic account is perhaps most plausible, at least on the face of it, are ones that explicitly concern practical human affairs – that is, politics and morals. Socrates continues his account of how Protagoras would explain and defend himself on this theme:

wise and honest public speakers substitute in the community sound [*in the sense of 'healthy' or 'beneficial'*] for unsound views of what is right. For I hold that whatever practices seem right and laudable to any particular state are so, for that state, so long as it holds by them. Only, when the practices are, in any particular case, unsound for them, the wise man substitutes others that are and appear sound. On the same principle the Sophist, since he can in the same manner guide his pupils in the way they should go, is wise and worth a considerable fee to them when their education is completed. In this way it is true both that some men are wiser than others and that no one thinks falsely – by these considerations my doctrine is saved from shipwreck.

The Sophist must use his rhetorical powers to get the beneficial or 'sound' view accepted in the community as the right or just one. Thus it seems that in this version of Protagoras' doctrine, relativism is held to apply to some things and not others. It applies to justice and moral rightness ('whatever practices seem right and laudable to any particular state are so, for that state'), but not to what is ultimately beneficial or useful (for sometimes the community's views are 'unsound for them'). It is just like the sick man and his food: each man is right about how his food tastes to him, but his sensations may nevertheless be 'unsound', in the sense that it would be better for him if they were different. That, at any rate, is what Socrates envisages Protagoras saying.

Notice how the thesis of relativism has subtly changed from being about each individual man to being about 'any particular state'. It is now not what each person thinks about justice that is correct for him, but what each state or community thinks that is correct for that state or community. It is groups, not individual people, who cannot be wrong in their moral and political practices, so long as they continue to maintain them. This move ushers in some more of the problems endemic to relativism: how many people does it take to make a community that is big enough to qualify for the protection of relativism? And how much do these people have to agree about in order to count as a united community? What if only one man, or a minority of men, fails to share the views of the rest? Are such dissidents always merely guilty of a philosophical misunderstanding if they say that the majority is wrong about what is good or bad, as relativism implies? Or do they themselves count as a mini-community, qualifying for their own quota of guaranteed truth under relativism's generous redistribution of intellectual income?

The fact is that most people seem not to adopt a strictly relativistic attitude to disputes about justice and moral values, let alone all the other subjects of which relativism is supposed to be true. If they did, there would be no real disputes. And this fact is itself a problem for relativism, as Socrates soon shows. He points out that many people, himself included, do not agree that each man or each society is the measure of all things. Many people hold that there are indeed truths which are true for everybody. And according to relativism itself, they must then be correct to hold this, because relativism says that nobody is wrong in what he believes (except perhaps for beliefs about what is beneficial). It follows that relativism is, at best, true only for those who believe it. It may be true for Protagoras, but it is not true for Socrates, and thus Protagoras cannot say that Socrates is wrong to reject it. Indeed, if majority opinion is the criterion of truth, then even Protagoras would have to admit that his doctrine is false, because most people disagree with it. With Socrates' help, Protagoras has thus painted himself into a corner.

Remember, though, that all this is make-believe. The real Protagoras had been long dead by the time Plato's *Theaetetus* was written, and one cannot be sure how he would have responded to any of these criticisms. Besides, we are dealing with what was once a living intellectual movement. Such a thing does not simply lie down and die just because someone else apparently possesses the logical means to kill it. Faced with Socrates' refutation of him, Protagoras might have taken comfort from Gorgias' puzzle. For did that not show – as far as anyone could tell in those days – that a clever philosopher could refute anything if he put his mind to it? Better to ignore such refutations and press on.

Protagoras' idea that man is the measure of all things, and indeed all of the pragmatist and relativist notions of the Sophists, were to some extent practical responses to practical problems. The Greeks were increasingly aware of the diversity of moral beliefs and customs – the Sophists, since they were usually well-travelled, would have been particularly familiar with it. This moral diversity presented a problem of conflicting appearances just like the one noted by Democritus and Protagoras in connection with sensation and perception. Just as one man might find the wind to be unpleasantly cold while another finds it merely refreshing, so a Greek might find the idea of burning the dead perfectly honourable while some foreigners find it morally repulsive. The historian Herodotus, after noting just such a conflict of moral appearances, remarks that 'if anyone were to propose to all men that they should choose the best customs from all that there are, after consideration each nation would choose its own, so firmly is everyone persuaded that its own are by far the best'. Put like that, nothing could seem more reasonable and wise than to suppose that in fact no nation had 'the best customs'. 'Each to his own' was a more understanding philosophy.

This raised an interesting question that was explored by the Sophists. How did moral and political beliefs come to vary in the first place? The Sophists answered by citing a contrast between nature and human convention. Human customs, practices and moral beliefs were not dictated by nature (nor by the gods, which were generally regarded to be part of nature); they were freely developed according to local circumstances and to what suited each community best. Thus the Sophists held an account of the origin of society just like the story attributed to Democritus: legal and moral systems evolved for the maintenance of civilization. The rules of such systems were accepted by the members of a community as a binding and mutually beneficial social contract of the sort that was to be much discussed in the seventeenth and eighteenth centuries, most famously by Locke and Rousseau. As one leading Sophist, Antiphon, put it: 'the laws of men are adventitious, but those of nature are necessary; and the laws of men are fixed by agreement, not by nature'.

From a Sophist point of view, the freely accepted laws of man are thus quite a different thing from the unbreakable laws of nature. In fact they are all too different. Sometimes the demands of nature and of human law are in conflict. Antiphon goes so far as to suggest that 'most of the things which are just by law are hostile to nature'. He argues that if one follows the dictates of nature, one will do whatever helps one to thrive and is generally most advantageous. Providing one gets away with it, this is much to be desired from one's own point of view and thus from the point of view of nature. But the law often seeks to restrain self-interest for the benefit of the community as a whole. In this way and in others, 'custom, the tyrant of mankind, does much violence to nature', as the Sophist Hippias says in one of Plato's dialogues.

Antiphon makes the point that even if one is perfectly virtuous and not trying to win an unfair advantage over another, acting in accordance with the law may turn out to be against one's own best interests. For suppose one is wronged by someone, and instead of seeking illegal revenge and redress, one puts one's trust in the law. The wrongdoer may never be apprehended. And even if he is:

if the case comes to trial, the injured party has no more of an advantage than the one who has done the injury; for he must convince his judges that he has been injured, and must be able, by his plea, to exact justice. And it is open to the one who has done the injury to deny it; for he can defend himself against the accusation, and he has the same opportunity to persuade his judges that his accuser has. For the victory goes to the best speaker.

This last sentence is, in effect, the Sophists' motto. The idea that 'victory goes to the best speaker' is not necessarily a cynical or amoral encouragement to cheat in disputes, as Plato and the other enemies of the Sophists would sometimes have one believe. It can equally be seen as a simple statement of fact about the way courts work. Given that victory does indeed go to whoever can make the most convincing case (or can employ someone else to do so), the skills of the Sophist can evidently be a force for good, truth and justice. When used responsibly, they can help to redress the imperfections that are found in any legal system. Whatever one might think of the Sophist idea that morality is simply a matter of human convention, there is no denying that the procedures of justice as actually applied in any community are all too humanly imperfect.

The Sophist can make use of his skills to defend the innocent or prosecute the guilty just as well as the reverse. He can also help the community to improve its views by refining and criticizing them. No doubt some Sophists used their powers immorally, but these bad pennies can hardly have had a monopoly on wickedness. What the Sophists did specialize in, if not monopolize, was moral and political argument; and the fact that they did not content themselves with winning cases and teaching others to do so, but also reflected on the very basis of morality, is to their credit.

Naturally such reflection would often have bordered on the subversive. The questions they raised about the opposition between nature and convention invited unpleasant or shocking thoughts. Does justice exist only for the protection of the weak, and should the strong feel free to ignore it when they can? This was a question that Plato frequently addressed. If some conservative Athenians felt that the Sophists had opened a Pandora's Box, they were right. But it had to be opened. If you do not even ask a question, you cannot answer it. Plato, for one, later set out to put morality on what he saw as a firmer footing, by trying to arrange a remarriage of the ideas of nature and convention, as we shall see. He might never have bothered to do so if the Sophists had not unsettled him. Besides, even Plato had to admit that the best Sophists were not so much spreading subversive new ideas as bringing tensions that were inherent in traditional morality up to the surface. It was already clear in Hesiod – whose works were, with Homer's, the familiar centrepiece of education – that insofar as traditional morality rested on obedience to the presumed wishes of the gods, it was in fact based on a form of self-interest. People who do wrong will suffer because Zeus ensures their punishment; but if Zeus were to fail to enforce morality in this way, and unjust people therefore prospered, there would be no point in being moral. As Hesiod put it:

> The eye of Zeus sees all, and understands,
> And when he wishes, marks and does not miss.
> How just a city is, inside.
> And I would not myself be just, nor have my son
> Be just among bad men: for it is bad
> To be an honest man where felons rule;
> I trust wise Zeus to save me from this pass.

Trusting Zeus was a shaky foundation for morality; the Sophists were right to give the prevailing notion of justice a thorough inspection.

The Sophist style of teaching naturally encouraged the sort of sceptical open-mindedness that troubled some people and invited the nervously hostile mockery of Aristophanes. For by practising and teaching the art of argument, the Sophists were inevitably involved in searching out the reasons that could be given for and against various views, including moral, political and even religious ones. Once the rationalist knives were out, any traditional belief that put up a poor performance in the Sophist court could expect an unpleasant end. This made brothers of the Sophists and the first natural philosophers, much though the former disparaged the apparently pointless speculations of the latter. Both were sceptical naturalists: they tended to reject mythological explanations and beliefs that were accepted purely on the grounds of custom, tradition or religion. The *physici* looked askance at attempts to explain the world in terms of gods, and instead sought natural reasons why things should be as they are. The Sophists were similarly sceptical about the relevance of religion, which was after all rather hard to discuss rationally. As Protagoras said: 'About the gods I am not able to know whether they exist or do not exist, nor what they are like in form; for the factors preventing knowledge are many: the obscurity of the subject, and the shortness of human life.' The Sophists demanded to know the reasons that could be offered for moral views, and showed a generally naturalistic turn of mind whatever they inquired into.

What was intellectually exhilarating for them was bound to be disturbing for others, especially when there were such ingenious and powerful suppliers of arguments as Gorgias around. It must have been somewhat disconcerting to find an intellectual arms-merchant like Gorgias loitering on your doorstep. It is not surprising that people fought back with the laughter of *Clouds*, nor that Aristophanes should have cast Socrates as a champion Sophist, for Socrates was the best-known arguer in Athens. Aristophanes certainly presented an unjust caricature of Socrates. But equally, in the course of defending Socrates, Plato certainly caricatured the Sophists too. Having described the real Sophists, it is time to look at the real Socrates.

# PART TWO

# 10

# Philosophy's Martyr:
## *Socrates and the Socratics*

Socrates is the saint and martyr of philosophy. No other great philosopher has been so obsessed with righteous living. Like many martyrs, Socrates chose not to try to save his life when he probably could have done so by changing his ways. According to Plato, who was there at the time, Socrates told the judges at his trial that '[y]ou are mistaken . . . if you think that a man who is worth anything ought to spend his time weighing up the prospects of life and death. He has only one thing to consider in performing any action – that is, whether he is acting rightly or wrongly.' But unlike many saints, Socrates had a lively sense of humour; this sometimes appeared as playful wit, sometimes as pregnant irony. And unlike the saints of any and every religion, his faith consisted not in a reliance on revelation or blind hope but in a devotion to argumentative reason. He would not be swayed by anything less.

His friends told stories about how strange he was. After dinner one night, according to a dialogue of Plato, a young man who had been on military service with Socrates recounted how Socrates had

started wrestling with some problem or other about sunrise one morning, and stood there lost in thought, and when the answer wouldn't come he still stood there thinking and refused to give it up. Time went on, and by about midday the troops . . . began telling each other how Socrates had been standing there thinking ever since daybreak. And at last, toward nightfall, some of the Ionians brought out their bedding after supper . . . partly to see whether he was going to stay there all night. Well, there he stood till morning, and then at sunrise he said his prayers to the sun and went away.

Despite such uses of his spare time, Socrates had by all accounts an honourable military record.

Another friend described how, on the way to the dinner party at which the above story is told, Socrates 'fell into a fit of abstraction and began to lag behind'. Socrates then lurked in a neighbour's porch to continue thinking. 'It's quite a habit of his, you know; off he goes and there he stands, no matter where it is.' His other regular habits did not include washing; even his best friends admitted that it was unusual to see him freshly bathed and with his shoes on. He was shabby and unkempt, never had any money nor cared where his next meal was

SOCRATES.

coming from. He admitted to the court that 'I have never lived an ordinary quiet life. I did not care for the things that most people care about – making money, having a comfortable home, high military or civil rank, and all the other activities . . . which go on in our city.' But Socrates did not think that any of these trappings of a conventionally successful life were bad in themselves. Neither was he an ascetic in the ordinary sense of the term. He never preached abstinence (he could, said his friends, drink any of them under the table, though he was never seen to be drunk), nor did he urge others to live as simply as he did. A hardy and preoccupied man, he was just too busy to pay much attention to such things as clothing, food or money.

For most of the time he was busy talking to others, not just contemplating by himself. His discussions, it seems, were as intense as his fits of solitary abstraction. A distinguished general who knew him once said:

anyone who is close to Socrates and enters into conversation with him is liable to be drawn into an argument, and whatever subject he may start, he will be continually carried round and round by him, until at last he finds that he has to give an account both of his present and past life, and when he is once entangled, Socrates will not let him go until he has completely and thoroughly sifted him.

Socrates was poor, had no conventional achievements to his name and was of humble birth – his father was a stonemason and his mother a midwife. The fact that he nevertheless had an entrée to Athenian high society attests to his remarkable powers of conversation. Alcibiades, who told the story of Socrates' vigil at camp, compared his speech to the music of Marsyas, the river god 'who had only to put his flute to his lips to bewitch mankind'. The 'difference between you and Marsyas', Alcibiades tells Socrates, 'is that you can get just the same effect without any instrument at all – with nothing but a few simple words, not even poetry'. And:

speaking for myself, gentlemen, if I wasn't afraid you'd tell me I was completely bottled, I'd swear on oath what an extraordinary effect his words have had on me . . . For the moment I hear him speak I am smitten with a kind of sacred rage . . . and my heart jumps into my mouth and the tears start into my eyes – oh, and not only me, but lots of other men . . .

This latter-day Marsyas, here, has often left me in such a state of mind that I've felt I simply couldn't go on living the way I did . . . He makes me admit that while I'm spending my time on politics I am neglecting all the things that are crying for attention in myself.

The young Alcibiades was indeed 'bottled' at this stage of the dinner, so no doubt he was getting carried away. It is a telling fact that everyone got carried away when they talked about Socrates, whether it was Alcibiades singing his praises or his enemies ranting against him.

Alcibiades also wanted Socrates to love him. It was fairly usual for dealings between Athenian philosophers and young men to be tinged with homo-eroticism, especially among Plato's circle. Attracted by the youthful beauty of boys, an older man would happily hold their attention by spooning them wisdom. But both Plato and Socrates criticized homosexual intercourse; Alcibiades had at first been mortified when Socrates refused to return his physical affections. As Socrates had tactfully explained at the time, he resisted the advances of Alcibiades for ethical reasons, not because he was not attracted to him. Alcibiades was famously handsome and Socrates was famously ugly. It was an inner beauty that Alcibiades saw in him: 'I've been bitten in the heart, or the mind, or whatever you like to call it, by Socrates' philosophy, which clings like an adder to any young and gifted mind it can get hold of.'

Socrates poked fun at his own ugliness, and he could make something more than half-serious out of even such a light-hearted subject as that. Critobulus, a friend of Socrates, apparently once challenged him to a 'beauty contest' in which each man was to try to convince a mock-jury that he was better-looking than the other. Socrates begins the contest:

*Socrates*: The first step, then, in my suit, is to summon you to the preliminary hearing; be so kind as to answer my questions . . . Do you hold . . . that beauty is to be found only in man, or is it also in other objects?

*Critobulus*: In faith, my opinion is that beauty is to be found quite as well in a horse or an ox or in any number of inanimate things. I know, at any rate, that a shield may be beautiful, or a sword, or a spear.

*Soc*: How can it be that all these things are beautiful when they are entirely dissimilar?

*Crit*: Why, they are beautiful and fine if they are well made for the respective functions for which we obtain them or if they are naturally well constituted to serve our needs.

*Soc*: Do you know the reason why we need eyes?

*Crit*: Obviously to see with.

*Soc*: In that case it would appear without further ado that my eyes are finer ones than yours.

*Crit*: How so?

*Soc*: Because, while yours see only straight ahead, mine, by bulging out as they do, see also to the sides.

*Crit*: Do you mean to say that a crab is better equipped visually than any other creature?

*Soc*: Absolutely . . .

*Crit*: Well, let that pass; but whose nose is finer, yours or mine?

*Soc*: Mine, I consider, granting that Providence made us noses to smell with.

For your nostrils look down toward the ground, but mine are wide open and turned outward so that I can catch scents from all about.

*Crit*: But how do you make a snub nose handsomer than a straight one?

*Soc*: For the reason that it does not put a barricade between the eyes but allows them unobstructed vision of whatever they desire to see; whereas a high nose, as if in despite, has walled the eyes off one from the other.

*Crit*: As for the mouth, I concede that point. For if it is created for the purpose of biting off food, you could bite off a far bigger mouthful than I could. And don't you think that your kiss is also the more tender because you have thick lips?

*Soc*: According to your argument, it would seem that I have a mouth more ugly even than an ass's . . .

*Crit*: I cannot argue any longer with you, let them distribute the ballots . . .

Of course Socrates lost. He knew he could not really be said to be good-looking, and they were only having fun. This exchange (from a dialogue by another admirer, Xenophon) is not the sort of thing that would bring tears to the eyes of Alcibiades, unless perhaps they were tears of laughter. Nor yet does it show Socrates at his most sophisticated. Far from it: this is the Beginner's Socrates. But it is interesting to see how this simple banter has much of the Socrates that one meets in the weightier and better-known philosophical exchanges in Plato's dialogues.

First there is his characteristic method of interrogation. Instead of proposing a thesis himself, Socrates lets the other man do so and then draws out its consequences. As always with Socrates, the business begins with a request for an enlightening definition of whatever is being discussed – in this case, of beauty. Critobulus takes the bait and offers as his definition: '[*things are*] beautiful and fine if they are well made for the respective functions for which we obtain them or if they are naturally well constituted to serve our needs.' Then Socrates reels him in. He has no difficulty in showing that if this is what beauty is, then he himself is beautiful. Unravelling the accounts of others is how Socrates always played the game of dialectic.

The contest also shows Socrates' complex irony. He knows that he is ugly. He knows that Critobulus' definition of beauty is faulty. Yet he proceeds as if neither of these things were so: he seems perfectly happy to adopt the definition and to use it to prove that he is in fact good-looking. But he is not just trying to exploit Critobulus' words to win the beauty contest by foul means. He is not really trying to win it at all. While pretending to fight the contest, Socrates is in fact doing something else. By playfully adopting Critobulus' definition, Socrates demonstrates that he has failed to get to the bottom of what beauty is. It cannot be defined in terms of fitness and usefulness alone, since this would imply that Socrates' features are beautiful, which everybody knows they are not. Thus, while ironically pretending to convince Critobulus of his beauty, Socrates has in fact established the negative result that beauty cannot be what Critobulus says it is.

Socrates frequently and tiresomely denied that he knew anything about beauty or virtue or justice, or whatever else was being discussed. Such avowed ignorance was his trademark. Like his playful claim to personal beauty, these denials were partly ironic, though with a more serious purpose. Although he always claimed to have nothing to teach, his activities looked very much like teaching – enough so to get him hauled before the courts as a teacher with a malign influence. I shall now turn to the trial of Socrates and his defence, which show just what it was that made him so unpopular with some conservative Athenians, and so popular with most subsequent philosophers.

The trial of Socrates took place in 399 BC when he was nearly seventy. The charges were that he refused to recognize the official gods of the state, that he introduced new gods and that he corrupted the young. There was a vivid political background to the trial, but this does not mean that the charges were a sham and that the trial was really a political one. Politics, religion and education were all intertwined in the matter, and, however you looked at it, Socrates was saying the wrong things at the wrong time.

In 404 BC, five years before the trial, a twenty-seven-year war between Athens and Sparta had ended with the defeat of Athens. The Athenian democracy was overthrown and replaced by a group of men, subsequently known as the Thirty Tyrants, who were installed by Sparta. In the course of earning their name, the Tyrants murdered so many people that they lasted for only a year, though it was not until 401 BC that democracy was fully restored. Understandably, the democrats were still feeling rather insecure in 399 BC. There were plenty of reasons to be uneasy about the presence of Socrates in the city.

Two close former associates of his had been involved in the tyranny. One, Critias, was the leader of the Thirty and a particularly bloodthirsty man. The other, Charmides, was one of their deputies (both men were, incidentally, relations of Plato). Alcibiades had also turned out to be rather a liability. A headstrong and arrogant aristocrat, he was accused of sacrilegious high-jinks and profanity – committed, perhaps, while 'bottled'. Alcibiades heard about these charges while he was on a military expedition to Sicily. Rather than return to face them, he defected and treacherously fought on the side of Sparta instead. None of this looked good for these men's former mentor, Socrates.

In 403 BC, however, a political amnesty had been declared in Athens, so it would not have been possible to indict Socrates on explicitly political charges, even if anyone had wanted to. Besides, there were deeper causes for concern about his influence. During the long war with Sparta, Athenians had grown increasingly nervous about the home front. It was felt that intellectuals were weakening Athenian society by undermining its traditional views and values. Well might a man who captivated idle youths with his questioning about justice have aroused suspicion. The fact that there had been a hilarious caricature of Socrates as a bumbling but subversive teacher in a play by Aristophanes, staged in Athens twenty-four years earlier, did not help matters. And whatever truth there was to the rumour that Socrates disbelieved in the traditional gods – he seemed to deny the charge, but not convincingly – there was no doubt that he had an unorthodox approach to divinity. The way he talked about his *daimonion*, his 'guardian spirit' or personal 'divine sign', gave reasonable cause for concern that he did indeed 'introduce new gods', as the indictment put it. That would have been a grievous sin against the shaky democracy. The state alone had the power to say what was a suitable object for religious veneration; it had its own procedures for officially recognizing gods, and anyone who ignored them was in effect challenging the legitimacy of the democratic state. All of this Socrates was up against when he faced the 500 Athenian citizens who were to judge him.

Plato was at the trial; the *Apology* [or 'defence-speech'] *of Socrates* which he wrote a few years afterwards was probably his first work. There are reasons to believe that in this work Plato tried harder to represent the real Socrates than he subsequently did elsewhere, though he did not necessarily try to reproduce his exact words. So I shall rely on Plato (as I have done for much of the information about Socrates provided so far). There is no alternative. The Socrates of Plato's *Apology* is the only Socrates there is, or has been for nearly all of the history of philosophy.

From a legal point of view, Socrates' speech is a miserable performance. He begins by saying that he has no skill as a speaker; this is a standard rhetorical first move, but in this case one would have to agree with him, if his aim in speaking were simply to get himself acquitted. Almost everything he says to rebut the official charges is either irrelevant or else unpersuasive. For example, on the subject of religion he confines himself to mocking his accuser. He gets him to contradict himself by provoking him into saying that Socrates is a complete atheist who believes in no gods at all. But if that were so, Socrates points out, how could he also be guilty of introducing new gods? To the charge that he has corrupted the young, Socrates makes the unconvincingly convoluted reply that he cannot intentionally have done any such thing, since this would have been against his own interests. To corrupt someone is to harm him, he says, and if you harm someone then he will try to harm you back. So clearly he would not have risked that. This argument will have persuaded nobody.

Socrates knew that his judges were already prejudiced against him by the slanders of Aristophanes, and set out to correct these false impressions. He is not, he says, a man who teaches for money, like the professional 'Sophists' with whom Aristophanes has confused him. This seems to have been true enough: he did not charge a fee. But he did sing for his supper. He accepted hospitality in a tacit bargain for his edifying conversation, and apparently did no other sort of work. So the way he earned his living was not really different from that of the Sophists – not that either way of life would be regarded as inherently suspicious today. He also tried to dismiss the slander that he taught people how to win arguments by trickery when they were in the wrong. Far from it, he protested, for he did not know enough to teach anybody anything.

This is the main theme of the *Apology*, which is more of a general defence of his way of life than a rebuttal of the official charges. The nub of this defence is Socrates' claim that he has positively benefited the Athenians by subjecting them to his philosophical cross-examinations, but that they have failed to realize this and merely been angered by it, which is why he has ended up on trial for his life.

Socrates says that he is fulfilling the wishes of the gods when he goes about and argues with people. A friend of his once went to the oracle at Delphi and asked if there was any man wiser than Socrates. No, came back the answer, which threw Socrates into a frightful confusion – or so he says. For he always held that he was not wise at all. 'After puzzling about it for some time, I set myself at last with considerable reluctance to check the truth of it.' He did so by interrogating all sorts of people who had a reputation for wisdom or specialized knowledge. But he was always disappointed, because it seemed that there was nobody whose alleged wisdom could stand up to his questioning. He was always able to refute the efforts of others to establish some thesis of theirs, usually by highlighting some unwelcome and unexpected consequences of their views. He also questioned poets, but they could not even elucidate their poems to his satisfaction. After one such encounter:

I reflected as I walked away, Well, I am certainly wiser than this man. It is only too likely that neither of us has any knowledge to boast of, but he thinks that he knows something which he does not know, whereas I am quite conscious of my ignorance. At any rate it seems that I am wiser than he is to this small extent, that I do not think that I know what I do not know.

Then it dawned on him what the oracle must have meant:

whenever I succeed in disproving another person's claim to wisdom in a given subject, the bystanders assume that I know everything about that subject myself. But the truth of the matter, gentlemen, is pretty certainly this, that real wisdom is the property of God, and this oracle is his way of telling us that human wisdom has little or no value. It seems to me that he is not referring literally to Socrates, but has merely taken my name as an example, as if he would say to us, The wisest of you men is he who has realized, like Socrates, that in respect of wisdom, he is really worthless.

In other words, the superior wisdom of Socrates lies in the fact that he alone is aware of how little he knows. Of course, there is a little more to Socrates' wisdom than just that, as he is made to admit elsewhere in Plato's dialogues. Although, he claims, 'the arguments never come out of me; they always come from the person I am talking with', he acknowledges that he is 'at a slight advantage in having the skill to get some account of the matter from another's wisdom and entertain it with fair treatment'. He aptly describes himself as an intellectual midwife, whose questioning delivers the thoughts of others into the light of day. But this skill in elucidation and debate, which he obviously has in abundance, is not a form of real wisdom so far as Socrates is concerned. Real wisdom is perfect knowledge about ethical subjects, about how to live. When Socrates claims ignorance, he means ignorance about the foundations of morality; he is not asserting any general sort of scepticism about everyday matters of fact. His concern is solely with ethical reflection, and he cannot with a clear conscience abandon his mission to encourage it in others:

If I say that this would be disobedience to God, and that is why I cannot 'mind my own business', you will not believe that I am serious. If on the other hand I tell you that to let no day pass without discussing goodness and all the other subjects about which you hear me talking and examining both myself and others is really the very best thing that a man can do, and that life without this sort of examination is not worth living, you will be even less inclined to believe me. Nevertheless that is how it is.

His pious references to the wisdom of God (sometimes he speaks of a single God, sometimes of the gods) are apt to disguise how unconventional his attitude to divinity was. When he says that only God has wisdom, he seems to mean this figuratively, just as one might shrug and say 'God knows!' For consider how he sets about interpreting 'God's' words and trying to tease out hints of 'his' wisdom. The Delphic oracle was as authentic a voice of God as any available: yet Socrates did not just accept what it says but instead set out 'to check the truth of it'. He says elsewhere that 'it has always been my nature never to accept advice from any of my friends unless reflection shows that it is the best course that reason offers'; he seems to have adopted exactly the same approach to the advice of God. Presented with the divine pronouncement that no man is wiser than Socrates, he refuses to take this at face value until he has satisfied himself that a true meaning can be found for it.

He seems to be speaking in a roundabout way when he refers to his mission as divine, because the Delphic oracle did not explicitly tell him to go forth and philosophize. He does at one point say that his mission to argue and question was undertaken 'in obedience to God's commands given in oracles and dreams and in every other way that any divine dispensation has ever impressed a duty upon man'. But when he continues by saying that this is a true statement 'and easy to verify', his verification consists merely in arguing that his mission is a morally good thing. He does not give any evidence that God told him to do it. He probably came closest to the heart of the matter when he said, 'I want you to think of my adventures as a sort of pilgrimage undertaken to establish the truth of the oracle once for all.' It was his conscience and intelligence which told him to interrogate those who believed themselves to be wise. He could claim that this 'helps the cause of God' because such activities do help to confirm the Delphic pronouncement that nobody is wiser than Socrates. But the talk of God is largely a gloss, which serves to mark Socrates' high moral purpose and to win the approval of his hearers. His basic motive for philosophizing was simply that it seemed to him the right thing to do.

Socrates says he is influenced in his actions by what he calls his *daimonion*, a guardian spirit or voice which has been with him since childhood. This seems to have been the unorthodox divinity or 'new gods' referred to in the charges against him. Once again the advice of the *daimonion* is treated as advice to be reasoned with before it is endorsed, like the counsel of friends or the words of the Delphic oracle. The voice of the *daimonion* is pretty clearly what we would call the voice of cautious conscience. He says that 'when it comes it always dissuades me from what I am proposing to do, and never urges me on'.

The guardian spirit warned him off any involvement in politics, he says, because if he had made a public figure of himself, he would have been killed long before he could have done much good. That is why he chose to minister to the people privately:

I spend all my time going about trying to persuade you, young and old, to make your first and chief concern not for your bodies nor for your possessions, but for the highest welfare of your souls, proclaiming as I go, Wealth does not bring goodness, but goodness brings wealth and every other blessing, both to the individual and to the state.

This persuasion seems to have been rather strident at times. He implies that the Athenians should be 'ashamed that you give your attention to acquiring as much money as possible, and similarly with reputation and honour, and give no attention or thought to truth and understanding and the perfection of your soul'. He must have particularly annoyed them when he said, during his trial, that he thought he was doing the Athenians 'the greatest possible service' in showing them the errors of their ways. This was at a stage of the proceedings when he had already been voted guilty and was required to argue for a suitable penalty, to counter the prosecution's proposal that he be put to death. Typically, he treats this responsibility with irony. What he actually deserves for doing the Athenians such a service, he says, is not a punishment but a reward. He suggests free meals for life at the expense of the state. Such an honour was usually reserved for victors at the Olympic Games and suchlike; he has earned it even more than they have, he says, because 'these people give you the semblance of success, but I give you the reality'. He ends this part of the speech by suggesting a fine instead, at the instigation of Plato and other friends who offer to pay it for him. But the Athenians had already lost their patience. They voted for the death penalty by a larger majority than that by which they had found him guilty. This means that some of them, having previously found him innocent, were so enraged by his cheek that they either changed their minds or else decided to get rid of him anyway.

One story has it that as Socrates was leaving the court, a devoted but dim admirer called Apollodorus moaned that the hardest thing for him to bear was that Socrates was being put to death unjustly. What? said Socrates, trying to comfort him. Would you rather I was put to death justly?

As for the prospect of death itself, he was already very old and close to death anyway, so he says, and he had had a good and useful life. Besides:

to be afraid of death is only another form of thinking that one is wise when one is not ... No one knows with regard to death whether it is really the greatest blessing that can happen to a man, but people dread it as though they were certain that it is the greatest evil, and this ignorance, which thinks that it knows what it does not, must surely be ignorance most culpable ... and if I were to claim to be wiser than my neighbour in any respect, it would be in this – that not possessing any real knowledge of what comes after death, I am also conscious that I do not possess it.

If there were an afterlife, he added, he would get the chance to meet 'heroes of the old days who met their death through an unfair trial, and to compare my fortunes with theirs – it would be rather amusing'.

For all his talk of ignorance, and his insistence that he merely acted as a midwife for the ideas of others, Socrates did have strong beliefs of his own. Unfortunately he never wrote them down. For one of these beliefs was that philosophy is an intimate and collaborative activity: it is a matter for discussions among small groups of people who argue together in order that each might find the truth for himself. The spirit of such a pastime cannot accurately be captured in a lecture or a treatise. That is one reason why Plato and Xenophon (and several of their contemporaries whose works are now lost) chose to present Socrates' teaching in the form of dialogues. Dialogue had been his *métier* and dialogue would be his monument.

There are four main witnesses for the intimate thoughts of Socrates: Plato, Xenophon, Aristophanes and Aristotle. None of these men is quite what a historian might have wished for. Plato has by far the most to say on the subject, but as an objective guide to Socrates he suffers from the disability of having practically worshipped him. He is therefore likely to have exaggerated what he took to be his finest qualities. Also, in the course of some forty years of thinking and teaching, during which Plato's ideas naturally changed quite a lot, he paid Socrates the tribute of using him as a mouthpiece. To Plato, Socrates was pre-eminently wise, so whenever something seemed to Plato to be wise, he put it in the mouth of Socrates. Plato himself – or else a close associate – once described his dialogues as 'the work of a Socrates embellished and modernized'. This is double trouble, because not only does the Socrates in Plato's dialogues often speak for Plato rather than for himself, but he is also made to say rather different things at the various stages of Plato's literary career.

What about the other three witnesses? The failings of Xenophon (*c*.430–*c*.355 BC) as a source are quite different. He was not – like Plato – too much of a philosopher to act as a guide to Socrates, but rather too little of one. It is no crime to be a retired general turned gentleman-farmer, but such a man is perhaps not the safest custodian of the key to one of the world's great thinkers. Xenophon implausibly uses the figure of Socrates to pass on his own tips about farming and military tactics. He also depicts him as a boringly conventional goody-goody: 'All his private conduct was lawful and helpful: to public authority he rendered such scrupulous obedience in all that the laws required, both in civil life and in military service, that he was a pattern of good discipline to all.' A leading scholar of ancient philosophy has understandably referred to Xenophon as 'that stuffy old prig'. In fairness to Xenophon it must be said that anyone who admired an eccentric like Socrates as much as he did cannot have been all that stuffy. But Xenophon was certainly no Socrates himself, and he may often have failed to grasp both the strangeness of his character and what he was getting at. If Xenophon tried too hard to make Socrates respectable and a sound chap, then the playwright Aristophanes (*c*.448–*c*.380 BC) tried too hard to do the opposite. His Socrates is a slapstick fool who is intrigued by such questions as from which end a gnat breaks wind. Aristotle's disability in describing Socrates is simply stated: he was born fifteen years too late.

Yet it is Aristotle who holds a vital clue. Although he never heard Socrates' opinions at first hand, he studied for some twenty years in Plato's Academy and had plenty of opportunity to hear Plato's views from Plato himself. He was therefore in a position to disentangle the thinking of the two men. To a considerable extent, Aristotle's testimony lets one subtract Plato from his own dialogues and see the Socratic remainder. Aristotle was also much less in awe of Socrates than Plato was, and therefore managed to take a more dispassionate approach to his teachings.

The fact that the four main sources for Socrates were so different turns out to be something of a boon. It means that the features which are common to their various accounts are all the more likely to be authentic. And the more we know about each of the four and what he was up to, the easier it is to discount his bias and see the true Socrates loitering behind. By following up such clues, modern scholars have pieced together much of the philosophy of the man who literally argued himself to death.

It is simplest to consider the views of Socrates in relation to those of Plato. The approximate dating of Plato's dialogues, plus some information about his life, make it possible to retrace his steps on an intellectual journey that started in the company of Socrates but eventually left him far behind. At first Plato largely limited himself to recreating the conversations of his revered teacher. Gradually, Pythagorean and other mystical glosses were put on Socrates' ideas as Plato came increasingly under the influence of Italian Pythagoreans. And eventually Plato reached a point where he invoked the name of Socrates to expound on all sorts of subjects.

The important discussions of the real Socrates were exclusively concerned with how one ought to live. They were mostly about the virtues, of which there were conventionally held to be five: courage, moderation, piety, wisdom and justice. His mission was to urge people to care for their souls by trying to understand and acquire these qualities. This task was enough to keep Socrates busy, but Plato was much more ambitious on his master's behalf. He wrote many dialogues that do not focus on morality at all but which usually still have Socrates as the main speaker. For example, Plato's *Republic* starts out as a discussion of justice but ends up touching on practically everything that interested Plato.

Even when the real Socrates made a point of saying that he did not have a clue, Plato often plunged ahead and credited him with firm opinions. For instance, Socrates thought that what happens after death is an open question. But in the *Phaedo*, which purports to give Socrates' last words before he drank hemlock in prison, Plato makes him produce a whole barrage of proofs for the immortality of the soul.

Plato seems to have had few doubts about what would happen after death. He thought that the soul was separable from the body, that it existed before birth and that it would definitely continue to exist after death. Under Pythagorean influence, he held that while it was tied to a physical body during life it led a defiled and inferior existence from which it needed to be 'purified' and 'freed from the shackles of the body'. According to Plato in this dialogue, what the good man can hope to enjoy after death is reunification, or at least communion, with those incorporeal higher forms of existence that are conventionally called 'the divine'. The philosopher, in particular, should regard the whole of his life as a preparation for the blissful release of death. As we have seen, Socrates lived a shambling, poor and unconventional life that was certainly unworldly. But Plato was positively other-worldly, which is a rather different thing (and actually he led a mostly comfortable existence until escaping the shackles of his amply fed body).

Socrates pursued the virtues because he felt morally obliged to, here and now. Earthly life imposed its own duties, brought its own blessings and was not simply a preparation for something else. Plato's motives were less straightforward because he had at least one eye fixed on something beyond. One belief about virtue that the two men held in common is that the pursuit of goodness is not only a matter of acting in certain ways but also an intellectual project. Yet they saw this project differently. Socrates believed that coming to understand the virtues was a necessary precondition for possessing them. A man could not be truly virtuous unless he knew what virtue was, and the only way he might be able to get this knowledge was by examining accounts of the particular virtues. That is why Socrates went around questioning people and arguing with them. Plato believed in this argumentative search too, but he also interpreted it as something almost mystical. While Socrates saw the search for definitions as a means to an end, namely the exercise of virtue, Plato saw the search as an end in itself. To look for a definition was, for Plato, to seek the ideal, eternal, unchanging Form of whatever was under discussion; the contemplation of such Forms was itself the highest good. That is what he thought Socrates' questioning really amounted to and what it ought to aim at.

For Plato, philosophy was the ladder to this elevated world of the Forms, but not everyone could climb it. Its higher rungs were reserved for those who were especially talented in dialectical argument, an elite, like the initiates of cult religions, or the followers of Pythagoras who had been privy to the master's secrets. Socrates had a more egalitarian approach to knowledge and virtue. The unexamined life, as he famously said in his defence-speech, is not worth living, and this is not a fate to which he meant to condemn all but a chosen few. Anybody could examine his own life and ideas and thus lead a worthwhile existence. Socrates would happily question and argue with anybody, cobbler or king, and for him this was all that philosophy was. He would have had little use for Plato's Forms or the rare skills needed to find them.

One thing which led Plato to the mysterious Forms was his fascination with mathematics, again a Pythagorean matter and again a point of difference between him and Socrates. Above its gates, Plato's Academy was said to have had the words 'No one ignorant of geometry admitted here'; Aristotle later complained that for Plato's followers, 'mathematics has come to be the whole of philosophy' – a petulant exaggeration, but a pointed one. What struck Plato about the objects dealt with in mathematics, such as numbers and triangles, is that they are ideal, eternal, unchanging and pleasingly independent of earthly, visible things. Plainly one cannot see or touch the number four: it therefore exists in a different sort of realm, according to Plato. And the lines, triangles and other sorts of objects that figure in mathematical proofs cannot be identified with anything physical either. Particular physical lines and triangles are nothing more than approximations to ideal mathematical ones. A perfect line, for example, would have no thickness; but any visible line, or rim of a physical object, always will. Given the impressiveness of mathematics, Plato reasoned, other sorts of knowledge ought to copy it and be about ideal and incorporeal objects too. These objects of knowledge were the Forms.

In one of his dialogues, Plato used a geometrical example to argue that knowledge of the Forms, which for him meant all the important sorts of knowledge, is acquired before birth. The truths of pure reason, such as those of mathematics, are not discovered afresh but are painstakingly recollected from a previous existence in which the soul was disembodied and could encounter the Forms directly. Thus one does not strictly speaking learn these truths at all: one works to remember them. When a soul is born into a body, the knowledge which it previously enjoyed slips from memory: as Wordsworth wrote in his 'Intimations of Immortality', 'our birth is but a sleep and a forgetting'.

Wordsworth was not particularly thinking about geometry, but he liked the general idea. To illustrate this theory, Plato makes 'Socrates' elicit some apparent knowledge of geometry from an uneducated slave-boy. This is supposed both to confirm the Platonic idea that some knowledge is recollected from an earlier existence and to show why the teaching of Socrates is indeed, as Socrates had claimed, really like midwifery.

The problem which 'Socrates' sets the slave is that of determining the sides of a square of a given area. He starts by drawing a square whose sides are two feet long, and whose area is thus four square feet, and asks how long the sides would have to be if its area were instead eight square feet. At first the slave ignorantly reasons that the sides would have to be twice as long as those of the original square, i.e., four feet. By drawing another diagram, 'Socrates' soon shows him that this must be wrong, since the area of such a square would be not eight but sixteen square feet. The slave is surprised to learn that he does not know as much as he thought he did. 'Socrates' notes that at this point 'we have helped him to some extent toward finding the right answer, for now not only is he ignorant of it but he will be quite glad to look for it'. Next, with the aid of further diagrams and by asking the right questions about them, Socrates gradually leads the slave to work out the answer for himself: the sides of a triangle with twice the area of the original one would have to be the same length as a diagonal drawn across the original square – which, in effect, boils down to the famous theorem of Pythagoras. Bingo: since Socrates never actually told him this, the slave must have 'known' it already.

This little episode does not really prove Plato's theory of recollection, as Plato himself acknowledged. But the story does illustrate a distinctly Socratic thesis about knowledge and how it can be imparted. Socrates' questions to the slave are indeed leading ones (and the diagrams help, too), yet it is nevertheless true that the slave comes to see the answer for himself. He has not simply been told it as one might be told how many feet there are in a yard or what the capital of Greece is. He has come to appreciate something through his own intellectual faculties. So Socrates can modestly make his usual claim that he has not handed over any knowledge himself but has just acted as a midwife to bring it out of somebody else. And there is another thing: as Socrates points out, in order for the slave to know this piece of mathematics properly, it is not quite enough for him to work through the example just once:

At present these opinions [*of the slave*] being newly aroused, have a dreamlike quality. But if the same questions are put to him on many occasions and in different ways, you can see that in the end he will have a knowledge on the subject as accurate as anybody's . . .

This knowledge will not come from teaching but from questioning. He will recover it for himself.

Repeated doses of Socratic questioning are called for. In other words, what the slave needs is exactly the sort of treatment that the real Socrates offered the largely ungrateful Athenians. As he says in the *Apology*, if anyone claims to know about goodness, 'I shall question him and examine him and test him'. Thus in his fanciful story of assisted recollection, Plato has given us a striking illustration of the sort of thing Socrates was doing when he claimed to help other people deliver their own opinions. It is as if Socrates were drawing out and firming up some knowledge that was already there.

This is all very well for Plato's example of his beloved triangles and squares. It is not hard to believe that a skilled questioner can bring a pupil to appreciate a mathematical truth without explicitly stating this truth for him – anyone who has had a good teacher will recognize this experience. But what about matters of justice and the other virtues, which is what the real Socrates was interested in? Ethics is messier than mathematics; it does not, for one thing, seem to have any proofs to offer. So presumably the business of learning about virtue will be quite different from the business of learning about mathematics.

Socrates knew this. He had no illusions about being able conclusively to prove any ethical doctrines. Quite the contrary, in fact, for he was forever insisting on his own uncertainty and the tentativeness of his inquiries. For example, before starting a defence of one thesis, he admits that 'sometimes, however, I am of the opposite opinion, for I am all abroad in my ideas about this matter, a condition obviously occasioned by ignorance'. No doubt he is wrong to maintain this thesis now, he says to his interlocutor, but let us follow the argument wherever it leads and perhaps you will be able to put me right. When

Socrates says earlier on in this dialogue that 'I am full of defects, and always getting things wrong in some way or other', he is partly just being modest. But he was quite clear that he had no mathematical-style proofs about virtue.

Does he ever get anywhere, then? Does he really succeed in delivering any knowledge about virtue? In one sense, yes. He does, albeit indirectly, lay out several pronounced and rather extraordinary views about virtue, which all slot together to form a theory of human life. As for whether he succeeds in convincing his hearers of this theory, the answer is generally no. But he does not really aim to do that anyway, because he is not absolutely sure that the theory is right, and besides people must find their own way to the truth about such matters. What he aims to do is to put opinions about virtue to the test, and this applies both to his own opinions and to those of the people he is talking to. The test is to be trial by dialectical ordeal: definitions or accounts of various matters are to be queried and thereby elucidated, and whatever seems to survive such questioning is provisionally to be accepted. The results yielded by this approach fall short of true wisdom in various ways, but it is nevertheless the best approach available. Such inquiry does lead to a sort of knowledge, so Socrates' bare-faced denials that he knows anything are partly ironic.

Most of the authentically Socratic investigations in Plato's dialogues wind up without settling on a final conclusion. Socrates ambitiously sets off to find out what, say, justice is; he argues away for a while; and then usually has to go home apparently empty-handed. But he is not really empty-handed. The discussions usually succeed at least in showing up something important along the way. For example, in one early Platonic dialogue, Socrates quizzes a man called Euthyphro on the nature of piety or holiness. Although Socrates does not manage to establish exactly what piety is, he does manage to show something interesting about what it is not.

The two men meet outside the law courts, where Euthyphro is about to prosecute his own father for unintentionally (though perhaps culpably) causing the death of a slave who had himself murdered another slave. Socrates is surprised that Euthyphro should want to pursue such a case. Euthyphro insists that although his family think it impious for a son to prosecute his father as a murderer, he knows what he is about. His family are ignorant about what is holy, whereas he has 'an accurate knowledge of all that'. He therefore has no doubts about the rightness of his action. Socrates wonders at Euthyphro's confident wisdom and asks him to share it and tell him what holiness is. At first Euthyphro says that it is what the gods love. But Socrates gets him to see that since the gods are commonly represented as having fierce disagreements, they presumably do not always love or approve the same things. This means that whether or not a god approves something cannot be the criterion of whether or not it is holy: one god might approve it and another not, in which case one would be none the wiser as to its holiness. So Socrates and Euthyphro amend the proposed definition and say that the holy is what all the gods agree in approving. But now a question occurs to Socrates: 'Is what is holy holy because the gods approve it, or do they approve it because it is holy?'

This is an excellent question, so good in fact that at first Euthyphro does not understand it. It comes down to this: would absolutely anything that the gods approved of count as holy, just because they approved of it, or are they bound to approve only of certain things, namely those which would count as holy whether they approved of them or not? Unfortunately Plato did not have the vocabulary to make this distinction absolutely clear. So when Socrates tries to explain it, his account gets tangled in irrelevant grammatical matters and is not altogether compelling. Yet Socrates does seem to have uncovered a dilemma about the relationship between religion and morality. If we ask the same sort of question about what is morally good instead of about what is holy, we can see that we are faced with a revealing choice: either goodness cannot be explained simply by reference to what the gods want, or else it is an empty tautology to say that the gods are good – in which case the praise of the gods would simply be a matter of power-worship. As Leibniz put it, at the start of the eighteenth century (by which time the gods had long ago dwindled to one God):

Those who believe that God has established good and evil by an arbitrary decree ... deprive God of the designation *good*, for what cause could one have to praise him for what he does, if in doing something quite different he would have done equally well?

The Socrates in Plato's dialogue did not develop the argument that far. But he does appear to have seen that moral values cannot simply be derived from considerations about what the gods want, since to do so would rob the gods (or God) of any distinctively moral authority. Euthyphro apparently accepts the point, though later he wavers and hurries into court before he can be pinned down. Thus Socrates does succeed in making useful progress, even though he does not finally settle the matter at hand.

Yet there is still something unconvincing about what Socrates says he is up to in arguments like this. Can his questioning, or indeed any sort of intellectual enterprise, really have the sort of practical benefits he claims? Even though he never professes to establish the whole truth about virtue, and although we can agree that he nevertheless manages to make some intellectual headway, it is hard to see how his interrogations can have the power with which he seems to credit them. The problem lies in his belief that discussing the virtues can lead one actually to become a better person. This is no casual aside: it is this very idea which Socrates invokes to justify subjecting people to his trying examinations. It is all for their own good, he thinks, not only because such discussions are worthwhile in themselves but mainly because having them is the only path to personal virtue. This sounds implausible, to say the least. Surely it is one thing to come to know that a principle of action is right and quite another to behave in accordance with it. Could not someone find out all sorts of things about virtue by talking to Socrates but still go off and be wicked? As we have seen, Critias, Charmides and maybe Alcibiades seem to have done just that.

Aristotle frequently attacked Socrates along these lines: 'We must not limit our inquiry to knowing what it [*virtue*] is, but extend it to how it is to be produced.' He accused Socrates of failing to distinguish between practical questions and theoretical ones:

he thought all the virtues to be kinds of knowledge, so that to know justice and to be just came simultaneously . . . Therefore he inquired what virtue is, not how or from what it arises. This approach is correct with regard to theoretical knowledge, for there is no other part of astronomy or physics or geometry except knowing and contemplating the nature of the things which are the subjects of those sciences . . . But the aim of the practical sciences is different . . . For we do not wish to know what bravery is but to be brave, nor what justice is but to be just, just as we wish to be in health rather than to know what health is . . .

Socrates had a sort of answer to this. He could have replied along the following lines: 'You are not being fair to me. The reason why Critias, Charmides and some other troublesome pupils failed to be virtuous is simply that they had not yet learned enough about virtue. If only we had got further in our discussions, these people would indeed have become just. Thus, while I agree that we not only want to know what virtue is but want to be virtuous ourselves, my point is that if we really did know what it was, virtue would follow of its own accord. As I keep saying, I do not yet know what it is; so I cannot yet produce it in myself, let alone in others. That is precisely why we must keep on looking for it.'

The main point of this reply is fair enough. We cannot say that Socrates' claim about what his methods could achieve has been refuted: it has never yet been put to the test, because he has not yet found out what virtue is. But even so, why should anyone believe him when he says that full knowledge of virtue, if we ever managed to get it, would itself produce virtuous behaviour? It sounds an implausible hypothesis when we consider how weak-willed, selfish and short-sighted people often are. People frequently think that something is morally wrong and yet do it anyway. Why should we think they would be any different if only they knew more?

Aristotle reckoned that Socrates suffered from an over-simplified picture of human psychology: 'he is doing away with the irrational part of the soul, and is thereby doing away also both with passion and character'. Socrates saw human action and emotion in largely rational or intellectual terms; he ignored impulses and wilful irrationality. 'No one', he said, 'acts against what he believes best – people act so only by reason of ignorance.' This explains the exaggerated importance that Socrates attached to inquiries about virtue. If the only reason why people fail to do whatever is best is that they are ignorant, then the cure for immorality would indeed be more knowledge.

On this subject, Plato seems for once to have been more down-to-earth and realistic than Socrates. He recognized an irrational part of the soul and saw it as often in conflict with the rational part. (In his more Pythagorean moments, he described this as a conflict between soul and body.) Producing virtue was thus for Plato not just a matter of imparting knowledge but of encouraging certain behaviour. In the utopian state described in his *Republic*, this involved careful training and discipline of the young and close attention to their early environment – even to the sort of music they listened to and the sort of stories they were allowed to hear.

Socrates himself evidently had no need of such training. He was by all accounts supremely disciplined and a master of rational self-control. Maybe that was the problem. Perhaps it explains why he seems to have had such impossibly high expectations for others and to have supposed that if only they really knew what justice was, they would immediately become just themselves. It has been said of Socrates that 'in the strength of his character lay the weakness of his philosophy'. This is a neat formulation, but the ideas of Socrates had rather more coherence than it suggests. Besides, it must be said that his implausibly rationalistic account of psychology was not the only problem anyway. Even if some wise person were as disciplined as he was, and had somehow been born with the irrational part of his soul missing, it is hard to see how this would automatically make such a person morally good. Could not someone be as rational as Socrates, as wise as he sought to be, but also as bad as Milton's Satan, who knowingly embraced evil with the words 'Evil, be thou my Good'? Not according to Socrates, who held (said Aristotle) that 'no one would choose evil knowing it to be such'. Not only did Socrates conveniently ignore impulsiveness and irrationality, he apparently declared that wilful immorality was simply impossible. He seems never to have met a fallen man, let alone a fallen angel.

Was he then just naive? Nietzsche wrote of the 'divine naïveté and sureness of the Socratic way of life', but what he seems to have had in mind is the clear-eyed focus of Socrates' vision, not any merely foolish innocence. Nietzsche thought long and hard about Socrates' habit of expressing himself in apparently naive propositions, and concluded that it was in fact 'wisdom full of pranks'. Nietzsche realized that it is important to bear in mind the circumstances in which Socrates conduc-

ted his discussions. Most of the paradoxical views that can be attributed to Socrates are based on things which he said to someone, or
which he agreed to, for a distinctive purpose and in a distinctive
context. He sought to teach – while denying that he taught at all – by
teasing, cajoling and provoking. He tried to uncover the truth about
things by playfully trying out various ideas on his hearers. And intellectual pranks were no small part of it. 'This was Socrates' Muse', wrote
Galen, a doctor and philosopher of the second century AD: 'to mingle
seriousness with a portion of lightheartedness'.

One cannot excuse all the implausibilities in his views by saying that
he did not really mean them. This might salvage an appearance of
mundane common sense for Socrates, but only at the cost of discarding
almost everything he said. One can, though, often interpret Socrates
better by bearing his unusual educational project in mind. I shall now
piece together the theory of human life that lies behind Socrates'
apparently naive and implausible pronouncements. What emerges is a
set of ideas that have proved to be, at the very least, extremely fruitful,
not only in edifying some of his immediate hearers but also in stimulating a great deal of subsequent moral philosophy.

Socrates' theory starts and ends with the soul; in the *Apology*, he says
that the most important thing in life is to look to its welfare. The soul,
he says elsewhere, is that which is 'mutilated by wrong actions and
benefited by right ones'. He does not mean the actions of others, but
those of oneself. To do good is to benefit one's own soul and to do
wrong is to harm it. Since the soul's welfare is paramount, no other
sort of harm is so important. Nothing that other people can do to you
can harm you enough to cancel out the benefit you bestow on yourself
by acting rightly. It follows that bad people ultimately harm only
themselves: 'nothing can harm a good man either in life or after death'.

Socrates therefore has no fear of the court which is trying him. He
will not stoop to dishonourable behaviour in order to win acquittal,
for 'the difficulty is not so much to escape death; the real difficulty is
to escape from doing wrong, which is far more fleet of foot'. One
reason why it is hard to stop evil catching up with you is that if
someone tries to do you wrong, it is often tempting to try to get your
own back on them. But since it is always wrong to do evil – which

would harm your soul whatever your excuse for doing it might be –
Socrates points out that one must never return evil for evil. In other
words, one must turn the other cheek.

This conflicts with old Greek moral conventions, according to which
it is acceptable to harm one's enemies, though not one's friends and
especially not one's family. The rigorous ethics of Socrates removes
such distinctions between people and enjoins a universal morality
instead. One striking thing about it is that it does so by appealing to
self-interest, not to the sort of altruistic feelings that are usually thought
of as the main motive for moral behaviour. Doing good is a matter of
looking after the part of yourself which matters most, namely your
soul. This is not like ordinary selfishness, though, because the only
way to achieve this sort of benefit for yourself is by acting justly and
practising the other virtues too. It cannot be gained by greedily putting
your own interests above those of other people, but only by putting
moral self-improvement above any other motive. Neither does this
unusual ethics rest on any hope of heavenly reward or fear of its
opposite. The benefits of virtue are reaped more or less immediately,
for 'to live well means the same thing as to live honourably' and 'the
just [*man*] is happy and the unjust miserable'. In Socrates' view,
happiness and virtue are linked, which is why it is in people's own
interests to be moral.

This is particularly hard to swallow. For one unfair fact of life is
that the wicked do sometimes seem to prosper, which rather darkens
Socrates' sunny landscape. But to Socrates' mind, the successful care
of the soul brings all sorts of good things that may not immediately be
apparent. He argues that there are unexpected connections between
some of the good things in life, and that happiness turns out to be a
more complicated matter than one might at first think. It might seem
that wicked people can enjoy all sorts of pleasures, but in fact there
are some that they cannot enjoy, and these are important enough to
cast doubt on the idea that such people can truly be said to be happy
at all. Intellectual pleasures allegedly come into this class, and there
are all sorts of other satisfactions which cannot be obtained without
the exercise of the virtues. To take a simple example: unless you
practise the virtue of moderation, you will not enjoy good health, and
will probably deprive yourself of many future pleasures for the sake

of a few present ones. So without exercising the virtues a man cannot be all that happy after all.

It turns out that among the aspects of the good life which are subtly and surprisingly linked are the virtues themselves. Socrates argues that they come as a package-deal or not at all. His arguments typically proceed by trying to show that some particular virtue cannot work properly unless another is present as well. Courage, for instance, requires wisdom. It is no good being daring if you are foolish, for such would-be courage will degenerate into mere rashness. And all the other virtues are intertwined in similar ways. One of them, namely the virtue of wisdom, plays a special part. For without some degree of wisdom, people will be too bad at seeing the consequences of actions to be able to tell what is right and what is wrong, which is the fundamental prerequisite for virtuous living. Without wisdom they will be unable to be truly happy either, because every benefit that has the potential to make one happy also has the potential to be misused and thus to do the opposite. One therefore needs wisdom both to reap the benefits of good things and to be virtuous.

For Socrates, the connection between virtue and wisdom was so close that he seems in some sense to have identified the two. They certainly seemed to run into one another. According to Socrates, if someone has any of the other virtues, he must have wisdom as well – because otherwise he would not have managed to be virtuous. And if he has wisdom, he must have all of the virtues – because, being wise, he will realize that he cannot be happy without practising all the other virtues too. As we have seen, Socrates thought that moral behaviour benefits the soul and that a person who acts wickedly is doing himself a spiritual mischief. If this is true, then anyone who is genuinely wise will realize this fact. Anyone who realizes it – and who values his own soul, as any wise person surely must – will therefore try to avoid doing wrong. This train of thought explains why Socrates held that nobody does evil knowingly, for if someone does wrong, the only plausible explanation for his doing so is that he does not realize that his actions will harm his soul. He is, in effect, acting out of ignorance. All in all, these sorts of considerations supported Socrates' idea that if his discussions helped people towards wisdom, he would thereby be helping them towards virtue too.

In one of Plato's dialogues, Socrates encapsulates much of his theory in the course of summing up a discussion with Callicles, a young aristocrat who was about to enter public life:

So there is every necessity, Callicles, that the sound-minded and temperate man, being, as we have demonstrated, just and brave and pious, must be completely good, and the good man must do well and finely whatever he does, and he who does well must be happy and blessed, while the evil man who does ill must be wretched.

Did Socrates really manage to demonstrate all of that? His hearers frequently shied at the logical jumps he effortlessly made himself. So much seemed questionable, particularly what he said about happiness. Aristotle was typically forthright in his objections on this point: 'Those who say that the victim on the rack or the man who falls into great misfortunes is happy if he is good, are, whether they mean to or not, talking nonsense.' At one point one of Socrates' hearers understandably remarked, in no doubt baffled tones, that 'if you are serious and what you say is true, then surely the life of us mortals must be turned upside down'.

That is precisely what Socrates aimed to do: to reshape people's moral ideas. Clearly this was not going to be easy. In order to succeed in doing it by debate, the discussions would have to be rather different from purely theoretical ones, for 'it is no ordinary matter that we are discussing, but how we ought to live'. A degree of exaggeration and simplification would sometimes be needed if the ethical point at hand was to be made forcefully. For example, when Socrates said that nothing can harm a good man, he did not mean to deny that various undesirable things can happen to the virtuous. He was trying to persuade his hearers to regard such misfortunes as less important than the misfortune of spoiling your own soul. When he said that the evil man is wretched, he did not mean that such a man could not occasionally enjoy a good night out. He was exhorting his hearers to appreciate the satisfactions of virtue, in the broadest sense of virtue, and perhaps to pity the man who could not enjoy them. And when he said that goodness brings wealth and every other blessing, he did not mean that if you behave yourself, you will get rich quick. In this context – in which he was more concerned to deny that wealth will automatically bring goodness than to persuade anyone of exactly the reverse – he was holding up a picture of the best sort of human life, in which all good things are pursued and enjoyed to the full, thanks to the exercise of practical wisdom and the other virtues.

This is indeed no ordinary set of dogmas; in fact, they are not dogmas at all. What I have called Socrates' theory of human life is not something which he explicitly expounded as such. These ideas are the ones on which he depended in his questioning of others, or which had apparently withstood trial by dialectical ordeal. The final goal, which perhaps would never be reached, was to achieve a sort of expert knowledge like the expert knowledge of skilled craftsmen, though not about shoemaking or metal-work but about the ultimate craft of living well.

What Socrates came out with in discussions should often be seen as nothing more definite than faltering steps on this road to expert moral knowledge. Sometimes the road twisted as he coaxed and prodded with irony, or tossed in an argument that seemed likely to propel his fellow-travellers in an interesting direction (or at least to make them stop and think). The result, as Nietzsche said, was wisdom full of pranks. And because it was a specifically moral sort of wisdom or knowledge that Socrates was trying to arrive at, his arguments are tinged with exhortation, idealism and appeals to the moral sentiments as well as to logic and common sense. That is why, considered in the abstract and as attempts at pure logic, they seem to have many implausible gaps of the sort Aristotle noticed.

Socrates does not just paint an inspiring picture of the ideal life. His style of talk makes an intimate marriage between exhortation and logic, which is why it stands as a contribution to argumentative philosophy rather than to preaching. Everything he says is presented in the context of an argument: reasons are demanded, inferences are examined, definitions are refined, consequences are deduced, hypotheses are rejected. This is the only approach serious enough to do justice to the matter of how one should live. Responsible exhortation must, for Socrates, be embedded in reasoned argument. A bare summary of his provisional conclusions, such as I have given here, cannot convey the strength of this marriage of idealism and down-to-earth logic. Such a summary inevitably reduces his thoughts to a shoal of beached propositions gasping out of their element. His thoughts flourished in the swim of discussion, and can be seen alive nowadays only in the setting of Plato's early dialogues.

Socrates was not an easy guru to follow, not least because a guru was one thing that he resolutely refused to be. Still, it is hardly surprising that after his death several of his friends wanted to carry on the good work somehow. Since it was, and is, no simple matter to say exactly what the good work amounted to, it should be equally unsurprising that these would-be successors of Socrates ended up championing very different causes. The greatest of his heirs was Plato. The rest were a mixed bunch. But three of them seem to have had a significant influence in one way or another.

Two of the men who were with Socrates when he died – Antisthenes of Athens, and Euclides of nearby Megara – went on to become founders or father-figures of schools of thought whose traces could still be seen hundreds of years later. The school founded by a third

ARISTIPPVS.

companion of Socrates, Aristippus of Cyrene in Libya (*c.*435–*c.*355 BC), has not lived on in the same way, which is no great loss. What Aristippus and his followers made of the teachings of Socrates is of interest mainly as an instance of how easily Socrates' followers could exaggerate and twist what they had learned.

The Cyrenaics who followed Aristippus were devoted to pleasure, but in a curiously philosophical way. Impressed by the rational self-control of Socrates, Aristippus turned his own self-discipline to the single-minded pursuit of gratification. While Socrates saw no reason not to enjoy the good things in life – provided, of course, that this did not interfere with his search for virtue – Aristippus saw little reason to do anything else.

After Socrates died, Aristippus became a sort of licensed court-jester to Dionysius I, the tyrannical ruler of Syracuse in Sicily, who is reputed to have died in a drinking-bout to celebrate winning the prize in a drama contest.

The basis of Aristippus' pursuit of enjoyment, riotous or otherwise, was apparently sincere and partly Socratic. Like most moralists, Socrates held that one must beware of becoming a slave to one's desires. Aristippus agreed. But his rather novel interpretation of this was to exert authority over his desires by getting them to work overtime for him. This made him happy; and what, after all, could be wrong with happiness? Had not Socrates dangled the promise of happiness as an incentive to virtue? There could not be much wrong with it, then.

Socrates had a somewhat high-faluting conception of happiness as a state of spiritual satisfaction obtained by noble living. Here Aristippus begged to differ. According to him, the form of happiness one should aim for was one's own physical pleasure. He regarded such pleasure as the only workable criterion of what is good and bad generally. He apparently held that it is impossible to have certain knowledge of anything but one's own sensations, a philosophical idea that had several defenders at the time. So pleasurable sensations, which were undoubtedly a good thing in some sense, even if nothing else was, may have seemed the logical thing for a philosopher to concentrate on in an uncertain world.

The pursuit of pleasure was thus a serious business. The philosopher's job was to engineer his desires and his circumstances in such a way as to maximize his pleasurable sensations, and to preach the wisdom of this way of life to others (who naturally ought to pay for such valuable advice). It took the self-discipline of a Socrates to do this difficult job properly, or so Aristippus seems to have thought, and it was important not to be distracted by other pursuits that might divert one from the only practical and intelligible quest in life, namely pleasure. Mathematics and science, for example, were no help and so should be ignored. Here once more the example of Socrates could be invoked, after a fashion, for did he not relentlessly pursue the matter of how to live, at the expense of all other questions?

Socrates would have enjoyed showing Aristippus and the other Cyrenaics where they had gone wrong. He would have wanted to know, for instance, what had happened to justice and the other virtues he had championed. He would also have rejected the ideas of the

ANTISTHENES

Cynics, though they were much more interesting. Like the Cyrenaics, Antisthenes (*c.*445–*c.*360 BC) and the later Cynics hijacked some of what they had got from Socrates and blew it out of proportion. 'A Socrates gone mad' is how Plato is supposed to have described the Cynic Diogenes, a follower of Antisthenes. But the Cynics still managed to keep more of their Socratic inheritance than did Aristippus, and indeed their main doctrine was the exact opposite of Cyrenaic indulgence.

Like Aristippus, Antisthenes thought that a Socratic strength of mind was needed for the pursuit of happiness. There the similarity with Aristippus ended. Antisthenes held that happiness was to be found not in satisfying desires, as the Cyrenaics maintained, but in losing them. He was impressed by Socrates' indifference to wealth and comfort, and turned this into an ascetic philosophy that positively embraced poverty. Socrates, after all, had said that nothing could harm a good man. Antisthenes drew the conclusion that so long as one was good, nothing else in life mattered at all. This certainly goes beyond Socrates, who never denied that wealth or possessions were, in their proper place, a better thing to have than to lack. His apparent indifference to them was largely a by-product of the demanding search for virtue and a healthy soul, not to mention mere absent-mindedness.

While Socrates was quite prepared to ignore ordinary ways and values when his principles demanded it, Antisthenes appeared to pursue unconventionality for its own sake. If something was neither virtuous nor wicked, then it did not make the slightest difference whether one did it or not. As can be imagined, this was a powerful recipe for eccentricity. Freed of the desire for possessions, and liberated from conventional behaviour, the wise man could wander around declaiming against society's foolish ways and generally making a spectacle of himself. He would console himself with the knowledge that conventional values are worthless and quite different from the natural values of the genuinely good life. Unfortunately, it was never made clear what natural values and true virtue actually involved. Antisthenes was much better at loudly saying what they were not.

Diogenes of Sinope, on the Black Sea (*c.*400–*c.*325 BC), came to Athens and was taken by the ideas of Antisthenes. But he thought that Antisthenes had failed to live up to his own teachings, which would not have been surprising. Diogenes made up for this magnificently, especially in eccentricity and unconventional living. One of the best-known tales about early philosophers says that Diogenes lived in an earthenware tub; another says that he set a fashion among the Cynics for public masturbation. True or not, the scores of stories about his wacky words and deeds show what a disconcerting impression he made. He revelled in the nickname of 'the dog' (*kyon*), which is how the Cynics, or 'dog-men', got their name. It was given to him because he sought the uncomplicated, instinctive and shameless life of an animal – animals being the true exponents of 'natural' values. He had a sharp tongue and was quick to savage those he disagreed with, which may also have contributed to his nickname. He was particularly hostile to Plato and liked to play practical jokes on him. He apparently turned up at one of Plato's lectures brandishing a plucked chicken in order to heckle him contemptuously on a point of definition – a low-life echo of Socrates' 'wisdom full of pranks'.

Diogenes' disturbing renunciation of conventional life evidently did not go so far as to make a hermit of this 'Socrates gone mad'. Life was too busy for that. There were people to be persuaded, examples to be set, there was preaching to be done and practical advice to be given. His activities seem to have made him quite popular. When his tub was destroyed, the citizens of Athens are said to have clubbed together and bought him a new one. His sincerity and the simplicity of his life seem to have been respectfully admired from a safe distance, although his teachings were far too radical to attract more than a small number of committed followers or to have any direct political effect. He taught that happiness consisted in satisfying only the most basic needs and in disciplining oneself not to want any more. Everything else was to be renounced – riches, comfort, ordinary family life – because none of it made one a morally better person. All the restrictive trappings of civilization in the city-state, from taboos against incest or eating human flesh to the institution of marriage, social-class barriers and traditional religion, were to be overcome for the same reason. The ideal society would be a loose community of spartan, self-sufficient, rational beings who indulged in any and every form of relationship to which all parties consented, unbound by conventional prohibitions.

Much of what Diogenes said was meant to shock; he probably did not make a regular habit of breaking all the taboos he condemned. But he did want to jolt people into examining their lives. Over the years, and especially in the first two centuries of the Christian era, Cynicism attracted all sorts of wandering hippies and free-loving, back-packing beggars, who were keener on general denunciation and on ridiculing society than on philosophy or doing good. Such people, and the satirical and sarcastic literature that was influenced by the movement, gave rise to the modern meaning of 'cynical'. But the earliest Cynics, Bohemian though they were, earnestly saw themselves as moral teachers and seem to have performed a useful service. Crates of Thebes (*c*.365–*c*.285 BC), for example, gave away his sizeable fortune to become a pupil of Diogenes. He apparently made house-calls as a sort of therapist or pastor, offering a service of moral guidance that was not available to ordinary people from any other source – certainly not from the formal schools of philosophical research set up by Plato and Aristotle. Hipparchia, the sister of a pupil of Crates, was desperate to join Crates in his unconventional life, but had to threaten her well-off parents with suicide before they would let her go. They eventually consented, and she 'travelled around with her husband and had intercourse publicly and went out to dinners'.

Euclides, the last of the followers of Socrates to be considered here, was so devoted to the master that when Athens banned the citizens of Megara from entering the city, he is said to have dressed up in women's clothes and slunk in under cover of darkness to be with him. Euclides shared not only Socrates' interest in the nature of moral goodness but also his passion for argument. While Socrates often seemed prepared to follow a promising line of reasoning wherever it led to, Euclides was interested in logical arguments for their own sake, especially paradoxical ones. One opponent spoke of 'wrangling Euclides, who inspired the Megarians with a frenzied love of controversy'.

Frenzied or not, the intellectual curiosity of the Megarians led them to come up with some of the most enduring riddles about logic and language. Eubulides, a pupil of Euclides, is credited with several, including the most famous one, commonly known as the Liar. This is the paradox presented by someone who says 'This statement is false'. The problem is what to say about such a statement; arguments about its truth tend to go round in a dizzying circle. For example, if it is false, then the speaker spoke truly because that is what he said it was. On the other hand, if he spoke truly, then it must be false because what he said is that it was false. Thus if it is false, it follows that it is true; and if it is true, it follows that it is false. This riddle is easier to make fun of than it is to solve. It has a remarkable ability to bounce back in the face of any proposed solution. One can sympathize with the poet Philetas of Cos, who is said to have worried about it so much that he wasted away, becoming so thin that he had to put lead weights in his shoes to stop himself blowing over. The epitaph on his gravestone read:

> O Stranger: Philetas of Cos am I,
> 'Twas the Liar who made me die,
> And the bad nights caused thereby.

It may be hard to see the puzzle itself as profound, but attempts to get to the bottom of it certainly have been. The Liar has stimulated a great deal of work on the nature of truth and linguistic meaning, by mathematical logicians and by linguists who look at the formal structure of languages. It seems, however, to have caused no further casualties. One eventual by-product of an interest in the sort of 'self-reference' involved in the paradox – the paradoxical statement is curiously about itself – was Gödel's Theorem, one of the most significant results of modern mathematics, which shows that there are certain limits to mathematical proof.

The pupils and successors of Euclides turned Megara into a real-life version of the farcically exaggerated 'logic factory' portrayed in

Aristophanes' play about Socrates. The fact that to some sceptics their work seemed like mere 'wrangling' and controversy for its own sake, which no doubt some of it was, recalls the reception that Socrates' incessant arguments about virtue got from some of the less intellectual citizens of Athens. One reason why Euclides would have felt it was his task as a philosopher both to hold forth about moral goodness and to get involved in abstruse logical questions was his admiration for Socrates' view that knowledge is the path to virtue. Socrates may not himself have discussed logic, but Euclides probably felt that doing so was one way to continue the search for wisdom. In particular, if one understood the process of argument, then this would presumably help one to carry on the good work of Socratic examination.

All these schools of philosophy that flowed from Socrates shared his idea that wisdom brings virtue and virtue brings happiness. They evidently differed over what they took happiness to involve – indulgent pleasure in the case of the Cyrenaics, ascetic discipline in the case of the Cynics. But they agreed that philosophical reflection of some sort was the way to find it, and that such an occupation amounted to the good life. The ethical views of these philosophers were all rather individualistic (to an extreme, in the case of Diogenes) and one can see how the unusual example of Socrates' life could have led to this. But in the case of the Cynics, at least, there was a clear break with Socrates over the ties of social obligation and about loyalty to the values of the city-state. The Cynics stressed a contrast between the life of virtue and the life enjoined by the city in which one happens to be born or live. In one sense Socrates did this too, but in another sense he did not. He certainly would have accepted that the individual must follow his own conscience, not the city's dictates, when those dictates are unjust. But he sought to better the life of the city, not to relinquish it altogether. He urged the Athenians to live justly together and to improve their laws and behaviour where necessary, not to abandon the whole enterprise of civilization and lose respect for the law.

Socrates made it clear that, although you must disobey the laws if they are unjust, you must nevertheless submit to punishment if caught, which is exactly what he himself did when he was condemned. Some friends gave him the chance to escape prison and flee Athens before execution; one of Plato's early dialogues, the *Crito*, deals with this episode and gives Socrates' reasons for rejecting the offer. As well as feeling a moral obligation to the legitimate authority of the city and the due process of law, Socrates loved Athens and did not relish life anywhere else. Some of the things he is made to say in Plato's dialogues suggest that he had misgivings about democracy as a form of government; this has led to him being sometimes described as anti-democratic. But it was really Plato who had those misgivings, as he did eventually about all the forms of government he came across. Socrates himself showed every sign of deep loyalty to the constitution of Athens. He often praised the city and its institutions, and seems never to have left it except on its military service. On the question of whether he approved its type of democracy, Socrates voted with his feet – or rather, showed his preference by failing to do so. There were many other states with non-democratic governments to which he could have emigrated. Perhaps most embarrassingly for those of his opponents in his own time who would have liked to cast him as an enemy of democracy, it was well known that he had risked death under the anti-democratic Tyrants by refusing to take part in the arrest of an innocent man.

Socrates was, if anything, too democratic for the Athenians. It was this aspect of his character and teaching which led to the exaggerated individualism of some of his imitators. His attitude to religion and morality can be seen as ultra-democratic. Nothing is to be taken for granted, especially not if it is handed down by an authority which puts itself above the moral reasoning of the people, be that putative authority in the form of Zeus or of a human tyrant. Every man must work out for himself what is good and right, and nobody can escape the obligation of examining himself and his life. The result of such discussions between citizens should ideally be a just society with just laws, arrived at through such collective self-examination. In the Socratic dream of democracy, individual conviction would lead to collective agreement – not about everything, presumably, but at least about the outlines of how to live.

Socrates was no politician. He felt he could play his part only by debating with individuals, one by one or in small groups: 'I know how to produce one witness to the truth of what I say, the man with whom

I am debating, but the others I ignore. I know how to secure one man's vote, but with the many I will not even enter into discussion.' Over the years, the votes for Socrates have steadily accumulated as Plato's dialogues have carried his debating, or a semblance of it, far beyond fifth-century Athens and its dinner-parties. There are now at any rate few who would disagree with one thing that Socrates told his judges: 'If you put me to death, you will not easily find anyone to take my place.'

# II

# The Republic of Reason:
## *Plato*

In the middle of his masterpiece, the *Republic*, Plato tries to define philosophy by elaborating on the etymological meaning of *philosophia*, which is 'love of wisdom'. This alone is too vague, so his first suggested improvement is to say that a philosopher is one who loves all wisdom and not just some of it: he must be 'one who feels no distaste in sampling every study, who attacks his task of learning gladly, and cannot get enough of it'. Yet this is still not precise enough, for it would include all those undiscriminating people who merely 'always want to hear some new thing'. It would include, for example, those who 'run about to all the Dionysiac festivals, never missing one, either in the towns or in the country villages'. 'Are we to designate all these, then, and similar folk and all the practitioners of the minor arts as philosophers?' No, says the character of Socrates, who acts as the voice of Plato in this dialogue. Although indiscriminate lovers of sights and sounds do bear a certain likeness to philosophers, genuine philosophers are those 'for whom the truth is the spectacle of which they are enamoured'. This means that they are interested not just in true or beautiful things but in Truth and Beauty themselves. To explain this idea, Plato invokes his theory of Forms, which takes us to the heart of Platonism.

Lovers of sights and sounds 'delight in beautiful tones and colours and shapes and in everything that art fashions out of these, but their thought is incapable of . . . taking delight in the nature of the beautiful in itself'. Such a person – like, indeed, most people – 'believes in beautiful things, but neither believes in beauty itself nor is able to follow when someone tries to guide him to the knowledge of it'. According to Plato, unphilosophical people live in a dream-like state, because they confuse fleeting phantoms (namely beautiful objects) with the reality (which is Beauty itself). The true philosophers are those who have woken up out of this particular dream. They realize that there exists, separately from the physical world and independently of our subjective opinions, an ideal realm of Forms, of which the things we see are imperfect copies or approximations. The job of the true philosopher is to use rational inquiry to grasp these transcendent realities and focus on the particularly interesting ones.

Whenever one comes across the term 'Platonism', it is always something like this picture of a transcendent reality that is being alluded to. For example, when today's mathematicians try to describe the nature of mathematical objects (such as numbers) or of mathematical truth, they often fall back on the ideas and the name of Plato. Thus Roger Penrose writes:

I imagine that whenever the mind perceives a mathematical idea, it makes contact with Plato's world of mathematical concepts. (Recall that according to the Platonic viewpoint, mathematical ideas have an existence of their own, and inhabit an ideal Platonic world, which is accessible via the intellect only . . .) When one 'sees' a mathematical truth, one's consciousness breaks through into this world of ideas, and makes direct contact with it.

Since he holds that the truths of mathematics are thus to be found in a Platonic realm, and that mathematics is the basis of all scientific knowledge, it follows for Penrose that 'the workings of the actual external world can ultimately be understood only in terms of . . . Plato's ideal world "accessible via the intellect".'

This goes too far for most contemporary mathematicians. But many of them recognize that some form of Platonism is at least tempting when it comes to explaining our knowledge of mathematics. To modern minds, Platonism is certainly far more attractive when applied to mathematics than when applied to most other things. It is one thing to believe in the objective existence of the number six in 'an ideal Platonic world, which is accessible via the intellect', but quite another to believe in the objective existence of an ethereal Beauty. It seems very strange to hold, as Plato did, that there exists not only a Form of Six and a Form of Equilateral Triangles, but also a Form of Beauty, a Form of Justice, a Form of Tables, a Form of Chairs and presumably a Form of Guinea-Pigs. If this bizarre theory of Forms is the answer, what can the question have been?

The theory developed to satisfy several needs: there is no one question that it was designed to answer. It seems to have undergone various changes in the course of Plato's intellectual career and indeed some people think he abandoned it towards the end. His later works discuss sophisticated objections to the theory, though it is unclear whether or not Plato believed he could answer them. The main idea, however, is fairly constant. We have already seen some of what led him to it in our discussions of earlier thinkers and of Plato's interest in mathematics. Plato's desire to find an underlying level of reality that is unchanging and that can be grasped by rational thought reflects his attraction to the ideas of Parmenides. These ideas provided him with, among other things, a welcoming intellectual framework for his Orphic and Pythagorean beliefs about the purification of the soul, which was to be achieved via the rational contemplation of a reality beyond the inferior physical world. From Heraclitus – or rather from what Plato's friend Cratylus said about Heraclitus – came the stimulus for Plato's idea that the incessant changes of the physical world pose a problem about knowledge that can be solved only by invoking something fixed like the Forms. Without the Forms, thought Plato, the world would be too messy to make sense of. And from Socrates and his search for definitions of ethical concepts came some support for the idea that there are objective truths about morality, which philosophers should strive to discover. Plato has Socrates express the belief that 'things are not relative to individuals', but must instead have 'their own proper and permanent essence; they are not in relation to us, or influenced by us, fluctuating according to our fancy, but they are independent'. In other words, the Forms set absolute standards and show that the 'relativism' of the Sophists is mistaken.

Plato uses language that is reminiscent of Parmenides in a passage in his *Symposium*, which is probably the earliest of his dialogues to appeal to the Forms. This dialogue is set up as an after-dinner discussion in which several friends, including Socrates, take turns to deliver speeches on the nature of love. The centrepiece is the speech made by Socrates and the account that he says he heard from a priestess named Diotima – who, he says, taught him everything he knows about love. Diotima tried to explain that the pursuit of love ought to consist of several stages, each of which can be seen as leading to the next in an ascent to the appreciation of Beauty itself.

It all starts (so Socrates reports her as saying) with the love of a particular person's body. By considering the similarity of this body to those of other beautiful people, the lover 'must set himself to be the lover of every lovely body, and bring his passion for the one into due proportion by deeming it of little or of no importance'. The next stage is to realize that 'the beauties of the body are as nothing to the beauties of the soul', so that the lover will come to love beautiful souls or characters even if they are housed in ugly bodies. This chaste sort of love – 'Platonic love', as it is sometimes now called – 'will quicken in his heart a longing for such discourse as tends toward the building of a noble nature. And from this he will be led to contemplate the beauty of laws and institutions.' Next the lover must focus on the sciences in order to come to know the 'beauty of every kind of knowledge'. Soon he will begin to make out the thoroughly Parmenidean Form of Beauty itself:

And now, Socrates, there bursts upon him that wondrous vision which is the very soul of the beauty he has toiled so long for. It is an everlasting loveliness which neither comes nor goes, which neither flowers nor fades, for such beauty is the same on every hand, the same then as now, here as there, this way as that way, the same to every worshipper as it is to every other.

Nor will his vision of the beautiful take the form of a face, or of hands, of anything that is of the flesh. It will be neither words, nor knowledge, nor a something that exists in something else, such as a living creature, or the earth, or the heavens, or anything that is – but subsisting of itself and by itself in an eternal oneness, while every lovely thing partakes of it in such sort that, however much the parts may wax and wane, it will be neither more nor less, but still the same inviolable whole.

Diotima's image of the lover's ascent to the Beautiful has often been echoed in Western literature: it has been borrowed by mystical philosophers, by early Christian writers such as Origen and St Augustine, and by countless love-poets. This description of the Form of Beauty as an unchanging, immortal whole that is always and everywhere the same shows the Platonic Forms to be very similar to Parmenides' One, but reborn, multiplied and brought into relation with the physical world. While there was, of course, only one One for Parmenides, for Plato there was a different Form corresponding to each general term or concept, not just to 'beauty'. And while the physical world of changing things was simply an illusion as far as Parmenides was concerned, for Plato it was real enough, albeit inferior in various ways.

The physical world bears the marks of the superior Forms, each thing 'partaking' in the Forms it exemplifies. A good man, for example, would 'partake' in the Forms of Good and of Man. It is this relationship between physical objects and Forms which, according to Plato, prevents the physical world from being a chaotic jumble and renders it comprehensible. Remember the river in Heraclitus' famous saying: if it is always changing, how can we speak of one river, or manage to find out anything about it? If everything in the physical world is in a state of flux – as Plato argued that it was – how can we know what anything is? Plato got such a nasty shock from the cold and turbulent waters of Heraclitus that he leapt straight up to his safe, dry land of Forms. Genuine knowledge, he held, can be obtained only of what is unchanging and is stable enough to be pinned down. And only something like a Form could be constant enough for that.

Perception and common sense on their own give people mere fallible 'opinion'; for genuine, certain knowledge one must look to the Forms as well. How does one do that? By using the faculty of reason to supplement what the senses tell us. In practice, this is not as obscure a business as the mystical imagery of Diotima might suggest. Everybody can do it to some extent, at least for some of the Forms. Even the ordinary man in the street, or on the riverbank, may have a pretty good knowledge of rivers. And insofar as he can say clearly and truly what a river is, i.e., give a general account of what all rivers essentially have in common, he thereby has some apprehension of the Form of River. Plenty of other Forms, though, are more interesting and more difficult: the Forms of Justice, Goodness and Beauty, for example. Working out a true account of these will require the faculty of reason to work overtime. A sound knowledge of these Forms can be sought only by dialectic – that is, the use of co-operative, logical argument to test ideas and what one has learned through observation. Plato once described the process of dialectic thus: 'when names, definitions, sights and other sense-impressions are rubbed together and tested amicably by men employing question and answer with no malicious rivalry, suddenly there shines forth understanding'. When Socrates tussled over definitions, he was, according to Plato, in effect looking for the Form of what he was trying to define. (As we have seen in the previous chapter, Plato seems to have held that people know the Forms before they are born. But since they forget everything when they are born, their knowledge has to be dug up all over again using the dialectical methods of Socrates.)

To see how dialectic uncovers the Forms, consider a piece of typically Socratic examination, concerning justice – which, in Plato's language, is broader than modern legalistic notions and means 'doing the right thing'. Socrates is examining the idea that to give someone back what you owe him is the paradigm of justice. This seems straightforward enough. But, says Socrates, what if someone lends you a weapon and then goes raving mad? Should you still give it back to him? No, because he is likely to go off and do harm with it. So sometimes it is right to give back what you owe and sometimes it is not. This variability is an example of the sort of Heraclitean 'flux' that makes reference to stable Forms so necessary for Plato. According to him, the nature of justice cannot change from one moment to the next in this way; so 'giving back what you owe' cannot be what justice is. Socrates must keep on looking until he comes up with something that is correct not only sometimes but always. When he finds such a thing, that will be the stable Form of Justice.

This snatch of dialectic is from the *Republic*, which can be seen as one long discussion about justice. When we see the theory of Forms put to work in this way, the theory loses many of its mystical overtones. Finding a Form sounds no more baffling an enterprise than investigating a concept. Indeed, that is all it is when Plato gets down to doing it rather than talking about what it is.

I shall shortly sketch the main arguments and findings of the *Republic*. Plato uses this dialogue to enlarge on Socrates' idea that the just man is happy and the unjust man wretched. It aims to fill in some of the gaps in the arguments which the real Socrates offered, and to paint a picture of human psychology and of a utopia that is his best-known creation (though no modern person would want to live in it). After that I shall discuss Plato's *Timaeus*, which contains his account of cosmology. This was for many centuries virtually the bible of natural science. Together, the *Republic* and the *Timaeus* give Plato's answer to the problem posed by the Sophists about the relationship between man, with his apparently arbitrary laws and conventions, and the world of fixed, impersonal nature. But first it is worth looking briefly at Plato's life to piece together something of his own nature.

Plato came from a rich and well-connected family. His father traced his descent from the last king of Athens, which is about as noble as you could get (except that this particular king may well never have existed). As a brilliant student from such a background, it was only natural that Plato should cherish hopes of a political career. He was soon disappointed, not because he failed to come up to expectations but because politics itself did. Writing about it later, long after he had first been swayed by the high ideals of Socrates, Plato says he 'withdrew in disgust from the abuses of those days'. Some years after this early disenchantment, an ill-fated opportunity arose to try to put his political ideals into practice in the Syracusan empire. Plato later counted himself lucky to have escaped this tragicomic episode with his life. It might have consoled him to know that the Academy he had

PLATO.

founded in Athens some years before, and to which he then devoted himself instead, turned out to last for about 900 years in one form or another.

Plato's first chance to enter politics had been in the time of the Thirty Tyrants who briefly came to power after Athens was defeated in the Peloponnesian war. Two of his relations were in this unpleasant government and they invited him to join them. Plato was ambitious, and only in his twenties, but he clearly saw the Tyrants for what they were and turned them down. One particular sin that he held against them was that they tried to involve Socrates – 'the justest man of his time' – in their doings. Things seemed to get better for a while in Athens when the democracy was reinstated. At first, Plato thought that his moment had come. But he was horrified when 'some of those in control' then brought about the trial and death of Socrates. This was a nasty lesson in what could happen under a democracy, from which Plato's political opinions never recovered.

His ambitions of public life in Athens were crushed. He had had enough of waiting for the right moment and for a better government. He says that he

finally saw clearly in regard to all states now existing that without exception their system of government is bad . . . Hence I was forced to say . . . that . . . the human race will not see better days until either the stock of those who rightly and genuinely follow philosophy acquire political authority or else the class who have political control be led by some dispensation of providence to become real philosophers.

Plato was twenty-eight when Socrates, the 'real philosopher' *par excellence*, died in 399 BC. He did a great deal of travelling in the next few years, much of it to visit other philosophers and mathematicians. First he went to Megara to stay with Euclides, the follower of Socrates who shared (or perhaps stimulated) Plato's interest in Parmenides. The Megarian philosophers, as we have briefly seen in the previous chapter, were very interested in goodness and what exactly it was. By contrast, too many of the other people Plato saw on his subsequent travels in Italy and Sicily were mainly interested in having a good time:

I found myself utterly at odds with the sort of life that is there termed a happy one, a life taken up with Italian and Syracusan banquets, an existence that consists in filling oneself up twice a day, never sleeping alone at night, and indulging in all the practices attendant on that way of living. In such an environment no man under heaven, brought up in self-indulgence, could ever grow up to be wise.

It was no accident, thought Plato, that states ruled by such people tended to be unproductive, badly governed and violently unstable: 'It is inevitable that in such cities there should be an unending succession of governments – tyranny, oligarchy, democracy – one after another.' What he found more congenial in Italy were the Pythagorean communities of wise men and mathematicians, from whom he drew lasting friendships and philosophical inspiration; Archytas of Tarentum, a mathematician-philosopher-statesman, was a notable provider of both. It was probably in order to make contact with such men that Plato had made his Italian trip.

Another valuable friendship was made in Syracuse in the course of this first round of travels, though it ultimately proved to be a mixed blessing. Dion, a relative of the tyrannical ruler Dionysius I, nobly believed in 'liberty for the Syracusans under the guidance of the best system of laws'. Plato accordingly 'set before him in theory my ideals for mankind' and found Dion to be an eager recipient of his ideas. Once Plato had opened his eyes, Dion 'resolved to live for the remainder of his life differently from most of the Greeks in Italy and Sicily, holding virtue dearer than pleasure or luxury'. This enthusiastic reception helps to explain why many years later Plato returned to Syracuse during the reign of Dionysius II, with sorry results.

Dion was a fish out of water in the quarrelsome and corrupt court of Dionysius I, who was a patron of the pleasure-loving philosopher Aristippus – Socrates' most unlikely disciple. Plutarch described the atmosphere there as 'a regimen that counts pleasures and excesses as the highest good': just the sort of thing, in other words, that Plato could not stand. This first visit of Plato to Syracuse ended badly in some way. One account says that Dionysius I had him sold into slavery, from which he was rescued by friends.

When this phase of Plato's travels came to an end, he went back to Athens and founded what became known as the Academy. This would have been in about 387 BC, when he was forty. He bought some property about a mile outside the city walls, in and around a grove sacred to a hero, Academus, and there set up a collegiate institution of self-supporting intellectuals. It is hard to get a picture of daily life in Plato's Academy. By law it had to be registered as a religious fellowship dedicated to some deity: Plato chose the Muses, who in those days were responsible for all intellectual activities, not only the arts. Some of the Academy's more convivial activities would have mimicked the Pythagorean brotherhoods Plato saw in Italy. There were organized monthly dinners, perhaps like the occasional feasts at today's older universities. There may also have been a few educational courses open to the general public. Aristotle and others mentioned a lecture by Plato, possibly given at the Academy, on 'the good'. It was not a success. Whatever exactly they had been expecting, those in the audience were puzzled and cross at having to listen to a great deal of abstruse mathematics instead.

Most of the Academy's teaching, however, would have been intended for a well-off elite who were hungry for higher education. The range of subjects taught and discussed was immense – much wider, at any rate, than would nowadays be regarded as necessary to serve one of the Academy's main aims, which was to produce wise statesmen. In Plato's time, experts from the Academy were called on by at least four cities to write new laws and constitutions for them. It was one of his deepest convictions that such a job could be done best by those with a broad training. The Academy accordingly offered instruction in all areas of learning, from geography, botanical classification and political history to the most abstract philosophical doctrines about the Forms, much of the latter no doubt given by Plato himself. It became a renowned centre of research in mathematics and astronomy in particular. Two of the most important mathematicians before Euclid, namely Heraclides Pontius and Eudoxus of Cnidus, were associated with the Academy. And it was there that Aristotle, who started attending at the age of about seventeen, developed his very productive interest in biology.

Plato thought that certain natural gifts were required for the pursuit of learning. He stressed that anyone seeking wisdom in his way should be aware 'how many subjects there are to study, how much hard work they involve, and how indispensable it is for the project to adopt a well-ordered scheme of living'. Some of the Academy's students may well have subjected themselves to such discipline solely because they were itching to run a city and wanted to go about it in the right way; but surely not all that many. The various scholars who passed through the Academy cannot all have been aspiring or frustrated politicians.

Plato's conception of philosophy as the love of knowledge in its purest form must have appealed to some people in its own right. Plato himself felt the attractions of intellectual life for its own sake and not just as a preparation for politics. Nevertheless, he was nagged by a doubt about the Academic way of life: 'I feared to see myself at last altogether nothing but words, so to speak – a man who would never willingly lay hand to any concrete task.'

In 367 BC, when Dionysius II succeeded his late father in Syracuse, such a task presented itself. Dion persuaded the new king, who was about thirty years old, to send for Plato to advise and educate him. The old Dionysius had kept his son isolated and unschooled because he was fearful of plots to usurp him, and saw his own heir as a potential threat. Now the young Dionysius seemed eager to make his mark and earn some respect. Dion read this as an opportunity to make something worthwhile out of the Syracusan tyranny. Tempted by this prospect, and out of friendship for Dion, Plato therefore 'forsook my own pursuits, and they were not undistinguished, to come under a tyranny, a form of government seemingly inconsistent with my doctrines and my character'.

Reforming the Dionysian dynasty was bound to be a struggle and Plato never managed it. Dionysius II may not have been as vicious as his father, but he was no model student either. According to one account, 'The young king once kept up a drinking bout for ninety consecutive days . . . and . . . during this time his court gave no access or admission to men or matters of consequence, but drunkenness and raillery and music and dancing and buffoonery held full sway.' Plato and Dion tried gently to point him in the right direction, but their influence only made matters worse, because it fuelled jealousy and suspicion among those of Dion's political enemies who preferred the bad old days. Just four months after Plato's arrival, Dion was banished because the old guard convinced the king that Dion had been plotting against him. Plato stuck it out for another eighteen months or so and slunk back to Athens.

It is surprising, and perhaps a testament to his optimism, that Plato yet again returned to Syracuse some four years later. This time it was going to be different, or so he had been persuaded. This time Dionysius was mature enough to follow through his earnest desire to improve himself and his empire by the study of philosophy. He somehow convinced Archytas of Tarentum, and some other intellectuals whom he knew that Plato respected, to attest to his good intentions. Perhaps they believed his story; perhaps Dionysius himself believed it. But with hindsight it seems that he just wanted a few famous sophisticates to adorn his court.

In his pleas to Plato, Dionysius promised to allow Dion back and to treat him well. Plato was worried that more harm might come to Dion and his other friends if he ignored the summons, so he went. But in fact everything was even worse this time. He found Dionysius once more a bad student: stupid or lazy or both. Dionysius thought he knew it all already from his third-rate court-philosophers, which particularly annoyed Plato. The tyrant naturally broke all his promises about Dion – and even stole all his property – and Plato found himself virtually a prisoner. Somehow he escaped back to Athens and the Academy and did not make the same mistake again.

It is easy to suppose that the utopian state which Plato described in the *Republic* must have been the blueprint for what he had been trying to achieve in Syracuse. In fact the connections between the *Republic* and Plato's practical projects cannot be so neatly tied up. True, the *Republic*'s model city is said to be ruled by 'philosopher-kings', and Dionysius was supposed to become a better ruler by learning some philosophy. The *Republic* was indeed written before Plato's attempt to reform Dionysius. But it is no blueprint for any real city. For one thing, the term 'philosopher-king' in the *Republic* does not, as is sometimes supposed, denote merely a king who knows some philosophy, or a professional philosopher who somehow finds himself on the throne. A more accurate description of what Plato intended by that term would be: a particularly wise, able, balanced and virtuous military man who has been trained in science for a very long time and has a great deal of practical experience in politics and administration. Over-optimistic though he sometimes was, Plato was not so foolish as to suppose that any actual king could ever fit this bill, and certainly not a worm like Dionysius II.

The real point of Plato's utopia is stated in the *Republic* itself by the character of Socrates. 'It makes no difference', he says, 'whether it exists now or will ever come into being.' The ideal city is intended as a subject for reflection and argument. By considering the *Republic*'s discussion of it, a man can learn the truth about justice and about how to live; in particular, he will learn the truth of what the real Socrates was always claiming, namely that it is in one's own interest to be just. He will thereby come to live in this city of the mind: 'perhaps there is a pattern of it laid up in heaven for him who wishes to contemplate it and so beholding to constitute himself its citizen.'

The main argument of the dialogue starts with an encounter with an obstreperous and amoral character called Thrasymachus. Thrasymachus forcefully puts the case for naked self-interest, echoing some of the cynical ideas discussed by Sophists such as Antiphon. Morality is, he argues, just a set of rules imposed by the strong on the weak. If you can get away with breaking the law, then you should do so. Best of all, you should write the rules yourself and compel others to obey them. Call this 'unjust' if you like, but 'you must look at the matter, my simple-minded Socrates, in this way, that the just man always comes out at a disadvantage in his relation with the unjust'. In other words, justice or morality does not pay and Socrates is a poor fool to suppose that it does.

Socrates prods and pokes Thrasymachus' account of morality, but does not succeed in disposing of it. Thrasymachus goes off to be amoral and unpleasant somewhere else. For the sake of a good debate, Glaucon and Adimantus – two friends of Socrates – then powerfully restate the case for amorality. They want to see if Socrates can make a fuller reply and thus resolve the matter. In the course of playing devil's advocate, Glaucon considers a mythical shepherd, Gyges, who finds a ring that gives him the power to make himself invisible. With such a ring, says Glaucon,

no one could be found, it would seem, of such adamantine temper as to persevere in justice and endure to refrain his hands from the possessions of others and not touch them, though he might with impunity take what he wished even from the market place, and enter into houses and lie with whom he pleased, and slay and loose from bonds whomsoever he would, and in all other things conduct himself among mankind as the equal of a god . . . And . . . this is a great proof, one might argue, that no one is just of his own will but only from constraint . . . For if anyone who had got such a licence within his grasp should refuse to do any wrong . . . he would be regarded as most pitiable and a great fool.

Adimantus adds that, in replying to such ideas, Socrates should not try to defend justice merely by showing that it brings honour and respect from other people. That would prove only that it was in one's interests to have a reputation for justice, not that it was in one's interests actually to be just. If it were merely having a reputation for justice that was beneficial to the just man, then one might as well be wicked, so long as one managed to keep up appearances by being sneaky with it. Therefore Adimantus asks Socrates to demonstrate instead 'what it is that . . . [*justice and injustice*] inherently does to its possessor . . . whereby the one is good and the other evil'.

This is a tall order, which Socrates wisely decides to meet in a roundabout way. He does it by shifting his focus away from the just person or the just soul and towards the just city. It will be more fruitful, he thinks, to look first at the city as a whole, because justice will be easier to make out in this larger context. Having determined what a just city is, by trying to arrive at an account of the ideal city, he plans then to look into the question of individual justice. If the two investigations converge, so that the just man and the just city turn out to be very similar sorts of things, he will rest assured that he has found true justice. And he is confident that, having found it, it will become clear how and why the just man is the happiest sort of man. Thrasymachus and his sort will then have been answered.

So first we have to say what the ideal city would be like. It will need, says Socrates (or we might as well say Plato), a sort of soldier-police of guardians to protect it against civil wars and rampaging invaders. Such security is the first prerequisite for any flourishing state. These guardians will be full-time experts in defence and law and order, for the best sort of city will realize the value of specialization. All citizens will do the sort of work for which they have the highest natural aptitude, regardless of birth, and women may rise to the top just as easily as equally qualified men. This was a revolutionary idea for the time. In Plato's Athens, women were kept as uneducated breeders and housekeepers who were virtually the property of their fathers or husbands. Plato was far from being an enlightened feminist by modern standards: he shared the then-common belief that women were in general worse than men at everything worth doing. But he says in the *Republic* that they should nevertheless be given the same opportunities as men, and that any woman who proved herself able should be allowed to rise through the hierarchy.

The society of the ideal city would divide into three classes: producers (e.g., craftsmen, farmers and traders) at the bottom; then guardians; then rulers, who would be chosen from among the best guardians. If the child of a producer shows the right sort of promise, he or she will join the guardians; any guardian child who falls short will, correspondingly, be relegated to the lower orders. Since the guardians and rulers will have a great deal of power over the majority, it is vital that they should be impeccably unselfish and beneficent. It is, after all, by failing to ensure that its rulers are virtuous that so many other sorts of societies come to an unhappy end. So Socrates takes trouble to specify the education and environment that the guardians must have. They will live communally and have no private property. Even their spouses and children will in effect be shared. They are forbidden to touch silver and gold, let alone possess it. All of this will ensure that they do not use their power to enrich themselves or come to put any private interest above the interests of the community as a whole.

It is important that their characters and physical constitutions should be formed in the right way. Meticulous attention will be paid not only to their diet and exercise but also to what they study and even to what sorts of stories and songs they may hear. The Greeks held that music was a particularly powerful influence on character and thus on society, so it had to be watched with particular care. Socrates warned that 'a change to a new type of music is something to beware of . . . For the modes of music are never disturbed without unsettling of the most fundamental political and social conventions.' (Some morose modern conservatives, such as Allan Bloom in his *The Closing of the American Mind*, seem to have thought that the birth of rock music in the 1950s proved the point only too well.) As for the stories which the young guardian-class will hear, the main thing was that their heroes should set all the right examples. Socrates even goes so far as to specify the most inspiring forms of poetic metre. In general, the curriculum is designed to inculcate balance and virtue by subjecting the little would-be guardians to only the most uplifting materials.

All craftsmen whose products will be seen by these tender youths – from poets to designers of household furnishings – must follow strict rules. They must be forbidden

to represent the evil disposition, the licentious, the illiberal, the graceless, either in the likeness of living creatures or in buildings or in any other product of their art . . . that our guardians may not be bred among symbols of evil, as it were in a pasturage of poisonous herbs, lest grazing freely and cropping from many such . . . they . . . all unawares accumulate . . . a huge mass of evil in their own souls. But we must look for those craftsmen who by the happy gift of nature are capable of following the trail of true beauty and grace, that our young men, dwelling as it were in a salubrious region, may receive benefit from all things about them, whence the influence that emanates from works of beauty may waft itself to eye or ear like a breeze that brings from wholesome places health, and so from earliest childhood insensibly guide them to likeness, to friendship, to harmony with beautiful reason.

This stringent and high-minded attention to the details of upbringing would no doubt be pointless overkill in any real educational system. But it shows that Plato did not make the mistake for which Aristotle and others took the real Socrates to task, namely that of ignoring the role of character in determining moral behaviour. The guardians of the *Republic* would be virtuous, rational and generally benign because everything in their early life was designed to mould their characters to that end.

Imagine, then, a city run by these hot-house saints. Would it be full of the virtues – courage, wisdom, moderation and justice – as the ideal city ought to be? Socrates argues that it would. It would have courage because of the guardian-police, who are picked and trained for military excellence. It would have moderation or self-control because it would be well-regulated; as Socrates puts it, the desires of 'the multitude and the rabble' will be dominated and controlled 'by the desires and the wisdom that dwell in the minority of the better sort'. It would be wise because of its rulers, who are picked from among the best guardians and are highly educated in order to nurture their rational faculties. As for the virtue of justice, at this stage of the argument Socrates seems to hold that the essential thing is that each citizen should devote himself to the sort of life and work that suits him. This will lead to a harmonious, equitable, contented and therefore just society.

So the imagined city of the *Republic*, Socrates suggests, will exemplify all of the virtues. The idea that a just city will have all of its parts working harmoniously together, like a balanced and happy man, suggests to Socrates that the analogy between city and soul is worth taking further, and can be used to add more support to this picture of justice. Just as his city is divided into three strata (producers or artisans, guardians and rulers), may not human psychology be regarded as having three components? The soul, he thinks, has three parts: the appetitive, the spirited and the rational. These correspond to certain types of desires. The appetitive part is the part that is driven by lowly desires for food, sex and money; the spirited part wants honour (such as military honour); the rational part is driven by the desire for knowledge. It is no surprise that these three sorts of desires turn out to correspond precisely to the three classes: the rulers are dominated by reason, the guardian-police by the desire for honour, the rest – poor saps – by their base appetites. Just as a well-balanced man will not let his stomach or sex-organs rule his head, so a healthy state will be guided by those whose own souls are ruled by reason. Then everything will be in its proper place.

After Socrates has drawn these and other parallels between what is good for a city and what is good for a man, the discussion moves on to the question of how a city such as he has described might actually be brought about. (The main argument in defence of justice is resumed later when more has been said about the ideal city and its rulers).

One thing that Glaucon and Adimantus find impractical about Socrates' imaginary city is the equality of education and opportunity between men and women. Socrates manages to convince them that this is perfectly sensible and gets them to agree that, at least on this point, his proposed legislation for the city 'was not impracticable or utopian, since the law we proposed accorded with nature. Rather, the other way of doing things, prevalent today, proves . . . unnatural.' But this discussion of women leads on to another troublesome proposal

18

about the sexes which makes it particularly hard to see how Socrates' city could ever come about. This further proposal would today be condemned at least as vehemently as the equality of men and women would be applauded. It turns out that not only will there be nothing like conventional monogamous marriage or child-rearing among the guardians, but attempts will also be made to control their breeding so that the best will have sex only with the best, and any inferior offspring will be killed. The point of all this is to produce the finest guardians for the future.

To enable such selective breeding to proceed smoothly, the rulers are allowed to hide what is happening from the rest of the guardians in order to keep them sweet. The rulers will concoct ceremonies involving 'certain ingenious lots . . . devised so that the inferior man at each conjugation may blame chance and not the rulers' for the breeding partner whom he or she is allotted. When children are born, 'the offspring of the good' will be taken 'to certain nurses who live apart in a quarter of the city, but the offspring of the inferior, and any of those other sort who are born defective, they will properly dispose of in secret, so that no one will know what has become of them'.

Socrates is unhappy about the need for these lies. He pleads that they should be seen as medicinal: the nasty taste of such deception must be swallowed for the sake of the ultimate good of the people. He admits that he finds the whole thing a 'distasteful topic'. To understand how Plato's Socrates came to entertain this shocking project, two things should be noted. First, the guardians who are to have their love-lives and children hijacked by the state in this way are people who have been given unusual powers and responsibilities. Considering the authority that they would have to wield over the masses – there would, for example, be no independent courts to which the people could take their grievances – it no doubt seemed prudent to take every conceivable step to ensure their suitability for the job. The aim of the breeding project is, after all, only the public-spirited one of producing 'from fathers helpful to the state sons more helpful still'. Secondly, the rulers who are picked from among these guardians and permitted to lie in order to organize the unsavoury business of selective breeding are totally unlike any real rulers we can imagine. They are almost God-like. The idea that they might abuse their powers or be misguided in what they are doing is unthinkable for Plato. As for discreet infanticide of the deformed, this would not in itself have raised many eyebrows in Plato's time anyway.

When pressed further on the practicality of the whole enterprise, Socrates wriggles out by reminding his companions that 'our purpose was not to demonstrate the possibility of the realization of these ideals' in all their details. 'Do you think', he asks, 'that he would be any the less a good painter, who, after portraying a pattern of the ideally beautiful man and omitting no touch required for the perfection of the picture, should not be able to prove that it is actually possible for such a man to exist?' Socrates is prepared to defend the most important details of his utopia as desirable in theory; but the real point is to paint a thought-provoking picture, from which people can pick out the parts they believe to be useful models. He is not trying to start a revolution. Nevertheless, to satisfy his hearers' curiosity, Socrates is prepared to say what he thinks would be 'the smallest change that would bring a state to this manner of government'. For the ideal city to come into existence, he says, either philosophers must become kings or else 'those whom we now call our kings and rulers take to the pursuit of philosophy seriously and adequately'. This 'smallest change' to present arrangements would evidently be a radical one. But if he were allowed to try to realize his utopia by having just one wish granted, that would be the one likeliest to do the job.

Socrates had avoided bringing up this business of philosopher-kings before because he was understandably afraid of being laughed at. He is perfectly aware, he says, that most actual philosophers are either not particularly virtuous or else are totally useless. The idea of putting such people in charge of anything would be a joke. His type of philosopher-king, though, is not that sort of person at all. The training and selection that would be necessary to produce one would ensure that only the most extraordinary people made the grade. Later on in the *Republic*, he spells out exactly what he has in mind. After a conventional Greek education of music, poetry, elementary mathematics and gymnastics, the best students would have two or three years of military training, provided they were exceptionally virtuous and well-balanced as well as clever. The most successful would go on to do no fewer than ten years of advanced study in science, which in those days would largely have consisted of geometry, arithmetic, astronomy and harmonics. The best of these would then get five years of training in 'dialectic' or philosophical argument. This is a particularly tricky stage, because a student's dialectical powers can easily degenerate into pointless or misguided quibbling. That is one reason why Plato's rigorous educational plan ensures that the students will learn plenty of other things first. For those who get through this part of the curriculum, there then follow fifteen years of practical training in politics and administration. At the end of it all, the ageing trainees would be about fifty years old and would finally be ready to run things, as long as they had proved themselves 'altogether the best in every task and form of knowledge' and 'do not fall short of . . . others in experience and are not second to them in any part of virtues'. Those who have come through the philosopher-king programme with honours would spend most of their time on philosophy and would take it in turns to rule.

Put such people in charge, says Socrates, and you will get the sort of state I have been talking about. They will be in a position to see what is really best for man and so they will bring it about. Although, as we have seen, these people will be much more than just philosophers in any conventional sense, it is their philosophical gifts that Socrates wants to stress. Such talents are just about the last thing anyone would expect a good ruler to need, yet Plato thinks they are essential. So he tries to say more about what philosophical knowledge is, why it matters and what bearing it has on the leadership of men. This gives rise to the attempted definition of philosophy with which this chapter began and to Plato's famous allegory of the Prisoners in the Cave.

For Plato, the ideal philosopher is one who can see through mundane practicalities to appreciate the unchanging and objective nature of things, i.e., the Forms. Such genuine lovers of knowledge cannot but end up being good as well as knowledgeable, since all sorts of benefits accrue to 'a mind habituated to thoughts of grandeur and all time and all existence'. For example, 'a cowardly and illiberal spirit . . . could have no part in genuine philosophy' because the philosophical mind would be above such pettiness. As well as thus requiring and encouraging virtue by the very nature of its enterprise, genuine philosophy leads to goodness in another, more abstract way too. Philosophers are taught to be 'strivers after truth in every form'. And if they complete their pilgrimage their reward will be the sight of the pinnacle of truth, the highest of the Forms – which is the Form of the Good, or goodness itself.

Not even Socrates can say exactly what this is. But he can say a few things about it. In the language of the day, the notion of 'the good' was closely bound up with the idea of appropriate function, purpose or goal. In general, a thing was said to be good if it fulfilled its proper role, achieved its proper aim, or was complete (i.e., had reached its proper end). From Plato's perspective, there had to be a Form corresponding to this general idea of propriety, an essence of 'the good'. It follows that anyone who knows this Form will know everything about what is genuinely beneficial, i.e., what everything ought ideally to aim at. In other words he will always know what is best. Naturally the philosopher-kings described by Socrates are just such people. Their education, especially in dialectic, will have made them specialists in the Forms, so they are bound to be on intimate terms with this most important of them. And 'when they have thus beheld the good itself they shall use it as a pattern for the right ordering of the state'.

Glaucon and Adimantus are understandably eager for some hints about this enlightening Form. They press Socrates to say more about it. Unfortunately, the best he can offer them is an obscure analogy. The Form of the Good, he says, is like the sun. In particular, what the sun is to the power of sight, the Form of the Good is to the power of reason. What this means is that just as the sun illuminates things and makes them visible, so the Form of the Good somehow renders them comprehensible.

There are many questions one might ask about Plato's analogy between the sun and goodness itself. But for present purposes the most important point about this image is that it makes the knowledge of what is best seem just like perceiving something that is really there. At the conclusion of their education in dialectic – investigating, arguing, questioning, defining – the philosopher-kings would see the Form of the Good as straightforwardly as lesser mortals see the sun. Like the sun, this Form sits out there independently of us and our opinions. Plato's message is that there is nothing subjective or fallible about the philosopher-kings' ideas about what is best for their city. They will simply *see* what is right. Of course, there are no such wise people yet and there may never be any. This conception of the sun-like Form of the Good is intended to give us something to aspire to.

To contrast the knowledge of such hypothetical philosophers with the opinions of ordinary men (among whose number he counts himself), Socrates makes use of another analogy: the Prisoners in the Cave. Imagine, he says, a row of prisoners deep in a subterranean chamber. They are firmly chained so that they can look only straight ahead at the dark rock face in front of them. Far behind them is a fire, the only source of light in the cave. Nearer behind them, in front of the fire, people are moving about and carrying various objects. These cast flickering shadows on the wall in front of the prisoners. The prisoners have been manacled in this position for all of their lives: all they have ever seen is these shadows. Not only have they never seen real things, they have no inkling of their existence. This sorry state, says Socrates, is the human condition. The unseen real things in this story correspond to the Forms, whose mere shadows are what we see and take for reality. We are so deeply accustomed to this life that if we were liberated from our captive existence, we would not at first realize what had happened. Suppose, says Socrates, that one of the prisoners in the cave were freed from his chains and dragged outside. The bright light would hurt his eyes and at first he would want to turn back to his familiar half-light. He would be too dazzled to make out the things around him. 'And if . . . one should point out to him each of the passing objects and constrain him by questions to say what it is, do you not think that he would be at a loss and that he would regard what he formerly saw as more real than the things now pointed out to him?' So it is with real people: Plato's Socrates shows them the Forms, and they just blink in puzzlement.

The released prisoner would have to get used to his new surroundings gradually. First he would manage to discern shadows cast by the sun; then reflections in water; then he would begin to make out the solid objects of the real world. At night he would gaze at the comfortably faint light of the stars and moon. His sight might then be strong enough for him to look up towards the sun – and now he can start to make sense of the overall scheme of things: 'at this point he would infer and conclude that this . . . provides the seasons and the courses of the year and presides over all things in the visible region.' By this time he will realize that what he had been used to before in the cave were mere images. He will pity his former companions in the cave and 'what passed for wisdom there'.

And what would happen if he went back to visit the cave, presumably eager to release his fellows? Once again he would at first be handicapped. No longer used to darkness, he would be unable to make out the cave's faint shadows any more. His reappearance down below would

provoke laughter, and would it not be said of him that he had returned from his journey aloft with his eyes ruined and that it was not worth while even to attempt the ascent? And if it were possible to lay hands on and to kill the man who tried to release them and lead them up, would they not kill him?

Killing him might seem implausibly extreme, even for these deluded prisoners who have no clue about the real world. But remember that from Plato's point of view something like this is what happened to the historical Socrates. Socrates tried to enlighten the cave-dwellers of Athens and they killed him for it. The image of the returned man who wants to lead his fellows into daylight, but is met with hostility and incomprehension, is a metaphor for the puzzled contempt that some-times greets one who has just rushed back from an encounter with knowledge:

do you think it at all strange . . . if a man returning from divine contemplations to the petty miseries of men cuts a sorry figure and appears most ridiculous, if, while still blinking through the gloom, and before he has become sufficiently accustomed to the environing darkness, he is compelled in courtrooms or elsewhere to contend about the shadows of justice . . . and to wrangle in debate about the notions of these things in the minds of those who have never seen justice itself?

It would be by no means strange.

The fate of the returned ex-prisoner of the *Republic* is a small memorial to the real Socrates, whose talk about justice fell on stony ground.

Enlightened ex-prisoners must always return to the cave of human-ity, so the argument of the *Republic* continues. Just as people who are 'uneducated and inexperienced in truth' could never be trusted to rule over others, so those who have attained 'the knowledge which we pronounced the greatest' should not be allowed to escape their responsibility to pass it on and put it into practice. Having reached the enviable heights from which they can see what is right and best, the philosopher-kings must not be permitted to 'linger there . . . and refuse to go down again among those bondsmen and share their labours'. It may sound cruel to make the philosopher-kings return to the darkness once they have tasted knowledge, but 'the law is not concerned with the special happiness of any class in the state, but is trying to produce this condition in the city as a whole'.

Down you must go then, each in his turn, to the habitation of the others and accustom yourselves to the observation of the obscure things there. For once habituated you will discern them infinitely better than the dwellers there . . . because you have seen the reality of the beautiful, the just and the good. So our city will be governed by us and you with waking minds, and not as most cities now, which are inhabited and ruled darkly as in a dream by men who . . . wrangle for office as if that were a great good, when the truth is that the city in which those who are to rule are least eager to hold office must needs be best administered and most free from dissension.

How exactly will this best sort of city, with its wise but reluctant rulers, differ from all the other sorts of constitutions on offer? There are plenty of types of government to be seen in the world. The Cretan or Spartan type, which is ruled by the military; oligarchy, or rule by a rich elite; democracy, rule by the masses; and lastly tyranny, 'the fourth and final malady of a state'. These are the main types but there are also 'hereditary principalities and purchased kingships' and many other intermediate species. In fact, says Socrates, there seem to be as many sorts of government as there are sorts of people. He thinks that all these different states must correspond in some way to the different characters of their rulers. Having now said quite a lot about the philosophically enlightened rulers in his ideal city, he is ready to go back to his main task: analysing the various constitutions and the psychologies that go with them to find out about justice and how it leads to happiness.

Socrates arranges the four main types of government, plus his ideal type, into a five-storey hierarchy. Aristocracy – which means rule by the philosopher-kings – is the best and tyranny is the worst. Democracy turns out to be the next worst thing to tyranny; for Plato, even military dictatorship or government by a rich elite would be better than this rule of the rabble. Before jumping to any conclusions about the awfulness of Plato's politics, though, the fact that we tend to think of military rule and oligarchy as tyrannical forms of government, while Plato describes tyranny as something much worse than either, should alert us to the fact that things are not what they seem. None of these political terms corresponds exactly to its modern meaning, especially not democracy, though there is enough common ground between modern liberal governments and Plato's 'democracy' to make his discussion of it fascinating. As for 'aristocracy', in Plato's language this just meant rule by the best and most just sort of people. It had nothing to do with people having ancestors who were rich or did some favour for a king, which is in effect what it means nowadays.

The philosopher-kings, the Platonic aristocrats, are people who are in themselves ruled by reason; therefore the aristocratic state is one ruled according to the wisest principles. Next one down in the order of desirable political systems is military rule (called timocracy): the timocrats are ruled by a noble passion, namely the desire for honour, but this is not as noble as reason, so the state that they run is not as good as an aristocracy. Then comes oligarchy. The rich elite of oligarchs is dominated by an ignoble passion, the hunger for wealth. But they do have some virtues. They are thrifty and self-controlled, to some extent, in order to save money. This is not saying much, but it is at least slightly better than the next lot, the democrats, who have practically no self-control at all. They are dominated by their lowly appetites for food, drink, sex and immediate gratification in general. The democratic state run by such people is an undisciplined and chaotic mess. As for the tyrants at the bottom of the heap, they are not even restrained by the law. They take the vices of the democrats one step further by doing absolutely anything they feel like, and are particularly fond of murder. Obviously a state ruled by tyrants is the worst place to be (even if you are one of them, as we shall see).

Socrates describes how each of the top four types of government degenerates into the one below. Each contains the seeds of its own destruction. Even the ideal 'aristocracy' will eventually disintegrate. Sooner or later some guardians will break the rules of the mating game, perhaps unwittingly, and the stock of inferior guardians will increase. This will lead to trouble when the good guardians try to compromise with the less good ones and the city accordingly slides away from its harmonious ideal. The 'high-spirited' among them, with their 'contentiousness and covetousness of honour', will eventually push the virtuous and retiring philosophers out of the way. The resulting militaristic state – the timocracy – will sooner or later in turn succumb to civil strife, perhaps when its leading citizens run out of foreigners to conquer. The man who is too covetous of honour is bound to become rather keen on property too, and so the seeds of an oligarchic government will grow: 'from being lovers of victory and . . . honour they become lovers of . . . money, and they commend and admire the rich man and put him in office but despise the man who is poor'. It is easy to see that wealth is no real guide to political ability. 'Suppose men should appoint the pilots of ships in this way . . . and not allow a poor man to navigate, even if he were a better pilot . . . A sorry voyage they would make of it.' The downfall of such an oligarchy is guaranteed by the fact that there is bound eventually to be strife between rich and poor: a class-struggle. Discontent will be fomented by money-lovers who have fallen on hard times, and envy will lead the poor masses to rise up and install a democracy. The pursuit of money will thus have destroyed the oligarchy from within, just as the pursuit of freedom will ultimately end the democracy that follows it.

The victory of the poor masses, the democracy which liberates them from the various elites who ruled over them before, will no doubt be heralded as a victory for freedom. But Socrates argues that it is no such thing. The appetites that are given free rein in such a society will inevitably lead to extreme slavery, not extreme freedom. It will seem attractive enough to start with: the democratic city will be 'chock-full of liberty and freedom of speech' and 'everyone would arrange a plan for leading his own life in the way that pleases him'. Like 'a garment of many colours, embroidered with all kinds of hues, so this, decked and diversified with every type of character, would appear the most beautiful' of cities. There will, of course, be no room for philosopher-kings under the patchwork quilt:

the tolerance of democracy . . . its disdain for our solemn pronouncements made when we were founding our city . . . tramples underfoot all such ideals, caring nothing from what practices and ways of life a man turns to politics, but honouring him if only he says that he loves the people!

The sort of democracy Socrates is describing is in one sense more democratic than anything we know. It is the ultimate democracy. Power will be distributed not by elections – today considered the essence of democracy – but by drawing lots, i.e., at random. This may sound too extreme to be worth considering, but it is close to how Athenian democracy worked in Plato's time. Much of the state's business, and many trials, were in the hands of magistrates who were picked at random for a term of one year. Many bigger political decisions were determined by the votes of whoever happened to turn up at the relevant mass-meeting. True, there were constitutional safeguards which were supposed to ensure efficient government in Athens (magistrates, for instance, had to pass a simple exam and could be voted out of office). But to Plato's mind the natural weaknesses of such a system could best be brought out by imagining the rule of the people to have been taken to its logical extreme.

To get to the bottom of democratic ideas, Socrates proposes to look at the character of a typical democrat. This will show up the characteristic vices and virtues of democracy. Just as the ultimate democratic state will tolerate everything and everyone, so the democratic spirit will be equally indiscriminate:

he establishes and maintains all his pleasures on a footing of equality . . . and so lives turning over the guardhouse of his soul to each as it happens along until it is sated, as if it had drawn the lot for that office, and then in turn another, disdaining none but fostering them all equally . . . And he does not accept or admit into the guardhouse the words of truth when anyone tells him that some pleasures arise from honourable and good desires, and others from those that are base, and that we ought to practise and esteem the one and control and subdue the others, but he shakes his head at all such admonitions and avers that they are all alike and to be equally esteemed.

A democratic man, like democracy itself, assigns 'a kind of equality indiscriminately, to equals and unequals alike'. Everything will seem to be as worthwhile as everything else, and so open-mindedness will naturally become empty-headedness. Star-struck by the idols of liberty and equality, the democrat will be a merrily befuddled enthusiast for every passing fancy:

day by day indulging the appetite of the day, now winebibbing and abandoning himself to the lascivious pleasing of the flute and again drinking only water and dieting, and at one time exercising his body, and sometimes idling and neglecting all things, and at another time seeming to occupy himself with philosophy. And frequently he goes in for politics and bounces up and says and does whatever enters his head. And if military men excite his emulation, thither he rushes, and if moneyed men, to that he turns, and there is no order or compulsion in his existence, but he calls this life of his the life of pleasure and freedom and happiness and cleaves to it to the end.

The democrat thus becomes a slave to his desires. The end may come sooner than he thinks, because the love of freedom will snowball. If all freedom is good, all compulsion is bad: the citizens will become 'so sensitive that they chafe at the slightest suggestion of servitude and will not endure it':

the father habitually tries to resemble the child and is afraid of his sons . . . The teacher . . . fears and fawns upon the pupils, and the pupils pay no heed to the teacher or to their overseers either . . . while the old, accommodating themselves to the young, are full of pleasantry and graciousness, imitating the young for fear they may be thought disagreeable and authoritarian.

Socrates jokes that the spirit of autonomy and liberation will spread to dumb animals. Even 'the horses and asses' will 'hold on their way with the utmost freedom and dignity, bumping into everyone who meets them and who does not step aside'. Glaucon interrupts and says that this is exactly what happens to him when he ventures out into the countryside.

Maybe Socrates' remark about asses is not such a joke after all. The defence of animal rights has turned out to flourish mainly in democracies, though it is not, as in Socrates' little fantasy, actively pursued by animals themselves ('the exploited group cannot themselves make an organized protest against the treatment they receive', writes one contemporary animal-liberationist about today's injustices). It is an amusing exercise to find modern parallels for the symptoms of liberal society described by Socrates, from dieting fads to the acute sensitivities of politically correct language – or chafing 'at the slightest suggestion of servitude', as he put it. Whether or not any of these features of modern life as foreshadowed by Plato are as obviously undesirable as he assumed is quite another matter.

There is one part of Plato's prognosis which everyone will hope is wrong, namely that democracy leads to destructive chaos. Socrates argues that this will logically happen in the end because the appetite for freedom in all its forms will not always be satisfied within the law. (A minor modern example of this might be extremists who are prepared to threaten human life to secure liberty for laboratory gerbils.) The democratic spirits, he says, will 'finally pay no heed even to the laws written and unwritten, so that . . . they may have no master anywhere over them'. It is disrespect for the law, together with some other features of democratic life, that will accidentally let a tyranny come to power. It might happen like this, says Socrates. The naturally pushy and corrupt members of society will thrive and elbow themselves into prominence, because there is nothing to keep them down in a free-for-all democracy. Masquerading as loyal servants of the people, they will manage to fleece those who have accumulated wealth, keeping some of it for themselves. The wealthy will naturally complain at this expropriation and try to do something about it; but for this they will be accused of trying to subvert the state. Some charismatic leader will be acclaimed as the protector and champion of the common people against the plotting rich. Then things will get hot. Such a 'protector' will 'devise that famous petition of the tyrant – to ask from the people a bodyguard to make their city safe for the friend of democracy'. He and his private army will soon taste the blood of those they pronounce enemies of the state. The headlong descent into tyrannical and murderous rule will soon be unstoppable. The people, 'trying to escape the smoke of submission . . . would have plunged into the fire of enslavement' under tyranny.

Plato spends more time on the character of the tyrant than on any other type. It is after all the tyrant who lives the life described as most desirable by Thrasymachus in his attack on morality. What sort of happiness can such a man have? His mental life is, Socrates argues, literally a nightmare. In an anticipation of Freud, Socrates describes a type of repressed desire that can erupt at night. 'Our dreams make it clear that there is a dangerous, wild and lawless form of desire in everyone, even in those of us who seem to be entirely moderate or measured.' Such desires

are awakened in sleep when the rest of the soul, the rational, gentle and dominant part, slumbers, but the beastly and savage part, replete with food and wine, gambols and, repelling sleep, endeavours to sally forth and satisfy its own instincts ... in such case there is nothing it will not venture to undertake as being released from all sense of shame and all reason. It does not shrink from attempting to lie with a mother in fancy or with anyone else, man, god, or brute. It is ready for any foul deed.

While a balanced person can keep such desires in check for the most part, the tyrant is dominated by them night and day: 'either his nature, or his way of life, or both of them together make him drunk, filled with erotic desire, and mad'. His hunger for money will lead to a life of crime; he will be surrounded by flatterers fearful of his power. In general, he will mix with people only in order to get what he wants out of them, so friendship is one pleasure he will never know. Real peace and freedom are also unknown to him because the moment he stumbles he will be devoured by his terrified false friends. Like the city he rules, the soul of the tyrant must be 'full of slavery and unfreedom, with the most decent parts enslaved and with a small part, the maddest and most vicious, as their master'. Proceeding by suggestive analogies and largely plausible examples, Socrates paints the soul of the tyrant as necessarily poor, fearful, disordered and generally wretched:

so far from finding even the least satisfaction for his desires, he is in need of most things, and is a poor man in very truth, as is apparent if one knows how to observe a soul in its entirety. And throughout his life he teems with terrors and is full of convulsions and pains, if in fact he resembles the condition of the city which he rules.

The tyrant's fundamental problem is that he is 'ill-governed in his own soul'. He is ruled by the worst part of himself and is thus bound to be fundamentally unhappy. The happiest sort of man is the very opposite of this: he is ruled by the best part of himself, namely reason. Thus a complete conception of justice or right action – an answer to the question of how to live – has been arrived at. For individuals it lies ultimately in the harmonious ordering of the parts of the soul, i.e., of types of desires. Make sure that the desires for honour, money, sex and so on are all kept in their proper places and guided by reason, and you will have a righteous and happy man (or at least a man who has the main prerequisites for happiness). For cities as a whole, justice and happiness lie in the harmonious ordering, again guided by reason, of the parts of society – that is, the money-lovers, the honour-lovers, the knowledge-lovers and so on – which correspond to the parts of the soul. We can now see what was wrong with Thrasymachus' amoralism and lawlessness by seeing the whole picture. We see what his attitudes ultimately lead to and how far his sort of life or system of government is from the happiest one. Thus Socrates finally claims the victory that had escaped him at the beginning of the *Republic* when he had tried to tackle Thrasymachus' arguments head on.

To bring his own main argument to a triumphant end, Socrates gives two more considerations in favour of all that he has been urging. First, what is one to say to a money-lover or honour-lover – or indeed a self-indulgent, amoral tyrant – who simply denies that any other sort of life is in any sense superior to his own? The devotee of each type of pleasure will insist that his are the most satisfying. Socrates points out that the only person who is in a position to judge the different sorts of pleasures is the one who has experienced them all. This, he argues, is the philosopher-king, who must have travelled all these roads to get to where he is. He will, for example, remember from his childhood what it was like to be enslaved to the lowlier appetites. Also, his experience of life will be tempered by the faculty of reason. His education in dialectic puts him in the best position to evaluate evidence. So when the philosopher-king tells us that he has found the pleasures of reason to be the best, we should listen.

The second point is something on which Socrates is prepared to rest his case. The impure pleasures derived from lowly things cannot be satisfying in the end, because they are intrinsically unstable and therefore illusory. These are 'pleasures mixed with pains, mere images and shadow paintings of true pleasures':

those who have no experience of reason and virtue, but are always occupied with feasts and the like . . . never taste any stable or pure pleasure. Instead, they always look down at the ground like cattle, and, with their heads bent over the dinner table, they feed, fatten and fornicate. To outdo others in these things, they kick and butt them with iron horns and hooves, killing each other, because their desires are insatiable. For the part they're trying to fill is like a vessel full of holes.

The man who is ruled by reason has a more satisfying meal, because his appetite for knowledge takes him to a more rewarding feast. To return to the allegory of the cave, he has found his way to daylight and sees things as they really are. He therefore knows 'the good' for man – that is, he knows that man is not like the beasts but has a higher, better part, the cultivation of which brings him virtue, which in turn helps to bring solid happiness.

Plato then makes Socrates indulge in a mathematical flight of fancy by which he bizarrely seeks to prove that a philosopher-king is precisely 729 times happier than a tyrant. The less said about this presumed joke the better (even the arithmetic is wrong: by Socrates' own lights the answer should in fact have been 125 times happier). The *Republic* ends in an anticlimax, with a discussion of the fate of the human soul and a curiously hostile digression on certain sorts of poetry. But by this stage the serious work of the *Republic* has already been completed.

What people most often take away with them from the *Republic* is the extraordinary city with its implausible philosopher-kings that Plato uses as the vehicle for his argument. Some twentieth-century critics, writing with the twin evils of Hitler's fascism and Stalin's communism in view, have argued that Plato's state is a totalitarian abomination whose only virtue is to have been the first of its misguided kind.

Plato deserves rather better than that. First one must remember that his main purpose was not to design a state at all: it was to exploit the analogy between city and soul in order to get a broad picture of the relation between justice and happiness. His analysis of tyranny, for example, is there mainly to cast light on the psychology of the unjust man, and the philosopher-kings are there as ideal examples of the very opposite sort of person. The ever-present moral of his tale is that justice and the best sort of happiness are to be found together in the rule of reason. Everything else in the book is more or less incidental. Towards the end Socrates explicitly says that the very best state of affairs would be for each person to be ruled by reason 'preferably indwelling and his own, but in default of that imposed from without'. In other words, the whole civic apparatus of the ideal city with its carefully educated and controlled guardians is in fact a second-best option, to be entertained only if people cannot manage to rule themselves properly. It is worth stressing that the 'utopia' described in the *Republic* is therefore in one sense not Plato's ideal at all. What he is really urging, he says, is no more than what guides a prudent parent:

we don't allow [*children*] to be free until we establish a constitution in them, just as in a city – by fostering their best part with our own best part – until we equip them with a guardian and ruler within them to take our place. Only then do we set them free.

According to his own principles, Plato would have been perfectly happy with the constitutional arrangements of a modern democracy – that is, with setting the people free – provided these arrangements were capable of delivering justice and happiness. It is just that he would have been very sceptical about their ability to do so.

Plato's attitude to the democracy of his time was evidently very different to that of the historical Socrates. Although Socrates apparently never bothered to weigh up the various sorts of constitution explicitly, we have seen that he was devoted to the Athenian democracy, whereas Plato and his 'Socratic' mouthpiece could see in it only aimless chaos and the seeds of an even worse tyranny. To modern minds, Plato misses all the virtues of constitutional liberty. Even if he was not primarily arguing for any particular political system, and even if the city he describes is only a second-best for him, it is plain that he did not sufficiently appreciate the dangers of putting too much power in the hands of an elite. He also seems insensitive to the idea that people might want to find happiness for themselves, not be steered towards it by 'guardians' of their welfare. Kindly old man though Plato is, adults do not want to be treated like children. In short, Plato appears to be untouched by the values of diversity and individualism that are prized in contemporary Western democracies.

Plato does not simply ignore such pluralism: his treatment of democracy aims to address it directly, by painting it as haphazard, indiscriminate and only superficially satisfying. Let people pursue any aim they happen to choose and they will just end up enslaved to every passing fad. Far from being masters of their own destinies, they will, he thinks, be at the mercy of all sorts of untoward influences and seductive ideologies. As for the powerful guardians he talks about, Plato would remind his critics that their training would make them 'expert craftsmen of civic liberty'. So there is no need to worry about possible abuses of their power. To the charge that no real people could ever be trustworthy and wise enough to fulfil this role, he would reply that he knows this perfectly well and has himself already pointed out that such an aristocracy of the wise is bound to fall apart sooner or later. By reminding us that he is only theorizing about ideals, Plato can wriggle out of some of the practical-minded accusations against him – at least for a while.

But the ideals themselves are suspect. When Plato argues that 'unity is the greatest blessing for a state' it is hard to escape the verdict that he has taken a good thing too far and has sacrificed diversity on the altar of discipline. As Aristotle said: 'There comes a point when the effect of unification is that the state . . . will . . . be a very much worse one; it is as if one were to reduce harmony to unison or rhythm to a single beat.' Relying on the metronome of the philosopher-kings to mark time – however clever they are – could easily be dangerous for the city. As Aristotle put it, even if the few philosopher-kings are better and wiser than any member of the multitude, it could be that the people 'when they meet together may be better than the few good, if regarded not individually but collectively, just as a feast to which many contribute is better than a dinner provided out of a single purse'. The citizens might march over a precipice (albeit in step) which they might have been able to avoid if their own views had been consulted occasionally. Might not the very fact that the philosopher-kings will, as designers of the city, have a different perspective on it to that of the inhabitants be a drawback in itself? Aristotle pointed out that 'there are some arts whose products are not judged of solely, or best, by the artists themselves . . . the user . . . of the house will actually be a better judge than the builder'. Perhaps the art of politics is one such art.

Plato would reply, once more, that his hypothetical philosopher-kings are imagined to be ideally good and ideally wise, so these objections do not apply. But do the notions of ideal goodness and ideal wisdom even make sense? Part of the trouble can perhaps be traced back to Plato's conception of the Form of the Good, and the imagery of the sun and the cave which suggest that this Form can eventually be seen as clear as day by a philosopher-king. Maybe goodness is not like the sun after all: maybe it is not something that a person can see if he just manages to stand in the right place. What if there is no single, all-encompassing truth to be known about what is best for man? And even if there were, how could we ever be sure that any person or class of people had found it? Any doubts about either of these questions must in turn cast doubt on the desirability of Plato's city, even as a second best. It gives too much power to too few people, who may not be able to know best in the way that Plato thinks. Perhaps there can be wisdom but not perfect wisdom, goodness but no Form of the Good.

Fortunately for Plato and for us, plenty of his insights and arguments about justice and happiness survive this necessary scepticism. Still, the streets of his city in the *Republic* must remain dark and deserted, because from our point of view his Form of the Good is permanently eclipsed.

One thing that Plato had tried to establish in the *Republic* is that the Sophists' alleged conflict between morality and self-interest is really an illusion. It is based on a crude and incomplete picture of self-interest, because it turns out that the soul of man is naturally constituted so as to lead its happiest existence when ruled by reason and the other virtues. Seen in the right perspective, living the moral life emerges as being to a man's advantage. It could thus be said that nature itself is on the side of morality and reason because it punishes the immoral and irrational man with unhappiness. The *Timaeus*, which I turn to now, tells a related story on a larger scale. It shows the inanimate natural world as also happily ruled by reason, because it was fashioned by an intelligent being (a 'Master-Craftsman' or God) and bears the marks of his rational design. Plato tried to give an account of all these marks, from the movements of the planets to the movements of the bowels.

For the first twelve centuries of the Christian era, the *Timaeus* formed the basis of most cosmology in the West. Indeed from the fifth century AD onwards, partial Latin translations of it provided the only generally available systematic account of nature until the scientific works of Aristotle, among others, were translated into Latin in the twelfth century. Some of the dialogue's popularity was due to the fact that the God of the *Timaeus* could, at a pinch, be interpreted as the God of Genesis. Reading Plato without biblical blinkers, we can see that this required plenty of imaginative interpretation; but the Christians were happy to provide it. The main differences between Plato's God and the biblical one are these: his God is not the most important thing in the universe (the Forms are, and God must take his cues from them); he is not the only God but has many assistants; he is not omnipotent but must co-operate with various natural forces; he did not create the universe from scratch but used materials that were already to hand; he has no particular interest in people – in fact he gave the job of making them to his juniors in order to keep them at arm's length.

Considering all this, one might wonder why medieval Christians bothered to perform their posthumous conversion of Plato. But the temptation to hijack the only detailed 'scientific' account of the world was evidently irresistible, and besides there were plenty of other things in the *Timaeus* to keep them happy. Referring to the Master-Craftsman and his works, Plato wrote that 'the world is the fairest of creations, and he is the best of causes'. The *Timaeus* insisted that the order of the universe and the meticulous planning that seemed to lie behind it pointed to a higher and rational purpose of some sort. Almost every explanation offered in the dialogue returns to the notion of purpose, so the *Timaeus* suited theological ideas much better than the blind, mechanical universe of Democritus, Epicurus and Lucretius would have done. The following typical piece of eighteenth-century theologizing closely echoes the language of the *Timaeus* in the inferences it draws from the motions of planets and the paths of comets. It is by Isaac Newton:

it is not to be conceived that mere mechanical causes could give birth to so many regular motions . . . This most beautiful system of the sun, planets, and comets could only proceed from the counsel and dominion of an intelligent and powerful Being.

In fact, blinded by his faith, Newton had temporarily overlooked his own laws of motion. These explain precisely how 'mere mechanical causes could give birth to so many regular motions'. Immanuel Kant (1724–1804), who is mainly remembered as a philosopher but was also one of the most informed writers on mathematical physics and astronomy of his day, understood this better than Newton himself. Kant pointed out three drawbacks of such attempts to pull a Christian rabbit out of a celestial hat. First, much of the apparent harmony of nature follows necessarily from the laws of matter; so any Being offering further 'counsel and dominion' is permanently in danger of being made redundant as more and more laws come to be understood. Secondly, seeing nature primarily in terms of the purposes of an intelligent being can make scientific inquiry lazy, because the scientist is tempted to stop asking questions as soon as he thinks he has found the divine purpose of something. And lastly, any argument in the style of Newton or Plato can take one only so far; it might point to a Master-Craftsman who has organized pre-existing matter, but it cannot reach further back to an original Creator of the sort described in the Book of Genesis. Similar criticisms of 'physico-theology', as Kant called it, were brilliantly developed by the sceptical philosopher David Hume (1711–76) at around the same time.

These sceptical attacks would not have posed any problem for Plato, whose aims in the *Timaeus* were not primarily religious in any modern sense. His goal was to improve on the crude explanations of the earlier naturalists, not to lay a smooth path for later Christians. Where he thought that his predecessors from Thales to Democritus had gone wrong was in focusing too hard on the question of what sort of stuff things are made of. While these men fixed their gaze on elements and atoms in their search for causes, a quite different and more important sort of cause was slipping past them. The Pythagoreans had had an inkling of this fugitive cause in their talk of the mathematical patterns in nature. Anaxagoras caught a glimpse of it in his fleeting mention of *Nous* – mind, intelligence or reason. Plato's new agenda for science had already been laid out in a speech he put in the mouth of Socrates, quoted in connection with Anaxagoras (page 87). The key thing was to make use of the idea of a rational plan, an intelligible pattern, in terms of which the functions of things would become clear. The example of man bore this out: physiology and mechanics were at most half of the story when trying to explain a man's actions; a good explanation would also have to say what his goals were – i.e., what he was trying to achieve. Something similar was true in the case of inanimate things, too, which is what the naturalists had failed to realize.

We saw that the thought of Anaxagoras, who hardly made any scientific use of his concept of intelligence or reason, was marked by a hostility to superstition. Presented with a deformed animal's head, he refused to read any supernatural message into the event but merely explained it as a physiological effect and moved on. Is Plato not just returning to the superstitious ways of the *theologi*, the myth-makers, in looking for notions of purpose – and divine purpose at that – in natural events? Not really. The sort of purposes which Plato wanted to invoke were in one important sense the exact opposite of what the myth-makers had been talking about. The trouble with the pseudo-explanations of the *theologi* was that the gods they introduced were capricious. Poseidon caused earthquakes because he felt like it. Such events were therefore impossible to predict or to fit into any general pattern. So science was impossible. But the purposes which Plato found in nature were much more rational than Poseidon's whims, and the whole point of looking for them was to establish an overall pattern and thus a genuine science. Plato did not debase the art of rational explanation by conjuring up gods to account for particular everyday events.

He tried to explain his new story in the language of a myth, and it is not clear how literally we are supposed to take it all. The main narrator of the *Timaeus* describes the Master-Craftsman as taking a bowl and using it to mix a sort of world-soul which is then liberally sprinkled about. With soul in a bowl on the menu, it is plain that at least some of these delicacies are not meant to be swallowed whole. There has been plenty of dispute over whether Plato's God or Master-Craftsman is himself meant to be understood literally, or whether he is just supposed to suggest an analogy between the works of man and the works of nature. The Platonic God sometimes seems to be as abstract and impersonal as the Form of the Good and not like a personal being at all; the two seem at least to be very close relations. This question of interpretation could not be resolved even by Plato's own pupils, so there is not much hope of directly answering it now. But we can dissolve the question, to a considerable extent, by remembering how different Greek ideas of rationality, mind, purpose and divinity are from our own.

Plato's universe was ruled by reason; that was certainly the main message he meant to convey in the *Timaeus*. But what did he mean by reason? It will help to go back to what he says about human reason in the *Republic* and elsewhere. For Plato, being rational does not primarily mean being cool, calculating and intellectual. Greek reason is not cold; it is hot. It has been aptly defined as 'that in man which enables him to live for something'. It is what lets him identify and set appropriate goals and then focus his life on achieving them. It is not an absence or suppression of desires, but the faculty that harnesses them so that they can work together in the best possible way, dangling the carrot of some 'good' or aim to urge them on. Thus in the *Republic* the best and happiest sort of man is said to be ruled by reason, meaning that he organizes his life around pursuing the goal that will ultimately benefit him, not letting any stray, impulsive appetites divert him from this course. Society is ruled by reason when it is similarly organized by those who are themselves best organized. How, then, might such a conception of directed, active reason show itself in the context of lifeless matter? In the 'information age' some contemporary physicists have found it useful to describe the universe as if it were a gigantic computer – processing information (i.e., events) according to the instructions in its 'software' (i.e., the laws of nature). In the machine age, beginning in the eighteenth century, the workings of nature were characteristically described in mechanical terms: its admirable ingenuity lay in the exact repetition of its movements and the fine-tuning of its parts. The Greeks were craftsmen, not makers of machines or dealers in information. For them, the application of intelligence was most typically displayed when some artefact was fashioned out of yielding materials:

craftsmen do not each choose and apply materials to their work at random, but with the view that each of their productions should have a certain form. Look, for example . . . at painters, builders, shipwrights, and all other craftsmen . . . and see how each one disposes each element he contributes in a fixed order, and compels one to fit and harmonize with the other until he has combined the whole into something well ordered and regulated.

For something to be well-ordered and regulated, then – for it to exemplify reason at work – is for it to be put together in such a way that all its parts are harmoniously orchestrated according to a clear 'form' or pattern. The key to Platonic rationality, whether its traces are found in a man, a ship, a city, or the universe as a whole, lies in the skilful adaptation of means to ends. Inanimate things can be seen as harmoniously orchestrated, as well-adapted means, and this is at bottom what Plato has in mind when he speaks of rational purpose in the natural world. It works, its parts all fit together, it seems to be good of its kind. This is the craftsman's picture of rationality and purpose.

What sort of job would a God do in such a picture? The biblical God would march in with his sheaf of blueprints – the Forms or patterns to work from – and propose to build and launch a world. But such a position is not available in Plato's universe. The Forms or blueprints for the natural world exist already. We have already seen in the discussion between Socrates and Euthyphro that moral values, which are the most important of the blueprints for a good world, cannot just be whatever a God chooses them to be (page 151). By pursuing the crucial question, 'is what is holy holy because the gods approve it, or do they approve it because it is holy?', Plato shows that his God's hands are tied; such matters must be determined independently. The same is true for every Form, from the Form of the Worm to the Form of the Good. There is for each thing, quite objectively and prior to God, some way that is the best way for it to be, if it is to flourish and to perform its natural function. The job of Plato's God is thus largely the ceremonial one of marrying matter and form by following the instructions in the blueprints provided. A vital task, if you suppose that otherwise the world would never get round to developing in accordance with these plans, but one at which many other gods would turn up their noses if they were not allowed to bring their own Forms and personal ideals with them when they turned up for work.

All ancient Greeks, whatever their philosophical views, shared a conception of divinity that is relevant for understanding Plato's God, and in particular the question of how far the account of his actions given in the *Timaeus* is to be read as if it were a literal, fundamentalist Bible story. The Greeks were much more at home with the idea of divinity, a set of qualities that are found in nature, than with the idea of a God, a being wholly set apart from nature. We have seen that all sorts of things were commonly called divine on account of their permanence, their power and their superiority to the characteristically human. The basic use of 'divine' among the Greeks was to speak of such things. And the idea of a divine personal being derives from this usage, rather the other way round. As one commentator on Plato puts it:

Where the Christian says that God is love or that God is good he is first asserting, or taking for granted, the existence of a mysterious being, God, and making a qualitative judgement about him. He is telling us something about God. With the Greek the order was frequently reversed. He would say that Love is god or Beauty is god; he is not assuming the existence of any mysterious divinity but telling us something about love and beauty, the reality of which no one could deny. The subject of his judgement, the thing of which he speaks, is in the world we know.

From Plato's point of view, someone who denies the existence of divinity – an atheist – is one who mistakenly believes that there is no order or purpose in the universe greater than man. Plato's Master-Craftsman, or senior god, may well be the greatest personification of this order and purpose, this beautiful and efficient functioning; but whatever else he might be, he is something which exists in the universe rather than a distant creator of it all. Just as this God inherits the matter he has to work with, he must bow to the Platonic Forms – to Order, Beauty and Goodness themselves. These are the true sacraments of the Platonic religion. With this point established we can proceed to the influential myths of the *Timaeus*, and see that it does not make all that much difference to the fundamentals of Plato's philosophy whether or not he supposed that such a Master-Craftsman literally existed.

The *Timaeus* was intended as the start of a three-part sequel to the ideas of the *Republic*, which had been written quite a long time earlier. The trilogy was supposed to embellish the discussion of the *Republic*'s city by telling a story about how such a place might come about and how it might fare in its dealings with other cities. In particular, the story would tell of a titanic battle long ago with an empire called Atlantis, which lost the war and sank under the sea. Plato's invention of Atlantis was so vivid that scholars and lunatics have looked for it ever since. Oddly, many of them transformed it into a sort of utopia, whereas Plato describes Atlantis as an evil empire of tyrannical enslavers. The planned trilogy was never finished. What we have in most of the *Timaeus* is some detailed story-telling about the earliest days of the world, given in a series of long monologues by a character called Timaeus of Locri (in Italy), who may have been modelled on the Pythagorean Archytas of Tarentum.

In the preamble to his lectures, Timaeus insists that there can be no certain knowledge of the matters he is about to discuss: 'Enough if we adduce probabilities as likely as any others, for we . . . are only mortal men, and we ought to accept the tale which is probable and inquire no further.' With that caution out of the way, he soon plunges into a rather definite and precise account of the cosmos. God, or the Master-Craftsman, made the pleasingly ordered world we see because he was good and he wanted everything else to be as good as possible too. It is implied that there was some primitive sort of world before, but that it was a very poor specimen. Since this God was a sound Pythagorean, the recipe book he used to cook up the world was a geometry text, of which his copy seems to have had substantial annotations by Empedocles and Democritus.

The main thing was to ensure regularity, because regularity was good and rational. Plato knew that there were just five regular solids in geometry, i.e., five types of symmetrical figures that can be constructed out of identical plane surfaces. These are the tetrahedron (a pyramid of four equilateral triangles), the cube (made of six squares), the octahedron (eight equilateral triangles), the icosahedron (20 equilateral triangles) and the soccerball-like dodecahedron (12 pentagons). Such paragons of symmetry were too good to leave rotting in the larder, so God used these geometrical building blocks as models when moulding all forms of matter. The first four were used to make Empedocles' elements: fire, earth, air and water respectively. Earth, for example, was made cubical in construction since cubes were thought to be the stablest of the regular solids, and God needed a stable base to work with. The fifth solid was reserved for association with the cosmos as a whole, because the dodecahedron is the closest of the five to a sphere ('a figure that has the greatest degree of completeness and uniformity').

The planet earth is an unmoving globe at the centre of the cosmos, with the sun, moon and other planets circling around it at various speeds and inclinations. Their motions trace a larger sphere, itself revolving and forming the boundary and outer skin of the cosmos, in which the stars are embedded like jewels in a canopy. Plato seems to have realized – probably by learning from his colleague in the Academy, Eudoxus – that the observed irregularities of planetary motion can in principle be accounted for in terms of the compounded effects of several uniform motions. Uniform rotation was the best and most complete sort of motion, so that was picked as the basis of the astronomical scheme. Timaeus says that the sight of these mighty, regular movements gives people their ideas of time ('a moving image of eternity') and of mathematics. This may even be why God made them.

At one level, all earthly events consist in the interaction of the four elements, and all earthly substances are composites of them, much as Empedocles had said. Deeper down, Plato took a leaf out of the atomists' book and accounted for the properties of each element and substance in terms of the shapes of the particles it is made of. Thus fire is painful to the touch because of the sharp points of its constituent tetrahedra. But Plato's particles are neater and more mathematical than Democritus' atoms, because those came in an irregular jumble of shapes rather than just Plato's five special ones. Another difference is that Plato's particles are not unsplittable and basic: they are in turn made up of triangles, and the transformations of the elements are to be explained by reference to the recombination of these Pythagorean pieces. It seems that the triangles themselves could in turn be analysed into numbers in some suitably Pythagorean fashion.

This curious mathematical fantasy underlines the biggest difference between Democritus' picture and Plato's, at least as far as the structure of matter is concerned. The ultimate 'building blocks' of Plato's system are not literally building blocks at all. They are not solid, but are ideal, mathematical shapes. This reflects the fact that what Plato's God is up to is not the creation of absolutely new matter out of nothing – no craftsman could achieve that – but the imposition of form and structure in a suitably rational way. He is working with formless (and unexplained) raw material and somehow giving it mathematical shape so that it can turn into sophisticated and well-ordered things. The triangles and regular solids which Timaeus describes are not God's bricks and mortar, but the models on his architect's plans.

God's work is always an uphill struggle. Even when he has made his elements, he cannot altogether bend them to his will. He is not omnipotent. He has to contend with the fixed laws of nature and the intrinsic properties of things. For example, he can choose to make air, but he cannot choose to make it melt earth. Timaeus speaks of God, personifying reason in action, as having to persuade and negotiate with natural forces and hard facts. This recalcitrant side of nature is referred to as 'necessity' (*ananke*), the word used by Democritus to mean the mechanical inevitability of physical causes operating without purpose. Plato's Timaeus acknowledged that there were such causes, but was convinced that this was not the whole story: 'Mind, the ruling power, persuaded necessity to bring the greater part of created things to perfection, and thus . . . through necessity made subject to reason, this universe was created.' Thanks to successful persuasion on the part of reason, necessity agrees – where it has room for manoeuvre – to work in useful ways.

The Master-Craftsman is not the only divine thing in the universe. The astronomical bodies count as divine because they are deathless and self-sufficient, and there are also the junior gods, made by the Craftsman, whom Timaeus half-seriously and somewhat sceptically is prepared to call by the names of Zeus, Chronos, Hera and all the rest. Their job is to take some diluted portions of the 'world-soul' (which the Craftsman ladled out to enable the heavenly bodies to move and to imbue the cosmos with some form of intelligence) and make men out of it. They are to do this by combining some of this divine substance with physical bodies which they are to engineer according to his specifications. The Craftsman tells the junior gods that he feels he had better not do this job himself:

if they were created by me and received life at my hands, they would be on an equality with the gods. In order then that they may be mortal – do ye, according to your natures, betake yourselves to the formation of animals, imitating the power which was shown by me in creating you. The part of them worthy of the name immortal, which is called divine and is the guiding principle of those who are willing to follow justice and you – of that divine part I will myself sow the seed, and having made a beginning, I will hand the work over to you. And do ye then interweave the mortal with the immortal and make and beget living creatures, and give them food and make them grow; and receive them again in death.

There are to be three 'tribes' of these living things: men, women and animals, all riding a cycle of reincarnation. The first generation will all be men, of whom those who lead spiritually inferior lives will come back as women, birds, beasts or (worst of all) fish. Thus the less mathematical side of traditional Pythagoreanism gets a look-in, too.

Every turn of the wheel of reincarnation has its reason. Those of the first-generation men 'who were cowards or led unrighteous lives may with reason be supposed to have changed into the nature of women in the second generation'. Thus reincarnation is held to explain the generally presumed 'fact' that women are less brave and morally upright than men. A similar line of thinking explains the existence of birds, who were 'created out of innocent light-minded men who, although their minds were directed toward heaven, imagined, in their simplicity, that the clearest demonstration of the things above was to be obtained by sight . . . and they grew feathers'. Birds, in other words, are ex-people who had no idea of rational understanding and who thought that the way to understand things was just to get a close-up look at them. So they were sent twittering up to the heavens, where they are physically closer to eternal things and yet further from comprehending them. Animals exist because some people were so far from knowledge that 'they never considered at all about the nature of the heavens', and 'in consequence of these habits of theirs they had their front legs and their heads resting upon the earth to which they were drawn by natural affinity'. As for fish, Timaeus says:

these were made out of the most entirely senseless and ignorant of all, whom the transformers [i.e., *the junior gods*] did not think any longer worthy of pure respiration, because they possessed a soul which was made impure by all sorts of transgression, and instead of the subtle and pure medium of air, they gave them the deep and muddy sea . . . And hence arose the race of fishes and oysters, and other aquatic animals, which have received the most remote habitations as a punishment of their outlandish ignorance.

This moralistic zoology comes at the very end of the dialogue, when Timaeus is letting off steam (what is said about women hardly squares with the equality they are given in the more serious discussions of the *Republic*). Before this fanciful story-telling comes much detailed explanation of human physiology and psychology. Here Plato tried to weave the latest findings of the contemporary medical schools, and some common observations, into his rational scheme of things, explaining the beneficent purpose of each facet of the body. For example, in the course of his treatment of bone, marrow, sinews and flesh, Timaeus says that 'on the joints of the bones, where reason indicated that no more was required, he placed only a thin covering of flesh, that it might not interfere with the flection of our bodies and make them unwieldy because difficult to move'. Among other things, Timaeus goes into stomach-churning detail about various organs and their role in conducting internal negotiations between reason, passion and appetite. Thus the lower intestine is said to be provided in order to hold food for a reasonable length of time, so that we are not perpetually eating and 'thus producing insatiable gluttony and making the whole race an enemy to philosophy and culture'.

Like Democritus, Plato's Timaeus tries to explain human sensation in terms of atomism. The feeling of cold, for example, is said to be caused by large particles of moisture fighting their way into the body, struggling for room with the moisture within and thereby producing shivers and shudders as we are shaken by this battle. As in all the similar accounts by Plato's predecessors, the whole picture of the relation between mental and physical phenomena shows a primitively materialist conception of soul or mind: soul is some sort of material stuff swilling around inside. It may be invisible and somehow more refined than anything else, but it does seem to have physical properties – it gives off 'vapours', for instance. Moral defects and unpleasant sensations are together explained in physical terms (and in a way which is intended to find some truth in Socrates' implausible thesis that nobody does wrong on purpose):

no man is voluntarily bad, but the bad becomes bad by reason of an ill disposition of the body and bad education . . . And in the case of pain, too, in like manner the soul suffers much evil from the body. For where the acid and briny phlegm and other bitter and bilious humours wander about in the body and find no exit or escape, but are pent up within and mingle their own vapours with the motions of the soul, and are blended with them, they produce all sorts of diseases . . . they create infinite varieties of ill temper and melancholy, of rashness and cowardice, and also of forgetfulness and stupidity.

This scheme of semi-liquid 'humours', as popularized by Plato, is one of the many elements of the *Timaeus* that was painted into the common-sense picture of the world at a time when the dialogue was the main source of scientific learning. The fact that the *Timaeus* was so influential inevitably made it a millstone around the neck of Plato's reputation when the ancient and medieval pictures of the world came to be erased. Whatever people believed, they believed because of Plato; therefore whenever they were wrong, it was all Plato's fault. One modern historian of science, George Sarton, wrote that 'the influence of the *Timaios* was enormous and essentially evil' and that it had 'remained to this day' – this was in 1952 – 'a source of obscurity and superstition'. By 'superstition' this writer seems mainly to have been thinking of astrology, the popularity of which he oddly blames on Plato. There is, of course, a great deal in the *Timaeus* of what we can now see to be fantastic rubbish, which is hardly surprising since it was written nearly 2,400 years ago. True, it is a literary dialogue, much of it written in overtly mythological terms, and is thus open to many interpretations. Nevertheless, it does seem to us that it contains plenty of red herrings swimming up the underwater equivalent of blind alleys, and that many of its shortcomings can be traced to Plato's determination to find purpose, order and function in nature. Aristotle's somewhat refined and demythologized version of this project later came to typify all that was wrong in pre-modern science.

How much mischief is the purposeful Master-Craftsman really responsible for? One thing that must be said in his favour, or rather in favour of the conception of nature that he represents, is the impetus he gave to the investigation of the messy details of the world. It is no coincidence that Aristotle, who sought purpose (though not divine purpose) throughout the living world, was the most successful empirical investigator of his day. He was recognized by Darwin as the father of biology – 'Linnaeus and Cuvier have been my two gods . . . but they were mere schoolboys to old Aristotle' – and it is hard to believe that Aristotle would have bothered to get his hands quite so dirty delving in the innards of squid if he had not believed that there were intricate and purposeful mechanisms to be found there. Consider, by contrast, the attitude of one who insisted that nature worked aimlessly and was impelled only by blind causes. Lucretius (*c.*99–*c.*55 BC) frequently inveighed against those like Timaeus who held that natural phenomena should be understood in terms of aims and purposes:

There is a fault in this regard which we earnestly desire you to escape . . .: do not suppose that the clear light of the eyes was made in order that we might be able to see before us; or that the ends of the calves and thighs were jointed and placed upon the foundation of the feet, only to enable us to march forward with long forward strides; that the forearms again were fitted upon sturdy upper arms, and ministering hands given on either side, only that we might able to do what should be necessary for life. Such explanations, and all other such that men give, confuse cause and effect and are based on perverted reasoning.

This anticipation of modern ways of thinking may be philosophically sound, but it is noteworthy – and again, presumably, no coincidence – that Lucretius felt no need to find out more about eyes, calves, thighs and forearms. If, like Aristotle, you believe in something like Plato's purpose-filled account of nature, you have a philosophical incentive to dissect things in order to find evidence for such an account in their intricate functioning. But if, like Lucretius, you are mainly concerned to refute superstitious and theological ideas, there is not much point in going out of your way to lift up stones when all you are going to find underneath them is a teeming mass of inexplicably sophisticated phenomena. At a time when genuine explanations for the complexity of nature (such as Darwin's) were simply not available, the hypothesis of a Master-Craftsman, whether taken literally or metaphorically, could be a useful spur to scientific inquiry.

The same was true to some extent in later, Christian times, when empirical investigations could be glossed as uncovering and thereby glorifying the works of Providence. For example, in the seventeenth century, William Harvey attributed his discovery of the circulation of the blood to his belief in the intelligent design of the human body. Robert Boyle, the great chemist, remembered asking Harvey what had induced him to propose this revolutionary idea:

he answered me that when he took notice that the valves in the veins of so many . . . parts of the body were so placed that they gave free passage to the blood towards the heart, but opposed the passage of the venal blood of the contrary way, he was invited to imagine that so provident a cause as Nature had not so placed so many valves without design; and no design seemed more probable than [*the circulation of the blood*].

Harvey's hunch paid off, so the Master-Craftsman with his rational designs has had his uses, even if he is in fact non-existent.

Even some twentieth-century physicists have found inspiration in the *Timaeus*, not in its talk of purpose or design but in the way it puts mathematics at the heart of cosmology. Thus Werner Heisenberg (1901–76) said that the geometric particles of the *Timaeus* played a crucial role in his own development of the ideas of quantum theory; he was not the only physicist to claim to see parallels between Plato's mathematical account of matter and today's quantum mechanics. And Sir Karl Popper (1902–94) has argued that Plato's most important philosophical achievement was his geometrical theory of the world, which Popper takes to be the common basis of the work of Copernicus, Galileo, Kepler, Newton, Maxwell and Einstein. Perhaps this is reading a little too much into the dialogue, but plenty of others have made up for such exaggerations by reading too little into it instead. Many people, relying on a conventional wisdom about Plato that seems not to be based on the text itself, have said that he dismissed the pursuit of scientific knowledge about the changing world, because he held such knowledge to be inferior to that of the eternal and immutable Forms. Plato did indeed regard the Forms as more important than anything else – the centre of his intellectual universe – just as the devout Newton regarded God as the most important thing in his, later universe. But it no more follows that Plato dismissed science than that Newton did. Timaeus clearly says that: 'A man may sometimes set aside meditations about eternal things, and for recreation turn to consider the truths of generation . . .; he will thus gain a pleasure not to be repented of . . . a wise and moderate pastime.' Plato would hardly have written the *Timaeus* if he had not agreed with his own main character on this point.

By focusing on what seem to be the main conclusions of Plato's most influential dialogues, the *Republic* and the *Timaeus*, we find out something about Plato's deepest beliefs. But we are thereby in danger of obscuring the Socratic side of the man who admired Socrates above all other thinkers. Like Socrates, Plato believed that truth emerged only through dialogue; that is why all his works are at least ostensibly in the form of dialogues, and why all but two of them – one of these exceptions being the *Timaeus* – engage in genuinely exploratory discussions. When he had his Socratic hat on, Plato tried not to lay down the law or be dogmatic.

Sometimes, however, he could not help himself. There were many things he wanted to say, especially to the naturalist philosophers from Thales to Democritus who saw nature as devoid of any real reason or purpose, and to the relativist and subjectivist Sophists. In Plato's view, the errors of the former led to the errors of the latter. It is because his various opponents failed to realize that nature itself in some sense follows a rational pattern that they mistakenly contrasted law, or morality, on the one hand and impersonal nature on the other, as if these were completely different things. For Plato, they are essentially similar because they both embody the workings of reason. As one speaker put it in Plato's last work, the *Laws*, law and morality are 'natural, or no less real than nature, seeing that they are products of mind' – not the human mind, of course, but the mind of nature. The *Timaeus* is supposed to show how nature is a product of intelligence (or at least how it behaves as if it were) since it embodies intelligent adaptation to goals or functions. And the *Republic* is supposed to show how the welfare of man depends on discovering and following the course which the rational construction of nature has made to be in his own ultimate interests. Plato's project was to suggest, by example, how such a discovery might be within man's reach if only he would copy the example of Socrates by pursuing the right questions in the right way.

After his death, Plato's Academy moved back and forth between the two poles of his philosophical personality. Sometimes its leaders defended and developed what they took to be his positive doctrines; at other times they followed the more tentative, questioning and Socratic aspect of his thinking – notably in the so-called 'sceptical' phases of the Academy under the leadership of Arcesilaus (*c*.318–*c*.243 BC) and later of Carneades (*c*.219 *c*.129 BC). Long before that, however, Plato's best pupil, Aristotle, had begun a philosophical movement of his own that overshadows any other Platonic offshoot.

# 12

## The Master of
## Those Who Know:
## *Aristotle*

If Aristotle had never existed, it would be pointless to try to invent him. Nobody would believe that there could have been such a man, and quite right too. Considering the lost works of ancient polymaths such as Democritus and some of the Sophists, one cannot help feeling that even if these men did spread themselves thinly enough to write all the books they are supposed to have done, what was in them cannot have been up to much. The case of Aristotle, however, is different: his surviving works run to almost one and a half million words. There is good reason to think that this is no more than a quarter of what he wrote; all of his works that were polished for publication have been lost, including several dialogues in the style of Plato. But what is left today is more than enough to put him in a class of his own. Any credible description of the impressiveness of his work would be an understatement.

The surviving works are treatises that Aristotle used as the basis of his teaching at a research institute which he set up in Athens in 335 BC, known as the Lyceum. These include books dealing with ethics, political theory, rhetoric, poetry, constitutional history, theology, zoology, meteorology, astronomy, physics, chemistry, scientific method, anatomy, the foundations of mathematics, language, formal logic, techniques of reasoning, fallacies, and other subjects which it will be easier to describe later. There are also works of disputed authorship on 'economics' (this is really about household management) and mechanics, among others. Aristotle's treatises include the first disciplined treatments of what we now call sociology, comparative politics, psychology and literary criticism. His works on politics and poetry, not to mention his more purely abstract philosophical writings, are still studied today. But two of his contributions stand above the others for their originality and power: formal logic, which Aristotle invented from scratch, and biology, of which he was by far the most influential investigator until Darwin evolved.

Aristotle's father was a doctor, and biology was Aristotle's first love. About a fifth of his extant writings describe the physiology and behaviour of some 540 zoological species, based on his own dissections and observations and the reports of others. It is an embarrassment to subsequent zoologists how long it took them to add substantially to Aristotle's painstaking studies, though they have sometimes covered their embarrassment by hooting over the mistakes that inevitably crept into his works. Parts of his accounts of the digestion of ruminants and the reproductive systems of mammals were not bettered until the sixteenth century; some aspects of his approach to the heart and vascular system remained orthodoxy until the eighteenth century; and his descriptions of the habits of octopuses and squid were not improved upon until even more recently.

Like every great scientist, Aristotle was sometimes led astray by hasty generalizations. For example, he concluded that worker bees cannot be female, because they have stings and 'nature does not give weapons for fighting to any female'. He also said that men naturally have more teeth than women. Some people have wondered why he never asked Mrs Aristotle to open her mouth so that he could check. But few adults of either sex would have had a full complement of teeth in those days. Aristotle seems to have been misled by his observations of cows, bulls, stags and does, in which the male does indeed have more impressive equipment. In general, Aristotle's successes were more remarkable than his failures. One modern history of embryology lists fourteen of Aristotle's most important findings in this area, of which it says eleven are true and three false. On a couple of biological points about which Aristotle was for centuries regarded as having been mistaken (concerning a species of dog-fish and a type of squid, among others), he has actually turned out to be right.

The science of formal logic is a very different sort of investigation to zoology. Plenty of people enjoy observing animals, but most people are unnerved by formal logic – if they ever come across it. Logic does not involve any of the careful description of nature that Aristotle loved, but it does involve the sort of rigorous classification that he used in biology. He put this skill to good effect by sorting and sifting various types of logical inference, which nobody else seems to have even thought of doing before. It was Aristotle's logical researches that ultimately led to the development of digital computers and computer-languages, via a twisting road in the history of mathematics that passes through several interesting landmarks and oddities, including a demented mystic from Majorca who designed a machine for converting infidels after the Crusades had failed, and an extremely boring board-game invented by Lewis Carroll. When a nineteenth-century scientist, John Herschel, wrote that 'speculations apparently the most unprofitable have almost invariably been those from which the greatest practical applications have emanated' he did not yet know of what is perhaps the outstanding example of this, namely the applications of formal logic. Everybody knows what computers are; what exactly logic is will be explained later.

We may be impressed by Aristotle, but educated people of late medieval times ate, drank and breathed him. For hundreds of years, secular higher education consisted largely of imbibing and commenting on his treatises. When Dante (1265–1321) referred in his *Divine Comedy* to 'the master of those who know' there was no need to mention Aristotle by name. More than 300 years later, Descartes could still say, grumpily: 'How fortunate that man was: whatever he wrote, whether he gave it much thought or not, is regarded by most people today as having oracular authority.' Aristotle still leaves his mark in the twentieth century, not by the survival of his main doctrines but in the fossils of his concepts which are left in our language and in our thought. The following notions, for example, derive from him, mostly via Latin translation: potential, dynamics, energy, substance, quality, essence and category.

These concepts and many more are echoes of the medieval university lecture room, which was itself echoing Aristotle. The extent of his influence in those dim halls of scholasticism may be gauged from the fact that for a number of centuries, fundamental criticism of him was largely confined to whispering at the back of the classroom while old Aristotle droned on at the blackboard. In 1641 Descartes wrote privately to a friend, to whom he was sending some new work:

I may tell you, between ourselves, that these six *Meditations* contain all the foundations of my physics. But please do not tell people, for that might make it harder for supporters of Aristotle to approve them. I hope that readers will gradually get used to my principles, and recognize their truth, before they notice that they destroy the principles of Aristotle.

The scientific backlash against Aristotle, when it came, was sometimes vicious and often exaggerated. A poet and dabbling scientist, John Dryden, wrote the following lines in the year of his election to the Royal Society, one of the earliest of the European organizations dedicated to clearing away Aristotelian scholasticism and furthering new knowledge:

> The longest tyranny that ever swayed
> Was that wherein our ancestors betrayed
> Their free-born reason to the Stagirite [*Aristotle*],
> And made his torch their universal light.

It was Aristotle's chemistry, physics and cosmology that fell loudest and hardest in the seventeenth century, to the blows of men such as Galileo and Boyle. Aristotle's science, except for his biology, was condemned as not just barking up the wrong tree but lost in the wrong forest. So indeed it was. But plenty of the seventeenth century's anti-Aristotelian invective unfairly branded him with the sins of his slavish and inferior followers. This is particularly true of the attacks by Francis Bacon (1561–1626), a hero of the Royal Society whose writings served as a rallying point for the scientific revolutionaries.

Bacon is still often described as a prophet of the scientific revolution, though he frequently did not know what he was talking about and had a remarkable ability for looking the wrong way when something interesting was going on. By all appearances he would not have noticed a major scientific discovery even if it had, like Newton's proverbial apple, hit him on the head. He overlooked the work of his own doctor, William Harvey, who discovered the circulation of the blood; he condemned the theory of magnetism propounded by his acquaintance, William Gilbert, as occult nonsense; he ignored Galileo and Kepler because he failed to understand their mathematics, and he could not see the point of Copernicus. Nevertheless, as a propagandist he had an honourable role in turning the tide against the old world-view of Aristotle and scholasticism.

Bacon made two main criticisms of Aristotle. First, he claimed that Aristotle's physics was terminally diseased with malignant concepts and crippled theories. Bacon was right about that (though in fact he never shook off some of them himself). Second, he claimed that Aristotle habitually ignored facts and disdained observation because of his blind adherence to the theories he had cooked up. This was the most influential of Bacon's criticisms and it is entirely wrong, though it is still often endorsed by people who do not bother to read Aristotle before repeating it.

Here is Aristotle himself, just after he has drawn the mistaken conclusion about worker bees quoted above:

Such appears to be the truth about the generation of bees, judging from theory and from what are believed to be the facts about them; the facts, however, have not yet been sufficiently grasped; if ever they are, then credit must be given rather to observation than to theories, and to theories only if what they affirm agrees with the observed facts.

In general, he wrote elsewhere, 'We must survey what we have already said, bringing it to the test of the facts of life, and if it harmonizes with the facts we must accept it, but if it clashes with them we must suppose it to be mere theory.' This is not just a pious statement of intent; it is exactly what Aristotle tried to do in all his extant scientific work. The truth is that Aristotle was moved by the same open-minded curiosity as the members of the Royal Society, but because they thought of themselves as revolutionaries they had to convince themselves otherwise. What needed updating was not so much the methods of Aristotle as his conclusions, which, since he had been dead for 2,000 years, he was unable to do for himself. It was not his fault that later thinkers turned his conjectures into their dogmas.

Galileo understood this better than Bacon. He acknowledged that Aristotle 'not only admitted experience among the ways of forming conclusions about physical problems, but even gave it first place'. Consider the case of sunspots, whose discovery was a cruel splash of acid on the Aristotelian world-picture (this picture had been venerated for over a thousand years by Galileo's time). Aristotle had noted that 'in the whole range of times past, so far as our inherited records reach, no change appears to have taken place in the outermost heaven'. That is to say, nothing much ever seemed to happen to the stars. Aristotle provisionally concluded from this that the only form of change to be found outside the earth's atmosphere was uniform circular motion, and that there was therefore a radical difference between the turbulent earthly realm and the serene and unblemished heavens. This idea turned out to suit the religious purposes of the Middle Ages very well, for such a division between heaven and earth seemed to be echoed by Scripture. But when Galileo looked through his telescope and saw irregular sunspots besmirching the surface of the sun, he realized that the heavens were not so perfect and immutable after all. He also realized that Aristotle would have changed his mind about the earth and the heavens if only 'his knowledge had included our present sensory evidence'. The medieval philosopher-priests would then have had to base their religious fantasy on something else. Of course, nobody can prove that Aristotle would definitely have changed his mind if he had seen what Galileo saw. But neither is there much reason to suppose that he would have refused to do so.

There was, however, one genuinely revolutionary difference between Aristotle's approach to scientific knowledge and the one that was successfully championed by Bacon. It lay in the two men's attitudes to technology. Aristotle had no conception of such a thing: for him, the knowledge of nature was a desirable end in itself and had nothing to do with inventing labour-saving gadgets. Bacon, by contrast, was the prophet of the technological society. He may not have understood much science, but he knew what he wanted and he dimly perceived that science was the way to get it. Mother Nature had to be mastered and put to work for the benefit of man. In the course of campaigning for this novel project, Bacon urged the need for more experiments, more systematic observation and more scientific co-operation. None of these things was exactly new in itself, but his exertions on their behalf were a useful corrective to medieval tradition.

Bacon gave a lot of thought to the methods of winkling out and evaluating the data of empirical inquiry. Unfortunately he was not very good at it himself, but his principles are sound, as far as they go. He believed that in propounding them he was offering a new technique which would replace the canons of scientific method advocated by Aristotle. Bacon believed, as generations believed before him, that Aristotle had proclaimed science to be simply a matter of concocting a few plausible-sounding general principles and then deducing as much as you can from them without bothering to check the facts. This rumour took hold at a time when the only available works of Aristotle were parts of some of his treatises on logic, and it is based on mis-readings of them. What Aristotle was held to have said is not what he actually said.

That goes for many of the subjects he wrote about and is often still true today. For example, many students of drama believe that Aristotle stipulated that a good tragedy should observe the so-called 'three unities' of place, time and action (roughly, that it should depict one main action, happening in one place, and occurring over a period that is no longer than the performance itself). In fact these rules were invented by a seventeenth-century Italian critic in a commentary on Aristotle. Aristotle himself would not have recognized them. Nor would he have recognized some of the bizarre cosmology and physics which have been foisted on him. According to one layman's guide to science, Aristotle held that the human race is the purpose for the existence of the whole universe – i.e., that everything exists for the sake of man. This is complete fiction, but it is par for the course. Even a respected history of science asserts that Aristotle explained the acceleration of falling objects by arguing that a plummeting body 'moved more jubilantly every moment because it found itself nearer home'. There are many strange-sounding things in Aristotle, but that is not one of them; he offered a respectably mechanical, though incorrect, explanation for acceleration. The list of misrepresentations of him could go on and on.

If someone is persistently misinterpreted, it is usually his own fault. It is probably because his writings are confused, contradictory, badly constructed or all three. Aristotle's treatises are not entirely free of any of these defects. But his good excuse for a long tradition of eccentric interpretation is that his writings were not prepared for publication, and that translations of them (often second-hand, via Arabic and other languages) trickled out in a confusing form. It was often hard to understand the parts until they could be seen in the context of the whole. This does not excuse the odd things people still sometimes say about Aristotle today. But such is the reward of being so famously influential that few bother to read what you actually wrote.

'The master of those who know' – often just called 'the Philosopher' in late medieval times – was born in a backwater, the undistinguished town of Stagira in northern Greece, in 384 BC. His father was hereditary court-physician to Amyntas II, King of Macedonia, and if his father had not died young, Aristotle might well have carried on the family trade and become a doctor himself. As things turned out, he went to Athens at the age of seventeen and joined Plato's Academy, where he stayed for the next twenty years. Although he seems to have been an enthusiastic follower of Plato at first, he moved far beyond him later on. 'Plato is dear to me,' he is supposed to have said, 'but truth is dearer still.' Perhaps it was because Plato wanted a more orthodox suc-

ARISTOTELES.

cessor than Aristotle that his star pupil was passed over for the headship of the Academy when Plato died in 347 BC; the job went instead to Plato's nephew, Speusippus. Aristotle left Athens at this point and stayed away for twelve years. In 343 BC, family connections at the Macedonian court got him the job of tutor to Alexander the Great, who at that time was not great at all but only thirteen. Much of Aristotle's biological fieldwork was done during his travels of this period. It is said that when Alexander later became king, he used his power to help his old tutor get specimens: 'Orders were given to some thousands of people throughout the whole of Asia Minor and Greece . . . to see that he [*Aristotle*] was informed about any creature born in any region.' In 335, a year after Alexander was crowned, Aristotle returned to Athens and set up the Lyceum while his former pupil set off on his conquests. Aristotle stayed in Athens teaching, supervising research and writing his treatises for the next thirteen years.

When Alexander died in 323 BC there was an anti-Macedonian revolt in Athens; like other city-states, Athens had come increasingly under the sway of Macedonia during Alexander's reign. Aristotle, who was too close to the Macedonian regime for comfort, was indicted on trumped-up charges of impiety and left Athens before he could be brought to trial. After what had happened to Socrates, it is said that he did not want to let the Athenians 'sin twice against philosophy'. He died in exile a year later.

Few of Aristotle's treatises are easy to read today, but his methodical style is almost disconcertingly up to date when compared with the writings of any earlier Greek. Aristotle writes like a modern-day professor, which is no coincidence because today's academics are direct descendants of a line that dutifully copied his approach. He usually starts by defining his subject-matter and saying precisely which questions he is out to answer. Then he looks at earlier answers, untangles them and weighs up objections. He draws distinctions to try to unstitch ambiguities and confusions, gives his verdict on which problems remain to be solved, argues for some answers of his own, says where he thinks their limitations lie, relates them to his accounts of other topics and then recaps. It can be hard work to cope with the deluge of arguments that pour off Aristotle's pages, but at least you always know roughly what he is trying to do.

Marching through each intellectual battlefield, Aristotle was optimistic about the possibility of winning knowledge. He had no time for self-confessed 'sceptics' who say that one must always suspend judgement because truth is unattainable. 'All men by nature desire to know,' he said, and he had little doubt that this desire could eventually be fulfilled. He believed that people have 'a natural instinct for what is true, and usually do arrive at the truth'.

Nevertheless, Aristotle was far from satisfied with the way in which his philosophical predecessors had looked for truth. They often asked the wrong kinds of questions, he said, and they sometimes muddled up different sorts of questions. According to Aristotle, there are four main things one should ask about something, and they need to be kept distinct. First, what is it made of? Second, what is its form (i.e., structure)? Third, what purpose does it serve? And lastly, what made it come into being or made it change? Only the last of these corresponds to the modern idea of a 'cause', but all four are usually referred to together as 'Aristotle's four causes' – the material, formal, final and efficient cause, respectively. To illustrate these four, consider a house. Its material causes are such things as bricks, mortar, wood and stone. Its formal cause is the arrangement of these components to fit a certain overall design. The final cause (or purpose) of the house is to provide shelter for people. And its efficient cause is its builder. This fourfold schema can be applied to all sorts of natural phenomena, not just to artefacts.

The earliest philosophers, according to Aristotle, paid too much attention to material causes and not enough to anything else. Whenever they wanted to explain something, they simply named their favourite substance – water, air, fire, or whatever – and seem to have been unsure what to do next. This is why they did not get very far. The reason why early accounts of the mind or soul seem so crude is that the only question which the early philosophers asked about it was what sort of stuff it was made of.

The Pythagoreans, by contrast, paid not too much attention to material causes but too little. They discovered some interesting answers to questions about form – in particular, they found how mathematical ideas can explain the structure or configuration of things – and then, in their enthusiasm, they ignored material causes in favour of these formal ones. That is why they seemed crazily to suggest that everything is numbers. Laudable though their mathematical ideas were, the Pythagoreans seem not to have realized that it was also necessary to go and find out about what sort of stuff things are made of, i.e. about material causes. To get the whole picture, one had to look at all four types of cause and not get too bogged down in any one of them.

As Aristotle saw it, one particularly serious flaw in the thought of many earlier philosophers, especially Democritus, is that they failed to notice the importance of final causes or purposes. In effect, Democritus answered all questions about material, formal and efficient causes by talking about variously shaped atoms careering through the void.

What are things made of? Atoms. What explains their forms? It is all a matter of atoms. What makes them move or change? Other atoms. But Democritus explicitly rejected any talk of purposes. And from Aristotle's point of view, this was a big mistake. To leave out the question of what something is for, of what its function is, is to fail to explain a great deal about it. One can see why a keen biologist like Aristotle would feel this lack particularly strongly. How can you explain the parts of plants or animals if you do not address the question of what functions these parts perform?

Plato did not make Democritus' mistake of ignoring such final causes. We have seen that he was so eager to stress the role of purpose in nature that he spoke of a Master-Craftsman organizing it all. But, according to Aristotle, although Plato appreciated the importance of final causes, he got into a frightful muddle about formal ones. The whole theory of Platonic Forms was the result of a confusion about what form was. As we have seen, for Plato the Form of something – the Form of a table or the Form of something beautiful – is a sort of non-physical entity that is separate from any particular table or beautiful thing. The fact that a certain arrangement of materials is a bed is explained by the fact that it is an imperfect copy of the Form of Bed. Likewise with beautiful things: Plato makes his mouthpiece, 'Socrates', say that a beautiful object 'is beautiful because it partakes of that absolute beauty, and for no other reason'. Aristotle was much too down-to-earth to be attracted by this sort of talk. To say that there are such Forms or absolutes is, Aristotle wrote, 'to speak abstractly and idly'. They do not really explain anything. For this and other reasons, he insisted that the form of something should not be thought of as a separate object that is somehow twinned with it. It is more like an aspect or feature of the object, not something that exists in its own right.

Aristotle used this conception of form to provide a new theory of the soul's relation to the body. He did not think of the soul as some sort of ghostly substance temporarily occupying the body, as in the Orphic type of belief adopted by Plato. Instead he thought of it as whichever arrangement of physical characteristics makes the body alive and capable of perception and thought. In other words, to have a soul was to have a body that was organized so that it worked in certain ways. In one sense, then, Aristotle was a materialist, because he denied that what made a person alive and human was the presence of any substance other than matter. Matter was the only stuff involved. On the other hand, he certainly did not think that the answer to the question 'What is the soul?' was simply 'A lump of flesh'. To say this would be to repeat the mistake of the earliest philosophers, like Thales, who never distinguished between form and matter. Having a soul is a question of form, not of matter, so to ask what sort of stuff the soul is made of is to miss the point. Similarly, Aristotle argued, 'we can dismiss as unnecessary the question whether the soul and the body are one: it is as though we were to ask whether [*a piece of*] wax and its shape are one'.

There was, however, still a glimmer of old Plato's ideas in some of what Aristotle said about the soul. Plato thought that people had a divine spark in them which existed before birth and would continue after death. This spark, the soul, was somehow connected with the faculty of reason, which we have seen to be in some sense the governing principle both of the universe as a whole and of the life of the happy and virtuous man in Platonic philosophy. Aristotle, too, held that reason is the best thing in us. In his ethical writings, he argued that exercising this faculty provides the path to the highest happiness. So far, so good. But he also said that reason is the one immortal part of the soul. How can this be? Since the soul is, for Aristotle, the form of the living body, it follows that it cannot exist either before or after the body does. The soul must cease to exist when the body dies – just as the shape imprinted on a piece of wax melts away when the wax itself melts. So the immortality of reason, whatever exactly it amounts to, cannot provide any sort of personal immortality. It is not clear why Aristotle spoke of reason as immortal. One can only assume that the idea is a deep splinter of Platonism in his flesh.

This is one of several points at which echoes of the master's doctrines can be heard in the pupil's writings. Although Aristotle rejected Plato's division of reality into one inferior realm occupied by ordinary physical objects and another superior one occupied by the ideal Forms, there are still traces of the old Platonic scheme of two worlds. Aristotle's distantly visible heaven is sometimes reminiscent of Plato's invisible realm of Forms. When Aristotle speaks of 'the loftier interest of the heavenly things that are the objects of the higher philosophy', you would hardly guess that he was talking about astronomy. It sounds more like Plato singing the praises of the ideal Forms that his philosophers are supposed to study.

Modern popular books about space often begin with similar high-flown talk. They usually express awe at the immensity of the universe when compared with our humble immediate surroundings. In Aristotle's case, though, it was not the size but the apparent perfection of the heavens that impressed him. For him, astronomy was much more than just another branch of science, because astronomical bodies (except the earth, comets and meteors) were regular in their motions, unblemished, unchanging, eternal and therefore divine. This made them quite unlike the objects studied by the more lowly branches of knowledge such as biology or terrestrial mechanics. Stable and unchanging things were higher up the cosmic scale of perfection. It was typical of Aristotle to think in terms of such a scale; he was always keen to discover hierarchies. When left alone with a pile of intellectual bricks, his playful mind always built them up into a pyramid, and usually found an especially good one to balance on top. At the top of the pyramid of mortal living things was man; at the top of the pyramid of mental faculties was reason; and at the top of the pyramid of physics teetered the immutable heavenly bodies.

Thus, like Parmenides, and like Plato, Aristotle seems to have thought that to be unchanging and eternal is to be intrinsically superior. Yet when it came to the question of knowledge of mundane and mortal things, Aristotle disagreed utterly with Parmenides and was not really on Plato's wavelength either. Parmenides said that there just were no such things, so there was nothing to know about them. All that existed was the unchanging One. Although Plato did not go that far, he did think that knowledge of the unchanging Forms was better than any other sort of knowledge. In principle, Aristotle agreed with Plato that the knowledge of mundane things was somehow inferior. But only in principle. In addition to the fact that Aristotle's 'superior' knowledge was about astronomy, not about abstract Forms, he also recognized that however desirable the knowledge of unchanging things might be in theory, it seemed to be very hard to get any of it in practice. So one had to make do with mundane knowledge, and look on the bright side:

Of substances constituted by nature some are ungenerated, imperishable, and eternal, while others are subject to generation and decay. The former are excellent and divine, but less accessible to knowledge. The evidence that might throw light on them is furnished but scantily by sensation; whereas respecting perishable plants and animals we have abundant information, living as we do in their midst, and ample data may be collected concerning their various kinds, if only we are willing to take sufficient pains ... in certitude and completeness our knowledge of terrestrial things has the advantage.

Aristotle and his students at the Lyceum did their best to exploit this advantage by collecting, sorting and trying to explain the abundant information that lay around them, not just in biology but wherever the means existed to satisfy man's natural 'desire to know'. In addition to their scientific work, they amassed the details of 158 political constitutions, made collections of barbarian customs and beliefs, com piled sporting almanacs (an important form of history in those days), histories of philosophy and records of dramatic and musical perform- ances. Aristotle was also a renowned collector of books; the Lyceum seems to have had a collection of anatomical diagrams, maps and perhaps biological specimens as part of its library.

What Aristotle says in praise of his favourite study, zoology, illus- trates the fundamental difference between him and Plato. Plato had a pessimistic attitude to the everyday world. Everything in it seemed to him to fall pathetically short of the standards set by the ideal Forms. The philosopher's job was to convince people of this depressing fact and persuade them to transcend this world, at least in their own minds, and learn to love the Forms instead. Aristotle, by contrast, was an optimist. While Plato wanted to leave the dark Cave of physical reality and find something better, Aristotle said that the Cave was not so bad once you turned the lights on – particularly if you started dissecting the animals in it. The beauty which Plato appreciated best in unrealized, unworldly ideals, Aristotle saw all around him.

It was worth studying even the lowliest living things, 'for each and all will reveal to us something natural and something beautiful'. What particularly struck Aristotle was the fact that 'absence of haphazard and conduciveness of everything to an end are to be found in nature's works in the highest degree'. By 'conduciveness to an end', what he had in mind was the way many things in the living world are apparently arranged so as to work towards a goal. They can be explained in terms of his 'final causes'. For example, the parts of an eye all work together in such a way as to produce sight. So seeing seems to be the final cause, or purpose, of an eye – its parts do what they do 'for the sake of' sight, as Aristotle often put it, and that is the key to understanding them. Lions have sharp teeth for the sake of killing and tearing meat; plants send their roots downwards, rather than upwards, for the sake of reaching moisture; and so on. Aristotle acknowledged that not everything in the natural world could be described in this fashion. Some features of living things are not 'for the sake of' anything. They are the way they are by accident and for no reason. But to Aristotle it was striking how much of the world appeared not to be the product of blind chance.

He foresaw an objection to this way of talking. Perhaps the wonders of biology were really an accident and the appearance of purpose was illusory:

why shouldn't nature work, not for the sake of something, nor because it is better so, but just as the sky rains? The gods do not send rain in order to make the corn grow: it comes of necessity. The vapour that is drawn up is bound to cool, and, having cooled, to turn into water and come down again. That the corn grows when this has happened is merely coincidental – Why should it not be the same with the parts in nature, e.g., that our teeth should come up of necessity – the front teeth sharp, good for tearing, the molars broad and useful for grinding down the food – merely [*as*] a coincident result?

Aristotle rejected this alternative account as just too improbable: 'For teeth and all other natural things either invariably or for the most part come about in a given way; but of not one of the results of chance or spontaneity is this true.' It might happen by accident that some creatures were born blessed by fortunate features, but surely not to such an extent and with such almost invariable regularity. If chance were responsible for well-designed teeth, for example, it ought also to have produced plenty of hopelessly bad ones too. Yet if you look around you, you see precious little of such hit-and-miss diversity.

Aristotle was essentially right about this: it is no accident that nature is so regularly beneficent. For example, the fact that sharp teeth are good for lions to hunt and eat with is indeed part of the explanation for why they have them, and this is mainly what Aristotle was getting at. He was sure that usefulness played a role in biological explanations, though he did not know the real reason why this was so, because he did not know about Darwinian natural selection. In the case of lions, for example, what Aristotle did not realize was that lions with sharp teeth will have flourished at the expense of less fortunate ones and will consequently have outbred them, so that the lions he observed will have been the descendants of the fortunate ones and will consequently have their good teeth. Add in these crucial Darwinian details, and you see why the fact that such teeth serve a useful purpose helps to explain why today's lions have them. Aristotle was stumbling along the right track.

Having the Darwinian details does not mean that we can do without Aristotle's final causes. Quite the reverse: the mechanism of natural selection spells out how nature involves final causes, not how it can dispense with them. This fact has been obscured by the religious and obscurantist uses to which Aristotle's secular and basically simple concept of final causes have been put. Darwinian natural selection does indeed show how it is unnecessary to postulate any sort of God, or occult mechanism, or conscious intelligence in biological nature in order to account for its generally beneficent working. But Aristotle's final causes never involved any of those things in the first place. Later 'Aristotelian' theologians certainly invoked such things, and would have found some support in Plato for doing so, but that is another matter. Aristotle himself took pains to insist that when he said that a physiological feature of plants or animals was 'for the sake of' some goal or purpose, he did not mean that there was any sort of conscious deliberation or planning going on – not on the part of the creature itself, nor on the part of God or personified Nature. Bacon, and many others since, have said that Aristotelian final causes are a piece of juvenile rubbish that has to be cleared out of the way before any grown-up science can move in. This may be true of the pseudo-Aristotelian final causes of some of his followers, but not of Aristotle's own.

To get clear about what Aristotle himself meant by final causes, it helps to know what he thought their scope was. He held that explanations in terms of purpose could work in just three sorts of ways. First there were the intelligent actions of living things, such as when an animal pursues some prey in order to eat it, or when a man goes for a walk because he wants some exercise. The animal had a meal in mind, the man some air. That is why they did what they did. Nobody has any problem with that sort of 'purpose', or 'final cause'. Equally uncontroversial is the second class of final causes: those involving artefacts, such as a house. The reason why we can speak of final causes, or purposes, in explaining why a house has, say, a certain sort of roof is that the person who built it will have had certain aims. Like the hungry animal or the health-conscious person, he will have had a plan and a purpose in mind. He may have built it that way in order to keep the rain out, for example, in which case we can say that the roof is the way it is 'for the sake of' protecting its inhabitants from rain. Nothing odd about that either. The third class of final causes is the one that fills the pages of Aristotle's biology. It covers the explanation of those features of living things that perform some useful function for the creature concerned, such as the intricacies of the eye, the shape of the teeth or the root-system of a plant. As Aristotle stressed, the big difference between this physiological sort of case and the other two is that it does not involve any mental activity, e.g., any goal envisaged by a living creature. Nevertheless, eyes, teeth and roots do serve a purpose for the organisms of which they are part, even if that purpose is not part of any conscious plan; and you cannot understand the way they work unless you understand what they are doing. This is what Aristotle realized, and why his biological explanations spoke of final causes. He did not know *why* the parts of the eye exist and function 'for the sake of sight' – he just knew that they did.

One should not be misled by the terminology of 'final' causes into thinking that Aristotle regarded them as in any sense ultimate. To him they were the most beautiful sorts of causes to apprehend, but he certainly did not think that once one had found the final causes of a phenomenon, everything else was unimportant. Other things would still remain to be investigated, such as its 'causes' in the modern sense of the word, i.e., the prior circumstances which brought it about. He was not trying to abolish these 'efficient' causes and replace them with final ones. Nor were Aristotle's final causes ultimate in the sense that they revealed some overall plan of the universe. Many later thinkers believed that the universe was created by God for man's benefit and that He had arranged things to serve the purposes of His favourite creatures. Certain animals and plants, for example, existed for man to eat (it was in this spirit that a British clergyman argued in 1836 that God had laid down the earth's deposits of coal so that man could eventually burn them). But all this was entirely foreign to Aristotle's way of thinking. There were no such links between different species in his universe – and besides, as we shall see, Aristotle's God would not have cared two hoots for man. Very occasionally, Aristotle wrote loosely in ways that gave an excuse for such odd ideas, though only a very slight one. Sometimes he wrote as if nature were an intelligent being who designed the wondrous mechanisms of biology. But the contexts make it plain that he was speaking figuratively, as contemporary biologists also frequently do in a similar way. Construed literally, such an idea does not fit the body of his work at all. Admittedly, Aristotle once casually wrote that plants 'exist for the sake of' animals and that animals exist for the sake of man. But again the context shows that he did not mean to imply anything more than that the one lot could, as it happens, make good use of the other, for example by eating them.

The upshot of all this is that when the scientific revolutionaries of the seventeenth century rejected the purpose-filled universe of their medieval predecessors, they were not really overthrowing Aristotle but rather returning to him. When Descartes said, 'I consider the customary search for final causes to be totally useless in physics,' he was not disagreeing with Aristotle, though he probably thought that he was. In biology, his talk of one thing being 'for the sake of' another reflected nothing more mysterious than his conviction that questions of function and organization were more interesting than the crude sorts of questions about matter that obsessed the first *physici*.

Once the true Aristotle has been fished out of the 'Aristotelianism' of the Middle Ages (and sometimes beyond), it can be seen that there is very little in his conception of the purposefulness of nature that cannot be accommodated by modern scientific ways of thinking. Except for one thing. It is a rather big thing, though its oddity turns out to have more to do with Aristotle's conception of what is living and what is inanimate than with his ideas about purpose. Aristotle thought that the motion of at least some astronomical bodies could be explained in terms of a purpose, namely their desire for God – 'the love that moves the Sun and the other stars', as Dante put it in the closing words of the *Divine Comedy*. Comic this certainly seems to be, in a rather different sense from the one intended by Dante. How does love move a star? At first sight this seems to throw away all the sensible things Aristotle said about final causes. It apparently supports the traditional picture of him as someone who held an occult view of nature in which the behaviour of a simple physical object, such as the fall of a stone, could be explained in terms of its desires or aims. Indeed, what he wrote about the movements of the heavenly bodies is a major reason for the popularity of that interpretation of him.

But it is still a misinterpretation. The crucial fact is that Aristotle regarded stars and planets as more like animals than like stones. Unlike stones, they were alive. If they were alive, they might be capable of a sort of mental activity. And given this idea – bizarre in itself to us, but less so if, like any ancient Greek, your notion of divinity quite naturally covers the stars – it is not so strange that he should also have regarded them as capable of being motivated by desires. The love that moves the stars is thus like the appetites which make animals move towards their prey. The actions of the stars are influenced by their love of God just as people's actions are influenced by their earthly paramours. Whatever other criticisms one may make of this story, what Aristotle says about the heavenly bodies is at least consistent with the rest of his perfectly sensible account of final causes.

One might well wonder, though, how he came to talk about the love-lives of stars in the first place. Aristotle often said that his conclusions on astronomical matters were tentative, and this was the most provisional part of all. Nevertheless, he felt driven to these remarkable ideas about God and love and stars by the rest of his physics, and in particular by what seemed to him to be powerful considerations about the nature of motion and change. The love that moves the stars was a consequence he simply could not see how to avoid. Aristotle had painted himself into a corner.

This was partly because he wanted to be in that particular corner.

The vague idea that there is a God who somehow contributes to the activities or nature of the universe was, Aristotle thought, a belief so widely held that it counted as one of the accepted facts which it was the business of a good scientist to explain. The then-common belief that the heavens were in some sense alive was similarly indubitable. It was impossible to believe that practically everybody could be wrong about such things. If the best physical theories he could think of pointed in that direction – and the God they led to was pretty minimal as supreme beings go, which suited Aristotle's relatively relaxed religious opinions – then all the better from every point of view. There are a few places in which his physics seems to be distorted by stretching to reach this predetermined theological conclusion, but not many of them. On the whole, Aristotle's picture of the universe fits together very neatly, which is one main reason why it proved to be so popular. I shall now look at the outlines of that picture, leading up to Aristotle's extraordinary romantic finale in the heavens.

For Aristotle, physics was the study of change. Its first task was to steer a middle course between the absurdities of Parmenides, who thought there was no such thing, and those of Heraclitus, who seems to have thought there was little else. To find an account that avoided these unhelpful extremes, Aristotle went back to the basics by asking what exactly a 'change' is. It must always involve three things, he said: something which changes, a state to which it changes, and a state from which it changes. Consider a bowl of cold water that is being heated: we have the bowl of water and we have the two states of cold and hot, the change being the water's switch from the former state to the latter one. Not all changes are exactly like this example; the states need not involve tangible qualities like heat and cold. In addition to changes of quality, there are also changes of place (i.e., motion), changes of quantity (i.e., growth or diminution) and changes of substance (i.e., generation or destruction, birth or death). But in each type of change you have the same three essential components: something which changes, plus the 'before' and 'after' states.

This gives Aristotle the basis for improving on Heraclitus. Heraclitus had had a great deal to say about the ubiquity of change, but precious little to say about what it was that did the changing (e.g., the bowl of water). This omission is as odd as Lewis Carroll's disappearing Cheshire cat, which left its smile long after its face had gone. You cannot have a smile without something to do the smiling. Similarly, if there is change going on, there must be something which is changing. This must in some respect stay the same during the change, so change always involves some sort of stability. Even if a bowl of water changes its temperature, it still remains a bowl of water. It follows that complete flux – i.e., the total absence of stability – cannot be the basis of nature in the way Heraclitus seems to have held that it was. That would imply a smile without a cat.

Change involves not only the notion of stability but also of potential, because there are limits to what can change into what. A seed can turn into a plant but not into a statue; it is a potential plant but not a potential statue. In general, when a piece of matter changes from one state to another, what happens is that a potential state becomes an actual one. These now-familiar twinned notions of potentiality and actuality were invented by Aristotle, and they provided a main part of his answer to Parmenides. For various reasons, Parmenides had held that *being* cannot come from *not-being* and that this impossibility is precisely what 'change' – ludicrous concept that it was – seemed to imply. But Aristotle argued that this talk of *being* and *not-being* was too crude and vague. What change involved was a passage from potentiality to actuality, and only in that clear and unproblematic sense was it a passage from *not-being* to *being*. First the water is potentially hot, then it is actually hot. First the seed is potentially a tree, then it is actually a tree. No logical mystery there.

Having clarified the notion of change and made it intellectually respectable, Aristotle proceeded to look more closely at the material factors involved. What exactly is the material stuff which changes? The atoms of Democritus and Leucippus were no good, because matter was infinitely divisible (or so Aristotle argued) and thus there simply were no such ultimate particles. Plato's geometrical atoms were even worse, because they were abstract, non-material things which should never really have strayed into this part of physics in the first place. They belonged in pure mathematics. So Aristotle went back to something like the old Milesian 'opposites' of hot, cold, moist and dry; this seemed to be the basic set of qualities involved in all the changes to be seen on earth and in the atmosphere. They at least were something you could get down to work with.

The four possible pairings of these qualities yielded Empedocles' four elements: fire (hot and dry), water (cold and moist), earth (cold and dry) and air (hot and moist). Everyday objects, including living things, were mixtures of these four, and each object behaved according to the characteristics of the element that predominated in it. Unlike Empedocles' elements, each of Aristotle's had the potential to turn into any other when the four basic qualities shuffled around – for example, when moist things dried out, warm things cooled down, and so on. That is one reason why alchemy flourished in medieval times, for nothing Aristotle said ruled out the possibility of base metals turning into gold if the conditions were right. Aristotle, however, was not interested in getting rich through physics. He just wanted to explain the workings of natural things. The principal engine of change in the various transformations of elements was the heat of the sun. This was the first observable link in the chain of change that stirred up everything else and produced the interplay of the four basic opposites.

Measurement played little part in this system of physics, which is the main reason why it is such a dead-end. Aristotle's juggling of his elements was an impressive feat at times, but the show was bound to get boring after a while because there was no way to take it any further. He dealt primarily in absolutes – hot/cold, up/down, heavy/light, and so on – not in measurable matters of degree, and as long as he was wedded to the idea of such absolute opposites it was impossible for his concepts of physical qualities to become scientifically exact. Where Aristotle's books on physics soar is in their discussions of the concepts of time, space, motion and infinity, which include some proposed solutions to Zeno's paradoxes. These more abstract areas were for one thing more susceptible to a treatment that was at least partly mathematical. His account of dynamics, for example, presents the first quantitative laws attempting to link the factors governing the speed of moving objects. The results are famously wrong, largely because Aristotle stuck too closely to the data of common-sense observation, without introducing enough of the sort of idealizations that Newton found so useful (such as that of frictionless movement in a perfect vacuum).

Aristotle's failure to make an imaginative leap and develop anything more like Newtonian or Galilean mechanics had more to do with a desire to stay true to the facts than with the sort of disregard for them alleged by his seventeenth-century critics. For example, he did not realize that a complete theory of motion required one positively to discount some aspects of common sense, which can be misleading, in order to formulate precisely accurate laws. Strange as it may sound to modern ears, his lack of interest in developing sophisticated experiments in physics also stemmed from much the same impulse to stick closely to the phenomena, not from any laziness or complacency about his theories. He took it that the job of a 'natural philosopher' was to find out what things do naturally. From his point of view, to interfere with nature by setting traps for it in the manner of a modern experimentalist would be to play false and just confuse matters. It would change the picture rather than revealing it. Dissection in biology was one thing, but there too, artificial experiments could only distort the way things naturally behaved.

Aristotle's treatment of motion is a good example of this passive approach and of his overriding interest in what is natural. When he looked around him, it seemed to Aristotle that there were two sorts of motion: natural and enforced. Each element had its own form of natural motion, defined as the direction in which it would travel if released and left to its own devices. Earth and water would naturally move towards the centre of the universe, which was the middle of our planet. Air and fire had a natural tendency to travel in the opposite direction. That is why an apple (which has earth as its predominant element) will fall downwards when the stem supporting it breaks, whereas the flames of a fire will naturally shoot upwards. This explained heaviness and lightness: heavy things were those with a predominance of earth or water and which therefore had a tendency to move downwards; light things had the opposite tendency because of their different constitution. The tendency of heavy things to move towards the centre of the earth also explained why the earth was not flat but spherical. Aristotle already knew that the earth was round – he inferred this from several observations, such as that it casts a curved shadow on the moon – but the theory of natural motion added a good explanation for how it came to be that way. Since heavy matter would have arrived from all over the place to congregate at this one point (because it was the centre of the universe), this matter would have agglomerated equally in all directions around the centre and thus produced a sphere. Water did not have so much of a tendency to move downwards as earth did, and air was not quite as upwardly mobile as fire, so water tended to congregate on the surface of the earth (the oceans), air tended towards the lower atmosphere, and fire higher up. In this sense, everything had its natural place.

This did not mean that everything always stayed in its natural place, or indeed that it had ever been there. This is because the world is busy and complicated and there are all sorts of things that can interfere with the natural motion of a particular thing. One heavy body might be supported by another and thus be prevented from heading for the centre of the earth. Or some air might be heated and thus rise, carrying some leaves with it for a while and therefore counteracting their natural propensity to fall by subjecting them to enforced motion in the opposite direction. One of the things that can interfere with natural motion is a living being such as a person. Someone might pick up an apple and throw it in the air, for example, thus imposing an enforced motion on it. Similarly someone might beat down the naturally rising flames of a fire. Living things were of course themselves subject to the same natural and enforced motions as any other physical things; but most of them also had the power to move themselves. In fact, this was the defining characteristic of animal life. For Aristotle, the signs of life were nutrition, reproduction, sensation, the power of locomotion, desire, imagination and reason. The more of these a creature had, the higher it sat on the ladder of nature. Only people had all of them, which is why they counted as the highest form of life on earth; but all creatures higher up than plants could move themselves. These movements could be explained by final causes: they were 'for the sake of' something. Creatures moved in order to satisfy their needs or desires, aided by sensation and (if they had them) imagination and reason to tell them where to go. In general, everything that moves is moved by something: higher forms of life are moved by their own desires and appetites, while everything else receives its motion from something external.

One might at first think that this provides Aristotle with a quick route to God. If everything inanimate is moved by some external motion, must there not then be a First Cause who started it all off? Not for Aristotle. For one thing, he argued that the universe had always existed, so there was no First Anything. This was one of the aspects of his thought that the Christian, Jewish and Islamic philosophers of the Middle Ages were not at all happy about. Aristotle thought that there was a God, of sorts, but not that He had made the world or kicked off its movements with a First Push. Several medieval philosophers – most famously, St Thomas Aquinas (1225–74), whose views became Catholic orthodoxy – tried to put Aristotle right on this point and prove the existence of God as a First Cause who made everything and started it moving. But Aristotle's own routes to God were not so direct. To find the simplest of them, one must move on to the other half of his world-picture: the part which deals with the heavens, and in particular with their type of motion.

As we noted earlier, Aristotle was struck by the fact that nobody had ever noticed any significant change in the heavens, just an endless revolving of bright, distant objects. One could certainly see for oneself, or so he thought, that the heavens were marked by uniform circular motion. And that itself was a remarkable fact which required some explanation, because uniform rotation did not seem to be natural for anything down here on earth. The earthly elements and everything made of them tended to move in straight lines, unless something got in their way, held them back or imposed a contrary, enforced motion on them. So it seemed to Aristotle that there had to be a fifth type of substance (or 'quintessence' as it was later called) which naturally moved in circles. This would account for the fact that heavenly things behave differently from earthly things: it is because they are made of a different sort of stuff. He sometimes called this stuff 'aether', borrowing an old term for the fiery substance of which the stars and planets were traditionally supposed to have been made.

God comes into the picture when one asks what moves these heavenly bodies. The hypothesis of a fifth substance, whose natural motion is rotatory, explains why they move in circles rather than in straight lines; but it does not explain why they move rather than remain still. Even if they have been moving forever, as Aristotle thought, one still wants to know why they move. Aristotle argued that it cannot be any ordinary physical push which keeps them going. Such a thing could not, for one thing, be powerful enough to maintain eternal motion. And there was a deeper problem, according to Aristotle: whatever it is that moves the heavenly bodies must itself be motionless, since otherwise we should have to look for something to move that too, and we would never get to the bottom of it all. Earthly motion could ultimately be traced back to the influence of the heavenly bodies (for example, via the sun's heat, which stirred things up), but somewhere the chain had to end. It followed that whatever moved the heavens did not itself move: it was some sort of Unmoved Mover. The next step was to explain how such a thing might work.

One way sprang to mind. Remember how animals were said to move as a result of their own aims. If a lion sees a zebra, wants to eat it and so moves towards it, the zebra will count as a cause of the lion's movement even if it does not itself move (indeed, the lion may be rather keen that the zebra should stay rooted to the spot). In this way, the object of a desire can act as an Unmoved Mover, which shows how the problem of the heavenly bodies might be solved. If they could have desires, or something like them, then the object of these desires could be the cause of their movement. It would be a final cause in Aristotle's sense, not an efficient one – it would be the goal of movement, not a push that started it off – and it could itself be motionless. This would neatly explain how something can cause the eternal motion of the heavenly bodies without raising a potentially endless series of questions about what moves the mover. It would also conveniently find the grain of truth in the respectably traditional idea that the heavenly bodies are somehow alive. Several ideas led Aristotle to the conclusion that any celestial Unmoved Mover would have to be simple and unchanging if it was to do its job properly. He also offered ingenious proofs that it would have to be everlasting and have no physical size or shape. And because the heavens are perfect, the sort of desire to be found up there will be a very intellectual sort of love and rather unlike the appetite of a lion for his midday zebra. All in all, this beloved Unmoved Mover begins to sound distinctly god-like.

Aristotle sometimes changed his mind about the various details of all this. At one stage he seems to have thought that it was the stars and planets themselves which desired the Unmoved Mover. Later he concluded that the desiring was done not by them but by the 'outermost heaven', that is, the gigantic translucent sphere in which, according to all leading Greek astronomers of the time, the furthest stars were embedded. This sphere rotated because it was moved by its desire for the Unmoved Mover, and it carried the stars around with it. The motion of this studded sphere was mechanically transmitted to smaller concentric spheres inside it, which carried all the other heavenly bodies (there was one sphere per planet, plus some intermediate spheres). The whole thing worked like clockwork, and managed to wind itself up because it was alive and motivated by a form of desire. Hence 'the love that moves the stars'. When Aristotle came to work out some of the smaller points he suggested that there might have to be dozens of Unmoved Movers to account for all the observed astronomical movements; but this was far from certain. What he was fairly sure about was that the motion of the outermost heaven required a senior Unmoved Mover, and that this obscure object of astronomical desire captured the element of truth in the conventional belief in a senior God.

What else could one say about this God? Aristotle had no time for the idea of gods that were like overgrown people, with their own desires and interests in lesser beings. They certainly did not perform any sort of actions in the world, as superstitious accounts (and Judaism, Islam and Christianity) would say. Aristotle's cool and logical mind stripped away all such anthropocentric ideas about divinity:

We assume the gods to be above all other beings blessed and happy; but what sort of actions must we assign to them? Acts of justice? Will not the gods seem absurd if they make contracts and return deposits, and so on? Acts of a brave man, then, confronting dangers and running risks because it is noble to do so? Or liberal acts? To whom will they give? It will be strange if they are really to have money or anything of the kind . . . If we were to run through them all, the circumstances of action would be found trivial and unworthy of gods. Still, every one supposes that they *live* and therefore that they are active; we cannot suppose them to sleep like Endymion. Now if you take away from a living being action, and still more production, what is left but contemplation?

The activity of the god who moves the outermost heaven by inspiring its love consists entirely of intellectual contemplation – the purest exercise of reason, which was the best thing there was. What He thinks about is Himself, since nothing else is worth thinking about if you are God.

To modern minds, this whole physico-theological edifice is a contraption of unsurpassed absurdity. But Aristotle would undoubtedly return the compliment. Even if he could be persuaded of our physics and astronomy, he would never have stood for the God of the Bible or the Koran. To him, the idea that there was a being who one morning conjured up the universe out of nothing and then busied himself handing out rewards and punishments to its measly inhabitants would not have been worth a moment's serious consideration. As far as Aristotle was concerned, the traditional gods of mythology were a childish fantasy. Reducing their number to one and bringing His morals up to date would not have amounted to a significant improvement.

One does not have to be a devotee of a rival god to see that there are yawning gaps in Aristotle's argument for his Unmoved Mover. His analogy between the motivating desires of animals or people on the one hand and of astronomical objects on the other is obviously a little stretched, to put it mildly. More damagingly, it simply does not follow that what the heavenly bodies desire actually exists. A lion might believe there is a zebra in a nearby thicket and pounce at it, only to find that there was no zebra. In such a case the imagined zebra still counts as the final cause of the lion's movement: the lion pounced 'for the sake of' the zebra which he thought was there. It is the goal or aim of his movement, and yet it does not exist. Perhaps the heavenly bodies are similarly deluded. Perhaps they move because of their love for an Unmoved Mover who turns out to be imaginary. Aristotle's argument for the existence of God fails because he cannot rule out this possibility.

Aristotle had other reasons for believing in the Unmoved Mover and so might not have been too troubled by this criticism. Consider, for example, the following line of thought. Time cannot have a beginning or an end because that would mean that there was a time before time and a time after time, and both of these ideas are gibberish. So time must be everlasting. It follows that change is everlasting too, because time is simply a way of measuring change, and thus it does not make sense to speak of a period of time in which there is no change going on. If that is right, Aristotle argued, there must be something which ensures that there is no end to change. He offered reasons for thinking that only something immaterial, everlasting and perfect could guarantee this, and that such an entity could not while away its endless hours with anything less than pure intellectual contemplation. Thus Aristotle had another route to God. His chain of argument is highly questionable in every detail, but it is typically neat, drawing on ideas developed in other parts of his writings and fitting them all together. The result is an intricately tooled and comprehensive world-picture that held the attention of dozens of generations.

Most of Aristotle's abstract discussions about motion, time, change and the Unmoved Mover are to be found in his treatises on physics, cosmology and biology. Such reflections were an intrinsic part of science as a whole; they arose naturally in the course of his attempts to understand the world. But they also cropped up in another context that is now sometimes regarded as far from the territory of science. Several of Aristotle's arguments on these subjects were developed in a set of treatises to which a later editor gave the name of *Metaphysics*. At the time, this term simply denoted that these books came after (*meta*) the ones that were classified as 'physics'; it was merely a librarian's term. But the word has since taken on a life of its own. By medieval times, 'metaphysics' had come to denote a special branch of inquiry that was radically different from 'natural philosophy' (i.e., science). 'Metaphysical' came to mean 'transcending physics'. For some later philosophers who were sceptical about the possibility of such transcendence, especially David Hume in the eighteenth century and the logical positivists in the twentieth century, 'metaphysician' became more or less a term of abuse. A metaphysician was one who concocted abstruse and sophistical conundrums; his work was mere intellectual doodling that could not lead anywhere because it ignored empirical evidence and scientific knowledge. 'Metaphysical' is now also sometimes used to mean 'occult'.

To understand what Aristotle was up to in this work, it is best to ignore such later connotations of the term. The fourteen of his books collected together under the title of *Metaphysics* are a rag-bag of topics. They include a lengthy attack on Plato's pseudo-mystical account of mathematics, in which Aristotle argues that numbers, points, triangles and so on should be considered as abstractions in the mind rather than as mysterious objects which somehow exist in their own right. They also include a lexicon in which Aristotle explores the various senses of thirty of the central terms used in his investigations, such as 'substance', 'disposition', 'quality', 'opposite', 'whole', 'impossible' and 'false'. In other parts of the *Metaphysics* he expounds his doctrine of the four causes and relates it to the ideas of earlier thinkers; he develops his ideas about the difference between form and matter; he talks about the principles of classification and definition and discusses the concepts of unity and diversity; he tries to work out some mathematical details of astronomy; he talks about his God; and – among other things – he attacks scepticism and relativism, and discusses such basic logical principles as 'no proposition is both true and false at the same time'.

These are very disparate bedfellows, it seems, but there was one theme which united at least most of them in Aristotle's mind. In a couple of places in the *Metaphysics*, he speaks of a subject which he calls 'First Philosophy'. Roughly speaking, it seems intended to cover the most general of principles, causes and concepts. It deals with universal questions that are common to all areas of investigation, from arithmetic to zoology, in an attempt to find the truths which 'hold good for everything that is'. The investigation of the four causes and the concepts of form, matter, potentiality and so on are general enough to count as First Philosophy, because they have a very wide range of application. Basic logical principles obviously do too. Why astronomy and theology belong in the same bag, as Aristotle says they do, is not so clear. It has something to do with the fact that these subjects deal with the highest or most perfect sorts of things, which are ultimately responsible for what goes on in the earthly realm. His main thought about First Philosophy seems to be that it deals with whatever sort of knowledge is most required for the attainment of wisdom – i.e., what the true lover of knowledge will be keenest to get. He takes it that it must therefore tell one about the most important objects (God and other unchanging, eternal things) and the most important (i.e., general) truths and concepts.

The most general concept of all is being, or existence, which is the one thing that absolutely everything has. One might at first think that *being* is indeed so general a concept that it is impossible to say anything specific about it, but Aristotle manages to come up with quite a lot.

After clarifying the many senses in which one might say that something 'is' so-and-so, or just 'is', he tries to find out whether there is some one fundamental type of existence on which all the others depend. He argues that there is: the existence of everyday physical things such as trees, rocks, plants and animals. Aristotle holds that all other types of existence are parasitic on that. For example, when we say that something is large or red or beautiful, the beauty or redness or size may be said to 'exist' only insofar as there is some particular object which has these characteristics. The characteristics cannot just float around on their own. This view is in sharp contrast to Plato's theory of Forms, according to which the Form of Red and the Form of Beauty are more real than any particular red or beautiful thing. In Plato's universe, the existence of Forms is the primary sort of existence, and the world of physical things is a confusing flux that is merely an imperfect reflection of these realities. From Aristotle's point of view, this puts the cart before the horse. Such muddled talk gets in the way of a proper understanding of what it is for something to exist, which is one of the most general of all questions and thus a required topic for the pursuit of wisdom.

Aristotle's attack on Plato's account of mathematical entities is part of this general investigation of the types of existence. So is his discussion of relativism and scepticism, both of which can be seen as radical and rather defeatist responses to the problem of determining what sort of things there are in the world. But there is little point in struggling to link everything Aristotle says in his *Metaphysics* into one clearly defined project. For one thing, he thought of First Philosophy as a science that is marked off from the others largely by its generality. There is therefore bound to be considerable overlap between parts of First Philosophy and the more general and theoretical parts of specialist branches of inquiry, such as physics. That is why the Unmoved Mover, for example, crops up both in Aristotle's *Physics* and in his *Metaphysics*.

Since what later philosophers have meant by 'metaphysics' is often very different from what Aristotle meant by 'First Philosophy', it is worth stressing that he did not think that First Philosophy involved any special techniques of rational insight. Later metaphysicians sometimes thought of the subject as somehow leapfrogging over the normal methods of scientific inquiry so that it could prove, by pure reason, fundamental truths about the world which the plodding sciences could not reach for themselves. The metaphysician is therefore a sort of super-scientist. But this was not Aristotle's way. According to him, one who studied First Philosophy was 'above the natural philosopher' only in the sense that 'nature is only one particular genus of being', i.e., because First Philosophy is concerned with all types of existence (including mathematical existence and divine existence) and not just the existence of natural things. It too was a conventional science, just a very general, diverse and particularly rewarding one.

One area of inquiry that frequently overlaps with First Philosophy, or metaphysics, is logic, which may be defined as the science of reasoning and proof. Aristotle had good grounds to stray into such matters when investigating the most general and abstract questions. If First Philosophy is the most general of sciences, logic is in one sense the most sweeping part of all. It is a tool to be used in all inquiries, as well as being fascinating in its own right. As Aristotle says, a seeker after wisdom 'must inquire also into the principles of deduction'. He was the first to do so systematically and thereby invented the science of logic.

Aristotle defined deduction as a piece of discourse in which 'certain things being stated, something other than what is stated follows of necessity from their being so'. To get straight to the heart of this idea, consider the following unlikely train of thought:

> All snarks are boojums
> All boojums are frabjous
> *Therefore*
> All snarks are frabjous

All these words except 'all', 'are' and 'therefore' are nonsense. Yet anybody can see that there is a sense in which it is right. The conclusion follows logically from the premises. If snarks are boojums, and if boojums are frabjous, then it 'follows of necessity' that snarks are frabjous too. In fact there aren't any snarks, frabjous or otherwise, but that is irrelevant to the question of what follows from what. The nonsense-words in this reasoning bring home an important fact, namely that whether or not a deductive argument is valid – that is, whether or not its conclusion follows – does not depend on whether or not the premises are actually true. Aristotle was the first to ask what it does depend on, and to give the right answer.

What he saw is that the validity of an argument like this depends on a type of form or structure that can be revealed simply by ignoring the details of what the argument is about. Take away the snarks and the rest, and you are left with a skeleton called a logical form:

All A are B
All B are C
*Therefore*
All A are C

It does not matter what *A*, *B* and *C* stand for: whichever terms you substitute for them in this pattern, the result will be a valid deduction. That is to say, if the terms you pick for *A*, *B* and *C* make the first two statements true, then the third will automatically come out true as well. The argument about snarks and boojums fits this pattern, so it is valid.

There are, of course, also plenty of invalid patterns of argument. As Aristotle says: 'That some deductions are genuine while others seem to be so but are not, is evident. This happens with arguments, as also elsewhere, through a certain likeness between the genuine and the sham.' Here is a sham one:

No snakes are pigs
No pigs can fly
*Therefore*
No snakes can fly.

All of these statements are true: neither snakes nor pigs can fly, and no snakes are pigs. Yet the argument is invalid, and Aristotle's notion of logical form can prove it and explain why. This argument has the form:

> No A are B
> No B are C
> *Therefore*
> No A are C

If this were a valid form, it would be impossible to find As, Bs and Cs which make the premises true but the conclusion false. Yet it is possible to do this. Let *A* stand for birds, *B* for pigs and *C* for things that can fly. Then we have:

> No birds are pigs
> No pigs can fly
> *Therefore*
> No birds can fly.

This is obviously invalid because it has put together two truths and produced a falsehood. Birds are never pigs, and pigs can never fly, but birds clearly can fly. Thus, just as 'All *A* are *B*, all *B* are *C*, therefore all *A* are *C*' is a valid argument-form, so 'No *A* are *B*, no *B* are *C*, therefore no *A* are *C*' must be a sham, invalid one. The counter-example about birds proves it.

This sort of use of general symbols, such as *A*, *B* and *C*, is now very familiar, especially from mathematics – and even song:

> See how the Fates their gifts allot,
> For A is happy – B is not.
> Yet B is worthy, I dare say,
> Of more prosperity than A.

Just as one can formulate general truths of arithmetic by using symbols that stand for numbers but not for any particular number – as in $x+y = y+x$ – so Aristotle was able to formulate general truths about logic by using symbols to stand for terms but not for any particular term – his *A*s, *B*s and *C*s. Aristotle seems to have been the inventor of the 'variable', as this form of notation is called, at least in this sort of use. Mathematicians had apparently not yet got round to using it for numbers, though they did use letters to label the lines of geometrical figures, which was perhaps the germ of Aristotle's brilliant idea.

The sort of general logical truths on which Aristotle focused were about the following four types of statement: All *A* are *B*; No *A* are *B*; Some *A* are B; Some *A* are not *B*. He argued that every assertion boils down to a statement with two terms (a subject, *A*, and a predicate, *B*), and must be either affirmative or negative and either particular or universal, thus yielding these four possibilities. The first general truths he came up with about these sorts of statements had to do with swapping around the subject and predicate terms, *A* and *B*. He noted that you can validly swap them in 'No *A* are *B*' and 'Some *A* are *B*', but not in 'All *A* are *B*' or 'Some *A* are not *B*'. For example, if no *A* are *B*, then it follows that no *B* are *A* (e.g., if no politicians are trustworthy, then no trustworthy people are politicians). Likewise, if some *A* are *B*, then it follows that some *B* are *A* (if some lawyers are careless, then some careless people are lawyers). But if all *A* are *B*, it does not follow that all *B* are *A* (all cats are animals, but not all animals are cats), and if some *A* are not *B*, it does not follow that some *B* are not *A* (some animals are not cats, but it does not follow that some cats are not animals).

Aristotle seems to have assumed that all interesting forms of deduction could be expressed as arguments like the ones above about snarks, pigs and birds. That is, they could be arranged into trios of statements consisting of two premises and one conclusion, in which each statement is one of his four types (i.e., All *A* are *B*, No *A* are *B*, Some *A* are *B*, Some *A* are not *B*). Arguments of this sort became known as syllogisms; according to Aristotle's main way of classifying them, there were 192 possible permutations, of which fourteen were valid. Armed with this system of classification, Aristotle established some general rules about syllogisms. Two of the simplest rules are: every valid syllogism has at least one affirmative premise (i.e., either 'All A are B' or 'Some A are B'); and every valid syllogism has at least one universal premise (i.e., either 'All A are B' or 'No A are B').

He argued that four of the syllogisms were 'perfect' or 'complete', in the sense that their validity was immediately apparent to everyone, and he used various methods to relate each of the other ten valid forms of syllogisms to one of these four. Given that the four perfect forms were valid, he demonstrated that the other ten must be as well.

By deriving all valid syllogistic forms from the four perfect ones (and arguing that these four were, in turn, instances of a single general principle, which I shall not discuss), Aristotle built an impressive system of logic about which even he, uncharacteristically, boasted. Until the end of the nineteenth century, almost everyone who was interested in such things seems to have thought that it could not be improved on in any major way. All that remained was to learn it up properly. Students in the Middle Ages learnt bizarre mnemonic poems to help them ingest the almighty syllogistic revelation:

> Barbara celarent darii ferio baralipton
> Celantes dabitis fapesmo frisesomorum;
> Cesare campestres festino baroco; darapti
> Felapton disamis datisi bocardo ferison.

This spell-like quatrain, consisting of the names of syllogisms, contains coded messages telling the student which ones are valid and exactly how to relate each of them to one of the perfect four.

The discovery that there was more to logic than Aristotle's syllogisms took a remarkably long time coming. In 1787, Kant wrote that Aristotle's logic was 'to all appearances a closed and completed body of doctrine'. A once-popular logic text by a nineteenth-century archbishop stated that the Aristotelian syllogism is 'the form to which *all* correct reasoning may ultimately be reduced'. In 1843, J. S. Mill could still write that Aristotle's perfect syllogisms were 'the universal types of all correct ratiocination'. But in fact by this time an English mathematician and philosopher, Augustus de Morgan, had clearly demonstrated that, far from being universal, Aristotle's logic could not even prove that a horse's head is an animal's head. That is to say it could not account for the validity of inferences like 'horses are animals, therefore a horse's head is an animal's head', because such deductions cannot be expressed as Aristotelian syllogisms.

In general, it turns out that although Aristotle's system of syllogisms is largely adequate for dealing with deductions involving his favourite sorts of statements – 'All *A* are *B*', 'Some *A* are *B*' and so on – it cannot be applied to many other useful forms of reasoning. For example, it cannot deal with compound statements, like 'If the power has failed, then the clock will have stopped', so it does not cover deductions such as:

> If the power has failed, then the clock will have stopped
> The clock has not stopped
> *Therefore*
> The power has not failed

The study of deductions like this one is called propositional logic, because it needs to use variables to stand for whole propositions like 'the power has failed', whereas Aristotle's logical system uses only *A*s and *B*s to stand for subject and predicate terms like 'bird' and 'flies'. In propositional logic, using *P* to stand for 'the power has failed' and *Q* for 'the clock has – or will have – stopped', the logical form of this deduction can be displayed as 'If *P* then *Q*; Not *Q*; therefore, Not *P*'.

Shortly after Aristotle's time, some members of the school of philosophers known as Stoics studied such deductions and developed a system of logic that could deal with them, up to a point. But since the Stoics were generally seen as rivals to Aristotle, and since Aristotle was seen as extremely wise, it was generally assumed that Stoic logic must be wrong. It was therefore largely ignored. In fact the two systems of logic are not rivals but complementary. As later logicians eventually came to realize, Aristotle's logic needs to be supplemented by the propositional logic of the Stoics, and vice versa.

Aristotle's logic also needs to be expanded to cope with statements involving so-called 'relative' terms that express relationships between two or more objects, such as ' – is taller than – ', ' – is equal to – ' and ' – is the father of – ', because his syllogisms cannot deal with them. (De Morgan's example of the horse's head comes into this class because it involves the relation ' – is the head of – '.) The need for a logic that could cope with relations was realized by Galen, a Greek philosopher and doctor of the second century AD, who falteringly worked out the beginnings of such a system. But most of his logical work, like that of the Stoics, was neglected and lost, perhaps because nobody could see how to square it with Aristotle. Such complications would, for one thing, have meant a lot more mnemonic verses to learn. Until the end of the nineteenth century, few realized that logicians ought to have paid a lot more attention to the Stoics and Galen, and a bit less to Aristotle.

Several features of modern logic were anticipated by the polymathic seventeenth-century philosopher, Leibniz (1646–1716). His logical works were not published until long after his death, and it was some time before his hints were taken up. Leibniz was one of the first people to grasp the full significance of Aristotle's use of variables. He saw in Aristotle's syllogisms of *As* and *Bs* 'a kind of universal mathematics whose importance is too little known'. He knew that Aristotelian syllogisms could not express every sort of deduction, but he believed that an expanded logical system could do so if it built on Aristotle's insights, particularly if it found a way to harness mathematical techniques. Ever since he was nineteen, Leibniz had dreamed of a universal language that could establish laws of reasoning in a mathematical style:

The only way to rectify our reasonings is to make them as tangible as those of the Mathematicians, so that we can find our error at a glance, and when there are disputes among persons, we can simply say: Let us calculate, without further ado, in order to see who is right. If words were constructed according to a device that I see possible, but which those who have built universal languages have not discovered, we could arrive at the desired result by means of words themselves. But in the meantime there is another less elegant road already open to us – [*It*] consists of making use, as mathematicians do, of characters, which are appropriate to fix our ideas, and of adding to them a numerical proof.

He believed, with wild optimism, that the use of such a calculus could resolve all intellectual debates. This clearly went too far, since most disputes are not about points of logic but about points of fact, and anyway not even all logical truths can be proved mathematically in the way Leibniz envisaged. However, his desire to create 'a language whose signs or characters would play the same role as the signs of arithmetic for numbers and those of algebra for quantities in general' was prophetic.

Leibniz's idea of a calculating language was partly stimulated by the gloriously eccentric project of Ramon Lull (1232–1315), a libidinous courtier who became a monk after a particularly unfortunate amorous encounter. Lull thought that Moslems, and presumably any other doubting Thomases, could be brought to see the truth of Christianity if only they could be made to appreciate all the various combinations of virtues possessed by the Christian God. He developed various mechanical devices and diagrams for displaying combinations of symbols which stood for the attributes of God, such as 'goodness', 'eternity' and 'greatness'. Just pondering such gadgets would, apparently, do the trick. The logical needle in this haystack of lunacy is the idea that the manipulation of symbols can play a part in, or at least represent, the process of reasoning. It started Leibniz thinking about how logic might be reduced to a purely mechanical process and thus be used to reach conclusions as irrefutably as mathematicians sometimes do.

Thomas Hobbes (1588–1679) had already expressed the idea that reasoning really amounted to a form of calculation:

By ratiocination I mean *computation*. Now, to compute, is either to collect the sum of many things that are added together, or to know what remains when one thing is taken out of another – all ratiocination is comprehended in these two operations of the mind, addition and subtraction.

Hobbes had neither the mathematical ability nor the inclination to take this idea any further. Leibniz had both, but still did not get very far. He drew some parallels between arithmetical formulas and ordinary statements, toyed with a sort of arithmetic of concepts and proposed some axioms from which a complete logical system might be deduced in the style of Euclid's geometrical proofs. But, like most of his many projects, he did not stick with it for very long. The task was taken up by two more dedicated English mathematicians, George Boole (1815–1864) and Augustus de Morgan (1806–1876). Boole sketched an algebra of classes, which could be used to express Aristotle's syllogisms, and an algebra of propositional logic. De Morgan developed a rudimentary algebra of relations. And finally it became possibly to prove that a horse's head is an animal's head.

Later on in the nineteenth century, more or less the finishing touches to basic logic were provided, independently, by an American philosopher, C. S. Peirce (1839–1914), and a German mathematician, Gottlob Frege (1848–1925). Frege was posthumously awarded all of the credit, though his notation was unusable and recent scholarship shows that his work played a smaller role in the development of logic than most history books say it did. In 1910–13, Bertrand Russell and his former teacher, A. N. Whitehead, published their *Principia Mathematica*, which synthesized and developed the best work in what was coming to be known as mathematical logic. From that point onwards research in logic and computation intertwined, as they had done in the mind of Leibniz. In the 1920s, mechanical procedures – that is, rules of the sort that can be followed by a machine – were devised for testing whether the theorems of *Principia Mathematica* followed from its axioms. This was a key step on the road to computer-languages, which are the descendants of logical calculi. In 1938 it was demonstrated that the lay-out of switches in electrical circuits could fruitfully be regarded as corresponding to formulas of propositional logic, with 'on' and 'off' construed as 'true' and 'false' respectively (just as Boole equated 'true' and 'false' with '1' and '0' in his algebra of propositions). Nowadays some parts of the diversified science of mathematical logic and formal systems are studied by pure mathematicians and other parts are studied by computer scientists. Philosophers pop up randomly in all areas of the subject.

It all began with Aristotle's *A*s and *B*s, but plainly a lot had to happen before today's comprehensive logical calculi and computer-languages could arrive on the scene. Perhaps the main reason why Aristotle's own logic was too narrow lies in what led him to it in the first place. Most of the advances in logic in modern times have been made by people who were interested either in clarifying mathematical proofs or in transforming all logical inference into a sort of mathematics, or both. Aristotle's aims were different. It seems that his approach to logical deduction was influenced not so much by any special concern with mathematics, nor by a desire to study all the diverse forms of reasoning, but by a particular interest in the sort of arguments used by Socrates. Aristotle's syllogisms seemed to fit the inquiries of Socrates like a glove; the trouble is that they do not fit much else.

The Socratic investigations in Plato's dialogues always seemed to end up talking about whether a certain class of things did or did not have a certain property. Were all examples of justice examples of returning what was owed? Were all things loved by the gods holy? In debate, Socrates would often ask for a definition stating what all instances of, say, justice, had in common. If his victim tried to get away with a few remarks about what was true of merely some examples of justice, Socrates would object that he was interested in what justice *is*, so he needed to know what was true of *all* just acts. With luck, he would secure agreement to a thesis of the form, 'All acts of justice are so-and-so', from which he could proceed to draw out logical consequences, consider apparent exceptions and formulate new generalizations. Aristotle seems to have been struck by the fact that such discussions always involved statements about all, some or no *A*s and whether or not they were *B*s. And that may be why, having done a brilliant job at analysing such statements, he never bothered to look beyond them in his logical work.

The investigation of the syllogism with its *A*s and *B*s was only part of Aristotle's writings on logic. It was the most original part, but there were other influential things too, some good and some not, which were studied with inexplicable enthusiasm in the Middle Ages – partly perhaps because of the historical accident that they were the first of his works to be translated into Latin. One treatise, known as the *Topics*, is largely a manual of tips for use in competitive argument, a popular spectator sport in Aristotle's day. This has an appendix on various kinds of fallacies and how to see them coming before one falls for them. Aristotle argued that the sort of training offered in the *Topics* was useful for serious purposes, such as scientific research, because it would make it easier to spot the difference between good and bad reasoning. It contains some sophisticated analysis, but Aristotle also offers unedifying hints on how to trip up your opponent: try being long-winded, talk very fast and do your best to make him lose his temper. To modern minds, this does not have a lot to do with logic. Two other treatises discuss some preliminaries to logical study: one deals with various types of propositions, their relations to one another and some problems about truth and meaning; the other deals with the various types of terms of which propositions are composed.

A more consequential logical treatise investigated 'scientific syllogisms'. It was more or less regarded as the Bible of scientific method until the Renaissance, which is very surprising when one reads its commandments. Aristotle's discussion of the 'first principles' from which all scientific demonstrations ought to start seems to have been modelled on geometry with its practice of deriving theorems from a set of primary definitions, basic postulates and indubitable axioms. He apparently held that every science could ultimately be squeezed into the form of pure mathematics, because he said that genuinely scientific knowledge consists of 'necessary' truths (ones which cannot fail to be true) and that these truths are all about eternal and unchanging things. At first sight this is incomprehensible: how can it be squared with his own biological inquiries? There is, for example, nothing eternal about a dogfish, yet Aristotle seems to have been interested in finding out about them nonetheless. Was this not science? It looks as if Aristotle has reneged on his own criticisms of Plato and gone back to the Platonic view that knowledge of immutable and unworldly things is the only real sort of knowledge there is.

Aristotle did not give enough detailed examples for one to be absolutely sure what he was up to in his remarks about first principles and scientific demonstration. But what he seems to have been describing is an ideal at which each branch of science ought to aim. The most highly developed science of the day was geometry, so Aristotle seems to have assumed that with luck every other branch of inquiry would end up looking much like that. It would consist of a body of truths arranged into a chain of deductions in such a way that one would see how each derived result could not fail to be true, as in geometry. As for dogfish and eternity, Aristotle's idea seems to have been that an advanced science would be primarily concerned with whatever was universally true about each species of object, and in that sense would deal with eternal truths as geometry does. Individual cows, for example, cease to be ruminants at their deaths, but it remains an essential truth about the species (according to Aristotle) that cows are ruminants. Daisy would die, but the class of bovine ruminants would go munching on. So zoologists could rest assured that the 'theorems' of their science would stay as eternally true as those of geometry.

Aristotle's account of science as a geometrical-style progression of syllogisms is a piece of hopeful anticipation: it pretends that all the data have already been gathered in, and moves eagerly on to the interesting question of how to arrange them into axioms, definitions, theorems and so on. Aristotle seems to have been aware that this meant his account could not yet be applied to any actual science (except of course geometry itself) because not enough research had been completed. That is presumably why he never attempted the thankless task of translating his own scientific work into syllogisms, except for occasional samples by way of illustration. As for collecting scientific data in the first place, there is, from Aristotle's point of view, not much specific advice one can give beyond 'Go and find out'. It was a matter for the insight and hard work of the experienced researcher, not the abstract ingenuity of the logician. So Aristotle was not really offering an account of practical scientific method at all. It was more like a form of book-keeping for the man who already knew everything. In later centuries, Aristotle's ideas about all this were abused by people who pored over his logical treatises but disdained (or did not know about) his scientific ones. These medieval scholars wanted to skip the research and focus on the syllogisms. Such idle stirring of definitions and deductions is what got 'Aristotelian' scientific method a famously bad name with the likes of Francis Bacon.

Thus both main parts of Aristotle's logic innocently caused trouble later. His general theory of the syllogism eventually outlived its useful-ness and held back the development of deductive logic, because his admirers were so impressed by the fact that he had said the first word on the subject that they assumed he must have said the last word as well. And his theory of scientific demonstration, or 'scientific syllogisms', led to an underestimate of the role of empirical research, because other admirers took Aristotle's abstract investigation of what an ideal science might look like to be an excuse for abandoning fieldwork rather prematurely.

'It is the mark of an educated man', wrote Aristotle, 'to look for precision in each class of things just so far as the nature of the subject admits.' Exactness might be a plausible thing to aim for in mathe-matics, for example, but elsewhere it would often be naive to look for more than rough generalizations. Aristotle sometimes forgot his own good advice, but when it came to ethical and political subjects, he was well aware that there were no precise axioms to be had:

the whole account of matters of conduct must be given in outline and not precisely . . . matters concerned with conduct and with what is good for us have no fixity, any more than matters of health. The general account being of this nature, the account of particular cases is yet more lacking in exactness; for . . . the agents themselves must in each case consider what is appropriate to the occasion, as happens also in the art of medicine or of navigation.

Life is too complicated to navigate by means of just a list of Dos and Don'ts. If you tried to write down a complete set of rules about how to live, they would have to be so complicated and hedged with qualifications as to be no practical use. True, there are a couple of hard and fast rules – do not murder, do not steal – but they cover only the boringly easy questions, and are more or less true by definition. (Only killings that are wrongful count as murder, so 'do not commit murder' is not much more informative than 'do not do wrong'.) What is needed to tell good from bad in a confusing world is character, experience and balanced judgement from the man on the spot. These will steer him through the difficult cases and help him see what to aim for in life.

This practical-minded and flexible approach is very different from Plato's favourite way of talking about morality. If, as Aristotle plausibly thinks, it is not simply a matter of formulating general rules, then ethics cannot be quite so intellectual a business as Plato makes out. Plato held that the nature of the 'the good' could be discerned in the abstract by reflecting on what various instances of goodness have in common. After almost a lifetime of gruelling study and tedious preparation, his philosopher-kings would catch a glimpse of the Form of the Good and would then be able to reel off answers to any question about what was good and what was not. Then they could write laws for everyone else, and that was that. No more ethical problems. As we have seen, Plato did not expect any of this actually to happen, but the moral of the tale was plain enough: get hold of the Form of the Good – or 'goodness itself', as he often called it – and the rest is details.

This was too neat for Aristotle. He was understandably puzzled about what this Form of the Good had to do with anything. For one thing, Plato's picture assumes that goodness is a single thing: a good man, a good house and a good chicken were all supposed to be united by their relationship to this Form. Aristotle objected that this cannot be right, because there are many different senses in which things are said to be good (or bad) and they vary widely according to what is being talked about. How could there be any useful notion of 'goodness itself' when the idea of goodness could be applied to so many different things? At any rate, it was a bit suspicious that nobody ever seemed to make use of any such general criterion or measure of goodness. If you want to be a good doctor, you study medicine, and if you want to be a good carpenter, you get to know about wood and tools. The Form of the Good does not come into it. Presumably something similar is true of the art of living: if you want to know how to excel at that art, then what you must look into is the details of human character and the distinctive circumstances of human life.

This is what Aristotle aimed to do in his writings on ethics. Since his method was, as in all his investigations, to account for the facts as they were generally perceived to be, and to build on and refine accepted views about them, it is not surprising that he turned out to be less of a moral revolutionary than either Socrates or Plato. As we have seen, Socrates was guided not primarily by traditional *mores*, but by a driving conscience that told him above all to avoid doing harm. The need to preserve and enhance the purity of his soul meant a saintly existence of turning the other cheek, among other irregularities. In Plato's case the demands of conscience were dressed up in more intellectual clothes as the requirements of 'goodness itself'. His ideals remained more comfortably abstract, but they still set unusually high standards, at least in theory, and some of the reforms he argued for in the *Republic* – such as the equality of women and a regime of enforced poverty for the leadership – were shockingly innovative.

Aristotle found less to quarrel with in the conventional values that were praised by educated and enlightened people of his time. This did not make his moral philosophy boring, because it is one thing to agree with conventional *mores* but quite another to be able to explain and make sense of them. Indeed, he went so far in this attempt as to try and justify the institution of slavery, which other Greek thinkers merely accepted as an inevitable fact of life and mostly passed over without comment. Aristotle preached what others practised and kept quiet about, which may be morally conservative but is also intellectually adventurous. All in all, if the moral philosophy of Socrates and Plato may be compared to trying to rewrite some of the rules of a club, Aristotle was more concerned to shed light on the club's existing constitution, and to see how the members could best be made to behave in accordance with it. This is not to say that he unthinkingly accepted all traditional values: he acknowledged that 'old customs are exceedingly simple and barbarous . . . The remains of ancient laws are quite absurd.' Old rules 'ought not always to remain unaltered'. But, on the other hand, change must be made very cautiously, because 'a readiness to change from old to new laws enfeebles the power of the law'.

Aristotle's first question about ethics and the art of living is: 'What is "the good" for man?' This does not just mean 'What makes a man morally good?' or 'How ought people to behave when their own interests conflict with those of others?' He was interested in a broader question and not just in what we would call moral behaviour. When he asks about 'the good' for man, he is asking 'What is the aim of human life? What makes it complete?' It is, he says, more or less a truism that the answer to both these questions is *eudaimonia*, which is usually translated as 'happiness'. This translation makes the answer sound unconvincing to modern ears; surely there is more to life than feeling good? But actually *eudaimonia* means 'happiness' only in a very broad sense of the English word, for it implies successful, admirable living and all-round good fortune, as well as a contented state of mind. A brash self-help book from the top of the best-seller lists in those days might well have borne the title, *Eudaimonia for Everyone: How to be Successful, Admired and Generally as if Blessed by the Gods*. So it was not unreasonable for Aristotle to suppose that people would agree that *eudaimonia* is the aim of life. Still, the real task, he says, is to find out exactly what this amounts to.

According to Aristotle, the masses tend to believe that the aim of life is pleasure. Yet that would be a lowly sort of existence, suitable only for beasts. People of 'superior refinement and active disposition' seem rather to identify it with honours and reputation, of the sort you might get from a successful career in public life. And that is a rather superficial approach to life for a different sort of reason. Such honour merely reflects what other people happen to think: can perfect happiness for oneself really depend on the capricious attitudes of other people? Besides, people want to be honoured not just by anybody but by those of good judgement, and not just for any old thing but for their merits. It therefore seems back to front to regard public acclaim itself as more valuable than the virtues which it is supposed to be recognizing. People are admired because they are admirable, not admirable because they are admired. So honour and acclaim cannot in themselves be the aims of life.

This leads to the thought that perhaps the aim of life is to possess all the virtues (or 'varieties of excellence', which in Greek means the same thing), whether they are publicly recognized or not. But this cannot be quite right either. Firstly, it is too passive. Aristotle regarded the virtues as dispositions or capacities, and one could in theory have a wonderful set of those without ever actually doing anything. Secondly, even if one acted virtuously and exhibited all forms of excellence, this might still not be enough, because one might happen to suffer great misfortunes – illness, ruin, the loss of friends and family. Such an unfortunate man 'no one would call happy'. Such blows in life take the bloom off *eudaimonia*. Aristotle also quickly disposes of the idea that wealth could be the key to the good life. Money is desirable only for what it can do, as a means to an end.

To make more progress, Aristotle suggests it might be useful to take a closer look at what sort of thing a person is. According to his way of thinking, this should tell us about the 'function' of man, which should in turn show us what it is for that function to be performed well:

just as for a flute-player, a sculptor, or any artist, and, in general, for all things that have a function or activity, the good is thought to reside in the function, so would it seem to be for man, if he has a function. Have the carpenter, then, and the tanner certain functions or activities, and has man none? Is he naturally functionless? Or as eye, hand, foot, and in general each of the parts evidently has a function, may one lay it down that man similarly has a function apart from all these?

As we have seen from Aristotle's biology, to ask for the function of a living thing (or a part of a living thing) is simply to ask what it typically and naturally does. Thus the function of an eye is to see, and so 'the good' for an eye is for it to see well. Now there are all sorts of things which man naturally does. He eats, breathes, perceives, sleeps, acts, thinks and so on. But most of these things are also done by other creatures as well, and thus do not count as part of man's distinctive function. What we are left with when we have subtracted these shared activities, says Aristotle, is reason or intelligence. It is those of man's activities which in one way or another involve intelligence that mark him off from other creatures, so it is here that the function of man and therefore the key to *eudaimonia* will be found.

Man typically and naturally makes plans, has motives, calculates consequences, tries to work things out, performs intentional actions and reflects on and studies things. These all involve intelligence. It follows that 'the good' for man involves doing each of these things well, or 'in accordance with the appropriate [*form of*] excellence'. That is to say, the activities and behaviour of a good and happy man will exhibit the virtues appropriate to each sphere of intelligent action and rational thought. He must behave in this way not just once or twice but in the context of a complete life, 'for one swallow does not make a summer, nor does one day; and so too one day, or a short time does not make a man blessed and happy'. We have already seen that ill-fortune can take the bloom off *eudaimonia*; thus to count as having the very best sort of existence, a man will also need a reasonable supply of good fortune and to be 'sufficiently equipped with external goods', some of which, like health, are necessary preconditions of well-being, and others, like wealth, are useful tools for the performance of noble acts.

Still, it is virtuous activity which is the main thing, so one must look more closely at that. Aristotle divides the main forms of human excellence into two groups: virtues of character (i.e., moral virtues) and intellectual virtues. Both sorts of virtue are connected with reason. The intellectual virtues, such as skill at planning and intellectual insight, are embodiments of reason itself. And the moral virtues, such as courage and generosity, are said to 'listen to' reason, or be guided by it. While the intellectual virtues are involved in dispassionately formulating plans, calculating consequences and weighing up circumstances, the moral virtues incline one to act in certain ways. They make one want to do certain things. Thus the two sorts of virtue work hand in hand to produce right action.

Aristotle argues that the moral virtues are neither innate nor unnatural. They are best regarded as acquired dispositions that are reinforced by repeated use. To have a generous character, for example, is to choose to act generously whenever the appropriate opportunity arises, and the more you take such opportunities, the firmer your disposition to generosity becomes. Vices are just like that too. A mean man is one who regularly chooses to behave in a certain way, and the more he does it, the more hardened a miser he becomes. Because vices are thus the result of past choices, Aristotle held that each person is morally responsible for his vices. He acknowledges that once a habit has become ingrained, you cannot just snap out of it; but he insists that people are ultimately to be held responsible for the habits they have let themselves get into.

If virtue and vice are both acquired dispositions to want to act in certain ways, what marks the essential difference between them? Aristotle argues that it lies in the fact that in each sphere of life one can go wrong in two opposite ways: roughly speaking, one can go wrong either by doing or feeling too little, or by doing or feeling too much. The vices either 'fall short of or exceed what is right in both passions and actions', so each virtue consists in an ability to steer a middle course between the two vices that stand either side of it. Take, for example, those circumstances calling for confident and fearless action. On one side of the virtue of bravery stands rashness, and on the other side stands cowardice. On one side of modesty stands shamelessness, on the other side shyness, and so on through all the virtues of character. In general:

moral excellence is concerned with passions and actions, and in these there is excess, defect, and the intermediate. For instance, both fear and confidence and appetite and anger and pity and in general pleasure and pain may be felt both too much and too little, and in both cases not well; but to feel them at the right times, with reference to the right objects, and in the right way, is what is both intermediate and best, and this is characteristic of excellence. Similarly with regard to actions also there is excess, defect, and the intermediate ... excess is a form of failure, and so is defect, while the intermediate is praised and is a form of success.

Aristotle is not just singing the uninspiring praises of moderation here. That is not what finding 'the intermediate' means, because some occasions call for extremes of behaviour and emotion. For example, if something is thoughtlessly and outrageously selfish, one should be very angry about it, not meekly placatory. One can, after all, suffer from an excess of moderation. Finding the intermediate is rather a matter of finding the emotion or action that is neither too much nor too little for the circumstances at hand. It is precisely because this 'intermediate' can be determined only by reference to concrete circumstances that Aristotle holds that ethics cannot just be a matter of knowing general rules and principles. The intellectual virtue of practical wisdom needs to be applied on the spot in order to find the appropriate, 'intermediate' course.

Aristotle argues that this way of looking at virtue and vice can be applied to matters concerning courage, temperance, money, honour, friendliness, anger, pride, truthfulness and shame, among other things. He even applies it to joke-telling: to have the virtue of wit, he says, is to steer the narrow course between buffoonery and boorishness. One place where he runs into trouble with this approach is where he discusses justice, which he divides into distributive justice (i.e., the distribution of goods and honours), rectificatory justice (the righting of wrongs) and reciprocal justice (fair exchange). His attempt to tie all these things into one bundle gets rather tangled, as he more or less acknowledges. Still, some of the analyses of legal and economic concepts in his discussion of justice have been so influential that they now seem obvious. One recent commentator points out in this context that 'Aristotle's works are full of platitudes in much the same way as Shakespeare's *Hamlet* is full of quotations.'

To sum up the story so far: the good life will require a certain minimum of material comfort and general good fortune, but the crucial thing is to do all the characteristically human things well and from the right motives. Such a life will bring the sort of pleasures that a wise man judges to be best. A new twist is added to the story when it emerges that one particular activity is even more valuable than the rest, so that the very best form of life would be the one devoted to that. This activity turns out to be *theoria*: intellectual contemplation, or the pursuit and enjoyment of truth for its own sake. This is a convenient thing for a philosopher and scientist to hold. It is rather like hearing a baker maintain that the best sort of life would be a life of baking bread. Whether it is a convenient thing for Aristotle to hold, given his supposedly down-to-earth approach to the question of how to live, is an intriguing question. The shadow of Plato – and even of Pythagoras and Orphism – seems to be falling over Aristotle at this point.

Aristotle believes that 'the life according to intellect is best and pleasantest, since intellect more than anything else *is* man'. He has already established that it is intelligence or reason which marks man off from the other creatures. He now offers several arguments to show that a capacity to engage in the disinterested pursuit of truth is the 'best thing in us'. For one thing, it is the one activity we share with the gods. As we saw when considering what the Unmoved Mover does with his time, the only activity appropriate for a deity is contemplation (see page 246). And there are several other considerations which make this the likeliest candidate for the ultimate aim of life. It provides pleasures that do not wax and wane as others do, but can be enjoyed more or less continuously; these pleasures are 'marvellous for their purity and enduringness'. The life of contemplation is also the most self-sufficient, which is supposed to be a mark of the best life. You do not need to depend on anything or anyone in order to get it. It seems to be the only activity which is loved for its own sake, since everything else (or so Aristotle claims) is done in the expectation of gaining something over and above the pleasures of the activity itself. Lastly, it is an activity of leisure, which is for Aristotle another sure sign of the best sort of life.

There is room for dispute about what exactly Aristotle's *theoria* involves. In the case of man, it is not clear whether it will include active scientific pursuits of the sort Aristotle himself excelled at, or whether it must be limited to inactive contemplation (as it presumably is in the case of God, who does not need to go and get a closer look at anything). Either way, it is clearly very near or even identical to the sort of disinterested pursuit of knowledge which the Pythagoreans praised as the true path to salvation. In the Pythagoreans, in Plato and in Aristotle, the capacity for *theoria* is the one divine spark in mortal nature that provides a window to eternity – though it seems that in Aristotle's case, one can only look through this window, not climb out of it, since there is no personal immortality.

Aristotle's praise for *theoria* was thus not a wholly novel development in Greek ethics. But what he and other philosophers said about it must have stood out as more than a little odd. Greek moralizing has its background in Greek literature, especially in the tragedies of Sophocles and above all in the epics of Homer, whose stories everyone could be expected to know. The lives of the familiar heroes of these works provided the common currency and starting point of Greek thought about 'the good' for man. From these works one learned that practical wisdom and various other virtues were all components of the model life, but that these ingredients did not guarantee *eudaimonia*, because things could always go wrong (and in tragedies they always did). It is in their praise for the virtue of *theoria* that the philosophers came furthest from the *Iliad* and the *Odyssey*. Odysseus had plenty of practical wisdom, of the sort which Aristotle argued was essential for a good life; but *theoria* was not exactly up his street. He did not poke out the Cyclops' solitary and unusual eye because he wanted to dissect it or formulate syllogisms about its working parts. Homer's works would have been very different if his heroes had kept taking time off for contemplation and the pursuit of knowledge; they were more likely to take time off for sulking, as Achilles did. It is also hard to see how *theoria* is supposed to fit in with the virtuous life as described by Aristotle, let alone that portrayed by Homer. If such an elevated pastime is the most desirable one for man, where does that leave the worldly blessings, good fortune and mundane virtues like courage, wit and all the rest which Aristotle has been talking about? As we have seen, Aristotle's gods do not bother themselves with such earthly irrelevances as justice. So why should man?

There is a conflict here; but it is, from Aristotle's standpoint, not so much a flaw in his theory of human life as an ineradicable conflict in the human condition itself. For man has a composite nature, as the Orphics, Pythagoreans and Plato said. On the one hand he is a mortal animal living among others of the same kind. As such, he must practise the human virtues, if he is to live this life well. And he will naturally want the necessities of life and the good fortune to enjoy them. On the other hand, man has something that not only distinguishes him from the animals but also gives him a share in what a divine life must involve. Given this fact, 'we must not follow those who advise us, being men, to think of human things, and, being mortal, of mortal things, but must, so far as we can, make ourselves immortal, and strain every nerve to live in accordance with the best thing in us'. The virtuous life is a balancing act, with the demands of humanity on one side and the demands of divinity on the other.

Aristotle acknowledges that an existence of pure contemplation or inquiry 'would be too high for man; for it is not in so far as he is man that he will live so, but in so far as something divine is present in him'. As a man he will mostly have to settle for happiness 'in a secondary degree' by living in accordance with the everyday virtues that 'befit our human estate'. Still, the idea of the contemplative life as the ultimate form of happiness gives us a focus for our ideas of perfection. No doubt we will regularly fall short of this ideal, and also even fail to live up to the more mundane 'secondary' virtues. But if we at least know what we are trying to do, then 'shall we not, like archers who have a mark to aim at, be more likely to hit upon what we should?'

This may seem a disappointingly academic conclusion. No doubt it is useful to have a target to aim at, but one was expecting a little more than that. Aristotle was, after all, supposed to be the practical one: he clearly said that 'we are inquiring not in order to know what excellence is, but in order to become good'. On closer examination, however, it turns out that Aristotle's approach to the matter is, if anything, all too practical, because it emerges that his answer to the question 'How can I become good?' is: 'If you weren't brought up to be good, then you will have to be forced to be good by the state.' For Aristotle, ethics is a sort of prologue to politics, and it is politics that delivers the goods. Ethics studies the forms of excellence to be found in the best people's characters and actions, and thereby reveals the aim of a worthwhile life. Politics studies the laws and constitutions that will encourage such excellence and let it flourish. It is therefore politics which is the 'master art' that produces happiness and goodness on a commercial scale. Aristotle was under no illusions about the power of mere rational argument. Virtue, as he tries to show in his work on ethics, is a matter of character, and character is largely a matter of habits: 'It makes no small difference, then, whether we form habits of one kind or of another from our very youth; it makes a very great difference, or rather *all* the difference.' So it is up to legislators to 'make the citizens good by forming habits in them'. A select few of the citizens will arrive at a 'conception of what is noble and truly pleasant' – perhaps by reading Aristotle's treatment of ethics – and will manage to act in accordance with it. But in general 'it is through laws that we can become good'.

I shall not examine Aristotle's writings on politics, in which he investigates the particular laws and forms of society that might achieve this. (On constitutional matters, he spends a great deal of time attacking communism and ends up somewhat grudgingly advocating a limited form of democracy.) Instead, the last part of this chapter will briefly look at some of his views on poetry. It turns out that poetry also has a role to play in making us good, at least indirectly.

If they were asked whether history or poetry is more like science, most people today would answer 'history'. After all, history is supposed to be fact and poetry is not. But Aristotle would have said that poetry is more like science, and that this is exactly why poetry has greater moral significance than history. This paradox is not hard to explain once we recall what Aristotle thought science was about and what he thought ethics was about.

We have seen that according to Aristotle the mark of a highly developed science is that it deals with the universal or essential truths about each type of thing – for example, that all cows are ruminants. One of his favourite ways of putting this was to say that science is concerned with 'that which is always or . . . for the most part'. It has little interest in chance events, incidental details and passing oddities (which is one of the drawbacks of Aristotelian science, but that is another story). Now history is the very opposite of this, according to Aristotle, because it is full of happenstance and is not guided by the search for general truths. It is therefore unscientific in his sense. History deals with particular things that just happen to have happened. But the best poetry, such as the works of Homer or the tragedies of Sophocles, cuts through irrelevant circumstances to focus on universal truths about life and human nature. Good poetry (which includes good drama) draws our attention to the essential characteristics of various human types by limiting the behaviour of its heroes and villains to what one would expect to find in such people 'always or for the most part'. It follows that 'poetry is something more philosophical and more worthy of serious attention than history; for while poetry is concerned with universal truths, history treats of particular facts. By universal truths I mean the kinds of things a certain type of person will probably or necessarily do in a given situation.'

The idea that poetry focusses on character does not fit much of what we call poetry, but it does fit most of what Aristotle regarded as the best sort, such as the *Iliad* or *Oedipus Tyrannus*. Ethics, too, is concerned with character and action, and since poetry simulates or imitates these things, it can hardly fail to have some sort of moral significance. By conjuring up certain types of people and actions, and by skilfully prompting us to take certain attitudes towards them, the best type of poet tones up our virtuous dispositions by putting us on a sort of mental exercise-machine. Virtue, after all, 'consists in rejoicing and loving and hating rightly', and in desiring virtue we are concerned to 'acquire and to cultivate . . . the power of forming right judgments, and of taking delight in good dispositions and noble actions'. Poetry can help to cultivate these things, because 'feeling pleasure or pain at mere representations is not far removed from the same feeling about realities'.

Still, Aristotle did not regard poetry in general as primarily a tool for self-improvement nor the theatre in particular as a preacher's pulpit and nothing more. The purpose of poetry, and indeed of all the fine arts, was simply to produce pleasure by means of various types of imitation, even if it did inevitably also have a moral dimension. It is natural for man to imitate things and to take delight in the products of imitation. Aristotle did not share the stern and sometimes bizarre disapproval of these pleasures expressed in Plato's *Republic*. Plato held that most poetry made one emotional and weak; it encouraged all the wrong things; it should, on the whole, be banned. At the end of the *Republic* Plato makes the character of 'Socrates' raise philosophical objections to the whole enterprise of artistic imitation, on the grounds that it distracts attention from the really important things in life, namely the ideal Forms. Given that the physical things which man erroneously takes to be reality are just shadows dancing on the wall of a cave, the representations to be found in the arts are even further removed from reality. Pictures and poems are imitations of physical things, and physical things are in turn imitations of the Forms. So poetry, drama, music and the visual arts are imitations of imitations, shadows of shadows. Art is a cave within a cave.

It seems that Plato could not make up his mind about just how bad a thing this cave within a cave was. Sometimes he said merely that poetry should be censored and that politically correct forms of it could be allowed an airing (this should probably be regarded as his considered view). At other times he said that it must be banned altogether, except for 'hymns to the gods and the praises of good men'. When Plato was in this sort of mood, even Homer had to go. Aristotle agreed that young children should be protected from some types of poetry; Plato, even in his relatively moderate moments, wanted to treat everyone like children, which was typical.

While Plato's main advice to poets was to get lost or else pick safer subjects, Aristotle's treatise on the topic has the more positive and practical aim of explaining how good poetry works.

Drawing on a wide knowledge of poems and plays, he tries to analyse their virtues and explain how they achieve their pleasurable and uplifting effects, which leads to his much-discussed definition of tragedy, the most important subject dealt with in his incomplete treatise on *Poetics*:

Tragedy is ... the imitation of an action that is serious, and also, as having magnitude, complete in itself; in language with pleasurable accessories, each kind brought in separately in the parts of the work, in a dramatic, not in a narrative form; with incidents arousing pity and fear, wherewith to accomplish its *catharsis* of such emotions.

(There is a long-standing controversy over what he meant by 'catharsis'; I shall return to this later. For now it is enough to note that its main meanings in most Greek contexts of the time were 'purgation' and 'purification'.)

What must the characters and plot of such a drama be like? The central hero should be basically good, since otherwise the audience will not pity him in his misfortunes. He should be fairly prominent, presumably because a fall from a great height is all the more pitiable.

Also, since sympathetic fear is evoked only by the plight of someone 'like ourselves', the hero must be as virtuous as the audience no doubt take themselves to be, but no more. Another reason why the hero of a tragedy must not be too good is that otherwise his unhappy ending will merely disgust us as an undeserved injustice. He must have some flaw or make some momentary error – give way to a rash impulse, for example. And this must be what brings about his fall, otherwise the misfortune that overtakes him will be a meaningless piece of bad luck and not a fitting subject for a serious play. Clearly, the tragic poet has quite a tightrope to walk. In addition, the characters must be lifelike and consistently portrayed, even if inconsistency is part of their nature, in which case they must be shown as 'consistently inconsistent'.

As for the plot of a good tragedy, pity and fear should be evoked not just by some horrible stage-effect such as blood and gore but by the story itself. In a well-made play, it is the unfolding of events that really does the trick. The two most important plot devices by means of which tragedy plays on our feelings are 'reversals' and 'discoveries'. A reversal occurs when an action or event produces the opposite of what was intended or expected – for example, when the messenger in *Oedipus* brings news that he believes to be good but which turns out to have dreadful implications. The messenger incident in *Oedipus* also happens to be an example of the sort of discovery on which the plot of a tragedy hinges, because it produces the revelation of Oedipus' true parentage, which is the key calamity of the play. It is best, said Aristotle, if reversal and discovery arrive combined in this way; but the crucial thing is that everything should develop believably out of what has come before, so that there is nothing inexplicable about what happens as the horror grinds to its piteous and fearful conclusion.

It is evident that Aristotelian tragedy is no mere morality play in which a villain gets his gratifying come-uppance. Provided the writer has done his job well, one leaves the theatre not cheering that justice has been done but in a rather more tranquil and perhaps reflective frame of mind. Why is this? Aristotle had plenty more to say about poetry, but nothing perhaps so interesting as what he does not say about the state of *catharsis* which tragedy produces. How is it that we take a sort of pleasure in this artificial stimulation of pity and fear when it is positively unpleasant to feel either of these things in real life? Plato raised this question but never answered it. Aristotle's theory of *catharsis* would have contained his answer, but the full treatment that he promised was either lost or never written. One can, however, make a few informed guesses about it.

According to the simplest theory, what tragedy provides is a purgation in a pseudo-medical sense. It flushes out the unpleasant feelings of pity and fear in a gratifying evacuation. But that crude idea would not have made sense for Aristotle, because he would not have thought it desirable to get rid of pity and fear. According to him, it is right to feel these emotions on certain occasions; the best sort of person will feel them in the right amounts at the right time. The emotions need educating, not expelling. Perhaps, then, a better explanation of *catharsis* can make use of the concept of purification, which is another of the word's basic meanings. Since a tragedy is designed to make one experience pity and fear in a carefully constructed set of circumstances, perhaps we should regard the experience as one which refines our emotional responses by giving us an entertaining form of practice in directing them at the right things. One recent commentator on Aristotle suggests that the pity and fear aroused by watching *Oedipus*

might lead a timorous man to realize that his own fears are exaggerated, and that his own misfortunes are not so terrible; yet the same play might arouse in a powerful and confident person, prone to feel and behave arrogantly towards others, the thought that even the mightiest ruler might one day need the sympathy and help of those weaker than himself.

Whatever their characters and personal circumstances, the members of the audience will thus experience an educational 'purification' of their responses; they will feel a certain sort of pleasure in so doing because, according to Aristotle, it is naturally enjoyable to watch 'imitations', especially if one learns something from them. Although an Aristotelian tragedy is not a simple sort of morality play, that does not mean that it is no sort of morality play.

The moral and emotional effects of literature, and the relationship between the two, remain enough of a mystery for it to be sad that one can only guess at what Aristotle thought about it all. If he had written a book on goldfish and it had become lost, we could be confident that we had not missed much. In the case of his treatment of the effects of poetry, it is hard to be so sure.

Another missing part of his treatise on poetics – a part which almost certainly was written – is his treatment of comedy. There are some attempted reconstructions of it based on early secondary sources, and there is also an engaging fantasy on the subject in Umberto Eco's thriller, *The Name of the Rose*. In this novel, Aristotle's lost work on comedy is discovered in the Middle Ages by a Benedictine monk. He finds its contents so horrifying in their implications for Christendom that he devotes his miserable life to protecting the world from any knowledge of it. (Because the monk is a librarian he cannot bring himself to destroy the book, until the fatal *dénouement* of his own drama.)

Before the book is part-eaten, part-burned, some of it is read out. In an amusing reversal of what the real Aristotle had said about tragedy, this text sets out to show how comedy 'in inspiring the pleasure of the ridiculous . . . arrives at the purification of that passion'. It proceeds to analyse how this mirror-image of tragedy produces laughter by

likening of the best to the worst and vice versa, from arousing surprise through deceit, from the impossible, from violation of the laws of nature, from the irrelevant and the inconsequent, from the debasing of the characters, from the use of comical and vulgar pantomime, from disharmony, from the choice of the least worthy things.

The monk's objections to such comedy are similar to those expressed in Plato's *Republic*: laughing at comedies makes us cynical, shallow and ignoble. But the monk also goes much farther. He thinks that a serious analysis of comedy, such as the one found in this supposed tract, could set a bad example and have awful social consequences:

if one day somebody . . . were to raise the weapon of laughter to the condition of subtle weapon . . . if one day . . . the art of mockery were to be made acceptable, and to seem noble and liberal . . . if one day someone could say (and be heard), 'I laugh at the Incarnation,' then we would have no weapons to combat that blasphemy . . . This book would have justified the idea that the tongue of the simple is the vehicle of wisdom.

Why should he think that one book could have such a large effect?

Because it was by the Philosopher. Every book by that man has destroyed a part of the learning that Christianity had accumulated over the centuries. The [*Church*] fathers had said everything that needed to be known about the power of the Word, but then . . . the divine mystery of the Word was transformed into a human parody of categories and syllogism. The book of Genesis says what has to be known about the composition of the cosmos, but it sufficed to rediscover the *Physics* of the Philosopher to have the universe reconceived in terms of dull and slimy matter . . . Before, we used to look to heaven, deigning only a frowning glance at the mire of matter; now we look at the earth . . . Every word of the Philosopher, by whom now even saints and prophets swear, has overturned the image of the world.

From the point of view of an especially narrow-minded and conservative Christian living in the later Middle Ages, that might be a fair summary of some of Aristotle's effects on Western thought. After his main works had been rediscovered in the twelfth century, and before Christianity found ways to assimilate them, they were viewed with suspicion and sometimes banned. Aristotle championed logic and rationality, which threaten to overturn blind faith. He championed the careful study of earthly things, which distracts man from thoughts of the heavens. The monk continues: 'But he had not succeeded in overturning the image of God. If this book . . . had become an object for open interpretation, we would have crossed the last boundary.' That is, if intellectuals had paid as much attention to this work of Aristotle's as to some of his other ones, the world would have become too anarchic and light-hearted for a Christian God. This is a wild fantasy, certainly. But only of a work of the revered Aristotle could one even entertain the idea that it might have had so great an impact.

# PART THREE

# 13

# Three Roads to Tranquillity: *Epicureans, Stoics and Sceptics*

Aristotle died one year after his former pupil, Alexander the Great. By common convention, Alexander's death in 323 BC marks the start of a new era in ancient history, the 'Hellenistic age', which has a convenient terminus nearly 300 years later with the picturesque death of Cleopatra, the Roman annexation of Egypt and the rise of a new empire as Greece gave way to Rome. Alexander's achievement had been to carry Greek culture into far-flung territories in a ten-year rampage south to Egypt and east to India. After his death, leaving no clear successor to run an empire that had anyway been too quickly assembled to stay in one piece, the newly enlarged Greek-speaking world became a patchwork of monarchies ruled by Alexander's former generals (Cleopatra was the last ruler of the dynasty established by Ptolemy Soter, one of Alexander's generals in Egypt). Now that it was spread thinly over a wide area, Greek culture inevitably became diluted in a soup of foreign ideas and religions. Alexander's former domain became a Hellenistic world rather than a Hellenic one – that is to say, it was Greek-ish rather than purely Greek. Athens ceased to be the centre of the intellectual map, as Alexandria in Egypt, Antioch in Syria, Pergamon in Asia Minor and later Rhodes in the eastern Aegean became rival centres of learning. Athens remained unchallenged as the capital of philosophy until well into Christian times. But philosophy itself was changing; it had a wider, more cosmopolitan audience to satisfy. The Hellenistic period brought a new era in philosophy as well as in general history.

It was in those days that Western philosophy came to be seen as above all a guide to life and a source of comfort:

Empty are the words of that philosopher who offers no therapy for human suffering. For just as there is no use in medical expertise if it does not give therapy for bodily diseases, so too there is no use in philosophy if it does not expel the suffering of the soul.

So said Epicurus (341–271 BC), the most famous of the new Hellenistic philosophers, and on this point he spoke for all of them. There were three main new schools of thought: the Epicureans, the Stoics and the Sceptics. On the whole, if an Epicurean said one thing, a Stoic would say the opposite and a Sceptic would refuse to commit himself either way. But there was something about which they could all agree: philosophy was a therapeutic art, not just an idle pastime for people who were too clever by half.

Epicureanism and Stoicism were to some extent popular creeds in a way that the drier teachings of Plato and Aristotle could never be. The Platonic and Aristotelian schools continued to exist in one form or another throughout the Hellenistic period, doing research and teaching an elite. They certainly had something to say about how one should live, but not perhaps much that could readily be understood and even applied by the ordinary man in the market-place. By contrast, many of the new Hellenistic philosophers were keen popularizers. Indeed to some critics their teachings were all too easy to understand. Cicero, a Roman orator and statesman whose sympathies lay instead with the more academic school founded by Plato, later wrote that the fact that Epicureanism was 'so easily grasped and so much to the taste of the unlearned' just went to prove how vague and inconsequential it was. Many Athenians had evidently not seen it that way. With a reputation for having something intelligible to say about life, the new philosophers could attract large crowds in Athens, especially for their funerals.

The new schools of thought owed more to Socrates than they did to Plato or Aristotle. It was Socrates who had stressed the practical relevance of philosophy. Its point, he urged, was to change your priorities and thereby your life. The Hellenistic philosophies tried to deliver on this Socratic promise. In particular, they claimed to be able to produce the sort of peace of mind and tranquil assurance that Socrates himself had conspicuously possessed. But in their hands the ideas of Socrates were shaped to suit a more inward-looking perspective. Socrates may have been famously tranquil in adversity, but he never claimed that such tranquillity was itself the aim of life. The Epicureans, Stoics and Sceptics regularly spoke as if it were. They all praised something called *ataraxia* – untroubledness, or freedom from disturbance – as if it were the ideal state of mind. Socrates had argued that a good man cannot be harmed, because the only sort of harm that matters is the harm you do to your own soul by being bad. The new Hellenistic philosophers gave this a more subjective twist: the wise man will not let himself be troubled, for the key to wisdom is knowing what not to care about.

We have already seen that, although Socrates was plainly a man with a message, there was room for dispute about what that message was (see page 160). Two of his companions, Aristippus and Antisthenes, apparently derived their very different philosophies from the words and life of the master. The pleasure-loving Aristippus was a forerunner of Epicureanism, and the ascetic Antisthenes a forerunner of Stoicism. So both of these Hellenistic philosophies could think of their doctrines as Socratic in some sense. The Sceptics, too, could claim descent from Socrates. Socrates was always saying that he knew nothing, though he didn't mean it literally; the Sceptics said the same, and apparently did. Socrates was always questioning any ethical ideas he came across; the Sceptics did the same, and did not limit their persistent probing to ethics.

The new Hellenistic schools were more wide-ranging than Socrates had been, but their strict sense of priorities still reflected the narrow focus of his interests. Socrates was not exactly gripped by scientific questions; nor, apparently, did he have much to say about logic, knowledge, the mind or many of the other philosophical topics that were discussed in the schools of Plato and Aristotle. For Socrates the question of how to live seems to have been the only one worth asking. Although Stoics, Epicureans and Sceptics did address themselves to all sorts of intellectual matters, they insisted that the sole point of doing so was to be able to live a happy life. All wisdom was thus held to be subordinate to ethics, as it had been for Socrates. The Epicureans and the Stoics expounded theories about many things; the Sceptics happily set to work on any doctrines that fell into their disputatious jaws; but the new schools always professed ulterior, curative motives for the pursuit of inquiry.

The Epicureans claimed that the point of inquiry was to crush dangerously false beliefs. They said that one of the main obstacles to happiness was irrational fear and that the best cure for such fear was a dose of sensible physics and a spot of logical exercise. For example, by demonstrating that the mind was nothing but a collection of atoms which would disperse when life departed, they held that the fear of death could be conquered and life thus enjoyed all the more. The Stoics claimed that the point of inquiry was to help man to live a life 'in accordance with nature'. Such a life was the key to happiness, and it would of course be impossible to pursue without an understanding of what nature was like. For instance, the Stoics held that one prerequisite of a happy life was the knowledge that everything is determined by fate, because knowing this fact would produce the right attitude of acceptance and resignation. Thus it was necessary to delve into various scientific matters in order to prove the existence of fate. As for the Sceptics, they held that the aim of inquiry was to make people suspend judgement on each question, in order to stop worrying about it. The way to do this was to demonstrate that one could argue every question both ways, which was no easy task, so the Sceptics got as deeply involved in intellectual matters as anyone else. The result is that all three schools of philosophers ended up discussing physics, and many other things that Socrates had apparently shunned, and yet their motives for doing so always boiled down to a search for happiness and tranquillity.

This fact affected the way they looked at scientific questions. The Stoics and Epicureans were naturally drawn to topics that promised to shed light on man and his place in nature. Thus while they were more than happy to speculate about the general nature of the universe, or to argue about fate and natural causes, they had little desire to follow Aristotle up the digestive tract of the cow. As far as they were concerned, zoology was a topic with little philosophical pay-off. Sometimes their ulterior motives for inquiry were embarrassingly evident. The Epicureans were often quick to accept any old explanation for a phenomenon just so long as it could be explained away and thus not be frightening any more. The Stoics tended to be unhealthily interested in fortune-telling because it seemed to confirm their belief in fate. In general, none of the new schools shared Aristotle's disinterested intellectual curiosity or his polymath's passion for accumulating accurate information. Some of Aristotle's followers at the Lyceum continued his tradition of genuine, open-minded research, but they were the exceptions among Athenian philosophers and comparatively speaking they did not amount to much. In Hellenistic times it was not the philosophical schools of Athens which earned a place in the history of science. The real action was now elsewhere.

The new kingdoms that had been carved out of Alexander's domain were larger and richer than the old city-states like Athens and Sparta. They could afford to sponsor the arts and sciences out of the royal purse, which they did on a grand scale. The kings competed for the prestige of attracting the best people in as many fields of learning as possible. The Ptolemies in Egypt, for instance (who ruled from the death of Alexander until the Roman annexation in 30 BC), collected eminent intellectuals for their research institute at Alexandria in the same way that they collected rare manuscripts for their famous Library. They showered such men with grants and salaries and offered other practical help (doctors, for example, were given bodies from the state prisons to dissect). Such bribery paid off. Euclid and Archimedes were the scientific giants of the third century BC – indeed, of the whole ancient Greek world – and they both worked at Alexandria.

In mathematics, astronomy and medicine (and in engineering, from giant catapults for warfare to a rudimentary steam engine), virtually all the scientific achievements of the Hellenistic period took place away from Athens and away from the people who are now remembered as philosophers. When the Epicureans and Stoics talked about nature, their type of theorizing had more in common with today's ruminative popular-science writing, or today's philosophy of science, than with research at the cutting edge. Most of the Hellenistic philosophers painted nature with a broad brush and were not too concerned with details. As a result, it is often said that it is at this point in Western history that philosophy and science momentously diverged, thus ending the joint project that had been begun by men like Thales and Anaximander three centuries earlier.

But this idea of a sudden break between science and philosophy gives too simplistic a picture of the relation between the two. If there had been some such magic moment when they started to go their separate ways, one would expect there to be agreement about when that moment came. Yet one finds a wide range of conflicting answers to the question of when science split away from philosophy. While some say it happened in Hellenistic times, others say it happened with Pythagoras in the sixth century BC. Some say it was in the time of Parmenides at the beginning of the fifth century BC; some in the time of Socrates about fifty years later. Others say it was not until the time of Galileo, early in the seventeenth century. One writer argues that the split was not complete until Kant in the eighteenth century. Another says it did not really take hold until the nineteenth.

There was, it is safe to conclude, no such magic moment at all; yet each of these answers points to a significant stage in the development of intellectual life. Take Pythagoras first. Whatever else he may also have been, he put himself forward as a mystical sage who could reveal the meaning of life and death to his initiates, which does not sound very scientific. So here, already in the sixth century BC, is one sort of model for the philosopher who wants to be something more than a scientist. A different and ultimately more influential sort of model was provided by Parmenides of Elea and his pupil, Zeno. They reflected on and criticized some of the concepts that the earliest philosopher-scientists had used but had never really examined, such as motion and change. Thus the Eleatics emphasized another facet of philosophical thinking that could arguably be taken to distinguish it from most everyday scientific work, namely abstract reflection on fundamental concepts. As for Socrates, he was widely credited with 'bringing philosophy down from the heavens' and setting her in the cities of men. That is, he talked about ethics and politics rather than about cosmology. But the shift of focus he thereby effected in philosophy has been exaggerated, as we have seen (page 86), for other people soon tossed philosophy back up to the heavens again.

The seventeenth century brought a number of changes in the way that searchers for truth went about their everyday business. The natural sciences became both more mathematical and more dependent on experiment and systematic observation. The specialization that had become noticeable in Hellenistic times intensified. But none of this would have been seen in the seventeenth century as prompting a conflict, let alone a divorce, between science and philosophy. In those days nobody would have understood what could be meant by such a thing. For, despite the revolutionary changes it was undergoing, what we call 'science' – the systematic investigation of nature – was still regarded as a branch of philosophy. It was called 'natural philosophy' ('science' usually meant simply 'knowledge' or 'skill'). The mathematical and experimental developments of the seventeenth century could be seen as causing a conflict between Aristotelian philosophy and newer philosophies, but not between philosophy *per se* and science *per se*.

Nor does one find any such conflict in the thought of Kant in the eighteenth century, though superficial readings of his works have suggested otherwise to some people. True, Kant contrasted the sort of information one gets from experience (i.e., from observations and experiments) with the results of abstract reflection, which he called 'pure reason'. But he did not think of science as exclusively concerned with the former and philosophy with the latter. Kant saw Newton's work, for example, as an intimate marriage of the two. It was not until later that the accumulation of knowledge forced a degree of specialization which is close to what we have today. In 1840 a British philosopher and historian, William Whewell, coined the term 'scientist', thus providing a neat way of distinguishing between those who produced the raw material for investigations of nature and those who tried to stand back and say something about what it all added up to. Even so, these roles could still be combined. Indeed, to this day it remains impossible to define them in such a way as to distinguish them absolutely. The borders between science and some parts of philosophy remain vague.

The upshot of all this is that the Hellenistic era may have been a milestone in the history of specialization, but it was not a turning-point. Although it was as an unscientific form of therapy that philosophy made the headlines in those days, and although some of the sciences meanwhile made headlines of their own, it would be wrong to think of science and philosophy as splitting like an amoeba, completely and forever, at that point in history. A lot of philosophy became more personal and introspective, and some of the sciences became more like a full-time job; but neither of these things was altogether new or by any means permanent. There had been specialists before and there would be polymaths again.

If the new Hellenistic schools were not altogether revolutionary, they did leave deep impressions on later thought, both by their styles of thinking and by their doctrines. The way that they offered comprehensive and popular philosophies of life, and the way they organized themselves into warring sects which tried to argue one another out of business, greatly affected the way later civilizations saw philosophy. When a well-known writer of Roman times like Cicero or Plutarch wrote about philosophy, it was the rival intellectual playgrounds of Hellenistic Athens that he mostly wrote about. Roman popularizations of Hellenistic philosophies (by Lucretius, Seneca and Marcus Aurelius, for example) have been among the most widely read philosophical works in European literature.

For a time, Stoic ethics was more or less the official philosophy of the upper classes in the Roman Empire; Stoicism also has loud echoes in Christianity. More importantly, it is barely an exaggeration to say that the modern era in science and philosophy began with the rediscovery of the ideas of the two other Hellenistic schools, Epicureanism and Scepticism. The 'new' philosophies which arose to challenge Aristotelianism in the seventeenth century had in fact very old Greek roots. Early in that century, physics was transformed by the rediscovery of Epicurus' version of atomism – his vision of an infinite and mechanical universe of interacting particles – and of his 'empiricist' approach to knowledge, with its emphasis on the importance of observation and experience. These were crucial components of the scientific revolution that overthrew the Aristotelian world-picture. So was the growing influence of scepticism. If modern philosophy had an official birthday, it would be on the day in 1562 when a key sceptical text was published in Latin, thus beginning a rejuvenation of the subject after the big sleep of medieval scholasticism. Some sixty-five years later, Descartes began to apply the method of 'systematic doubt' which he had learned from ancient scepticism, and philosophy has been shaped by the persistent questioning of the Sceptics ever since. More of that story will be told in the next chapter. But first an outline of the ideas of the three Hellenistic schools that sprang up in Athens after Aristotle's death.

\*

Like Pythagoras two centuries earlier, Epicurus (341–271 BC) came from Samos, an Ionian island off the south-west coast of Asia Minor. Also like Pythagoras, he founded the sort of commune that attracted hostile gossip. One rebellious former member sold his story: he wrote of Epicurus' 'notorious midnight philosophizings' and claimed that Epicurus vomited twice a day from over-eating. He wrote that Epicurus' acquaintance with philosophy was small and his acquaintance with life even smaller; that his health was so bad that for years he could not get out of his chair; but that he nevertheless enjoyed close relations with four women in the commune who were known by the nicknames of Hedeia ('Sweety-Pie'), Erotion ('Lovie'), Nikidion ('Little Victory') and Mammarion ('Big Tits').

EPICVRVS.

Mud like this has stuck to Epicurus – and, later, to Lucretius (*c.*99–*c.*55 BC), his best-known popularizer – ever since. The Romans commonly referred to Epicurus as 'the Pig'. St Jerome (AD 340–420) made the apparently groundless statement that Lucretius was driven mad by a love-potion and wrote his great Epicurean poem in a few lucid moments before committing suicide. John of Salisbury, a twelfth-century bishop, said that 'the world is filled with Epicureans for the simple reason that in its great multitude of men there are few who are not slaves to lust'. In the end, the name of Epicurus simply became synonymous with the excessive enjoyment of food, as in the words of a British wit, the Reverend Sydney Smith (1771–1845):

> Serenely full, the epicure would say,
> Fate cannot harm me, I have dined to-day.

But the truth about Epicurus and his followers seems be rather different. The commune that he established when he moved to Athens, in a house and garden just outside the walls of Plato's Academy, was in fact devoted to the simple life. It stressed the importance of an unadorned diet and condemned all forms of over-indulgence. As for sex, who knows exactly what Epicurus got up to with Sweety-Pie in his garden? But his official doctrine was largely against it: 'sex is never advantageous, and one should be content if it does no harm'. Lucretius said much the same, as we shall see. Ironically, it was probably the extremes of his passionate denunciation of sexual love which gave rise to the idea that he must have been driven out of his mind by a love-potion.

Still, one can easily see how the rumour-mill began and why later moralists and Christians lapped up the gossip. Epicurus did say that one needs first of all to be fed in order to lead a happy life. That could easily be quoted out of context and it no doubt was. His religion was theologically incorrect – his 'gods' were irrelevant swarms of atoms, and he was contemptuous of everyday religious beliefs. That in itself was bound to lead to trouble. Above all, his philosophy of life was explicitly focussed on 'pleasure', and that does not sound very virtuous.

It may be true, as one old history of European morals claims, that 'Roman vice sheltered itself under the name of Epicurus'. But when we look at what Epicurus himself says about pleasure, a picture emerges that would surprise those who know only the gossip:

when we say that pleasure is the end [*i.e., goal of life*], we do not mean the pleasures of the dissipated and those that consist in having a good time, as some out of ignorance and disagreement or refusal to understand suppose we do, but freedom from pain in the body and from disturbance in the soul. For what produces the pleasant life is not continuous drinking and parties or pederasty or womanizing or the enjoyment of fish and the other dishes of an expensive table, but sober reasoning which ... banishes the opinions that beset souls with the greatest confusion.

Epicurus' advocacy of 'pleasure' was a more sophisticated matter than the philosophizing of the luxury-loving Aristippus lolling at the banquets of Dionysius I. Unlike Aristippus, Epicurus did not focus on grabbing the fleetingly pleasurable sensations of the moment, but rather on ensuring a comfortable balance of satisfaction over dissatisfaction in the course of life as a whole. He was well aware of the dangers of cashing in pleasures today if such indulgence means a net loss of pleasures in the long run.

Moreover, he saw pleasure in a largely negative way: in its purest form it was just the absence of pain. This is because pain is not just somebody stamping on your foot and pleasure is not just a kiss from Sweety-Pie. According to Epicurus, if we look at what pleasure and pain really amount to, we see that we are constantly tossed between them. Either we are satisfied with something, which is to say we find it pleasant, or we are dissatisfied, which is to say we want something else or more of the same – and to want something is to feel a lack, which counts as a form of pain. So pain lurks around every corner, especially if one tries too hard to pursue a life of intensely agreeable sensations. This is not only because of such things as upset stomachs and upset rivals in love, but because the pain of unsatisfiable desire is never far away when one gives free rein to one's greediest appetites. The life of unalloyed pleasure, then, will have to be a rather quiet affair. It will be a life in which all potential sources of distress have been eliminated – a life of 'freedom from pain in the body and disturbance in the soul'. For Epicurus, that would be the ultimate pleasure.

Since freedom from distress is what Epicurus is really concerned with, his advocacy of 'pleasure' is not quite the threat to conventional virtue that philosophies of self-gratification are usually taken to be. According to Epicurus, if you concentrate on fending off pain, anxiety and fear, you will find that you are thereby living a virtuous life. For if you think about all the ways in which life can turn nasty, you will realize the 'impossibility of living pleasurably without living prudently, honourably and justly, and the impossibility of living prudently, honourably and justly without living pleasurably. For the virtues are naturally linked with living pleasurably, and living pleasurably is inseparable from them.'

For example, if you are truly dedicated to Epicurus' sophisticated form of pleasure, you will want to avoid committing any injustice, because 'the just life is most free from disturbance, but the unjust life is full of the greatest disturbance' – as Plato also argued in the *Republic* when he tried to show how unhappy a tyrant's life was bound to be. Also, a wise Epicurean will want to cultivate the art of friendship, which is lovingly praised again and again in the writings of Epicurus. This 'immortal' blessing, he argued, provides steady and lasting joys which can counterbalance some of the inevitable sorrows of life. In general, the amicable Epicurean community seems to have been marked by a natural generosity and benevolence: one of its maxims notes that 'It is more pleasurable to confer a benefit than to receive one.'

The fact that Epicurus describes virtue as a prudent course that will pay worthwhile dividends may make Epicureanism sound a self-centred philosophy. So in a sense it is, because it begins by appealing to the individual's desire to pursue pleasure and avoid pain. But this emphasis on the individual's point of view simply reflects the fact that what Epicurus was trying to do was reveal the secret of personal happiness. It does not follow that society, for all he cared, could go to pot. He might well have answered such an allegation by pointing out that if you reform each individual along Epicurean lines, by showing him where lasting satisfaction and calm is to be found, then society will look after itself. As he says: 'the undisturbed man causes no stress to himself or to anyone else', so a happy man makes a good citizen. Besides, when the Epicureans turned to address social and legal matters, the apparent self-centredness of their philosophy disappeared. Their treatment of such issues was expressed in terms of the pleasure and welfare of society as a whole.

The social philosophy of Epicurus, such as it is, is the main ancestor of the 'utilitarianism' of Jeremy Bentham (1748–1832) and John Stuart Mill (1806–73). Bentham began his treatise on morals and legislation with the Epicurean observation that 'Nature has placed mankind under the governance of two sovereign masters, *pain* and *pleasure*.' The principle of utility, most famously formulated by Bentham in terms of 'the greatest happiness of the greatest number', instructs one to produce a maximum of pleasure and a minimum of pain. Such a principle is supposed to guide the good utilitarian as he calculates the consequences of actions and policies in order to decide what to do, just as Epicurus spoke of a careful 'calculation and survey of advantages and disadvantages'. The main differences between Epicurus and the utilitarians are ones of emphasis and motivation. First, the Epicureans focussed on conquering fear and anxiety, whereas utilitarianism tends to be concerned with more positive measures of welfare. Second, while utilitarianism was specifically intended to guide law-makers and politicians, Epicurus warned his followers against any direct involvement in public life: 'We must liberate ourselves from the prison of routine business and politics.' Epicureanism might well have made a fine system for running the world; but Epicurus and his friends were inclined towards less stressful occupations.

Epicurus preferred to fight dangerous beliefs rather than rival politicians. He was after all a practitioner of philosophy, 'an activity which by arguments and discussions brings about the happy life'. The first step on the road to happiness was to secure basic comforts such as freedom from hunger. Although one might think that 'arguments and discussions' are not much help with that sort of thing, it turns out that they can be, for example by convincing us how little we really need. According to Epicurus, many of our problems in life are caused not by our actual circumstances but by our false beliefs about them: 'What is insatiable is not the stomach, as people say, but the false opinion [*that it needs*] unlimited filling.' Not only do we strive to get things that are in fact unnecessary or even undesirable, we are also afraid of things that are not there, and worry about things that won't happen. We are unnerved by superstitions because we do not understand how the world really works; we are oppressed by the thought of fate for much the same reason; and we are in a complete muddle about death, because we have not grasped what life is. Such anxieties and confusion cause the pains which do most to blot out the pleasures we could be enjoying. Philosophy, particularly in the form of scientific knowledge, is the answer for such 'fears concerning celestial phenomena and death and distress'.

Debunking the fear of death was a speciality of the house for Epicurus and his followers. They argued that tales about the unhappy disembodied souls of the dead must be scare-stories, because the mind or soul is a physical thing that does not survive the death of the body. Lucretius argued that the 'mind and spirit must both be composed of matter', and so must share the fate of the rest of the body, because 'we see them propelling the limbs, rousing the body from sleep, changing the expression of the face and guiding and steering the whole man – activities that all clearly involve touch, as touch in turn involves matter.

How then can we deny their material nature?' The main thing to grasp was the truth of Democritus' picture of life as a precarious assemblage of mechanically interacting atoms. According to this picture, when atoms are arranged in a certain way the result is a living creature that can think, feel, move about and so on. When this arrangement falls apart, and we die, there will be no thought or feeling left. So the state of being dead is not something we ever experience, either pleasantly or unpleasantly. The process of dying might sometimes be unpleasant, but the state of being dead cannot be so, 'seeing that when we exist death is not present, and when death is present we do not exist'.

Lucretius noted that for the dead person himself, being dead will be no different from not yet having been born. And the Epicureans had plenty of other reassuring observations on the subject: 'a correct understanding that death is nothing to us makes the mortality of life enjoyable, not by adding infinite time, but by ridding us of the desire for immortality'. Thus 'the wise man neither deprecates living nor fears not living. For he neither finds living irksome nor thinks not living an evil. But just as he chooses the pleasantest food, not simply the greater quantity, so too he enjoys the pleasantest time, not the longest.' Clear thinking shows that we do not need an infinite time in order to enjoy a complete life. In fact, worrying about death and longing for immortality just wastes the time we have got. So too does quaking and shuddering in a state of superstitious terror – for which, once again, the cure is Democritus' atomism. His account of the world shows us that signs and wonders in the upper atmosphere are a matter for atomic science, not for burning chickens and wailing at the sky. The universe is not ruled by gods but by atoms, and atoms have no interest in prayers and sacrifices. Actually, the gods are not interested in these things either, since they are busy enjoying a life of blessed tranquillity. The last thing they would want is to listen to the begging of anxious mortals, or to get involved in the administrative nightmare of organizing a good thunderstorm.

Although Epicurus spoke of gods, it is not clear in what sense he believed in them. Certainly he rejected tales of the gods intervening in everyday life and the sort of creation-story told in Plato's *Timaeus*. It was a proud boast of atomism that gods were not required in order to account for the workings of the natural world, a boast which Lucretius, for one, took great pains to justify with his ingenious and sometimes bizarre theories about everything from magnets to milk. To explain the apparently beneficent design of living creatures, the Epicureans adopted a crude type of Darwinian theory of natural selection, which they picked up from Empedocles (see page 80). Epicurean gods were not even needed to keep the heavens in eternal motion, as they had been in Aristotle's universe. Still, Epicurus agreed with Aristotle that the belief in gods was so widespread that it could not be altogether false. It turns out, however, that it was not altogether true either.

It seems that Epicurus' gods are nothing more than ghostly clusters of atoms. They are not solid beings like us, but have more in common with the streams of atoms which Epicurus and Lucretius talk about when they try to explain perception and imagination. When we see a tree, according to their theory, what happens is that the tree gives off a flimsy tree-shaped aura of atoms that enters our eyes. Every object continuously emits thin films of atoms, like a smouldering log giving off smoke, and this is how we manage to perceive things. Sometimes these atomic films mingle in the wind – 'they are delicate and easily join together in the air when they meet' – and they form a hybrid cluster, which is what gets into our heads when we have a hallucination or when we fancy that we see a creature like a centaur or a unicorn. Imagination and dreaming also involve fine swarms of atoms in the head: having a fantasy or a nightmare is a matter of having received some of the many free-floating atomic clusters from the air and sometimes jumbling them up further. Gods, too, are the flimsy mixed-up stuff of dreams. Our thoughts of gods are some sort of idealization, based on human-shaped images that stream in from the outside, plus ideas of perfection concocted on the inside. We think of gods as looking roughly like people – if we are ancient Greeks – because that is how they appear in our visions of them; and we think of them as enjoying a tranquil and undisturbed existence, because that, according to Epicurus, is what fits our ideal of the perfect life. Yet this way of talking seems to blur a crucial question: do these gods actually exist, or are they merely figments of the imagination?

The answer to that is, surprisingly, 'both'. Epicurus held that 'all impressions are true'. That is, everything which the senses tell us has some basis in reality. They never lie completely. So if the senses tell us that there are gods – which according to Epicurus they do, in our dreams and visions – then gods there must be. But we have to be careful what we conclude from these impressions of gods, because it is easy to misinterpret the messages that the senses give us. Although all impressions are true, 'opinions, on the other hand, are not all true since they are judgements which we make on the basis of our impressions, and we judge some things correctly, but some incorrectly, either by adding and appending something to our impressions or by subtracting something from them'. For example, when we have a dream about a unicorn, we should not jump to the conclusion that there is a solid creature wandering about with a spike sticking out of its horse-like brow. That 'opinion' or 'judgement' illicitly goes beyond the evidence, for in fact all that the senses are saying to us is that a unicorn-shaped stream of atoms has got into our heads. Similarly, although the senses provide us with dreams and visions of gods (or so Epicurus says), this does not necessarily mean that there are any solid beings striding around and hurling thunderbolts. Gods are real in the way that all our sensory images are real: they are clusters of atoms which enter our minds. They are real atomic images but not real solid bodies. That is why gods, and unicorns, can be described both as actually existing and as creatures of the imagination.

Yet if gods are real only in the way that unicorns are real, why does Epicurus not come clean and admit that he is an atheist? If some lunatic were to set up a temple to unicorns, Epicurus would presumably not go and pray in it. Why, then, does he pay lip-service to gods? Part of the reason is that openly denying them would not exactly have been a recipe for a peaceful existence in third-century Athens. Also, the gods were a useful vehicle for Epicurus' ethical ideals. To speak of them as leading a tranquil and undisturbed existence was a convenient way to express his deepest beliefs about life.

Epicurus may have been privately sceptical about gods, but he had no time for the general sort of scepticism that was becoming popular with some philosophers. Hence his idea that what the senses tell us is always true in one way or another: this was part of his answer to scepticism. The problem he was addressing went back to Democritus, who said that the senses paint a misleading picture of the world because they tell us that things are sweet, bitter, hot, cold, coloured and so on, whereas in fact there is nothing but 'atoms and void'. According to Democritus, qualities like taste and colour really belong in the mind, because they are just effects which the various configurations of atoms have on us. Now although Democritus did not himself draw the conclusion that we therefore have no firm basis for any knowledge of the world, others did draw this conclusion, and Epicurus thought it was time to call a halt to such nonsense.

His main point was that if you doubt everything the senses tell you, then you are up the creek without a paddle: 'If you fight against all sensations, you will not have a standard against which to judge even those of them you say are mistaken.' For example, suppose you see a tower in the far distance and it looks round, but when you get closer it looks square, and you conclude that its apparent roundness was an optical illusion. Can you say that the senses misled you about its shape? Not really, because although it was the senses which at first seemed to tell you that the tower was round, it is also the senses which later show you that it is square, when you get a closer look. If the senses sometimes lie, they also sometimes tell the truth. And you would not be able to tell that they were sometimes lying unless you could also sometimes tell that they were being truthful. In order to overthrow the senses you would have to find something more reliable than they are, but what could that be? Epicurus concluded that they cannot be overthrown, so one must somehow base one's knowledge on them after all.

The way to do that, he thought, was to be clear about how the senses work and what their limitations are. They work simply by registering the arrival of incoming atomic patterns, a job which there is no reason to doubt they do perfectly well. But although every sensation is equally valid when considered as a source of information about the thin streams of atoms that affect the sense organs, it is not equally valid when considered as a source of information about the solid objects (if any) which emit these fine atoms. This is because, as we have seen, the atomic patterns can get distorted in transit or in the mind. Lucretius discussed the example of the tower and said that what happens is that the fine streams of atoms it emits get disfigured as they travel the long distance through the air to our eyes. They get rounded off at the edges during transit, so what we receive is an image of a round tower. But when we see the tower close up, the atoms have a shorter distance to travel and do not get so misshapen. Epicurus said that some sensory impressions are more clear and distinct than others and that these are the ones to go by. Our dreams and hazy visions of gods, and our glimpses of very distant objects, for example, are not enough on which to base firm conclusions about the world outside. But some other impressions are. He had no definitive answer to the question of how one tells whether or not an impression is clear and distinct enough to rely on, but he did offer one or two helpful rules of thumb. One is that the closer you are to an object, the more likely you are to get reliable impressions from it.

By treating the evidence of the senses carefully, then, we can avoid misinterpreting them and so avoid ending up with false opinions about the world. Epicurus himself was guilty of one such false opinion on a quite magnificent scale. He said that the sun measures only about a foot in diameter, apparently because this is how it looked to him and because he could see no reason to suppose that it was too far away to judge. Still, this is not so much a fault in his principles as in his application of them. The fact that Epicurus was ludicrously wrong about the sun does not mean that the senses are ludicrously wrong about everything. His whole point is that it is people who make mistakes, not the senses. As Lucretius put it: 'do not trump up this charge against the eyes, for a fault which belongs to the mind'.

This remark underlines the way in which all of the Epicurean philosophy hangs together. It is always the mind which is at fault and the mind which needs therapy of one sort or another. Just as our unhappiness comes, on the whole, from our misguided beliefs about our situation and not from the way things are in themselves, so our perceptual mistakes should be blamed on our own faulty interpretations, and not on what the senses innocently tell us. In neither case is it nature herself who is the source of our problems, for nature is fundamentally benign. She even helpfully guides us about how to live, by placing us, as Bentham later put it, under the governance of the two sovereign masters of pleasure and pain. Nature has implanted in us an instinct to pursue the one and avoid the other, and it is ultimately by following these generously provided signposts that we will flourish. It is because we frequently do not know how to follow them, since we are polluted by false beliefs of various sorts, that we need Epicurean treatment to help steer us away from the pains of fear, anxiety and distress.

If taking the Epicurean cure is often a matter of impersonal atomic science, with its reassuring explanations of death, dreams and disasters, it can also sometimes be a matter of intimate counselling. The subject of sex provides one example. Lucretius tried to diagnose and treat what he took to be the deeply upsetting disease of sexual passion. Such passion is a bad thing because it produces the very opposite of the Epicurean's ideal of *ataraxia* or tranquillity: it is 'storm-tossed, even in the moment of fruition, by waves of delusion and incertitude'. By clinging to your passion, he wrote, 'you assure yourself the certainty of heart-sickness and pain. With nourishment the festering sore quickens and strengthens. Day by day the frenzy heightens and the grief deepens.'

According to Lucretius, sexual passion is bound to come to grief because it is a distortion of natural impulses by means of unrealistic desires and false beliefs. It stimulates desires which cannot be satisfied since they are based on illusion and idealization. For one thing, lovers want to (and apparently believe they can) consume and be united with the object of their passion, which is of course impossible:

Body clings greedily to body; moist lips are pressed on lips, and deep breaths are drawn through clenched teeth. But all to no purpose. One can glean nothing from the other, nor enter in and be wholly absorbed, body in body, for sometimes it seems that that is what they are craving and striving to do. At length, when the spate of lust is spent, there comes a slight intermission in the raging fever. But not for long.

Also, a lover tends to be blinded to the true mental and physical qualities of his beloved, overestimating her virtues and glossing over her defects. (Lucretius always referred to the lover as male and usually referred to the beloved as female.) The result of all this is not only private turmoil, frustration, anxiety and jealous suspicion, but also bad health, neglected duties and the loss of time, money and reputation.

Prevention is the ideal cure for this dreadful disease. One must always be on one's guard and look out for the early signs so as not to be enticed. If one is already ensnared in such a passion, the best advice is to concentrate resolutely on all the failings of one's paramour. If you think of her as a 'sprite', she is probably in fact a 'stunted runt'; if you think of her as 'delicate', she is probably 'half-dead with coughing'; if you tend to say things like 'she burns with a gem-like flame', the chances are she is in fact 'a waspish fiery-tempered scold'. You must bear all these things in mind. And even if she is a good specimen and worth all the praise, it helps to remember that there are plenty more where she came from, and that it was perfectly possible to live without her before she turned up. Lastly, don't forget that 'in her physical nature she is no different from the plainest of her sex. She is driven to use foul-smelling fumigants. Her maids keep well away from her and snigger behind her back.'

That should do the trick. Passion is unlikely to survive such cool reminders. Another piece of helpful advice is to 'Vent the seed of love on other objects.' Lucretius' imagery is not intended metaphorically: for him, the problem is partly the physiological one of an excess build-up of 'seed' in the sex organs. It needs to be disposed of, and a courtesan might provide a convenient receptacle. But not just anything can spark off the urge to vent this unhealthy accumulation. The swollen organs are stimulated or provoked only by the sight of certain human forms, such as 'an alluring face and a delightful complexion', and it is towards these forms that our frenetic attentions become directed. What happens in wet dreams is that atomic clouds forming such images of beauty enter our bodies and – as in all dreams – we take them to be genuine perceptions of solid human beings, because the mental faculties that could disabuse us of this illusion have been shut off by sleep. It turns out that it is not only in dreams that sexual desire is ultimately the pursuit of elusive phantoms. The fact that it is ignited by an influx of human images, both in sleep and in waking life, explains why amorous appetites are intrinsically unsatisfiable and therefore troublesome:

Food and fluid are taken into our body; since they can fill their allotted places, the desire for meat and drink is thus easily appeased. But a pretty face or a pleasing complexion gives the body nothing to enjoy but insubstantial images, which all too often fond hope scatters to the winds.

Since you cannot literally eat your beloved, your passion is doomed.

One might well conclude from this that it is Lucretius rather than the lover who is in need of some sort of treatment. Some love-stories, after all, do have happy endings, and they are sometimes quite nice in the beginning and even in the middle as well. Lucretius would reply that he is by no means condemning all forms of amicable attachment, only mad passion, or 'Venus', as he calls it. It is only the painful extremes of love which he seeks to diagnose and to treat. Nevertheless, he does seem to err on the side of caution in his attitude to personal relationships, for he prizes calm, stability and cool judgement above all else. There is never any hint that some sacrifice of the quiet life might occasionally be worthwhile. 'Live dangerously' is not a motto that is likely to have appealed to him, or indeed to any Epicurean. Plato sometimes described the intoxicating abandon of love as one of its delights – love could be a thoroughly desirable form of madness. For Epicurus and Lucretius, by contrast, nothing that was bound to end in tears could be worth even beginning.

One or two changes needed to be made to the Democritean theories about atoms that Epicurus and Lucretius used in order to explain the world to their anxious and confused patients. The most interesting novelty introduced by Epicurus was the 'swerve' – a tiny and unpredictable sideways jump which atoms sometimes made. This was supposed to solve two difficulties in Democritus' world-picture, one of them purely a matter of physics and the other having direct implications for human life. The first difficulty concerns collisions between atoms. For various reasons, Epicurus argued that Democritus' atoms would fall through empty space at the same speed and always straight downwards, each on its own trajectory. But how then would they ever bump into one another and join up to form ordinary physical objects? As Lucretius put it: without an occasional sideways swerve, 'no collision would take place and no impact of atom on atom would be created. Thus nature would never have created anything.' Epicurus concluded that there must be some randomness in nature, an unpredictable hop that took one atom into the path of another. Cicero called this idea 'a piece of childish fancy', but it is analogous to the indeterminacy or randomness found in modern quantum mechanics. The second problem, which was also to be solved by the swerve, is even more intriguing. Epicurus was apparently the first to state it, and it has become one of the central problems of philosophy.

It is the problem of free-will and determinism. If everything that happens is the blind and mechanical result of the motion of atoms, how can anybody be free? And how could anyone be held morally responsible for what he does? A person's actions will not really be 'his' actions at all, but just the inevitable result of atomic motions in his body. This was a particularly galling thought for Epicurus. The Epicureans thought that fortune-telling was a load of rubbish, but now it looked as if atomism itself implied that the future could be laid out like a pack of cards. Here was Epicurus, prescribing his scientific picture of the world as an antidote to the belief that people's lives were in the lap of the gods or in the hands of fate, and now the atoms themselves turn out to be just as bad as fate. In fact, Epicurus argued, Democritus' atoms were even worse than fate:

it would be better to follow the mythology about gods than be a slave to the 'fate' of the natural philosophers: the former at least hints at the hope of begging the gods off by means of worship, whereas the latter involves an inexorable necessity.

Lucretius also put the problem in terms of fate:

if all movement is always interconnected, the new arising from the old in a determinate order – if the atoms never swerve so as to originate some new movement that will snap the bonds of fate, the everlasting sequence of cause and effect – what is the source of the free will possessed by living things throughout the earth? What, I repeat, is the source of that will-power snatched from the fates, whereby we follow the path along which we are severally led by pleasure, swerving from our course at no set time or place but at the bidding of our own hearts?

If atoms sometimes swerved unpredictably, as Epicurus and Lucretius believed, then the 'bonds of fate' could be snapped. The 'everlasting sequence of cause and effect' was not so everlasting after all, and could be interrupted. Thus, by allowing room for atomic swerves in his physics, Epicurus thought he could avoid the inhumanly deterministic aspect of Democritus' theory. Some physicists in the twentieth century said much the same thing about the liberating possibilities of quantum mechanics. With the discovery of indeterminacy, wrote Sir Arthur Eddington in 1928, 'science thereby withdraws its opposition to freewill'.

The idea that randomness holds the key to the freedom of the will seems to be perennially tempting. But it is fraught with confusion. For what exactly are Epicurus and Lucretius saying? Are they saying that acts of will are random swerves of particles in the brain? If so, they seem to be saying that a person's actions count as free provided that they are unpredictable. But that cannot be right, because randomness is surely incompatible with the ideas of autonomy and of personal responsibility. As a recent British philosopher, A. J. Ayer (1910–89), pointed out:

if it is a matter of pure chance that a man should act in one way rather than another, he may be free but he can hardly be responsible. And indeed when a man's actions seem to us quite unpredictable, when, as we say, there is no knowing what he will do, we do not look upon him as a moral agent. We look upon him rather as a lunatic.

If Epicurus thought that acts of will are random swerves of atoms in the body, and that this fact is what gives people control over their own actions, then he was certainly in a colossal muddle. But that may not have been what he meant. It is possible that what he was trying to say is just that the existence of random hops in the movement of atoms shows that nature leaves various possibilities open, and thus does not determine absolutely everything. If an atom can be free to swerve in various directions, perhaps we too are free to exercise acts of will over our bodies, so that not everything we do is simply the mechanical and inevitable result of atomic cause and effect. If something like that is what Epicurus had in mind, then he was not necessarily confusing randomness with freedom. But if we cannot convict him of confusion, we must admit that his answer to the problem of free will does not amount to much. For he does not manage to say anything definite about what these acts of will consist in. They remain mysterious, and it is not clear how they fit into the atomic picture of the world. Perhaps in the end it would be too much to expect him to solve the problem of freedom when he had only just succeeded in posing it.

Or maybe he had more to say on the subject, but in a book that perished. Epicurus' main works, like those of all the Hellenistic philosophers, are lost to later generations who might have valued them more than their early custodians did. What survives intact are various popularizations that he wrote – 'for a comprehensive view is often required, the details but seldom' – and some collections of his sayings. This makes it hard for us to measure his intellectual sophistication against that of Plato or Aristotle. It is clear, however, that his whole style of thinking was a far cry from theirs. He distrusted technical terms, intricate proofs, abstractions and convoluted definitions, not just in popular works but altogether. These things, he thought, tended to seduce the mind away from the real world of nature that is revealed by the senses and explained by atomic science.

Epicurus was not in the same business as Plato and Aristotle; he did not even bother to try to refute them. Whereas they had dangled philosophical wisdom as a distant carrot at the end of arduous studies, no previous education was required in order to grasp the truths of Epicurean philosophy. Indeed, a philosophical education in the style of Plato or Aristotle was likely to be a positive hindrance. Wordy theorizing could easily lead one astray: 'we must grasp the things which underlie words, so that we may have them as a reference point against which to judge matters of opinion, inquiry and puzzlement'. A philosopher needs his feet planted firmly on the ground so as not to get swept away by a wave of words and drowned in a whirlpool of ingenious dialectical arguments. As one modern commentator put it, Epicurus aimed to 'keep thought always in the closest and most immediate relation with reality'. This meant coming to terms with the fact that, in Epicurus' words, 'all our notions are derived from perceptions, either by actual contact or by analogy, or resemblance, or composition, with some slight aid from reasoning'. The mind and its thoughts are material things, collections of atoms like everything else, and they are affected primarily by the influx of atoms through the sense-organs. It follows that whatever validity our thoughts might have as sources of knowledge must derive from this circumstance. Experiences of the world are 'the things that underlie words', and so all our talk and theorizing must be put to the test of experience.

This is the thesis of 'empiricism', which was enthusiastically revived in various forms in the seventeenth century. But it is not for any theory about knowledge or physics that the Epicureans have mainly been remembered, or would have wished to be. Their main legacy is the philosophy of life whose nature and benefits were warmly described by Lucretius, 200 years after the death of Epicurus and the fellow inhabitants of his garden:

When the winds are troubling the waters on a mighty sea it is sweet to view from the land the great struggles of another man; not because it is pleasant or delightful that anyone should be distressed, but because it is sweet to see the misfortunes from which you are yourself free. It is sweet too to watch great battles which cover the plains if you yourself have no share in the danger. But nothing is more pleasing than to be master of those tranquil places which have been strongly fortified aloft by the teaching of wise men. From there you can look down upon other men and see them wandering purposelessly and straying as they search for a way of life – competing with their abilities, trying to outdo one another in social status, striving night and day with the utmost effort to rise to the heights of wealth and become masters of everything. Unhappy minds of men, blind hearts! How great the darkness, and how great the dangers in which this little life is spent. Do you not see that nature shouts out for nothing but the removal of pain from the body and the enjoyment in mind of the sense of joy when anxiety and fear have been taken away?

Therefore we see that for the body few things only are needed, which are sufficient to remove pain and can also provide many delights. Nor does nature itself seek for anything more pleasing, if there are no golden statues of youths in the entrance halls holding in their right hands fiery torches so that evening banquets may be provided with light, or if the house does not gleam with silver and shine with gold and a carved and gilded ceiling does not resound to the lute, when, in spite of this, men lie on the soft grass together near a stream of water beneath the branches of a lofty tree refreshing their bodies with joy and at no great cost, particularly when the weather smiles and the time of year spreads flowers all over the green grass.

Epicureanism was a personal cult and continued to be so even after the guru himself had gone. On the 20th of every month, Epicurus' followers celebrated a festival to his memory in the house and garden which he left to a successor when he died in 271 BC. They recited some of his books from memory, just as they had done when the great man was still alive. They spread the gospel and tried to emulate his way of life. Nobody revered him more than Lucretius: 'You, who out of black darkness were first to lift up a shining light, revealing the hidden blessings of life,' he wrote, two centuries after the death of the master, 'you are my guide, O glory of the Grecian race. In your well-marked footprints now I plant my resolute steps.'

The Stoics were less of a one-man show. There were three main phases in the 500-year development of Stoicism, none of them dominated by any one thinker. The first Stoics took their name from the porch (*stoa*) in the Athenian marketplace where their official founder, Zeno of Citium (*c*.333–262 BC), held forth; but Chrysippus (*c*.280–207 BC), an ingenious philosopher who specialized in logic and physics, was just as much of an influence on the first phase of Stoicism as Zeno had been. If there had been no Chrysippus, went an old saying, there would have been no Stoicism. Chrysippus is believed to have written 705 books, not one of which survives (though there are quite a few fragmented quotations from them in other people's works). The best-known Stoic writings are those of three Roman writers, Seneca, Epictetus and Marcus Aurelius, whose works primarily offer moral instruction and consolation. They are the models of resigned 'stoicism' in the modern sense of the word. Marcus was a lenient and humane emperor of the second century AD, whose reign was spent in difficult times and who came to regard life as largely nauseating. Epictetus (AD 50–*c*.120) was a former slave who was much occupied with the nature of freedom and the things in life that cannot be enslaved, such as one's private thoughts. Seneca (4 BC–AD 65) was a public official, orator and dramatist who was exiled to Corsica after being accused, probably falsely, of adultery with the emperor Claudius' sister. He was brought back to educate the young Nero, was eventually commanded by Nero to commit suicide, and evidently had plenty to be stoical about. In between the 'early *stoa*' of Zeno and Chrysippus and these much later Stoics of the Roman Empire came the 'middle *stoa*' of Panaetius and Posidonius, two innovative thinkers who introduced Stoicism to the Roman world in the second century BC.

By Roman times, then, anybody who wanted to tread in the foot-prints of Stoicism had a choice of tracks to follow. They all led to roughly the same place, though: there was a core of ideas held in common by the various forms of Stoicism. The main ones come from a cocktail mixed by Zeno out of ingredients apparently picked up on his tour through the Athenian schools of philosophy. First and foremost among his teachers were the Cynics: from them came the idea that nothing much mattered except virtue. The trappings and values of conventional society were therefore to be rejected, or at least down-graded to the level of irrelevant distractions. Zeno endorsed the Cynics' hardy and resolute attitude to life, which made his philosophy sound like good solid stuff to the upper classes of Imperial Rome. (These upright imperial administrators were not so keen on the outrageous unconventionality of Cynics like Diogenes in his famous tub. Nor would they have been sympathetic to some of the more revolutionary, Cynic-inspired ideas in the political works of the first Stoics. These utopian books, usually entitled *The Republic*, like Plato's, described a world in which public buildings were not allowed, but incest, cannibal-ism and unisex clothing were.)

Zeno learned from the Platonists as well as from the Cynics. He seemed to like the thought behind Plato's creation-story in the *Timaeus*, according to which the world was designed and made by a beneficent intelligence. This idea made the miseries of life easier to bear up to: everything was ultimately for the best, even if on the surface it frequently appeared not to be. For the Stoics, as for Heraclitus, a key ingredient in the recipe for happiness was learning to live with the inevitable. As a later, Roman Stoic put it: 'Do not seek to have every-thing that happens happen as you wish, but wish for everything to happen as it does happen, and your life will be serene.'

This desire for serenity recalls the tranquil Epicureans, as does the same author's insistence that all of life's real problems are in the head:

It is not the things themselves that disturb men, but their judgements about these things. For example, death is nothing dreadful, or else Socrates too would have thought so, but the judgement that death is dreadful, *this* is the dreadful thing. When, therefore, we are hindered, or disturbed, or grieved, let us never blame anyone but ourselves, that means, our own judgements.

But the Stoic treatment for erroneous belief was very different from Epicurean therapy, both in substance and, at least in the early days of Stoicism, also in style. Unlike Epicureanism, early Stoicism had an academic side to it; Zeno had studied in the Platonic Academy and had picked up some of its ways. The Stoics were responsible for an explosion of philosophical jargon, as their critics were fond of pointing out, whereas Epicurus had said that one should always use the familiar words for things so as not to get lost in a thicket of specialist terminology. Many of the early Stoics were keenly interested in technical questions of logic, which the Epicureans on the whole steered clear of (though they did dabble in some abstract questions about language). Over 300 of Chrysippus' books were on various aspects of logic. This subject mattered to the Stoics because of the role it played in the production of knowledge: logic told you how to draw correct inferences from what you already know, and so helped to keep your judgements accurate. Chrysippus also plainly enjoyed the subject for its own sake and wrote a great deal about puzzles and paradoxes, such as the famous one about the man who says 'what I am now saying is false'.

In addition to matters of style and approach, large differences between Stoicism and Epicureanism emerge in their almost entirely opposed views of nature. Although the Stoics agreed with the Epicureans that most people do not realize what sort of universe they are living in, and so are bound to end up confused in their attitudes to life, they thought that the Epicureans were just as ignorant as anyone else – if not more so. There was just one thing the Epicureans were right about: that everything was physical. In opposition to Plato and Aristotle, both the Epicureans and the Stoics were firm materialists. There were not two worlds, as Plato had said, consisting on the one hand of ordinary physical things and on the other of ideal Forms and souls. According to the Stoics, Plato's ideal Forms were really just concepts in the mind, which is a physical thing, and so were themselves fundamentally physical. As for the soul, Plato was wrong to suggest that it consisted of some non-material stuff, and Aristotle was wrong to say that it was not made of any sort of stuff at all. For the Stoics and the Epicureans, it was made of the same material stuff as everything else. Still, on every other question about nature, the two Hellenistic schools were at loggerheads.

The Epicureans said that the world is the unplanned product of haphazard forces; the Stoics said it is rationally organized down to the last detail. The Epicureans said that the universe does not operate with any purposes in mind and that the gods are permanently on holiday; the Stoics retorted that a beneficent God, or providence, is thoroughly in charge and always on the job. The Epicureans said that the course of nature is not wholly determined in advance – there are, for instance, random swerves of atoms; the Stoics said that everything unfolds according to fate in an inexorable chain of cause and effect, and, moreover, that it will unfold in exactly the same way again and again in a cycle of cosmic creation and destruction. The Epicureans held that each person is completely free in his actions; the Stoics denied this, because of their belief in fate (though they still held that people are morally responsible for what they do). The Epicureans said that reality consists of atoms colliding by chance in the void to form everything we see; the Stoics said that matter is suffused with a sort of fiery breath (*pneuma*) that animates, organizes and directs it into various shapes and forms, and that atoms have nothing to do with it.

Like their ethics, the physics and cosmology of the Stoics were adapted from many earlier sources. They used the old four-element system of earth, air, fire and water instead of these new-fangled packets of atoms. Their sketchy stories about astronomical phenomena, the weather and all the other usual topics sure to attract the curiosity of ancient Greeks were variations on themes that had been familiar to the first naturalists two centuries earlier. The Stoics also seem to have drawn heavily on Heraclitus' unusual world-picture. He had promoted fire to a special status among the team of elements; their hot *pneuma* was similarly favoured. They spoke of *pneuma* and of God and of the organizing principle of nature as basically the same thing, which recalls Heraclitus' vague idea of a fire-like intelligence or soul that animates the world. Heraclitus apparently thought that the universe is destroyed and created over and over again, meeting its end each time in a cosmic bonfire before its embers spring once more to life. Whether or not he actually thought this – the idea may have been foisted on him retrospectively – the Stoics certainly did. And, given their belief that everything had been arranged by providence in the best possible way, it followed that each cycle of the world's history would have to be exactly the same. This is because there is only one best way to do things, so that is the course which providence will want to follow each time round. Why tinker with the perfect recipe?

The main novelty in Stoic physics was its use of the notion of complete mixture, or interpenetration, to explain how *pneuma* is breathed into the inert forms of matter which it activates. To understand this, consider the difference between two types of physical combination: solid particles stuck on to one another like bricks joined up to make a house; and substances mingled together like water mixed in with wine. For the Epicureans and other atomists, ordinary objects like trees, houses and people were assembled in the first sort of way. Their constituent atoms were affixed to one another but did not merge. For the Stoics, on the other hand, the physical world was a thoroughly stirred concoction in which substances become wholly intermingled. They held that different substances can interpenetrate one another and become threaded together to form homogeneous wholes. It is in this way that the hot, airy *pneuma* permeates all other matter and mingles with it. The world is thus a dense continuum of the various forms of matter, through which the ubiquitous *pneuma* ripples like waves across a pond.

On the question of how exactly *pneuma* acts to form and guide the world, one gets little more than mumbled excuses. The Stoics did not want to get bogged down in details. Yet some of their ideas have intrigued historians of science for the way in which they seem to anticipate later developments. It has been argued that the ripples of energetic *pneuma* which are spread throughout the physical world are analogous to the 'fields of force' that have featured in physics since the nineteenth century. And the intermingling of active *pneuma* and passive matter reminds some people of the equivalence of energy and matter in Einstein's theories. Indeed, it has seemed natural to some physicists after Einstein to describe the world in ways that would have made the Stoics nod in agreement:

Under all forms of matter and manifestations of life there beats the unity of energy according to Einstein's law. Yet this unified stuff of existence not only twists itself into the incredible variety of material things; it can also produce living patterns of ever greater complexity – from the gas bubble in the original plasma to the crowning complexity of the human brain.

Like Aristotle's physics, Stoic physics had some of its best moments when it turned to the concepts of space, time and infinity; but those quasi-mathematical matters need not concern us. What is of more immediate interest is the way the Stoics' overall view of nature bears on their philosophy of life, for that philosophy is their main legacy to the world.

The best-known mark of Stoicism is its attitude of resigned acceptance, which is an understandable attitude to take if the universe really works in the way the Stoics said it does. If fate rules the world, and much of what happens is out of our hands, then it makes sense to be realistic and to wish only 'for everything to happen as it actually does happen', as Epictetus put it. There is no point in getting worked up about things you cannot change. And there is no point in getting too attached to things you are bound eventually to lose. What you must do is avoid leaving any hostages to fortune. Any possessions whose capture would distress you should be handed over willingly before fate gets a chance to tear them away. You hand them over by ceasing to care about them, or rather by learning to care about them in a new way:

Never say about anything, 'I have lost it,' but only 'I have given it back.' Is your child dead? It has been given back. Is your wife dead? She has been given back. 'I have had my farm taken away.' Very well, this too has been given back. 'Yet it was a rascal who took it away.' But what concern is it of yours by whose instrumentality the Giver called for its return? So long as He gives it to you, take care of it as a thing that is not your own, as travellers treat their inn.

The way to cope with fate is to travel light. Regard anything you might lose as more or less gone already and you will be protected against the worst blows that fate can deal. Epictetus drew a distinction between the things which are under our control, namely our thoughts and desires, and those which are not, namely what happens to our bodies, our families, our property, our reputation and fortune in life. He argued that if you suppress or redirect your emotions in order to focus on what is in your power, and ignore everything else, then 'no one will ever be able to exert compulsion upon you, no one will hinder you – neither is there any harm that can touch you'.

'Withdraw into yourself,' said Marcus Aurelius. He spent much of his time as emperor keeping invaders at bay, and seems to have thought of philosophy as a similar exercise in self-defence. Seneca, too, advocated a tactical withdrawal to safer high ground: 'The happy man is not he whom the crowd deems happy, namely, he into whose coffers mighty sums have flowed, but he whose possessions are all in his soul.' This recalls Socrates' insistence that the welfare of the soul is the only thing that matters in life. Spiritual welfare meant moral welfare: virtue was the only thing that made the soul flourish, and vice was the only thing that could harm it. Some of the Cynic hippies took this to imply a wholesale rejection of conventional life, preferably by mocking and shocking those who could not see beyond it. The Stoics shared the Cynics' purist attitude to superficial things: 'I deny that riches are a good', wrote Seneca, sniffily, 'for if they were, they would make men good. As it is, since that which is found in the hands of the wicked cannot be called a good, I refuse to apply the term to riches.' But the Stoics took a more earnest and sober approach to morality than the Cynics, and a more public-spirited one than Socrates. It was not enough to make fun of those who did not grasp the importance of a pure soul – to put on rags and yell at them from a tub, as Diogenes had done, just to show how above it all you yourself were. Nor was it enough to reason quietly with one or two people at a time, as Socrates had done, hoping that they would come to see the light with the gentlest of help. You should enter public life, said the Stoics, to spread virtue and fight vice. Duty, discipline and self-control were the watchwords of this serious business.

The self into which Marcus had said one should withdraw was a 'rational, governing self'. It was like the universal intelligence that permeated and organized the world, indeed it was part of that all-pervading intelligence. The soul was an outpost of the rational empire of nature. Just as the well-run universe was governed by *pneuma*, so the wise and virtuous man would be governed by his rational soul. If he listened to it, and was not dragged off course by uncontrolled and misdirected passions, it would lead him to obey the first commandment of Stoic ethics: to live in accordance with nature. It would guide him to accept his part in the universal plan and play it to the hilt. The man who coped with fate by travelling light, who limited his concerns to matters of the soul and virtue, and who did his duty in the great scheme of things, was fit to be a model and hero for mankind.

Like the Epicureans, the Stoics set great store by having the right attitude to death. But while the Epicureans said that the right attitude was simply to ignore it – 'death is nothing to us' – the Stoics found death a useful reminder of man's fate and of the ultimate insignificance of worldly things. Marcus regarded the shortness of life as positively consoling: 'be not troubled; for all things are according to Universal Nature, and in a little while you will be no one and nowhere, even as Hadrian and Augustus are no more'. Also, it was good to know that when circumstances made it impossible to live up to the ideals of Stoic virtue, death was always an available option. Many of the Stoics inherited from their Cynic forebears a keen interest in the idea of suicide. The Cynics held that if one could not live a rational life, then one ought as a final resort to kill oneself; that way virtue need never be compromised. A few of their contemporaries seem to have taken this idea to extremes. One offshoot of a related school of philosophers argued that there was only one sure way to avoid the inevitable unpleasantness of life, and that was to commit suicide without delay. A philosopher called Hegesias earned himself the nickname 'the orator of death' for his energetic advocacy of this point of view. His lectures were banned after he was blamed for an epidemic of suicides. No Stoic went that far; but Seneca was obsessed with death, and seems to have held that suicide was the ultimate assertion of human liberty. What is the highway to freedom, he asked? Any vein in your body, came the answer.

Seneca was quick to find excuses for committing suicide – at least in his writings – which is hard to square with the dutifulness of mainstream Stoicism. In fact he never got round to it himself until it was forced on him, but he does seem to have advocated giving up the noble struggle rather easily. The attitude of Epictetus was more understandable for a Stoic. He held that since one should not really be concerned about what happens to one's body, most forms of suffering are not a good enough reason to commit suicide. There are circumstances which call for it, but in general so serious a step should be taken only at God's command. Yet sometimes even Epictetus forgot this hardy attitude and seemed to regard death as the acceptable way out of any old misfortune. He once compared deciding to commit suicide with simply choosing to walk out of a smoke-filled room. There is an old story which makes Zeno, the first Stoic, sound equally casual about it. It is said that one day he tripped over and broke his toe, whereupon he promptly committed suicide.

This tale was presumably made up as a caricature of Stoic views. The main reason why the Stoics were interested in suicide was that it was a powerful symbol for a philosophy that professed to rise above the selfish and indulgent ways of conventional society. The wise Stoic claimed to regard the difference between life and death as insignificant when compared with the difference between virtue and vice. A willingness to consider suicide showed that one had high ideals which would not be sacrificed at any cost, and that one was always willing to obey the will of God, or 'Universal Nature', however much it demanded. If there was any truth to the story about Zeno, it will have been that he took this little misfortune of his stumbling old age to be a sign that it was time for him to go.

Tales of noble suicides were a stock in trade of later Stoic literature. One classic example of Stoic heroism was the life and death of Cato the Younger (95–46 BC), particularly as described by Plutarch in his popular *Lives*. A leading opponent of Caesar, and renowned as a man of absolute integrity, Cato committed suicide rather than submit to an unjust tyrant who was plainly going to win. On his last night, according to Plutarch's version of events, Cato eloquently defended various Stoic theses during dinner, went off to his room to read Plato's *Phaedo* – in which Socrates argues that a true philosopher regards all of life as a preparation for death – and killed himself. He became a Stoic saint. Long after Stoicism had become defunct as a formal philosophical school in the third century AD, Cato was held up as a model of unbending good character, duty, charity and patience. His self-control proved that a Stoical mastery of the passions and dedication to virtue was indeed possible. Stoicism set high standards, but Cato showed they could be reached.

Yet the moralizing of the Stoics presents a paradox. If everything is ruled by Fate, what is the point in giving advice and setting an example to others, or even in trying to be a better person yourself? You cannot change anything or anybody. If everything is determined by a chain of physical causes, and if the mind itself is a physical thing, as the Stoics said, then how can even our thoughts and feelings be exempted from this iron necessity? Surely the Stoics were inconsistent in saying that some things are under our control and other things are not. If they are right about Fate, then nothing at all is under our control.

Some of the Stoics' enemies seized on this difficulty and tried to strangle Stoicism with it. For example, it followed from the Stoics' own doctrines, said these critics, that the misdeeds of man ought not to cause anger or be blamed on men themselves. They should rather be blamed on

a certain imperious necessity, which stems from fate; and this is the mistress and arbiter of all things, by which everything which will happen must happen; and for this reason punishments of criminals have been established by law unjustly, if men do not come to their evil deeds willingly, but are led to them by fate.

The Stoics, of course, did not agree with this diagnosis. They were just as keen as the Epicureans to establish that people were responsible for their own lives. If they were not responsible, there would be little point in offering them philosophical advice and treatment. The Epicureans had simply denied Fate, using their random 'swerve' of atoms to break the chain of physical cause and effect. They said that it was just not true that 'everything which will happen must happen'. The Stoics maintained that it was true, and so they tried to find a different way out of the apparent problem posed by Fate. Part of their answer is encapsulated in another little tale about Zeno: 'The story goes that Zeno was flogging a slave for stealing. "I was fated to steal," said the slave. "And to be flogged," was Zeno's reply.' In other words, the existence of Fate need not change anything. You can go on moralizing, punishing, blaming and praising as before. You just have to acknowledge that everything which happens, including everything which you do, is fated. Cato was fated to be a hero, Caesar was fated to be a villain, and Zeno, Chrysippus, Epictetus and the other Stoic philosophers were fated to go on about virtue, duty, reason and the rest of it.

The anecdote about the flogged slave gives only a rough caricature of the Stoics' response to the problem. Chrysippus recognized that to make any progress on this sort of question, one had to look more carefully at what exactly Fate was supposed to be. For him, it amounted to the idea that everything was the result of prior causes, i.e., that everything is the effect of an earlier event or circumstance. He pointed out that if this is what Fate means, then some of the attacks on Stoicism can be deflected. For instance, Plato's successors in the Academy used to taunt the Stoics with what was known as 'the lazy argument', which aimed to show that if there were such a thing as Fate then there would be no point in trying to do anything. The argument went like this. Suppose you are ill. Then either you are fated to recover or you are fated not to recover. If you are fated to recover, it would be superfluous to call a doctor; and if you are fated not to recover, calling a doctor would be no help. So either way it is pointless to get medical attention. This is like the 'fatalist' idea that there is no point in a soldier being careful, because either there is a bullet with his name on it or there is not.

Chrysippus spotted the fallacy in such arguments. It was true, according to him, that if you were ill then you would either be caused to recover or caused not to recover. But he pointed out that the attentions of a doctor might be part of what causes your recovery, so it does not follow that it makes no difference what you do. The trick in the fatalist 'lazy argument' is to overlook the fact that people's actions, like any other events in the world, can have effects and thus help to make the future. When you are deciding whether or not to call a doctor, you do not know whether you are going to recover or to die, and for all you know your actions may be what swings it one way or the other. Those actions may be fated in some sense, but this does not mean that they are irrelevant.

This answers the lazy argument: there is a point in calling a doctor, because this may well make your recovery more likely; there is a point in punishing people, because this may well discourage them from doing wrong in future; and there is a point in offering philosophical advice and therapy, because this may well make people happier. But it is not yet the whole story. For even if our actions can make a difference, it is still hard to see how we can really be held responsible for them. How can my thoughts and actions be under my control if they too have prior causes? Once more, Chrysippus saw that one has to look at the question itself more closely. In effect, he and the other Stoics maintained that there was one sense in which we are free and responsible, and another sense in which we are not. Before we think or do anything, what we are going to think or do is already fixed by earlier causes, so in that sense we are not free. But some of those causes have to do with our own characters, and in that sense our thoughts and actions are indeed our own.

Chrysippus illustrated what he was trying to say with a simple example. Take a cylinder and push it down a slope. Why does it keep rolling? Part of the cause of its movement is the fact that you pushed it: given this prior event, it is bound to roll. But another part of the cause lies in the fact that it is a cylinder and not, say, a cube. If it had been a cube, then your gentle push might not have been enough to get it moving, because its shape would have made it harder to roll. So part of the cause of its motion lies in its own nature: it rolls because it is a cylinder, not only because of the prior cause provided by your push. It is in this sense that some of the causes of our thoughts and actions lie in our natures. They can be explained by our own characters, just as the behaviour of a cylinder can be explained by its own shape. So our lives cannot entirely be explained by the actions of external forces.

Thus Chrysippus has managed to snatch back something from his enemies. But again one may wonder whether he has quite succeeded in salvaging the hulk of moral responsibility from the depths of Fate. Caesar may have been a tyrant because of his own character, but according to the Stoics this character was itself the product of Fate. How then can Caesar be held morally responsible for it, or therefore for his own actions? In the end, the Stoics' attempt to combine a belief in Fate with a belief in personal responsibility is not wholly satisfactory. There still seems to be a conflict between the two ideas. But it must be said in the Stoics' defence that they were not the only ones to nurse this apparent inconsistency in their bosom. In Aeschylus' tragedy, *Agamemnon*, the Chorus speaks of Zeus, the controlling power of nature, as 'the doer and source of all'. It asks, rhetorically, of the murder of Agamemnon: 'Could even this horror be, without his sovereign word?' But shortly after implicating Zeus – a name the Stoics often used for Fate – the Chorus also holds Clytemnestra responsible for the deed: 'of this blood who could absolve you?' Yet if Zeus or Fate directed events, how can Clytemnestra be blamed as well? On the other hand, if you look at the facts of the case, how could you fail to condemn her? 'O piteous mystery!', as the Chorus says.

One reason why the Stoics found it possible to live with the idea of Fate was that they also believed in Providence. Indeed, the two came to the same thing: the intelligence that rules the world is benign and always looking out for man. Everything has been arranged for the best. It may not always look like that on the surface, but the Stoics argued that a deeper understanding of nature reveals that there is a good reason for everything. Seneca said that adversity was sent to test us, and that it was therefore a blessing in disguise because it enables us to develop our powers of endurance and other Stoic virtues:

Why is it that God afflicts the best men with ill health, or sorrow, or some other misfortune? For the same reason that in the army the bravest men are assigned to the hazardous tasks – In like manner, all those who are called to suffer what would make cowards and poltroons weep may say, 'God has deemed us worthy instruments of his purpose to discover how much human nature can endure' . . . And so, in the case of good men the gods follow the same rule that teachers follow with their pupils; they require most effort from those of whom they have the surest hopes.

So the major misfortunes of life are not really misfortunes at all but opportunities for self-improvement. Chrysippus held that even such minor irritants as mice and bed-bugs are an example of this. Mice encourage the habit of tidiness, and bed-bugs prevent us from sleeping too much. Indeed he thought that mice and bed-bugs were let loose about the place by Providence precisely in order to provide such bizarre benefits. According to the Stoics, all sorts of things in nature had been arranged expressly with the interests of man in mind. Chrysippus said that pigs were made fertile in order to ensure us a regular supply of hearty meals. This is exactly the sort of back-to-front thinking, putting man at the centre of the universe, of which Aristotle has long been falsely accused. But it was the Stoics, not the true Aristotelians, who saw the signs of a kindly Providence at work in all the intricate mechanisms of nature. Indeed, so convinced were the Stoics by the apparent evidence of order and purpose in the world that they cited it as a proof of the existence of God.

It is just as well that the Stoics viewed the world as not such a bad place after all, because in the Stoic view of things there is no afterlife to right any wrongs one might suffer on earth. Providence is in charge down here already and will see us right, so there is no need for any reckoning-up later in heaven. Not only does Providence always bear the interests of people in mind, it is especially generous to good people, even while they are still alive.

This is one of the main differences between early Christianity and Stoic theology. The Christians could not swallow the idea that justice was satisfactorily done on earth. It seemed to them, as it seems to most others, that good people sometimes suffer and bad ones thrive. Yet the Stoics insisted that God or Providence protects the virtuous from the sort of misfortunes that really matter:

Evil of every sort he keeps far from them – sin and crime, evil counsel and schemes for greed, blind lust and avarice intent upon another's goods. The good man himself he protects and delivers: does any one require of God that he should also guard the good man's luggage? Nay, the good man himself relieves God of this concern; he despises externals.

The only really bad thing that can happen to you is to do evil, and by definition a good man does not do that. The good man cannot be harmed, as Socrates said. He can be robbed only of the sort of trivial things which, being virtuous, he will not be concerned about anyway. By means of this reasoning, Stoicism guarantees a happy life to the virtuous. But the Christians were not to be persuaded by such assurances of just deserts on earth. They preferred older ideas, such as those in the Greek mystery-religions, according to which bonus rewards would be enjoyed and extra punishments meted out hereafter in order to even things up.

The similarities between Stoics and Christians are, however, at least as striking as the differences between them. With the exception of the promise of a posthumous settlement of moral debts, all the ideas which Christians use to try to explain away the pain and suffering of a world allegedly ruled by an omnipotent God had already been exploited by the Stoics. In fact, many of the ethical doctrines of the Stoics seemed so close to those of the Christians that one medieval myth says Seneca actually became one.

The Stoic universe was more hospitable to biblical religion than any other Greek philosophy had been. True, the Stoics did not think that the universe had been created out of nothing by God – that would have been too much to ask of an ancient Greek, with his conception of the cosmos as eternal and of gods as part of it. Nor did the Stoics' materialist way of thinking leave room for any immortal souls. But it did see the universe as organized and ruled by a benevolent Providence who had a special interest in man and an upright sense of morals. Many of the supposedly distinctive aspects of Christian morality are to be found in the ethical writings of the Stoics. They taught that wealth, status and power – in fact all the things which separate men from one another – are ultimately insignificant. All men alike are smiled on by Providence, and the only thing that can raise one person above others is superior virtue, of which everyone is in principle capable. Thus the Stoics believed in the universal brotherhood of man: 'Nature made us relatives by creating us from the same materials and for the same destinies,' wrote Seneca. And, he continued, 'She planted in us a mutual love', which is the foundation of morality. You should not consider your own interests as distinct from those of others, said Epictetus.

The Stoic system not only enjoined a selfless devotion to the welfare of others, it also dwelt on the vanity of the world, and on the guiding inner voice of conscience. Epictetus stressed the importance of a pure heart. When a beautiful woman goes by, he cautioned, do not even let yourself *think* 'Her husband is lucky!' This struck a sympathetic chord with early Christian thinkers, as did several other Stoic themes, such as the importance of quelling turbulent passions which might distract one from the simple life.

The Epicureans, too, advocated a simple and quiet life, as we have seen. Indeed, practically every Greek thinker claimed to be in favour of this. (Who, one wonders, was left to live it up?) But although nature seems to have delivered the same message to both Stoics and Epicureans on this subject, it is clear that the 'Nature' whom the Stoics took as their guide had a quite different personality from the 'Nature' of the Epicureans. The Stoics' Nature, or God or Providence, was an earnest intelligence with the serious work of running a universe to do. Epicurean Nature was warm-hearted and not averse to a little enjoyment – provided, of course, that it was nothing too indulgent, for this might interfere with the pursuit of more refined and longer-lasting pleasures.

It has been said that Epicureanism and Stoicism appeal to two different types of character:

There have ever been stern, upright, self-controlled, and courageous men, actuated by a pure sense of duty, capable of high efforts of self-sacrifice, somewhat intolerant of the frailties of others, somewhat hard and unsympathizing in the ordinary intercourse of society, but rising to heroic grandeur as the storm lowered upon their path, and more ready to relinquish life than the cause they believed to be true. There have also always been men of easy tempers and of amiable disposition, gentle, benevolent, and pliant, cordial friends and forgiving enemies, selfish at heart, yet ever ready, when it is possible, to unite their gratifications with those of others, averse to all enthusiasm, mysticism, utopias, and superstition, with little depth of character or capacity for self-sacrifice, but admirably fitted to impart and to receive enjoyment, and to render the course of life easy and harmonious. The first are by nature Stoics, and the second Epicureans.

These neat profiles, written in Victorian times, make it an amusing game to spot the 'Epicureans' and 'Stoics' among one's friends. They catch some of the spirit of the two philosophies. But they are a little too neat to tell us much about the personalities of real thinkers who lived 2,000 years ago. For example, it is by no means clear that the leading Stoics were in fact the self-sacrificing philanthropists this picture would suggest. Seneca, who amassed enormous wealth under the patronage of Nero, certainly does not seem to have been one. It was his sudden recalling of large loans to leading Britons (which he had apparently pressed them to accept in the first place) that was one of the causes of Queen Boadicea's famous revolt against the Romans in AD 60. True, Seneca eloquently defended the official Stoic view that riches could not strictly speaking be regarded as a good thing, because only virtue itself was truly valuable. But he was most eager to point out that, once one had got this philosophical point straight, there was no reason to feel bad about being as rich as Croesus. 'Place me in the midst of sumptuous furnishings and the trappings of luxury; I shall not think myself one whit happier,' he proudly announced. Still, he continued, do not jump to any hasty conclusions about this; it by no means follows that one ought to give up such things. Why should one? It was no big deal either way, so if Seneca just happened to 'prefer to display the state of my soul clad rather in the toga and shoes than showing naked shoulders and with cuts on my feet' – which he did – then why not?

Marcus Aurelius was a nobler example of the benign and unselfish side of Stoicism than Seneca was. Actually, he was also in certain respects a better example of the 'Epicurean' personality than some Epicureans were. He seems by all accounts to have been amiable, kind and forgiving, especially for an emperor, whereas Epicurus himself did not altogether fit the Epicurean caricature. The old guru may have been easy-going and outstandingly genial among his followers and friends, but he seems to have been distinctly tetchy when it came to rival philosophers. The sunny disposition of the good Epicurean deserted him when it came to professional matters, for he regarded practically every other thinker as a rival and was especially ungracious about those from whom he had apparently learnt the most, such as Democritus.

If the Stoics and the Epicureans found it hard to live up to their respective official philosophies, the Sceptics must have found it nearly impossible to stay faithful to theirs. How could anybody be a complete sceptic and claim to be baffled by everything? How could one suspend judgement on all questions and live entirely without beliefs? Why, indeed, would anybody want to?

The Sceptical school of thought starts with Pyrrho of Elis, who was some twenty years older than Epicurus but died at around the same time (*c.*270 BC). Rather appropriately for a man who claimed to know nothing, little is known about him. It was not until 500 years after his death, and thus well after the end of the Hellenistic period, that the main surviving Sceptical texts were written. These were the works of Sextus Empiricus, who straddled the second and third centuries AD. Yet even at so late a date, the character of Scepticism remained essentially Hellenistic. That is to say, it was a philosophy of life which aimed to produce a state of *ataraxia* – freedom from disturbance – by teaching people what not to care about. Even in its latest and most sophisticated form, it still claimed to draw its inspiration from the distant figure of Pyrrho.

Pyrrho himself wrote nothing, but still made quite an impression on his contemporaries in Athens. His impact is attested by the usual round of barmy anecdotes, which mostly focussed on the alleged extremes of his detachment. 'He was always in the same mental state, so that even if someone left him in the middle of his talking, he would complete the conversation to himself.' When a friend fell into a ditch, Pyrrho passed him by without offering any help; the friend, being a true Sceptic himself, simply praised Pyrrho for his imperturbability. According to another of these stories, Pyrrho ignored all the apparent dangers of the world because he questioned whether they really were dangers, 'avoiding nothing and taking no precautions, facing everything as it came, wagons, precipices, dogs'. Luckily he was always accompanied by friends who could not quite manage the same enviable lack of concern and

PYRRHO.

so took care of him, pulling him out of the way of oncoming traffic and so on. They must have had a hard job of it, because 'often . . . he would leave his home and, telling no one, would go roaming about with whomsoever he chanced to meet'.

Two centuries after Pyrrho's death, one of his defenders tossed aside these tales and claimed that 'although he practised philosophy on the principles of suspension of judgement, he did not act carelessly in the details of everyday life'. This must be right. Pyrrho may have been magnificently imperturbable – Epicurus was said to have admired him on this account, and another fan marvelled at the way he had apparently 'unloosed the shackles of every deception and persuasion'. But he was surely not an idiot. He apparently lived to be nearly ninety, which would have been unlikely if the stories of his recklessness had been true. Still, one can hardly blame the gossips and satirists for taking Pyrrho's sceptical philosophy to what seemed to be its logical conclusion. The puzzling truth behind the half-serious anecdotes about him is that he urged people not to commit themselves to any opinions, and not to be misled into thinking that they knew anything. In *The Sale of Lives*, a satire by Lucian in the second century AD, various philosophers are put up for sale in a slave market. Diogenes the Cynic fetches a small price as a household pet; the obscure Heraclitus proves to be totally unsaleable even at rock-bottom prices; and Pyrrho obstinately insists on keeping an open mind about whether or not he has been sold, even while he is being carried off by his purchaser.

Extreme Scepticism seemed such a bizarre idea that it was assumed to have come from foreigners. Pyrrho apparently accompanied Alexander the Great's eastern expeditions as far as India and was said to have picked up a dose of Scepticism from the so-called 'naked philosophers' whom he met there. There are indeed some intriguing parallels between the ways of these Indians and the sort of life recommended by Pyrrho. The naked philosophers were ascetic sages, adherents of the Jain religion – a heretical branch of Hinduism – who regarded food and clothing as a hindrance to clear thinking, and often lived in forests to get away from it all. They believed it was perfectly all right to contradict oneself when describing the everyday world (which is probably why they had only a small impact on Indian philosophy). This was because they held that ordinary statements were only ever true in certain respects while being false in others. They believed that it was important to minimize the influence of sensation on the soul, so that just as one should not be troubled by feelings of pain or hunger, so too one should not take much notice of what one sees or hears. The naked philosophers' ideal of a saint was one who had managed to master this task and was as a result admirably tranquil, impassive and non-committal.

One account of Pyrrho's teaching makes it sound quite similar:

neither our sensations nor our opinions tell us truths or falsehoods. Therefore for this reason we should not put our trust in them one bit, but we should be unopinionated, uncommitted and unwavering, saying concerning each individual thing that it no more is than is not, or it both is and is not, or neither is nor is not. The outcome for those who actually adopt this attitude . . . will be first speechlessness, and then freedom from disturbance.

However, although the Indian naked philosophers may have been 'unopinionated and uncommitted' on many things, they were too dogmatic about religious and cosmological questions to count as full-blown Sceptics in the Greek sense. There were things which they claimed to know – for example, that the soul migrates after death, that the universe is eternal and uncreated, and that everything is alive and divine. These are just the sorts of subjects about which a true philosophical Sceptic would insist on keeping an open mind.

Besides, one does not have to go to India to find traces of scepticism. Many earlier Greek thinkers had shown sceptical tendencies by calling everyday beliefs into question. Back in the sixth century BC, Xenophanes had said that 'Nobody knows, or ever will know, the truth about the gods and about everything I speak of. For even if what one says happens to be right, one will not know that it is – it is all a matter of opinion.' He noticed that different peoples tended to describe the gods in their own images – 'The Ethiopians say that their gods are snub-nosed and black, the Thracians that theirs have light blue eyes and red hair.' This was a useful reminder of the fallibility of even the most dearly held beliefs, for presumably the Ethiopians and the Thracians could not both be right. Parmenides and Zeno of Elea had also in effect prepared the ground for Scepticism. They famously argued that people's most basic ideas about the world were hopelessly wrong: although everyone was sure that it was full of motion and change, in fact nothing moved, nothing changed and everything was really all one and the same thing. This unnerving doctrine led Timon of Phlius, a keen adherent of Pyrrho's Scepticism, to praise the Eleatics for having thereby underlined the illusory nature of everyday appearances. (Timon was scathing about philosophers whose thought was less congenial to the Sceptical point of view, calling them windbags and wafflers. He said that the founder of Stoicism, who had confidently expounded all sorts of doctrines, was 'less intelligent than a banjo'.)

The Sophists, too, had paved the way for Scepticism by undermining widespread beliefs. They were infamously relativist about ethical and political matters: according to them each society had its own values, and it was naive to think that one society was right and the rest were wrong. Some of the Sophists, such as Protagoras, had reacted against the wide range of theories about the world and about morality by saying that every man's beliefs could be regarded as true – but only for himself. This meant that objective knowledge was impossible: there was no question of establishing the real facts about things, because any old belief was as good as any other. Xeniades of Corinth, a philosopher from around Democritus' time, said that nothing at all is true. This seems to be the opposite of Protagoras' idea, but the upshot of the two philosophies is much the same. Whether all beliefs are as good as one another, as Protagoras said, or as bad as one another, as Xeniades said, there is no deciding between them and so they all enjoy equal status. According to some sources, Socrates was driven to a similarly Sceptical deadlock, at least as far as scientific questions were concerned. He could see no reason to prefer the views of, say, Empedocles to those of Anaxagoras, so he abandoned all inquiries into physics, cosmology and biology as hopeless. And, of course, he famously proclaimed that he did not know anything at all, even about the ethical matters in which he did show an interest. We have seen that this confession cannot quite be taken at face value; but Socrates' habitual probing and querying were nonetheless an influence on the techniques of later Greek Scepticism.

The doctrines of Democritus were also a stimulus to the Sceptics, as we have seen. Like Parmenides and Zeno of Elea, his picture of the world implied that it was not at all the way it appeared to be. In particular, the colours and smells and tastes which we perceive do not, according to Democritus, reflect the way physical objects are in themselves but rather the way their atoms affect our sense-organs. When we say that the sky is blue, for example, this is not a piece of knowledge but just an accepted convention. Such a yawning gap between appearance and reality was exactly the sort of thing a Sceptic could exploit in order to make any claim to knowledge seem impossibly ambitious. If the senses could not be trusted, then what could? Democritus was apparently not troubled by this question, but perhaps he should have been. How did he know that his own doctrine of atomism was true? What sort of evidence could he, or anybody else, use to make the leap from mere opinions to certain knowledge? For Pyrrho and his followers, the answer was 'none'. The leap could not be made.

It seems, however, that Pyrrho may have made rather an incautious leap himself. If Scepticism involves calling everything into question, then some of the things Pyrrho is supposed to have said seem puzzlingly inconsistent. According to some, he maintained that 'nothing is honourable or base, or just or unjust, and that likewise in all cases nothing exists in truth; and that convention and habit are the basis of everything that men do, for each thing is no more this than that'. Now, one can see how anybody who believes this sort of thing is likely to end up a Sceptic, for if everything is 'no more this than that', then there is nothing to know. But the trouble is that Sceptics are not supposed to have any beliefs – not even that everything is 'no more this than that'. How, then, could a Sceptic confidently claim that convention and habit are the basis of everything? Shouldn't he be saying instead that convention and habit *might be* the basis of every-thing, and that *for all he knows* everything is 'no more this than that'? Similarly, Pyrrho's friend Anaxarchus (the one whom he left lying in a ditch) is said to have compared everything he saw to stage-paintings, i.e., illusions, which implies not just that one cannot tell whether or not ordinary things are real, but that they definitely are not real. Again, this seems to go beyond what a consistent Sceptic has any right to assert. How does he know that everything is like stage-painting? Should a consistent Sceptic not suspend judgement about that too, and just say that things may be real or they may not and that he can't tell one way or the other?

This is what later Sceptics like Sextus Empiricus said, and they did their best to stick by this more consistently open-minded form of Scepticism. Sextus held that the Sceptic's job was to make people suspend judgement and 'live without opinions', by countering every positive reason for believing something with equally powerful reasons for believing the opposite, thus producing an impasse. The Sceptic was not selling any definite theory of the world – not even the theory that 'everything is no more this than that' – but rather providing a cure for all theories: 'Sceptics are philanthropic and wish to cure by argument, as far as they can, the conceit and rashness of the Dogmatists [*i.e., those who hold firm opinions*].' The idea that suspending judgement would make people more tranquil and contented came straight from Pyrrho. But the way in which this opinion-free life was to be achieved, namely by developing objections and counter-arguments to every doctrine that turns up, also owed something to a style of philosophizing that had developed in Plato's Academy.

Just before Pyrrho's death, a philosopher named Arcesilaus (*c.*315–*c.*240 BC) took over the headship of Plato's Academy and sparked off what is sometimes called its 'sceptical' phase. He had previously studied at Aristotle's Lyceum; legend has it that he moved over to the Academy because he was in love with one of the top men there. His predecessors in the job during the seventy-five years since Plato's death had devoted themselves to expounding and elaborating what they took to be Plato's doctrines, such as the creation-story in the *Timaeus* and the theory of Forms. But such priestly guarding of the ancient flame was not enough for Arcesilaus. He thought that the best way to continue the Platonic tradition was to be more like Socrates – that is, to question and to probe. He liked to copy Socrates by arguing people into a corner so that they would end up contradicting themselves. This was a popular sport in the Academy for roughly the next 200 years. It added a new intellectual depth to Scepticism, though Socrates himself would probably have condemned much of it as useless quibbling.

Much of Arcesilaus's probing was directed against the Stoics and in particular against what they had to say about knowledge and perception. He especially had it in for Zeno (Zeno the Stoic, that is, not Zeno the follower of Parmenides). According to this Zeno, some perceptions or impressions are so clear and distinct that they are self-evidently accurate. One can immediately tell that they reveal the world as it really is. Thus, provided one sticks to these superior impressions and refuses to be led astray by any other sort, one will have secure knowledge. But Arcesilaus soon poked holes in this notion of self-evidence. For one thing, he pointed out, 'no impression arising from something true is such that an impression arising from something false could not also be just like it'. In other words, an illusion could be just as convincing as the real thing (that, indeed, is the point of illusions), so you might not be able to tell the difference between them just by looking. A well-made wax model of an apple will have exactly the same appearance as a real apple: it will produce the same impressions on the mind. So how could there be such a thing as a 'self-evident' impression?

This technique of neatly dismantling philosophical doctrines soon caught on in the Academy; before long all sorts of theories were subjected to it. Dilemmas were posed, self-contradictions were alleged, unwelcome consequences were deduced. The Stoics and other victims worked to improve their theories in response to the Academy's attacks, then the Academics did their best to knock them down again. The Stoic doctrine of fate was pummelled from all angles: the 'lazy argument', which aimed to show that belief in fate implied that there was no point in doing anything, was a product of this sceptical phase of the Academy's history. As we have seen, the Stoics thought they had a reply to the lazy argument (see page 318), but the Academics had a reply to their reply, and so it went on. The Academics also took aim at the various arguments which Stoics wheeled out to prove that the universe was ruled by a divine providence. When the Stoics claimed that this or that feature of the world could not have come about without some supernatural guiding hand, the Academics punctured their reasoning and skilfully demonstrated that natural forces could well have been responsible instead. The Academics alleged that when the Stoics talked upliftingly about the 'rationality' of the universe, as they frequently did, they did not really have any clear idea of what they were talking about. This was largely true. The Academics also had a merry time refuting the Stoics' belief in astrology and other forms of divination, using some excellent arguments which St Augustine and others up to the present day have subsequently borrowed, though with depressingly little effect on popular belief.

Whenever Arcesilaus attacked this or that Stoic doctrine, or indeed anybody's doctrine, it was not that he was trying to establish any positive thesis of his own. He was just trying to show that neither side could yet safely claim to be in possession of the truth. He apparently even suspended judgement on the question of whether or not anything could be known. As with every other issue in philosophy, he argued that this matter had not been settled one way or the other. Some later critics alleged that when he went around refuting everybody he was simply showing off his famously effective powers of argument; it was said that 'in persuasiveness he had no equal, and this all the more drew pupils to the school, although they were in terror of his pungent wit'. From the surviving snippets of biography about him, we hear that Arcesilaus was lavish, flamboyant, openly lived with courtesans and was hungry for fame. But there is no real reason to deny that this colourful character was a sincere Sceptic. Indeed there is every reason to suppose that he was, because he went to the trouble of trying to show that it was perfectly possible to exist as one without making a disaster of everyday life.

All sorts of philosophers from Aristotle to David Hume have argued that too much scepticism makes life impossible. In 1748 Hume wrote that

a Pyrrhonian . . . must acknowledge, if he will acknowledge anything, that all human life must perish, were his principles universally and steadily to prevail. All discourse, all action would immediately cease; and men remain in total lethargy, till the necessities of nature, unsatisfied, put an end to their miserable existence.

Hume thought that a consistent Pyrrhonian Sceptic would not eat, drink or keep himself out of danger, because he would be incapable of deciding how to do any of these things. Should he put bread in his mouth or should he nibble a stone? Ordinary people believe that it is bread which is nourishing, but a Sceptic is surely committed to keeping an open mind about it. Should he step aside from a thundering horse, or under its hooves? A Sceptic would have to suspend judgement on all such matters and suffer the consequences. One ancient author made a similar point by asking: 'how is it that someone who suspends judgement does not rush away to a mountain instead of to the bath, or stands up and walks to the door rather than the wall when he wants to go out to the market-place?'

Arcesilaus and other like-minded philosophers had an answer to this. A bath does *seem* to be the sort of place where you could get a good wash, and this explains why a Sceptic will head towards one when he wants to get clean. If a mountain seemed to be such a place, then he would go there instead; but it does not, so he goes to the bath. A door does *seem* to be the best way out of a house, bread does *seem* to be nourishing, and being trampled by horses does not *seem* to be a good idea. According to Arcesilaus, even though a Sceptic will refuse to form an opinion about how things really are, he can still freely admit that they *appear* one way rather than another. As Timon once said: 'That honey is sweet I do not affirm, but I agree that it appears so.' Being human, a Sceptic is affected by appearances just like everyone else and so he will behave much like everyone else, at least in the essentials of life. He follows instincts, observes customs and generally acts in a sensible way, but he does so by habit or as a matter of human nature, not because he endorses any opinions about the world. As

CARNEADES.

Sextus later put it, a Sceptic follows 'laws and customs and natural feelings' but lives 'without holding opinions'. Thus if you were to ask him whether he definitely believes that bread is nourishing, a Sceptic would indeed say no, because he suspends judgement on the matter. But you will still find him in the larder.

It might well be asked in what sense someone can be said to be 'suspending judgement' about whether or not bread is nourishing if he is forever putting it in his mouth. We shall come back to that question later. The point for now is that Arcesilaus did at least try to explain how a Sceptic can live a tolerable life. One later head of the Academy, Carneades (*c.* 219–*c.* 129 BC), went even further in this attempt, though in doing so he rather watered down the Pyrrhonian prescription. He held that it was neither necessary nor possible to suspend judgement about absolutely everything. Although a Sceptic would not completely commit himself to any opinion, it was permissible for him – or so Carneades argued – to offer a weaker form of endorsement in certain cases and to agree that some beliefs are plausible.

The Academy was drifting away from Scepticism by this time, or so it seemed to some true-blue Pyrrhonists. On the surface, Carneades still behaved like a Sceptic: he 'adopted the practice of arguing on each side of a question, and used to upset all the arguments used by others'. But although he continued to perform the rites, he had apparently abandoned the faith. Philo of Larissa (*c.*160–*c.*83 BC), a later head of the Academy, seems to have strayed even further. He was said to have confidently asserted various things, even to have been positively in favour of some philosophical doctrines. This would never do for a true follower of Pyrrho – and at least one member of the Academy still regarded himself as that.

This was Aenesidemus, a radical who lived some time in the first century BC and who broke away from the Academy to re-establish a purer form of Scepticism. His Pyrrhonist revival did not exactly take the world by storm, not even the small world of philosophy. Just a couple of decades afterwards, Cicero wrote that Pyrrhonism was already extinct. A century later, Seneca was happy to report that it was still dead. But they were wrong. Although Pyrrhonism was never likely to become a mass-movement, it continued to develop after the time of Aenesidemus, and indeed had yet to reach its intellectual climax. This climax came with the writings of Sextus Empiricus, who was probably born in the latter half of the second century AD and whose works are the main source for a huge battery of sceptical arguments that have shaped Western thought from the seventeenth century to the present day. Many of the most interesting intellectual positions of the past four centuries may be seen as responses to these arguments, either as brave attempts to rebut them or as grudging attempts to come to terms with them. Sextus could not claim much originality for these sceptical patterns of reasoning, and he didn't. Many of them had already been used by Aenesidemus and others are apparently due to an almost entirely unknown figure from the first century AD called Agrippa. But the works of these two men do not survive, whereas Sextus' do; and since Pyrrho and Arcesilaus apparently never bothered to write anything down, Sextus is the only Sceptic who can now speak for himself.

It was in the first century AD that the sort of philosophers we have been referring to as Sceptics first actually called themselves that. In earlier days they had simply been 'Pyrrhonists', but from around the time of Agrippa they identified themselves as *skeptikoi*, which literally means 'inquirers' or 'searchers'. Sextus defined the revived philosophy of Pyrrhonism in terms of the three things that can happen if you look into any subject. You can think that you have found the truth; you can come to the conclusion that the truth cannot be found; or you can just carry on looking for it. Sceptics – 'searchers' – are those who are still looking. Aristotle, Epicurus and the Stoics are outstanding examples of people who think they have found the answers, at least about some things; Sextus calls them 'Dogmatists'. Pyrrho was the outstanding example of someone who resisted the temptations of Dogmatism and avoided answers like the plague.

Why do people become Sceptics and refuse to commit themselves? Because, according to Sextus, they have found that a welcome wave of tranquillity tends to follow in the wake of such open-mindedness. This discovery was, he thinks, first made by accident. The earliest Sceptics, says Sextus, were hoping to find tranquillity by finding out the truth about things. They were unable to find the truth, so they gave up and suspended judgement – whereupon they instantly started to feel better. Thus it turns out to be the suspension of judgement, and not the pursuit of inquiry, which brings contentment. Sextus illustrated the point with an anecdote about a painter called Apelles. Apelles was painting a horse and wanted to show foam at the animal's mouth. He tried all sorts of brush techniques until he lost his temper, picked up a sponge that he used to wipe his brushes, and flung it at the picture. Lo and behold, the impact of the sponge produced exactly the effect he had been trying for. Just so with the Sceptics: throwing in the sponge turned out to do the trick. 'When they suspended judgement, tranquillity followed as it were fortuitously, as a shadow follows a body.'

Sextus took pains to explain just what this suspension of judgement amounts to. The first thing to grasp is that real Sceptics do not endorse any philosophical thesis, not even that 'nothing can be known' or that 'everything is relative'. If you find a Sceptic saying things like 'everything is no more this than that' or 'for every theory about something, there is an equally good but different theory about it', he is merely expressing the fact that he has not yet been convinced by anybody's claim to know how things really are. It follows that you cannot catch a real Sceptic out by claiming that he is himself being too dogmatic. You cannot hurt him with the objection, 'How do you *know* that nothing can be known?' or 'How do you *know* that there are always equally powerful alternative views?', because he does not actually claim to know either of these things. Maybe one day there will be some real knowledge. Maybe one day somebody will come up with a theory that is more convincing than its alternatives. All the Sceptic is saying is that it seems to him that such a day has not yet come.

When a Sceptic argues against somebody by outlining a different point of view, he will not actually be endorsing this other point of view. He puts forward the alternatives just for the sake of argument. For example, when Sextus cites the large variety of beliefs among different nations, he is not trying to demonstrate that some or other of these foreigners are right and the Greeks are wrong. He is trying to unsettle the Greeks' confidence in their own views and merely inviting them to join him in keeping an open mind. That is why Epicurus' type of attack on Scepticism does not hit home. Epicurus and Lucretius said that a Sceptic who tried to cast doubt on everything would not have a leg to stand on: he would have no standard of correctness and therefore no basis for condemning any belief as false. But a real Sceptic does not try to prove that any of our beliefs are definitely mistaken. He just tries to make us question them, in the expectation that this will make us less dogmatic. The Sceptic does not want a leg to stand on. He wants to suspend his judgement in mid-air.

Sextus also tried to explain how this act of intellectual levitation can be combined with a basically normal life. He explained that the suspension of judgement is not supposed to apply to absolutely everything but only to controversial matters. Anything which people argue about, any subject of investigation or intellectual reflection, a Sceptic must leave open to question. But although he will suspend judgement about any disputed or obscure intellectual matter and will thus refuse to 'make firm assertions' about the ultimate nature or cause of anything, a Sceptic will happily say how things *appear* to him to be. He can state, for instance, that he *feels* hot or cold (or, to take Timon's old example, that honey *appears* to be sweet). He can say that bread *appears* to be nourishing, or that it *looks as if* the weather is about to turn nasty. The claim that Sceptics 'live without opinions' does not mean that they refuse to say trivial things like this. Such utterances do not count as expressions of an opinion about how things really are.

When we say that Sceptics do not hold beliefs, we do not take 'belief' in the sense in which . . . belief is acquiescing in something; for Sceptics assent to the feelings forced upon them by appearances – for example, they would not say, when heated or chilled, 'I think I am not heated (or: chilled)'. Rather we say that they do not hold beliefs in the sense in which belief is assent to some unclear object of investigation in the sciences.

The sciences do not bother to investigate and question subjective appearances such as whether or not an individual feels hot or cold. There is nothing unclear or controversial about such utterances, so a Sceptic is not expected to resist them. Sextus says that Sceptics happily 'go along with' everyday appearances in the way that a child unthinkingly follows his guardian. The guardian in this case is nature, which causes us to have certain thoughts, experiences and impulses. We have natural appetites and are naturally led towards the things which appear to satisfy them. Hunger, as Sextus put it, conducts us to food. And that is why a Sceptic may be found eating bread just like everyone else. Such behaviour constitutes a more or less unthinking and automatic response to appearances, i.e., to what we perceive or experience, just as a cow unthinkingly eats grass. Judgement does not come into it, so there is no judgement to suspend.

Just as a Sceptic is prepared to 'go along with' the appearance that bread is nourishing, so he will happily go along with the apparent fact that stepping over precipices or into the path of traffic is not a good idea. Thus, as Arcesilaus had argued when defending Pyrrho's reputation, Scepticism does not make it impossible to survive ordinary life without serious injury. In fact a Sceptic will lead a fairly conventional existence because he will also happily go along with the laws and customs that are passed down in his society, in order not to make trouble. Of course, if anybody is unwise enough to defend an explicit rational justification for these laws, or to pick a fight and criticize them, the Sceptic will feel obliged to rouse himself and offer arguments opposed to whatever this upstart is saying. He will do so in order to show that one must suspend judgement on whether any particular set of laws is the right one, because there is bound to be much to say on both sides of such controversies. Better not to make a controversy of it in the first place, and to continue to live in accordance with 'everyday observances' without making an intellectual fuss. The situation is similar in the case of religion. Sextus says that a good Sceptic 'in conformity with his ancestral customs and the laws declares that the gods exist – but, so far as regards philosophic investigation, declines to commit himself rashly'. Dogmatic proofs and detailed theological speculations must be contested. But Sceptics will respect 'from an everyday point of view' the piety that is natural to civilized men.

The Sceptic's unresisting attitude to 'everyday observances' extends not only to conventional customs and pieties and to matters that 'depend on passive and unwilled feelings and are not objects of investigation', but also to some forms of technical expertise. According to Sextus, the Sceptic should be happy to go along with the established results of certain practical sciences, provided that these sciences are concerned merely with collecting and collating observations and do not involve any dogmatic theorizing. For example, while the unsupported speculations of astrology are subjected to the full Sceptical treatment, the sort of astronomy practised by careful students of the heavens is regarded as acceptable, 'for this, like Agriculture and Navigation, consists in the observation of phenomena, from which it is possible to forecast droughts and rainstorms and plagues and earthquakes'. Similarly, it is acceptable for a Sceptic to use the formulae of geometry and arithmetic for practical measurements and reckoning, as long as he does not go in for questionable mathematical theories (such as Plato's theory that lines really consist of points) or wacky Pythagorean ideas about the significance of numbers.

Like several leading figures in the history of Scepticism, Sextus was a practising doctor. He was an advocate of the so-called 'Empiricist' approach to medicine – hence the second half of his name – which is a good example of the sort of expertise that Sceptics were prepared to tolerate. Empiricism began as a reaction to an impasse in the state of medical knowledge. The great doctor Hippocrates had held that medical practice ought to be based on a theory of the constitution of the body and the causes of its various unfortunate states. This sounds reasonable enough, but pretty soon there was a festering profusion of conflicting medical theories on offer. In around the first half of the third century BC, some doctors gave up trying to choose between them all and maintained that successful medical therapy did not need any theories. These were the Empiricists. Good Empiricist doctoring was just a matter of experience: you took care to observe which remedies had been effective against which symptoms in the past, and used these successes as your sole guide to treatment. There was no need to bother with the complicated and obscure matters which 'dogmatic' doctors (who were also called 'rationalists') went on about, such as the balance of the four 'humours' in the body (blood, phlegm, black and yellow bile) or the movement of invisible atoms through invisible pores in the skin. Similarly, you did not bother to look for 'hidden' causes when making a diagnosis. For example, if rabies was the problem, and if rabies had in the past always been observed to follow the bite of a mad dog, then that was all you needed to know about the causes of the condition. As for treatment, you tried whatever had worked before.

There was another anti-Dogmatic school of medicine that was more open-minded about the role of theories and the possibility of finding hidden causes. The so-called 'Methodist' doctors agreed with main-stream Empiricists that simple experience was enough to go on when treating a patient; but they thought it was at least conceivable that one would one day find some hidden or 'non-evident' factors to explain disease. Sextus pointed out that it was the non-committal Methodist school which provided the most appropriate medical philosophy for a Sceptic (perhaps he should have been known as Sextus Methodicus rather than Sextus Empiricus). For while Empiricists were adamant that hidden causes and obscure theories could have no role to play in medicine, Methodists suspended judgement about them.

It might be wondered where an Empiricist or Methodist doctor is to draw the line between evident causes and hidden ones. Both sorts of doctors need to be able to decide whether or not a particular factor is relevant, so they need to be able to distinguish between the acceptable observation of phenomena and the unacceptable investigation of 'unclear' matters. But how is this to be done? Surely what is evident to one person may be obscure to another: what an expert can see unthinkingly and in a flash, another may have to stop and think about. Thus it is not clear where the plain facts of experience end and questionable theories begin. Such puzzles may seem to pose a problem for Scepticism as a whole, because the Sceptics were always going on about the distinction between everyday experience (or 'appearances') and intellectual matters. Sceptics apparently need a way to tell the difference between these two sorts of things because they claim to suspend judgement only about the latter. For example, take some religious belief that is fairly widespread in a society but by no means universal; suppose some people go along with it unthinkingly while others argue about it. What should a Sceptic do? Should he suspend judgement on the issue, or should he follow the pious and unquestioning mob? How is he to tell whether or not this belief is intellectual enough to be worth doubting?

The Sceptics do not seem to have addressed this problem, but perhaps they had no need to. Remember that Scepticism was supposed to be a form of therapy, a useful cure for rashness and intellectual disturbance. So the answer to the question of what exactly it applied to would have been a practical one: Scepticism applies to whatever happens to need treatment. If it seems to a Sceptic that people are being so dogmatic about something that they are endangering their tranquillity, he will generously try to cure them by undermining the relevant belief. Likewise, if he finds that he himself is troubled by some question, he will administer his Sceptical remedies to himself so as to induce a calming suspension of judgement on the issue. And if doctors cannot stop quarrelling about the causes of some condition, a Sceptic will try to convince them to stick to the evident facts on which they can agree and to stop worrying about 'hidden' ones – for talk of these leads only to interminable disagreement. In general, he will decide what to call into doubt by seeing what causes trouble. He will presumably take the bad cases first. At the head of the queue will be the disputatious gaggle of philosophers, scientists and other 'professors' who have so much to say about the obscure truth behind everyday appearances. This unhappy lot definitely need the cure, so it is their dogmas which are the focus of most Sceptical writings. As for common beliefs, such as religious ones, they will get the treatment only if they cause problems.

Sextus said that the arguments which a Sceptic uses to dislodge dogmatic beliefs are like purgative drugs. They flush all the intellectual trouble out of one's system. Again like drugs, the Sceptic's remedies come in varying strengths: 'Sceptics . . . employ weighty arguments, capable of vigorously rebutting the dogmatic affliction of conceit, against those who are distressed by a severe rashness, and they employ milder arguments against those who are afflicted by a conceit which is superficial and easily cured.' One talent which a Sceptic particularly needs, however mild or severe the case under treatment, is 'an ability to set out oppositions'. That is, he needs to be good at displaying the diversity of perceptions, beliefs, attitudes and values in all of its conflicting variety. This is a great help in opening the mind by inducing a suspension of judgement.

Many of these 'oppositions' had to do with the external circumstances under which something is perceived, others with the physiological state of the perceiver. Some had to do with the perceiver's mental condition, others with the physical condition of the object. Some highlighted the varying effects of upbringing or environment on the opinions and tastes of different people. Others were about the different myths and laws prevailing in different places. But the point was always the same: the idea of displaying all this diversity was to show that what people think, say or feel – i.e., what *appears* to them to be true or *appears* to them to be good or desirable – varies according to circumstances. Thus, as Sextus says, 'it is no doubt easy to say what each existing object appears to be like to each person, but not what it *is* like'.

Having demonstrated that appearances vary widely, and that they depend on circumstances of various sorts, the Sceptic then pushes home his attack by asking what rational grounds a Dogmatist can possibly have for treating one set of appearances as superior to another and claiming that they present the world as it really is. Why does the Dogmatist say that the beliefs produced by *his* circumstances are the true ones? Whatever reply a Dogmatist makes to this challenge, the Sceptic is ready with a counter-argument. Suppose the Dogmatist tries to support his belief about how things really are by citing some other belief as evidence or proof of his opinion. The Sceptic will then try to force the Dogmatist into a corner by asking him, once more, to justify this evidence or proof. If the Dogmatist is inclined to offer yet another supporting belief, then another in support of that, and so on, the

Sceptic will point out that this chain of justifications must come to an end somewhere, or else it will in effect rest on nothing. And when the Dogmatist tries to rest his case on some final point, the Sceptic will attempt to show that he is making an unjustified assumption. Alternatively, the Sceptic might try to show that the Dogmatist is guilty of begging the question – i.e., of simply assuming the very point at issue and thus arguing round and round in a circle. (For example, one philosopher attacked Chrysippus on the grounds that he cited divination as evidence of Fate and Fate as evidence of divination.)

The Sceptic's therapeutic tool-kit is full of arguments designed to induce his weary opponent to suspend judgement. If all else fails, the Sceptic can simply fall back on the disconcerting fact of interminable human disagreement, in the hope that this itself will weaken his patient's rash Dogmatism. As Sextus points out, even if everyone we have ever heard of agrees about some question, there might be an unknown race (or, we might add, an alien species) that sees things differently. What could you say to convince them that you are right and they are wrong? People do not just disagree about their casual opinions and observations: experts frequently remain in conflict even after making exhaustive inquiries. As one expositor of Scepticism put it, those who

profess to hunt down the clear and the true in things, are divided into brigades and platoons and set down dogmas that are discordant not on some one chance point but on virtually everything, great and small, with which their investigations are concerned.

On thousands of topics in all branches of knowledge, including science, 'there have been countless inquiries, but up to the present time agreement has not been reached in any one of them on the part of all the inquirers'. If the experts cannot get to the bottom of things, what hope is there for anyone else? Better to suspend judgement.

One glaring fact stands in the Sceptics' favour: when they said that 'the Dogmatists' knew nothing, they were absolutely right. By our standards virtually all the theories of ancient thinkers (except mathematicians) are wrong. These people thought they knew various things, but they did not, which is exactly what the Sceptics had been saying. Yet, it will be said, the situation is very different today: the Greeks may have been hopelessly wrong about all sorts of things, but contemporary man knows a great deal. If the Sceptics had a point in the old days, they surely have less of one now.

Whether or not people ever really know things is a question that runs through much of the history of philosophy; more will be said about it later. However, it is worth noting at once that the sort of disagreements between experts that the ancient Sceptics smugly pointed out are very much still with us. Many scientific questions that puzzled the ancients have been more or less resolved, but their place has merely been taken by new controversies. Physicists may no longer argue about the number of elements or the existence of void, but their disputes about parallel worlds, worm holes in space-time and the state of the early universe, for example, are just as inconclusive. From medicine to cosmology, the sciences are full of open questions. Today's experts are confident that they are getting close to the truth, but then experts always have been – and not just on scientific subjects. Sextus used his battery of Sceptical arguments against the humanities of his day (against theories about music and grammar, for example). He would have had little difficulty in applying the Sceptical 'ability to set out oppositions' in newer fields such as economics, psychology or sociology.

Still, whether or not Sceptical arguments prove to be effective against modern 'Dogmatists', there are puzzling questions to be asked about the ancient Sceptics and what they thought they were up to. For example: what is so calming and therapeutic about always picking fights with people? If the Sceptic appreciates tranquillity, as he says he does, why does he spend so much time arguing? There is something a little suspicious about claiming to be a dedicated 'inquirer' or 'searcher' when you seem unwilling to accept any answers. In his *Historical and Critical Dictionary* (1697), Pierre Bayle wrote that 'All his life [*Pyrrho*] was searching for the truth, but he always managed things so as not to grant that he had found it.'

The Pyrrhonist may reply to this that the trouble and inconvenience of questioning every belief about how things really are are outweighed by the tranquillity that is produced by suspending judgement on such matters. The Sceptics presumably found that the pleasures of keeping an open mind were greater than the pleasures of thinking you have discovered the truth. For one thing, according to Sextus, there are emotional dangers in believing you have got to the bottom of things. This will make you think that you know what is genuinely good and what is genuinely bad, a state of affairs which is bound to leave you 'perpetually troubled'. For if you lack what you take to be truly good, you will exhaust yourself trying to get it. And if you do get it, you will still be far from tranquil. When people grasp what they have been striving for, 'they are elated beyond reason and measure, and they do anything so as not to lose what they believe to be good'. Scepticism is the only way to get off this treadmill. People who are wise enough to suspend judgement about what is genuinely good or bad 'neither pursue nor avoid anything with intensity; and hence they are tranquil'.

Sextus acknowledged that the Sceptical approach to life could not eliminate all sources of distress. Since Sceptics are human, they will find that certain unpleasant feelings are forced on them by circumstances: 'we agree that at times they shiver and are thirsty and have other feelings of this kind'. Nevertheless, good Sceptics minimize their suffering by managing to 'shed' any troubling opinions that would make them feel worse than they actually need to.

Unfortunately, Sceptics are also supposed to shed many of the opinions that make life enjoyable. In addition to suspending judgement about what is genuinely bad, they are supposed to suspend judgement about what is genuinely good as well. To us this seems too high a price to pay for tranquillity, because it means forgoing too many sources of everyday satisfaction. One would not be allowed, for example, to take pleasure in being promoted to a new job – for how does one know that getting this job is really a good thing? A Sceptic would say that for the sake of a quiet life it is worth suspending judgement on the matter and thus sacrificing the pleasure of believing that you have finally made it. After all, if you are so convinced that this job is a wonderful thing, you will always be worried about losing it. But that is hard to take. Most people would object that it is simply impossible to adopt so detached an approach to life's pains and pleasures without becoming positively inhuman.

Perhaps that was the point. It is worth remembering that although all the main Hellenistic philosophies were to some extent addressed to the needs of the ordinary person, part of what they aimed to give him was inspiration and ideals. Wisdom was not supposed to come cheap; the life of a sage was bound to be hard to live up to. Unworldly ideals are made to be watered down, and in due course Scepticism was. When the ideas of the ancient Sceptics were exhumed after more than a thousand years of neglect (see page 420), philosophers and scientists were selective in what they chose to learn from Pyrrhonism and what they chose to forget about. What they wanted to inherit were the virtues of open-mindedness, tolerance and intellectual caution, the Sceptic's willingness to go by experience and his healthy resistance to dogma. They were less interested in the radical Pyrrhonian project of 'living without opinions'. The end of the next chapter will describe how this Sceptical inheritance matured. But first we must look at some of what happened before it did so.

# 14

## The Haven of Piety:
### *From Late Antiquity to the Renaissance*

In AD 529, about three centuries after the death of Sextus Empiricus, a Christian emperor found a quick way to put an end to philosophical squabbles. This had been tried before. Sextus and other Sceptics had attempted to argue all 'dogmatic' philosophers into a tranquil silence, but most of them had been too sceptical of Scepticism to take any notice. The emperor Justinian now tried a more direct approach. He simply closed down the philosophical schools in Athens, and apparently wanted to ban non-Christian philosophy throughout the Roman Empire. His main aim seems to have been to stamp out paganism – he was said to have caused the forcible baptism of 70,000 people in Asia Minor alone – though he was also keen to squash Athens as an intellectual rival to his own imperial university in Constantinople. But whatever exactly led Justinian to close the schools, the days of open-minded rational inquiry were numbered anyway. The mystical and religious strains in Graeco-Roman thought had been growing stronger for quite a while: 'And so let me anchor, weary one, in the haven of piety,' wrote Proclus, the most eminent Greek philosopher of the previous century, in one of his hymns to the pagan gods.

Even among such non-Christian thinkers, the traditional marks of Greek philosophy were beginning to fade. The rationalistic spirit shared by Thales, Anaxagoras, Democritus and Epicurus; the habit of radical questioning shared by Socrates, the Sophists and the Sceptics; Plato's love of logical argument; Aristotle's wide-ranging intellectual curiosity – all of these qualities were dying, or at least mutating. Proclus was just as interested in magic and oracles as he was in geometry and Plato, and in this respect he was typical of his age. The old style of philosophy was already tiring long before Justinian's heavy-handed attempt to finish it off.

The closure of the Athenian schools in AD 529 was not in itself a momentous event. Two earlier developments had done far more damage to intellectual life: first the division of the Roman Empire into a Latin west and a Greek east in the fourth century, which soon cut off most Europeans from their Greek heritage; and second the destruction of the western empire and its civilization by assorted barbarians in the fifth century. Nevertheless, AD 529 is a convenient milestone for the history of philosophy. From round about this time, philosophy in the West remained more or less the slave of Christianity for about a millennium.

From the perspective of modern thought, it is tempting to see that lengthy interlude in terms of the tale of Sleeping Beauty. Having pricked its finger on Christian theology, philosophy fell asleep for about a thousand years until awakened by the kiss of Descartes. Many thinkers of around Descartes' own time believed something like this, though they tended to blame the influence of Aristotle as much as the influence of the Church for the decline of philosophy (and they did not yet credit Descartes with being the one who revived it). In 1651, Thomas Hobbes wrote that philosophy in the medieval universities 'hath no otherwise place than as a handmaiden to the Roman religion; and since the authority of Aristotle is only current there, that study is not properly philosophy (the nature whereof dependeth not on authors) but Aristotelity'. In 1605, Francis Bacon described 'the kind of degenerate learning' which

did chiefly reign amongst the schoolmen: who having sharp and strong wits, and abundance of leisure, and small variety of reading, but their wits being shut up in the cells of a few authors (chiefly Aristotle their dictator) as their persons were shut up in the cells of monasteries and colleges, and knowing little history, either of nature or time, did out of no great quantity of matter and infinite agitation of wit spin out unto us those laborious webs of learning which are extant in their books – cobwebs of learning, admirable for the fineness of thread and work, but of no substance or profit.

Two centuries after Bacon, by which time Descartes was widely seen as the man who had done the most to clear away the cobwebs, Hegel made a similarly damning judgement on medieval philosophy. He did

347

not damn it by what he said but rather by what he did not say. A mere 120 pages out of his 1,300-page chronological survey of philosophy are devoted to the 1,000 years of the medieval period; 1,200 years of ancient thought get 800 pages, and 200 years of modernity get nearly 400 pages.

Most of today's readers will have little cause to quarrel with Hegel's priorities. On the whole, the philosophical productions of the ancient and modern periods are not only much more creative but also more approachable for the contemporary reader than are the long-winded commentaries and dialectical exercises disgorged in the intervening centuries. Given limited time and space, most medieval philosophy is best left to slumber in its arguably dark and undeniably thorny forest.

Yet neither Hobbes nor Bacon should be taken too seriously on the question of what made medieval philosophy unflatteringly different. It was not just a matter of too much Aristotle or too much religion. And to imply that the best minds of the medieval West had produced nothing of any 'substance or profit' was going too far.

It is true that philosophy in the Middle Ages was primarily employed as the handmaiden of Christian theology; medieval philosophers themselves, all of whom were clerics and most of whom earned their keep as teachers of theology, would certainly not have objected to the description. But this handmaiden was allowed her days off. Several branches of philosophy came to be pursued without too much regard to the theological dividends of the investment. Besides, plenty of theological topics led naturally into philosophical ones. A discussion of the nature of the soul, for example, could soon become an inquiry into how the mind acquires its knowledge of the material world and how it is related to the body. A discussion of sin could turn into a treatment of free will. A discussion of God's foreknowledge could quickly lead on to the nature of time. In fact, many of the dogmas of medieval Christianity positively cried out for philosophical treatment. Christians were required to believe, for example, that a piece of wafer could become a piece of flesh while still looking like a piece of wafer, and that God could be three persons at once. Abstruse theories about matter, form and substance that seemed to make sense of such mysteries were therefore more than welcome.

The fact that medieval philosophy was intertwined with a religion that dominated many aspects of life had its benefits. Although it meant that the study of philosophy was constrained in ways that would today be regarded as intolerable, it also meant that the subject enjoyed the attentions of an immensely powerful patron. Because the Church was interested in philosophy, everybody who wanted to rise through her hierarchy – or even just to get a good education – had to be interested in it too. Unlike today, virtually every educated person studied it to some extent, under the guise either of theology or of natural philosophy or, most commonly, of logic. Philosophers, though they may officially have been called something else, were often important men. Today an eminent philosopher may aspire to advise a government committee on some relatively minor matter. In the Middle Ages, he could have had real power by becoming a cardinal, an archbishop or even the Pope.

He could also, of course, be imprisoned, excommunicated or worse if he came to the wrong conclusions. But the condemnations and bans that punctuate the course of medieval philosophy cannot quite be taken at face value. What they show is not that independent thought could easily be stamped out but rather that it could not. Why else would the Church have had to keep on trying? It tried the hardest and yet achieved the least in the Renaissance, when the trickle of unorthodox ideas was growing into a flood. And even when the Church's power had been at its height, ecclesiastical rulings could only ever slow the pace of intellectual change, not divert its course. In 1210, students at the university of Paris were forbidden on pain of excommunication to study Aristotle's scientific works, even in private. A few decades later these texts were compulsory.

The Church's grip on philosophy in the Middle Ages was not like the much more painful one exerted by Marxism-Leninism in Eastern Europe before the fall of communism. There are several differences between the two cases, but perhaps the most important one lies in the fact that alternative systems of thought were not withheld from students and teachers in the early Middle Ages as they sometimes later were under communism. They were not withheld because they did not exist, at least not in any easily usable form. Suppose, for a moment, that an imaginary intellectual of the early twelfth century had suddenly found himself freed of the limitations of a Church-dominated educational system and society. Suppose he had had time and money to research any subject he wanted, access to all the most up-to-date works in a language he could understand, and a supply of bright and equally liberated colleagues to talk to. What could he have done with this freedom? Where could he have turned to find inspiration and ideas? Only to the works of the ancient Greeks and the Arabic commentaries on them. And that is precisely what the actual intellectuals of the thirteenth century did, when they belatedly set out to recover and translate their Greek heritage. Did the Church then hamper the subsequent understanding and development of what had been unearthed? Arguably not: Westerners might well have been even slower to modify and ultimately transform this ancient heritage if they had not been forced by the demands of Christianity to examine it with a highly critical eye. Consider what happened in 1277 when the Bishop of Paris condemned 219 propositions derived from or apparently supported by the newly discovered Greek and Arabic writings. As we shall see, the long-term effect of such condemnations (similar ones were soon issued in Britain) was not to bind thinkers to the Church, but to start them thinking along new lines.

There is thus not much reason to think that abandoning Christianity in, say, the twelfth century would have brought a dramatic improvement to intellectual life in the Latin West. The fact is that learning had sunk to such a miserable state during the early Middle Ages that an overbearing Church would have been the least of a medieval thinker's problems. By the year 1000, medicine, physics, astronomy, biology and indeed all branches of theoretical knowledge except theology had virtually collapsed. Even the few relatively educated men, holed up in monasteries, knew markedly less than many Greeks had done eight centuries earlier. Most of classical literature, including Roman literature, was largely unknown, except to a handful of monks. The few mathematical jottings to be found are for the most part downright stupid. In short, Christendom was colossally ignorant. (The Arabs, meanwhile, had made striking progress in medicine, science, mathematics and philosophy ever since they began to translate Greek works into Syriac and Arabic in the eighth century.)

Nobody had killed the Greek inheritance; it had simply been allowed to waste away. Perhaps Christianity can be blamed for some of this neglect. After all, many influential early Christians had maintained that the only important thing to know about the world was that it was created by God. Any further details were irrelevant. St Augustine condemned 'the lust of the eyes' and 'perceptions acquired through the flesh . . . vain inquisitiveness dignified with the title of knowledge and science'. The dissection of human corpses in order to find out about anatomy was regarded as an impious impertinence, so serious medical research was out of the question. Some of the more liberal Church Fathers argued that the ancient Greeks were children of God and so might be worth listening to. But louder voices said that the Greeks had been born too early to know what really mattered in life, so they and their 'knowledge' could safely be ignored. Such an attitude can hardly have helped. On the other hand, neither can the fall of the Roman empire and the consequent demise of civilized life and school-ing in the depths of Europe's Dark Ages (around AD 450 750). Besides, the Romans were already proving to be somewhat half-hearted custod-ians of the Greek inheritance long before the empire went Christian. For that matter, by the third century AD so were the Greeks themselves.

If the Church was not quite as bad for intellectual life as it has sometimes been painted, what of that other stock villain in Hobbes' pantomime, Aristotle? The idea that Aristotle's thought dominated the Middle Ages needs one immediate qualification: practically all of his works were unknown for most of the period. With the exception of two minor treatises on logic, Aristotle's writings were not circulated until the last three centuries of the medieval era (i.e., 1150–1450). This final portion of the Middle Ages is, however, where most of the action was. Most of the sophisticated philosophical and scientific literature of medieval times was written then, in the wake of the translations of Greek and Arabic authors which had begun flowing from around the middle of the twelfth century. In fact, most of the best-known medieval philosophers, from Albert the Great to William of Ockham, lie squeezed within the compass of just 150 years. It was between 1200 and 1350 that the medieval world-picture as we know it best – the world-picture of Dante and Chaucer – took on its mature shape. And in those days Aristotle's influence was indeed supreme.

His concepts and terminology, as rendered into Latin, provided the currency for most academic exchange. If he had written about a topic, and he usually had, then his theories were the starting point for any advanced discussion of it. This was an age that tended always to look for a guiding authority to light its path. And when it came to academic matters, nobody could compete with the polymathic Aristotle for the job. For one thing, the newly emerging universities of the thirteenth century needed something to fill their curricula. His treatises fitted the bill. Writing commentaries on them was one of the main forms of philosophical activity in the universities: Albert the Great wrote about 8,000 pages of such commentary.

But Albert would never have found so much to say if he had always agreed with Aristotle. Christian doctrine made total agreement impossible. Aristotle said that the world had always existed; Christians knew that it had not. Aristotle said that the soul does not survive death; Christians knew that it did. What Aristotle said about the concept of substance seemed to imply that the Eucharist was a logical impossibility, which did not go down well. Aristotle's God was totally uninterested in what man got up to. This, too, was clearly a problem.

The reception of Aristotle's doctrines was always a cautious and critical affair. First of all they had, ideally, to be reconciled with the teachings of the Faith. This was not simply a matter of crossing out a few offending passages, but of creating a new synthesis of Christianity and Aristotelianism. The crowning achievement of this synthesis was the *Summa Theologiae* of Albert's best pupil, St Thomas Aquinas (*c*.1225–74). Aristotle's doctrines also had to be weighed against a few other venerable contributions, such as those of Platonism. (Plato's own writings – except for part of the *Timaeus*' creation-story – were largely unknown until the fifteenth century, but various ideas regarded as Platonic had come down through respected authors including St Augustine.) Furthermore, Aristotle's treatises arrived in the West together with voluminous and stimulating commentaries by Arab scholars. The Christian university teachers who set out to learn and pass on all this wisdom were hardly going to do so without having their own say as well. Thus Aristotle was by no means swallowed and regurgitated whole. When the best medieval thinkers agreed with him, they were not merely parroting his opinions but rather affirming that they themselves had come to the same conclusions.

Nevertheless, even when they wrestled with Aristotle, they mostly did so on his terms. This was what the Renaissance critics of medieval scholasticism most objected to. Nobody could blame Aristotle himself for being hopelessly out of touch sixteen centuries after he had died. But it was a bit much that his descendants in the late Middle Ages should treat the corpse of his philosophy as if it were alive and talking to them. These distant descendants may have added a Christian accent, but they still spoke the language of Aristotle. They may sometimes have looked at it from a different angle, but it was still Aristotle's world they lived in. Even when they questioned his conclusions, they were captivated by his concepts, categories and methods.

Aristotle would not have wanted such a degree of posthumous influence. As we have seen, he regarded his theories as tentative accounts that deserved to survive only insofar as they fitted the facts of experience (see page 224). He himself was animated by the spirit of open-minded inquiry: it was not he who let what was once a novel and liberating set of concepts become a prison for the mind. This brings us closer to the real problem with medieval learning. It is that the medieval professors allowed themselves to be tyrannized by books. The problem was not so much Aristotle's books or holy books but rather their attitude to books in general. Instead of putting ideas to the test of new experience, they were more inclined to put them to the test of old books.

This conservative outlook has a parallel in the expiring centuries of the ancient world, when the desire to acquire fresh knowledge and understanding degenerated into a concern merely to preserve and transmit what had been acquired before. Maybe this concern was aggravated in the early Middle Ages by the frustrating fact that there was so little left to transmit. One literary critic described the medieval intellectual as

a literate man who had lost a great many of his books and forgotten how to read all his Greek books . . . An exaggerated, but not wholly fake, model would be a party of shipwrecked people setting to work to try and build up a culture on an uninhabited island and depending on the odd collection of books which happened to be on board their ship.

The original cause of the shipwreck and of this ardent desire to cling to literary wreckage is not something which can be explained here.

But it is worth noting that when every copy of every book took longer to produce than it did to read, the survival of any text was bound to be both more precarious and more celebrated than we can easily imagine.

It is not hard to see how an obsession with texts and ancient authorities could lead to a form of scholarship that headed unerringly towards the arid and the convoluted. As he picked over his stock, our shipwrecked book-lover would soon realize that not all of his treasures said the same thing. In addition to the problem of reconciling scripture with the remnants of pagan learning, there were the problems of reconciling one Church Father with another, scripture with itself, and every commentator with every other commentator. It was a never-ending business. Whenever possible, it was best to try to show that the authorities were basically in agreement. Whenever it was not possible to produce a harmonious synthesis, one could try to find a middle path, or at least a piece of common ground. And when even this was impossible, one had to grit one's teeth, weigh up the pros and cons, and come down firmly and logically on one side or the other. Fortunately – or perhaps unfortunately, if you do not sympathize with his under-takings – one thing that our mariner managed to keep with him was ancient logic. This discipline offered a complete theory of analysis and debate, from a technical system of definition and classification to the study of pitfalls in argument. Unlike modern logic, it was not confined to the principles of valid deduction, though it covered them too. Logic in this broad sense was a cornerstone of medieval education, and its tools were applied in increasingly artificial ways to the grinding and polishing of texts.

In the universities, the practice of reconciling authorities evolved into a distinctive style of teaching and learning. Theologians in the early twelfth century had developed a technique known as the *quaestio*, in which the differing opinions of distinguished authors on some question were compared with one another and analysed. This seems to have started as a written exercise involving a statement of the question to be decided, brief arguments for and against various possible answers, comments on these arguments and then some sort of resolution. But it also came to provide the format for the oral debates or *disputationes* that were a major part of a university student's education. Each of these tournaments followed a predetermined pattern, though different patterns were followed at different times and in different settings. For example, in the Parisian faculty of theology in the mid-thirteenth century, a typical two-day event would go as follows. On the first day, selected students would play the role either of 'objector' or 'respondent', dealing with a simple yes-or-no thesis picked by the teacher. Authorities would be cited on both sides of the question. The objector would put forward arguments against the thesis and the respondent would retaliate with counter-arguments; the teacher would intervene now and then. On the second day, the teacher would summarize and resolve the issue by stating his answer and explaining how he had reached it. On special occasions, such as at Easter and Christmas, the students were free to choose the topics themselves. There were also debates organized for the younger students who had not yet proceeded to the study of higher subjects such as theology. These could be about questions in natural science, or more frequently in logic, and are reported to have sometimes got out of hand. According to some sources, hissing and stone-throwing were not uncommon. The fossils of these various types of debate can be seen in many of the main philosophical works of the period. Some are published records of actual tournaments, while others – like Aquinas's *Summa Theologiae* – were composed as textbooks but still followed a sort of *quaestio* format, trudging through the second reply to the fourth counter-argument to the third question, and so on. To the modern reader this style of treatment may seem almost designed to be indigestible. In fact it was designed to be helpful. The style was partly moulded and considerably reinforced by the circumstances of university teaching. With very little access to books of his own, and limited opportunity to take notes, the student needed to be fed material in memorable chunks. Also, his progress was measured largely by his performance in live debate. So he committed key quotes, stock arguments and standard debating manoeuvres to memory. The rigid division and classification of material was a helpful mnemonic device. Lectures, which always focussed on a text rather than a topic, also often followed an orderly and thus memorable pattern of question, argument, counter-argument and resolution.

Whatever its exact beginnings and original advantages, this style of teaching grew into a baroque monstrosity. Increasing emphasis was put on the ability to 'distinguish' the premises of an argument – i.e., to show that they were ambiguous and could be accepted as true in one sense but not in another. Disentangling many different senses of a proposition became a prized skill. As Aristotle's three-step syllogisms came to dominate the study of logic, ingenious thinkers expended much of their ingenuity on forcing interesting arguments into these ill-fitting three-legged trousers. As time went by, oral debates and the literature that reflected them became steadily less lively and more formal. By the early sixteenth century, the suspense of waiting to discover the 'right' answer in a debate was abolished in favour of a format in which the solution was given early on and yet the various arguments for and against still had to be plodded through afterwards. This back-to-front approach underlines the tendency of such performances to become exercises in logical skill for its own sake. The temptation to spend time on a point not because it was intrinsically interesting but because the debater had a clever answer to it was sometimes hard to resist.

According to popular myth, the scholastic style of philosophy quibbled itself to death in about the late fourteenth century. Histories of philosophy often lead one to think so, but in fact it was still very much alive in many universities as late as the seventeenth century. What happened was just that the universities and their methods ceased to be so interesting to later historians. After the spread of printed books from the middle of the fifteenth century, and for other reasons, intellectual life fanned out far beyond the confines of educational institutions. Particularly in science and philosophy, most of the innovators worked outside academia, and the spotlights followed them. None of the great post-medieval philosophers until Kant, who died in 1804, had much to do with any university (though Locke taught medicine at Oxford for a while).

The medieval professors quibbled themselves on to the unlit sidelines of philosophical history; death was a long time coming. But although their laboured approach, their narrow perspectives and their theological preoccupations severely restrict their appeal for later readers, one should not conclude that their philosophical work is marginal nit-picking and nothing else. The one thing which almost everyone has heard about medieval philosophy is that its practitioners used to argue about such trivia as how many angels can dance on the head of a pin. This story is worth a closer look, because the moral of the tale is the opposite of what one might expect.

The idea of sober calculations about prancing angels is a nice image, but it cannot be genuine. The puzzle is too easy to have occupied anyone for long. Since everyone believed that angels have no bodies, the answer to the puzzle of how many can dance on a pin was obviously 'none'. You cannot dance without a body. It is therefore not surprising that there is no evidence of anyone ever seriously addressing such a question. There were, however, some logical tournaments conducted in the universities purely for fun. One might compare these with modern end-of-term student debates: 'This House believes that cabbages are preferable to kings.' It is not impossible that the old anecdote about angels derives from some similarly light-hearted motion – in which case it is their detractors and not medieval philosophers themselves who lacked a sense of humour. But it is more likely that the tale began in the Renaissance as a caricature of a controversy about space and angels which was started by John Duns Scotus (*c.*1266–1308), one of the most important medieval philosophers. If so, the joke is still on the Renaissance wit, whoever he was, who first thought up the story. For the problem addressed by Scotus is essentially the same as one that later troubled Newton, and it remains an intriguing one in the foundations of physics.

It is known as the problem of action at a distance. How does an object exert an influence on something with which it has no physical contact? Newton was unhappy about the fact that the force of gravity which he postulated seemed to involve such disconnected action: the earth seemed to affect his famous apple without there being any intervening medium of contact. Scotus was similarly unhappy about the fact that angels – who were commonly held to be capable of causing physical events when God told them to – did not have bodies and so could not be in contact with anything. How, then, could they perform their divine missions? To solve this problem, Scotus had to rethink some of what Aristotle had said about the notion of place. His solution involved the idea that an angel can have a location in space even though he has no shape or size: like mathematical points (though

Scotus did not put it like this), angels can be given co-ordinates. It followed, or so Scotus thought, that they could be 'present to', or near, the material things which they affected, thus eliminating the puzzling phenomenon of action at a distance.

There are many obscurities in Scotus's account, but it was nevertheless an attempt to deal with a genuine problem of the day. If there is something absurd in his reasoning about the physics of angels, then the fault lies with the belief in angels, not with his style of reasoning about them.

If one immerses oneself in medieval texts, it is often possible to see great intelligence and a passion for understanding at work. The closer one looks, the more one finds evidence of acute thinking that manages to rise above its circumstances. Moreover, since most of the relics of medieval philosophy have still not been printed, let alone translated out of Latin, there will probably never be a shortage of specialists excitedly announcing that they have just found something remarkable in the haystack. Yet such close-up examination needs to be supplemented with the view from a broader perspective. Stand back to see the landscape of late antiquity and medieval times in the setting of what lies either side of it, and the comparison with what came before and what came afterwards is not flattering.

The rest of this chapter will trace the outlines of the story of philosophy and science from the decline of the ancient world to the birth of the new, pausing over a few personalities and turning-points along the way. It does not attempt to give a complete picture, or to mention everybody.

Go back to the time of Sextus Empiricus, the latest of the philosophers described in the previous chapter. He cannot have been a happy man. By the beginning of the third century AD, around the time when he was writing his defence of Pyrrhonist scepticism, the philosophical scene had turned into a sceptic's nightmare. It was an age of believers, not of doubters, and people managed to believe a great deal. While Sextus and a handful of others tried to play off the doctrines of Plato, Aristotle and the Stoics against one another, most thinkers preferred to try to combine them and then swallow the lot. Christianity, pagan mysticism, ghost-raising magic, Pythagorean numerological ramblings and assorted flavours of Eastern religion also turned up to join the feast.

If the first two centuries after Aristotle's death were marked by a spirit of competition between rival philosophies, the thinkers of late antiquity are notable for a spirit of reconciliation. This is not to say that everybody agreed with everybody or that philosophers managed to stop abusing one another. Still, most of the best thinkers from about the first century BC onwards were more concerned to look back in awe at the great philosophers of the past than they were to pick fights with their contemporaries. A few notable Roman writers settled on just one old philosophy: Lucretius settled on Epicureanism; Seneca, Epictetus and Marcus Aurelius on Stoicism. But although Lucretius stuck to the letter of Epicurus' writings, the Roman Stoics watered down the original ideas of the Greek Stoics with accretions from other sources. Such eclecticism was typical of the times. The main trend, especially among Greeks, was towards a synthesis of past wisdom that tried to show how much the different philosophies had in common. Antiochus of Ascalon, who was head of the Academy in Athens from 86–68 BC, proclaimed that Platonism, Aristotelianism and Stoicism all said the same thing. The orator Cicero, who went to hear Antiochus lecture, was another beachcomber. Sometimes his philosophical writings seem like those of a freelance Platonist, sometimes like those of a Stoic gone wrong. To add to the confusion, he described himself as a sort of sceptic.

Pythagoreanism started a small comeback around Cicero's time and its adherents tried to show that Plato got all his good ideas from Pythagoras. For good measure, these Pythagorean revivalists also claimed that Aristotle got all his good ideas from Plato, thus merging a large portion of classical Greek philosophy into a single body of doctrine. Another, even more ambitious, reconciling project was that of the Jewish philosopher, Philo of Alexandria (*c.* 25 BC–*c.* AD 45). His vast and sometimes befuddled commentaries on the Septuagint (a Greek translation of the Old Testament and Apocrypha) began a tradition of marrying holy scriptures to Greek philosophy that was continued by later Jewish, Christian and Islamic theologians. By the second century AD, pieces of Pythagoras, Plato, Aristotle, the Stoics and others were being combined in a jigsaw that came to fascinate pagans and Christians alike.

A philosophical textbook from this period, by a pagan teacher called Alcinous, puts many of the pieces together. The universe, he says, was created by a master-craftsman using the methods described in Plato's *Timaeus* (see page 204). It was 'fashioned by God as He gazed upon some Idea of the universe which was the model for it and of which it is a copy'. Although Aristotle had had no time for this sort of creation-story, his concept of an Unmoved Mover was borrowed by Alcinous to explain the incessant motion of the heavens: 'without motion himself, the primal God acts upon the cosmos as . . . the object of desire arouses desire while remaining motionless itself'. This God, again like Aristotle's, must 'contemplate eternally Himself and His own thoughts' because nothing else is grand enough to occupy Him. What exactly are these thoughts? Aristotle could not say, but Alcinous identified them with the ideal Platonic Forms that were the blueprints for the creation of the world. While Plato had regarded the Forms as independent entities that existed in their own right, Alcinous followed Philo in saying that they were merely ideas in the mind of God. This modification was useful to Christians, Moslems and Jews because it helpfully dispensed with Plato's notion that the Forms were somehow superior to God. In his resourceful adaptations and borrowings from earlier traditions, Alcinous also made use of the Stoic notion of a 'most marvellous providence' which guides the world according to man's best interests. This went some way towards making God less uninvolved with the world than Aristotle's disinterested and contemplative Unmoved Mover had been.

One way to get a clear view of God, said Alcinous, is to make the sort of intellectual climb described by the priestess Diotima when she spoke through Socrates in Plato's *Symposium* (see page 172). In Alcinous's version:

one contemplates first the beauty that resides in bodies and then passes on to the beauty of the soul, then to that which is found in customs and laws, then to the vast ocean of beauty, after which one conceives of the Good itself, the goal of love and desire appearing as a light and, as it were, shining upon the soul as it makes its ascent. To this one adds the notion of God because of His preeminence in honour.

Diotima's original climb up 'the heavenly ladder' culminated at 'the very soul of beauty'. But Alcinous here manages to get two rungs higher. From the Platonic Form of Beauty, he jumps straight to the Form of the Good, Plato's senior Form, which is compared in the *Republic* to the sun that shines on all things. And from the Form of the Good, Alcinous jumps to God. Indeed, God and the Form of the Good were spoken of as much the same thing in the second century AD, though Plato himself would have insisted that they were utterly different. For him, 500 years earlier, God had been a sort of soul, not an abstract Form. Philosophy studied the Forms and religion dealt with souls and gods. But now philosophical and religious themes were merging. What were once philosophical abstractions were beginning to take on a new shape as personalized deities and their divine thoughts.

A few thinkers of the second century copied the old Stoic habit of describing God as a sort of fire that permeated the universe. But this went against the grain. The dominant spirit of the times was opposed to materialism, and a fiery God just sounded too physical. Those who were swayed by Pythagoreanism tended to refer to Him as the 'One' – which, if He has to be a number, is presumably the best number to pick. These latter-day Pythagoreans were not quite monotheists, though. They held that there were inferior gods too, often borrowed from mythology, each of whom was assigned his own number. Numenius of Apamea, a Pythagorean contemporary of Alcinous, seems to have held that there were at least two main gods. There was a junior one who did the work of building the world, and a senior One, who would not dream of dirtying his hands with such a task. Numenius managed to cite Jewish, Egyptian, Persian and Indian scriptures in support of his Pythagorean and Platonic ideas. What was Plato, he once asked, but Moses in Greek?

The ghost of Plato occupied a special place in such compilations of past wisdom. It haunted the whole disintegrating feast of intellectual life. Typically, Alcinous billed his book as a 'summary of Plato's principal teachings' despite its evident borrowings from many other sources. In fact, all the main Greek philosophers from the third century onwards regarded themselves as Platonists of one sort or another. Plato's idea that the material world was a mere shadow of some superior reality gradually blotted out all alternative theories.

Aristotle's more down-to-earth views, and the hardline materialism of the early Stoics and Epicurus, did not have the same appeal to a civilization that was increasingly otherworldly in its philosophical and religious concerns.

Sometime during Alcinous' life (perhaps in around AD 120), a monument to the fading influence of Epicurus' materialism was erected in Oenoanda, a small town in southwestern Turkey. The inscriptions on it make it the strangest document in the history of philosophy. A prominent citizen called Diogenes erected a 100-yard colonnade on which he inscribed a treatise of perhaps 25,000 words in praise and belated defence of Epicurus. It was not intended as a vast memorial tombstone, but that is what it turned out to be. A few disciples of Epicurus are occasionally to be found over the next few centuries, but they were plucked from obscurity only to provide a target for Christian abuse. The citizens of Oenoanda demolished the colonnade some time in the third century and used its stones to build their houses. About a quarter of the text has been excavated and reassembled, including a prophecy of a coming golden age to be brought about by the acceptance of Epicureanism. A reworking of Epicurus' physics in the seventeenth century did indeed help to usher in the scientific revolution, but Diogenes was probably hoping for something a little sooner than that.

The inscription speaks of the 'salvation' that Epicureanism can bring. At least in this choice of term, Diogenes caught the spirit of his times. Philosophy was now generally seen as a path to spiritual salvation rather than as a recipe for tranquillity or as an intellectual exercise. One influential set of mystical writings defined philosophy as the business of 'learning to know the deity by habitual contemplation and pious devotion'. Contemporary religious movements such as Gnosticism typically focused on the inferior and illusory nature of the physical world, and on various not very intellectual ways of finding something better.

Diogenes' wall also described the Epicurean philosophy as a proof that natural science is of immense benefit to mankind. This idea struck no chord at all; few thinkers in the second century had any interest in science. Alcinous and his fellow 'Platonists' praised arithmetic, geometry and astronomy because Plato did, but they do not seem to have got much beyond idle praise. The Christians, as we have seen, had other things on their minds and were in any case suspicious of Greek learning. The great doctor Galen of Pergamum (AD 129–199) and his contemporary, Ptolemy of Alexandria, are two of the most impressive scientists of the whole ancient Greek world, but they were the end of the line. They had no successors for a very long time. Ptolemy was the most influential astronomer until the scientific revolution: his version of Aristotle's earth-centred universe went virtually unquestioned for 1,200 years. Galen's writings, based largely on his dissections of animals, were the source of practically all medical knowledge until modern times. He was a polymath in the old style who also made impressive contributions to philosophy, particularly in logic and in his attempts to answer scepticism. But neither Ptolemy nor Galen could have left such an enduring impression if they had not been the last of their outdated kind. Galen observed sadly that people knew less about the physical world than they used to, presumably because they were no longer so interested in it.

For a number of reasons, Greek science had failed to flourish under the Roman Empire. The Roman ruling classes had a curious but perhaps understandable mixture of disdain and awe for the intellectual achievements of their Greek subjects and slaves. On the one hand, no educated Roman could doubt that the Greeks were superior in the arts and sciences. Apart from anything else, they had a far more extensive and sophisticated literature than the Romans. Greek teachers were obviously the ones to employ, if they could be afforded, and Greek was the obvious language to use in higher education. Although the emperor Marcus Aurelius naturally conducted his imperial business in Latin, it was just as natural in those days that he should have written his philosophical *Meditations* in Greek. On the other hand, Roman pride dictated that the culture of a conquered race should be kept firmly in its place. The Romans, after all, had their own special talents and these deserved to come first. Roman interests and skills were more practical than theoretical: they were evidently happier building an aqueduct than constructing an argument. Their achievements make it hard to argue with this attitude. Roman sanitation and plumbing, for example, certainly saved more lives than any greater knowledge of Greek medicine could have done.

The educated classes did not discard Greek intellectual habits altogether, but neither did they embrace them wholeheartedly. As a result, their philosophy was second-hand and so was their science, and second-hand science means no real science at all. The Romans wrote and read encyclopedias and compilations of interesting facts, but on the whole they did not share the Greeks' drive to observe, understand, hypothesize, calculate and generally keep alive the spirit of inquiry. They were plodding accumulators rather than innovative thinkers. In his *Natural History*, Pliny the Elder (AD 23–79) boasted that he had assembled 'some 20,000 facts worthy of note, from 100 authors whom I have researched', adding 'I do not doubt that many facts have eluded me.' One of the many differences between this type of hoarding and Aristotle's investigations is that it would never have occurred to Aristotle to stop and count how many truths he had got in his sack.

Pliny said that he had also included in his book some valuable pieces of knowledge from his own experience – for instance: 'A surprising fact, but one easily tested, is the following: if one regrets inflicting a blow – and immediately spits into the palm of the hand responsible, the resentment of the person struck is lessened.' For Pliny, there was no real difference between science and story-telling. He tells the tale of Cleopatra's dissolving pearl, recounts the wondrous abilities of dolphins, and describes how he saw a woman turn into a man on her wedding day. There is also a great deal of relatively sober observation and classification about geography, zoology, botany, medicine and geology, but this keeps some odd company: 'The most carefully researched authorities are agreed that, in the consulship of Marcus Lepidus and Quintus Catulus, there was no finer house in Rome than that owned by Lepidus himself; but thirty-five years later, believe me, the same house did not even make the top hundred.'

The contents of an encyclopedia by Aulus Gellius (AD *c*.130–*c*.180), written about a century later, illustrate how the Roman approach to knowledge grew even more amateur, disorganized and whimsical. Here is a typical sample of Aulus Gellius' chapter headings:

For what reason our forefathers inserted the aspirate *h* in certain verbs and nouns
That it is uncertain to which deity sacrifice ought to be offered when there is an earthquake

That in many natural phenomena a certain power and efficacy of the number seven has been observed

The statement of men of the highest authority that Plato bought three books of Philolaus the Pythagorean, and that Aristotle purchased a few books of the philosopher Speusippus, at prices beyond belief

The strange thing recorded of partridges by Theophrastus, and of hares by Theopompus

Some interesting and instructive remarks about that part of geometry which is called 'Optics'; of another part called 'Harmony' and also of a third called 'Metric'

That those persons are in error who think that in testing for fever the pulse of the veins is felt, and not that of the arteries

The very witty reply of Antonius Julianus to certain Greeks at a banquet

This encyclopedia is more useful now than it was when it was written. It is a source of all sorts of antique information and stories which cannot now be found elsewhere, ranging from some of the early Stoic philosopher Chrysippus' ideas about fate to the now-famous tale of Androclus and the friendly lion. But perhaps the most revealing thing it shows us about the ancient world is how half-hearted, haphazard and derivative the approach to knowledge had become.

Even the few specialist texts on mathematics, medicine and astronomy produced by Greek intellectuals from the third century onwards tended to be compilations and commentaries on earlier work rather than original treatises. Most of the best purely philosophical writing of the next 300 years also took the form of commentaries. Some of this work showed powerful and novel thinking, but the fact that it was presented as glosses on venerable texts is a telling one. For the most part, philosophy and science seemed to be losing their nerve.

The most influential philosopher of the third century was an exception to this rule and did not merely write commentary. But his oral teaching was based around it, and he certainly fell in with all the other intellectual trends we have been noticing. This is Plotinus (AD *c.*205–270), a pagan teacher who studied in Alexandria and taught in Rome. His philosophy is otherworldly, deeply religious and entirely unmoved by scientific curiosity. Typically for his times, he tried to combine the ideas of many earlier thinkers while revering Plato above all. The mystically inclined thought of Plotinus inaugurated the final phase of Greek philosophy as it tottered over the brink of reason into occultism and religion. It was perfect for St Augustine (AD 354–430), who sometimes claimed that it contained everything that was important in Christianity except for the figure of Christ himself. It would be truer to say that Christian theology came to adopt many of Plotinus' ideas, partly thanks to the efforts of St Augustine.

Plotinus 'seemed ashamed of being in the body', said his pupil and biographer, Porphyry (AD *c*.232–305). Plotinus thought of earthly life as a second-rate sort of existence, like that of the manacled prisoners in Plato's gloomy Cave. Inspired by Plato's talk of immaterial souls and of the ideal Forms which earthly things dimly reflect, he urged his pupils to focus on a higher spiritual realm. What he tried harder than any earlier Platonist to achieve was a grasp of the relation between the lower and higher orders of reality. Plato himself did little more than gesture towards a higher world, but Plotinus tried to draw a map that would show how and where the two realms were connected. The resulting theory, with its rhapsodic descriptions of obscure hierarchies, was spasmodically revived later on in European thought. Historians since the nineteenth century have generally called it 'Neoplatonism' to mark the fact that it goes beyond anything found in Plato.

Plotinus knew that he was trying to describe the indescribable. The goal of his philosophy was union with a God-like One, which he claimed to have experienced himself now and then. But although he could report such fleeting experiences of union, their very nature meant that he could not say much about them. He held that the One was beyond rational comprehension. It was so far above everything else that no ordinary concepts applied to it. In a sense, he admitted, it was misleading to refer to it as the 'One', because this invited the unanswerable question 'one what?' The One (or whatever) could not even be called a being, because it was 'beyond being', to use a phrase of Plato. Plotinus wrote that 'nothing can be affirmed of it – not existence, not essence, not life – since it is That which transcends all these'.

The One transcends everything else because it is the source of everything else. One of Plotinus' favourite images for evoking the indescribable way in which everything comes from the One is 'emanation'. Reality streams out of the One like light emanating from the sun. But this analogy is imperfect because it does not capture Plotinus' idea of a hierarchy of realities. Perhaps a more useful image is that of a cascading fountain in which everything flows from a pinnacle, the One, down to successive tiers below it. This flow from the One must not be thought of as a physical process, though. Indeed it is not really a process at all, because it is timeless. What Plotinus is trying to express is a truth about what lies behind nature as a whole; he is not just describing a particular natural phenomenon that can be explained in terms of cause and effect.

There are three main tiers to Plotinus' metaphorical fountain, each one in some sense 'overflowing' to produce what is below it. Below the spout-like One comes the level of Intellect, and below that comes the level of Soul. At the level of Intellect we find Plato's ideal Forms, which are also regarded as living intelligences of some sort. Intellect is an overflowing of the One, and Soul is an overflowing of Intellect. Soul can itself be divided into several subsidiary tiers, the lowest of which creates or overflows into the visible universe. Matter on earth is the lowest of the low. It is furthest from the One, which Plotinus also calls the Good, and this means that it is evil. Evil is a purely negative concept for Plotinus, connoting the furthest possible distance from the One or Good.

There are many degrees of reality for Plotinus, just as there are many degrees of goodness. Some things are more real than others, and the closer they are to the One, the more real they are. By this curious expression he does not just mean, for example, that horses are 'more real' than unicorns because horses exist and unicorns do not. What he means is that there are many gradations of reality even among existing things. Even if unicorns actually existed, he would still put them low down on his ladder of reality because they would still be nothing more than physical things – and Plotinus did not think much of those. This idea is a sort of perfectionism carried to extremes. Nothing can be regarded as fully real unless it is in every sense complete and perfect, which no physical thing is. For Plotinus, only the One is absolutely complete. It is 'supremely adequate, autonomous, all-transcending, most utterly without need'. So only the One is absolutely real. Intellect is less real than the One, Soul is less real again, and we are not very real at all.

But there is no need to be depressed about this. We are not absolutely condemned to the lower depths of reality. Thanks to the fact that we have souls and the power of reason, we can in certain circumstances rise up towards the One. We do not make this journey physically, of course, because nothing about Plotinus' fountain and its cascading levels of reality is supposed to be physical. We make the journey with our minds. As we come to grasp how each level of reality depends on the one above it, so we ascend to those higher levels and perhaps eventually reach the One at the top. This idea of an intellectual climb that carries us further than our mere bodies could go parallels the priestess Diotima's talk of a contemplative ascent through increasingly abstract forms of beauty to 'beauty itself' (or 'beauty beyond beauty', as Plotinus sometimes called the One). If we achieve our end and get a glimpse of the One, then

the soul looks upon the wellspring of life, wellspring also of Intellect, beginning of Being, fount of Good, root of Soul

Our being is the fuller for turning Thither; this is our prosperity . . . Here is the soul's peace, outside of evil, refuge taken in the place clean of wrong

Our mental journey towards the One is a return, a journey home. Not only is it a pilgrimage back to the source of our existence, it also involves a discovery of our true selves. Plotinus says that 'When the soul begins again to mount, it comes not to something alien but to its very self.' This is because there are parallels between the highest parts of ourselves and the highest grades of reality. Plotinus regarded the upper grades of reality as mental rather than physical and held that reality flows from the One in roughly the same way that thoughts flow from our minds. That is, he believed that our own power of contemplation mirrors the mysterious process of 'overflowing' which gives rise to the world. Thus we are like the divine One. This recalls the Orphic idea that the soul within us is a dim but still living spark of divinity. It also recalls Aristotle's view that the activity of the rational part of our souls is the same as the activity of God.

Two things are needed in order to climb back up towards the One:

intellectual effort and moral virtue. For Plotinus, both of these are a matter of striving to ascend from earthly concerns to divine or transcendent ones. Yet it is not clear how far one is supposed to take such renunciation of earthly life. One Roman senator abandoned a career in politics in favour of philosophy when he heard what Plotinus had to say. But Plotinus certainly did not hold that one ought to hate the world or neglect the people in it. One should strive to appreciate the beauty in the visible world, he said, for this world is after all a manifestation or emanation of the One. One must be kind to everyone, because every soul is a child of God. And people should not think that they can get to the One without the passport of moral virtue. Plotinus attacked the idea that the soul's ascent to the One could be purely a matter of acquiring some secret about how the world works. This would not be enough on its own, because the One is also the Good and you cannot enjoy union with the Good without yourself being good.

Like any philosophy which stresses both ethical behaviour and otherworldliness, the thought of Plotinus seems to be pulled in two opposite directions at once. How much scope is there for a life of moral virtue if – 'almost ashamed of being in the body' – one barely lives a life at all? Could Plotinus' eminent pupil not have done more good in the world by remaining a senator? Another source of conflict in Plotinus is produced by the opposing attractions of mysticism and logic. He is a mystic and a rationalist rolled improbably into one. Plotinus usually tries to prove his views, and to do so he draws on a knowledge of earlier philosophy in a way that places him in the tradition of his rationalist predecessors. His arguments may nearly always be poorly expressed (even his adoring pupil, Porphyry, admitted that he was a very sloppy writer); they may be endlessly repetitive (even Hegel found that reading them 'is apt to prove wearisome'); and they would not convince many people nowadays. Nevertheless, inside Plotinus' tangled prose there is usually a piece of reasoning struggling to get out. For example, he does not merely assert that matter is unreal; he tries to show that this follows from the fact that we can easily be deceived about its properties, and from many other facts. Such reasoning may in the end be unconvincing, but it shows Plotinus' rationalist side. On the other hand, Plotinus admits he is trying to lead us beyond the reach of reason and logic: 'our way then takes us beyond knowing'.

Aristotle once said that everyone naturally desires to know. Plotinus was hungry for something more than knowledge, and he was prepared to cast off the sober methods of Aristotle in order to get it. Before he settled down to teach in Rome, Plotinus joined a military expedition to the east in the hope of gaining some enlightenment from Persian and Indian sages. Unfortunately the expedition was abandoned before it got very far, but Plotinus somehow managed to end up on the shores of Eastern mysticism anyway. To enjoy blissful union with the One, he said, we must abandon 'proof . . . evidence . . . reasoning process of the mental habit'. 'Such logic is not to be confounded with that act of ours in the vision; it is not our reason that has seen; it is something greater than reason.' The writings of Christian contemplatives such as Meister Eckhardt (*c.* 1260–1327) and St John of the Cross (1542–91), and also those of some Islamic and Jewish mystics, frequently echo Plotinus. Like them, Plotinus hungered for heaven. He looked forward to 'the time of vision unbroken, the self hindered no longer by any hindrance of body', when he could escape ordinary life and ordinary ways of thinking. Rational thought had its uses, but it was only a means to an end.

Because the philosophy of Plotinus is suffused with an intoxicated desire to express the inexpressible and to reach the unreachable, it is in one sense a religious philosophy. But in another sense it is far removed from any religion. Plotinus had no interest in magical rituals or any of the other conventional methods for invoking or appeasing the gods. He respected pagan beliefs and practices, and apparently believed in the efficacy of certain magical spells, but he thought that all these things were irrelevant to the One. To try to use worship, magic or prayer as a short-cut to the understanding of the One was, he thought, pointless and misguided. He never even bothered to mention Christianity. Plotinus' philosophy may have been unusually religious, but it is equally true that his religion was unusually intellectual.

The same cannot be said for his pupils and followers. Once Plotinus himself was gone, they soon gave in to some rather unintellectual temptations in their eagerness for a glimpse of the One. Porphyry could not resist the idea that magical practices and spells might provide some useful first steps on the road to the higher realms. He had a weakness for oracles, though he seems to have realized that as a good Plotinian he was not supposed to take much notice of them. In his *Philosophy from Oracles*, Porphyry managed to find a place in Plotinus' scheme of things for all the Olympian deities, plus the souls of divine and semi-divine heroes like Orpheus and Pythagoras. Porphyry even found room for Jesus as an enlightened spiritual teacher, though he was vehemently opposed to the main dogmas of Christianity and wrote a tract against this new-fangled religion. To his way of thinking, Christianity made the geographical mistake of putting Jesus where the One should be. As a keen follower of Pythagoras, Porphyry argued for vegetarianism on the grounds that its food is cheap, easy to prepare and thus less of a distraction from spiritual matters. He sometimes suggested that no food at all would be best. Like other Pythagoreans of the time, he was interested in the mystical powers of numbers and wrote several Pythagorean treatises. (He also wrote more conventional works including commentaries on Homer, Plato and Ptolemy, and an introduction to part of Aristotle's logic – this last work will turn out to be important later.)

Porphyry's own pupil, Iamblichus, who set up a school in Syria and died in around AD 330, dragged the Plotinian tradition even deeper into magic and superstition. Flying in the face of the mainly intellectual spirit of Plotinus, Iamblichus believed that an important part of philosophy lay in the performance of ritual acts that one should not even try to understand. Union with the One could be attained on the cheap

by the efficacy of the unspeakable *acts* performed in the appropriate manner, acts which are beyond all comprehension, and by the potency of the unutterable symbols which are comprehended only by the gods. Without intellectual effort on our part the tokens by their own virtue accomplish their proper work.

Iamblichus was keenly interested in a collection of mystical writings known as the *Chaldean Oracles*, which consisted of divine revelations together with some rather intoxicated commentary in hexameter verse. These *Oracles* had been written by a man called Julianus, who lived some time during the reign of the emperor Marcus Aurelius in the latter half of the second century. They became a sort of guidebook for invoking and making use of the gods, a practice known as 'theurgy', which one later philosopher of Iamblichus' ilk defined as 'a power higher than all human wisdom, embracing the blessings of divination, the purifying powers of initiation, and in a word all the operations of divine possession'. Julianus apparently knew spells for producing apparitions of the god Chronos, for thunderbolts, and for procuring out-of-the-body experiences. This sort of thing evidently ran in the family, for Julianus' father once conjured up the ghost of Plato.

When he was not performing 'unspeakable acts', Iamblichus was quite a scholar. In addition to a commentary on the *Oracles*, he produced commentaries on many of Plato's dialogues, several of Aristotle's treatises, and on the *Introduction to Arithmetic* by Nicomachus (a Pythagorean whose book remained the standard work on the subject for 1,000 years). Iamblichus also wrote mathematical treatises on acoustics and astronomy. Indeed, he announced his desire to 'attack mathematically everything in nature'. Although he does not seem to have been responsible for any notable conquests himself, such Pythagorean faith in the importance of numbers served as an inspiration to scientists such as Kepler in the sixteenth century.

The mixture of magician and proto-scientific thinker that we find in Iamblichus recalls the wonder-working figure of old Empedocles (see page 75), not to mention Pythagoras himself. Some later Platonists spoke of Iamblichus as divine, just as some of Pythagoras' followers had deified their master. But the main significance of Iamblichus in the history of philosophy is as a theologian rather than as a god. Like Porphyry, he tried to turn the dry concepts of Plotinus' system into living deities by identifying abstractions such as Intellect and Soul with gods from the Greek and Egyptian pantheons. He thus helped to create a philosophical theology for paganism which influenced the development of Christian thought. This project culminated in the work of Proclus (AD 410–485), who was head of the Plotinian philosophical school in Athens – the remnant of Plato's Academy.

Proclus' *Elements of Theology* is the last attempt in antiquity to provide an elaboration of the 'Platonic' system that had sprouted on Plato's grave. The format for this unusual book comes, curiously enough, from Euclid's geometry. Euclid began with a few assumptions and definitions about lines, planes, angles and so on and then deduced a chain of propositions about them. In a similar style, the *Elements of Theology* aims to demonstrate 211 propositions about the hierarchical structure of reality, the nature of time, existence, souls, the One and all sorts of subsidiary deities. Euclid's work (when suitably edited) still provides the basis for school geometry. But Proclus' *Elements* now seems like mumbo-jumbo. His universe is an arcane zoo in which pagan deities rub shoulders with barely comprehensible platoons of abstractions. In an attempt to insulate the divine and perfect One from contamination by the lower orders of existence, Proclus added many new intermediate levels of reality to a picture that was complicated enough already. Many of his innovations came grouped in triads, which sometimes gave Christians the impression that what he was really talking about was the Holy Trinity.

Although the background to Proclus' hierarchical world-picture comes from Plotinus, his approach to philosophy owes more to Iamblichus and the theurgy of the *Chaldean Oracles*. Plotinus' passive mystical visions of the One were replaced by an attempt actively to exploit the hidden connections which link the levels of reality and everything in them. In short, Proclus was a magician. He believed in all sorts of ritual practices involving herbs and stones, and incantations to invoke divine communion. He believed in dragons, in mermaids, and that statues of the gods could move if you said the right things to them.

Plainly, much had changed in the philosophical temper of Athens since classical times. Where were the heirs of Anaxagoras and Pericles, who had attacked the superstitious beliefs of their day and looked instead for natural explanations of apparently divine portents? Where were the heirs of Protagoras, who had said he knew nothing of the gods because such matters were too obscure for man to fathom? Where were the heirs of Socrates, who would only have spoken to a statue out of absent-mindedness? Proclus was evidently of a quite different cast of mind. He may have been well versed in the texts of Plato and Aristotle. He may have been active in many branches of learning – he wrote works of mathematics, astronomy, physics and literary criticism. But the science which he was most concerned to advance was that of salvation. His aim was to build a bridge between the gods who look down on the world and the souls who look up from it, a task that was best achieved by magic and religion. The job of philosophy was merely to explain spiritual truths which had already been arrived at by other means.

Like the axioms of Euclid's geometry, Proclus treated the basic premises of his theology as if they were beyond question. This is not because they were held to be self-evident, like Euclid's axiom that 'the whole is greater than the part', but because they came with the stamp of scriptural authority, namely the authority of Plato, Plotinus and the *Chaldean Oracles*. Proclus' philosophical works were attempts to elucidate what had been revealed in such sacred sources. As one modern commentator put it, Proclus' system 'would not have been created had there not been a religion to justify'. To supplement the stiff deductions of his *Elements of Theology*, Proclus also wrote prayer-like hymns summarizing its message in a more popular form. He was so assiduous in his observance of pagan rites and prayers at a time when the empire had officially become Christian that he got into trouble for it several times.

Just as Porphyry, Iamblichus and Proclus had converted Plotinus' philosophy into a pagan theology, so this theology was subsequently converted into a Christian one. The teachings of Proclus turned out to play an important part in the development of Christian thought, largely because of an audacious forgery. An anonymous Christian writer who was well acquainted with the works of Proclus, and who may even have been a pupil of his, wrote a handful of books purporting to be the work of Dionysius the Areopagite, a man who is mentioned in the Bible as having been converted by St Paul. This pretence gave the books an immense but spurious authority. Here was a theology whose pedigree apparently went back almost to Christ himself. After these works were translated from Greek into Latin in the ninth century by John Scotus Eriugena, an Irish scholar who was one of the few in the Latin West who still knew Greek, almost everyone who was anyone in medieval theology wrote about them. St Thomas Aquinas in particular paid much attention to them. The heavenly hierarchies described in the poetry of Dante and Milton come essentially from this 'Pseudo-Dionysius', whose forgery was finally uncovered in the nineteenth century. So do several leading ideas in Christian theology.

The pagan theology of Proclus needed some changes before it could be put to work for Christianity. The fact that it recognized many gods – indeed, more or less every god – was not too much of a problem, though. It was easy enough to see that the One was the true God. But there were other difficulties. For example, the main Neoplatonic hierarchy of One, Intellect and Soul seemed to delegate too much work to Intellect and Soul. The idea that each intermediate level of reality 'overflows' to produce the one below it seems to conflict with the Christian idea that God (i.e., the One) is Himself directly responsible for the creation of all things. Pseudo-Dionysius therefore recast the various intermediary beings in less demanding roles: the junior gods of Neoplatonic theology, for instance, now became angels with more restricted powers. They were all directly created by God and were incapable of creating anything themselves. Pseudo-Dionysius adapted the threefold hierarchies of Proclus to construct orders of precedence below God, each itself consisting of three groups of three. There was a celestial order and an earthly one. The celestial hierarchy contained Seraphim, Cherubim and Thrones; Dominions, Powers and Authorities; Principalities, Archangels and Angels. The earthly hierarchy, which had Christ at the top, covered the ranks and structure of the Church.

What Pseudo-Dionysius had to say about the knowledge of God was especially interesting to later theologians. He offered a sophisticated solution to the problem of describing a being who was supposed to be beyond understanding. The pagan Neoplatonists had maintained that terms like 'good' and 'wise' could not be applied to the indescribable One but only to elements below Him in the hierarchy of reality. This was clearly incompatible with the Christian doctrine that God himself is good and wise. Pseudo-Dionysius' answer was that, although God cannot be said to be good or wise in quite the way that people are, nevertheless a special type of wisdom and goodness can be applied to Him by virtue of the fact that He is the creator of these qualities in people. According to this theory, any positive quality that is manifested somewhere in Creation can be extended to the creator Himself (provided it is compatible with His non-physical nature: He cannot be said to be obese or blue-eyed, for example). People's goodness or wisdom will of course always be imperfect. And it is only these imperfect versions which we experience and which thus give meaning to our

375

terms 'good' and 'wise'. So to underline the fact that God's goodness and wisdom exceed their human counterparts, Pseudo-Dionysius suggested that we should really speak of God as 'super-wise', 'super-good', and so on.

Adopting an idea that was essentially invented by Proclus, Pseudo-Dionysius distinguished positive and negative ways of coming to understand God. The above method, which involves starting with the virtues found in Creation and saying that God has superior versions of them, is the positive way to build up a picture of Him. This method has its uses, but there is also another way – the *via negativa*, as Latin theologians later called it – which can take one closer to God. This consists of subtracting all everyday concepts from our idea of Him. Remove, for example, the notion of finitude that applies to all created things and we are left with its absence, infinity, which we can then attribute to God. True, we do not really know what infinity is. But we are well acquainted with its opposite: we are surrounded by manifestations of finitude, namely mortality, incompleteness and imperfection. So we learn something about God by seeing that none of these things applies to Him. Pseudo-Dionysius says that we can best approach God by 'denying or removing all things that are'. The point of this is to plunge us into a 'super-essential darkness' in which we are stripped of our ordinary ways of thinking and so try to grope beyond them. Such intellectual deprivation will leave us in a fit state to receive mystical enlightenment about the nature of God. *The Cloud of Unknowing*, an anonymous fourteenth-century classic of Christian mysticism, and many similar works, explore this theme of a negative method of coming to know God.

Going back to the positive way of knowing, in which God may be said to be 'super-good', 'super-wise' and so on, it might be wondered how Pseudo-Dionysius can avoid describing Him as 'super-evil' as well. If God is super-good because He made good people, why is He not super-bad for making bad ones? To evade this difficulty, Pseudo-Dionysius used Plotinus's idea that 'evil' signifies nothing more than distance from the One. It does not exist as a genuine feature of the world but is simply an absence of goodness. Thus it is a mistake to think of evil as part of Creation at all, so there is no reason to regard the creator as 'super-evil' because of it. Many later Christians endorsed this approach, as did St Augustine and others like him who had been influenced by Plotinus even before Pseudo-Dionysius came along.

Although his treatment of evil was a welcome contribution to Christian theology, Pseudo-Dionysius sometimes veered towards heresy. He was inclined, for example, to look for an indivisible One behind the Holy Trinity of Father, Son and Holy Ghost. Such tinkering with theological arithmetic leads into dangerous territory. Three persons in one somehow makes a trinity, but three persons plus one One definitely equals heresy. Divine creation was another subject on which the spirit of Neoplatonism led Pseudo-Dionysius astray. Even though he stripped Intellect and Soul of their productive powers and left creation solely in the hands of God, Pseudo-Dionysius still made the events described in Genesis sound too much like the automatic 'overflowing' of Plotinus' One. According to Plotinus, creation comes about because the nature of the One is so magnificent that it is bound to spill over and form lower orders of reality. This makes the whole business seem too impersonal and little more than a leak in the celestial plumbing. According to orthodox Christian doctrine, the act of creation was an intentional and voluntary one, which God could have chosen not to perform, but which He fortunately decided to go ahead with.

Pseudo-Dionysius always professed to agree with Christian dogmas on such matters. There is no reason to doubt the sincerity of his religious belief; yet part of him was still too at home in the Neoplatonic universe. He sometimes stretched the dogmas of the new religion to fit his philosophical preconceptions, though he was probably unaware of doing so. Without its bogus stamp of authority, his work would probably never have influenced Christianity in the way that it did.

St Augustine, by contrast, needed no pseudonym to smuggle his thoughts into the Christian canon. His absolute devotion to the Christian cause is evident in everything he wrote after his conversion in AD 386. The philosophers, he wrote, 'have said things which are true, but even them I would think to be no final authority'. Although Augustine found much to praise in what he took to be Plato's philosophy, he did not aim to produce a synthesis of Platonism and Christianity as Pseudo-Dionysius had done. He did not see Platonism as a rival source of wisdom to be reconciled with the true religion, but rather as a partial and imperfect anticipation of it. Augustine thanked divine providence for leading him to 'the Platonic books' (which were in fact works by Plotinus and Porphyry). They taught him, he said, to 'distinguish the difference between those who see what the goal is but not how to get there and those who see the way which leads to the home of bliss'.

When Augustine saw a conflict between Plato and God, he had no doubt where his allegiance lay. Nevertheless, he wrote that 'There are none who come nearer to us than the Platonists.' He speculated that 'If these men could have had this life over again with us ... [t]hey would have become Christians, with the change of a few words and statements.' The fact that Augustine, the most influential of early Christian thinkers, placed Plato and his pupil Aristotle far above all other Greek philosophers is one reason why these two Athenians have enjoyed such pre-eminence in the West ever since.

Augustine had been born in North Africa in AD 354, nearly sixty years before Proclus, to a Christian mother and a pagan father. His tortuous road from pride and depravity to Platonism and thence Christianity was famously described in his *Confessions*. As a student and later a teacher of rhetoric, he read some second-hand accounts of Greek philosophy in Cicero's works. Like Cicero, Augustine was particularly struck by the scepticism taught by Arcesilaus and Carneades, who argued that nothing can be known for certain (see page 330). After his conversion, when he had become sure that God had filled his mind with wisdom, Augustine claimed to be able to refute such sceptical arguments. But in his youth the main effect of his exposure to philosophy was to stimulate a hunger that he did not yet know how to satisfy: 'Truth, truth: how in my inmost being the very marrow of my mind sighed for you!' He eagerly followed Cicero's exhortation 'not to study one particular sect but to love and seek and pursue and strongly embrace wisdom itself, wherever found'. First he looked in the Scriptures, but found that they did not yet speak to him. They seemed 'unworthy in comparison with Cicero. My inflated conceit shunned the Bible's restraint, and my gaze never penetrated to its inwardness.' Instead he fell in with a sect of 'men proud of their slick talk, very earthly-minded and loquacious. In their mouths were the devil's traps.' These people were the adherents of Manicheanism, a religion Augustine ardently espoused for about a decade.

Mani, a Persian sage who regarded himself as an apostle of God, lived in southern Babylonia around the middle of the third century AD. The religion that he founded has elements of the much older Persian creed of Zoroastrianism, which spoke of an eternal battle between good and evil, and elements of Greek mystery-religions such as Orphism with their talk of purification and reincarnation. The central doctrine of Manicheanism is that good and evil are two mighty forces engaged in a more or less evenly matched struggle. Practically everything in life can be seen as a manifestation of this battle. The realms of light and spirit, which are personified by a good God, wage war against the realms of darkness and matter, which are personified by a bad one. This evil God created the earth and entombed our souls, which are sparks of light, in the prisons of our bodies. To Augustine, such a picture made better sense of the existence of evil than any other theory he had come across. It offered a straightforward answer to the puzzle of why God lets evil flourish, namely that He can do little about it because He is not quite the all-powerful being He is usually taken to be.

Manicheanism was not – in theory, at any rate – a licence for debauchery. On the contrary it aimed for a purgation of the soul by an ascetic life, vegetarianism and abstention from sex. Reproduction was to be avoided because it enlarged the evil God's empire by producing yet more bodies. Followers of Mani were supposed to enlist on the side of goodness and light by suppressing their earthly appetites. Nevertheless, with hindsight Augustine came to regard Manicheanism as a recipe for vice. Perhaps he and his friends had accepted an unusually lax version of it in which the ascetic life was required only of a few Manichean saints. Perhaps its emphasis on purgation left ample scope for sinning in order to have something to purge (Manicheanism certainly provided a convenient excuse for sin, because it taught that men's evil acts are determined by the stars). Or perhaps Manicheanism was just not engrossing enough to distract Augustine from base and vain activities. At any rate, Augustine later described his life at this time as

one of being seduced and seducing, being deceived and deceiving, in a variety of desires. Publicly I was a teacher of the arts which they call liberal [*i.e., grammar, rhetoric, logic, arithmetic, geometry, music and astronomy*]; privately I professed a false religion – in the former role arrogant, in the latter superstitious, in everything vain. On the one side we pursued the empty glory of popularity, ambitious for the applause of the audience, concerned with the follies of public entertainments and unrestrained lusts. On the other side, we sought to purge ourselves of that filth.

Mired in what he later saw as the confusions of Manicheanism, Augustine combined a lukewarm acceptance of Jesus as a son of Manicheanism's good God with a conviction that the Old Testament God was in fact Manicheanism's wicked God in disguise. In those dark days, the troubled Augustine was also involved in astrology and fortune-telling. When the time came to launch an assault on all this superstition and false religion, he found a good use for some of the sceptical arguments he had come across in Greek philosophy, particularly the attacks on astrology he had found in Cicero. But it was the message of Platonism that did the most to free Augustine's mind and lead him on to better things.

The belief which he was most pleased to be rid of when his spiritual recovery got underway was the belief that God and the soul are physical things. Manicheanism had been rather muddled about what counted as physical and what did not. On the one hand it condemned the heavier forms of matter typified by earth and human bodies; on the other hand it thought of the soul and the good God as manifested in light and fire – which are surely physical phenomena too. Thus it seems that the Manichees, like the Stoics, regarded spirit as a rarefied and relatively insubstantial form of matter, not as something completely different from it. A few early Christians, living at a time when the doctrines of the new religion were still being formed, thought the same. Tertullian (AD *c.* 155–*c.*222), for example, the first important Christian theologian to write in Latin, was persuaded by Stoic philosophy that God and the soul both consist of matter. Ironically, he wrote one of the most intemperate condemnations of such borrowings from philosophy:

Away with all attempts to produce a mottled Christianity of Stoic, Platonic and dialectic composition! We want no curious disputation after possessing

Christ Jesus, no inquisition after enjoying the Gospel! With our faith, we desire no further belief.

Tertullian seems to have forgotten where he got some of his own ideas from. Augustine, however, was quite willing to give credit where credit was due. It was, he acknowledged, Platonism that enabled him to put all forms of materialism firmly behind him.

The 'Platonic books' convinced him that the fundamental division in reality was between matter and spirit, not between good and evil. There was just one supernatural power, God, who made all physical things but was not in any sense physical Himself. Evil was not a rival supernatural force manifested in the grosser forms of matter. It was, as Plotinus had said, merely the absence of God's goodness. Suddenly everything started to make sense for Augustine. As he later put it:

the Platonists, coming to a knowledge of God, have found the cause of the organized universe, the light by which truth is perceived, and the spring which offers the drink of felicity. All philosophers who have this conception of God are in agreement with our idea of him.

Augustine began to study the works of Plotinus and other Platonists while he was teaching in Milan and attending the sermons of St Ambrose. Although some of his ideas about what Platonism involved were based on misunderstandings, Augustine thought he saw striking parallels between the God (or One) of Platonism and the God of St Ambrose. Both were absolutely supreme, absolutely good and absolutely non-physical. Augustine believed that this could not have been coincidence: he concluded that Plato must have got to know some of the Old Testament by word of mouth. He realized, however, that Platonism fell far short of Christian revelation. As he said, it showed what the goal was but not how to get there.

Platonism had, of course, nothing to say about Jesus or his role in salvation. It did not realize the importance of charity and humility. And, most of all, Platonism was wrong to assume that man could get anywhere by his own unaided efforts. No matter how much philosophical contemplation or mystical meditation he indulged in, man could not reach God until God chose to call him and he answered. The main mistake of all Greek thought was to believe that man did not need any outside help to see the truth or to do the right thing. The main message of Christianity, as Augustine saw it, is that man needs a great deal of help.

Having found that he himself fell into vice and error whenever he was left to his own devices, Augustine concluded that the same would be true of everyone else. Without God, man was nothing, could do nothing and knew nothing. Some later Christian thinkers watered down this extreme view and said that man could come to know a few things on his own. In the thirteenth century, St Thomas Aquinas contrasted the truths that can be reached by man's natural powers of reason with those that can be known only through divine revelation. For Augustine, however, there was no such distinction to be drawn. Every important piece of knowledge was a result of some sort of divine illumination in which God shone His truth into the minds of His creatures.

Augustine looked into his own mind to see the truths that God had left there for him. The first one he came across was the truth that he himself existed, which seemed to be a very special sort of truth because no sceptical reasoning could make him doubt it. While it was possible to be deceived about all sorts of things – he might, for example, believe that he was awake when in fact he was dreaming – it was impossible for him to be deceived about his own existence. How could he believe that he existed if in fact he did not? 'If I am deceived, I exist!' Augustine triumphantly announced. (Descartes later expressed the same idea in the famous words: 'I think, therefore I am'.) Introspection showed Augustine that there were various other things that he could not be wrong about, such as his own feelings. How could he be wrong about the fact that he loved certain things, for example? There were also some eternal and universal truths which could not be doubted: mathematical ones, for instance, like 'six plus one is seven'. Augustine asked where all these certainties sprang from and concluded that they could only have come from God. Thus, by pondering the contents of his own mind, he found many truths which not only evaded the doubts of sceptical philosophers but also pointed towards the existence of God.

Once he had satisfied himself that there were some things which sceptics were definitely wrong to doubt, Augustine jumped to the conclusion that scepticism was not worth worrying about at all. He simply assumed that God has somehow enabled us to know about the world and its contents. Augustine devoted a whole book to the subject of scepticism, but the only thing proved by this rambling work is that he had lost his appetite for questioning. Now that the Saviour has come, he wrote elsewhere, it is time for philosophers to stop their doubting. Augustine was no longer inclined to query what his senses told him, what other people told him, or – especially – what the Church told him. He had found the Truth.

In his old doubting days, Augustine had 'wanted to be as certain about things I could not see as I am certain that seven and three are ten'. These demandingly high standards soon slipped when he became a Christian. He was so impressed by the soothing power of God's word that he was now prepared to accept all sorts of things on faith alone. The doctrines of the Trinity, original sin, the resurrection of Jesus and the Christian recipe for salvation can hardly be said to enjoy the unquestionable status of the truths of arithmetic. Yet that did not stop Augustine believing in them. Although his work often shows a degree of philosophical acuity and intellectual curiosity, his primary interest is always theological, and it shows. All his philosophical discussions arise out of some religious question or other: his analysis of time, for example, is prompted by the question of what God was doing before He made the world; and his treatment of free will is prompted by a desire to absolve God of responsibility for human wrongdoing. Disappointingly, these discussions always peter out as soon as the theological puzzles that gave rise to them have been dealt with. Whenever Augustine finds a solution that he thinks will sit comfortably with Christian dogma, he simply switches off his intellectual curiosity and turns to another topic.

Augustine did more than anyone else of his day to develop a distinctively Christian framework for social and political values. But after his conversion he never again stood outside this framework to examine it objectively. He neither seriously questioned nor tried to justify the foundations of Christian belief. In the end, he therefore has more in common with the early mythologists or *theologi* than with the *physici* (natural philosophers) whom Plato and Aristotle thought it worthwhile to address. In one sense, Augustine turned back the clock of intellectual history. He returned to a version of the comforting supernatural stories which most of the first philosophers sought to dispense with, or at least to rationalize. Nobody with Augustine's overwhelming sense of the inadequacy of human reason and of man's need for blind leaps of faith can be counted as wholly committed to philosophy in its original Greek sense. This verdict would not have troubled him. Augustine would have been the first to agree that he was a Christian above all else.

By the time Augustine died in AD 430, about half of the population of the Roman empire were Christians; at the start of the previous century, probably not more than 10 per cent had been. The balance of power had shifted rapidly towards Christianity during Augustine's lifetime, and at the end of it Christians were on the whole more likely to be busy suppressing the views of their critics than to be suppressed themselves. In around AD 448, an anti-Christian polemic written by Porphyry was publicly burned. Many other pagan philosophers had written criticisms of Christian ideas, but not one of these works has survived intact from its trial of refutation by fire. The censored pagan philosophers of this period even have their own martyr in the form of Hypatia of Alexandria, who was tortured and killed by a Christian mob in AD 415. It seems that in medieval times, Hypatia's shocking story was regarded as too good to waste on a pagan, so elements of this embarrassing tale were recycled in the Christian myth of St Catherine of Alexandria. This lady was said to have been martyred after refuting fifty pagan philosophers who were sent to argue her out of her faith in a sort of dialectic joust. She seems to have been a fictitious mixture of Hypatia and unknown Christians. In medieval times, St Catherine used to be the patron saint of philosophers, but she later had her sainthood revoked on the grounds of non-existence.

Half of the truth behind this historical mix-up began to emerge in the sixteenth century, when the myth of St Catherine was punctured. But Hypatia started to attract her own myth-makers, who are active to this day. Her romantic legend has engendered dozens of plays, poems and novels; two feminist academic journals have taken her name. Ever since she got a good write-up from Voltaire and in Gibbon's *Decline and Fall of the Roman Empire*, she has enjoyed a secular version of canonization. Hypatia was, like her father, a distinguished mathematician as well as the leading Platonic philosopher of her day. She commanded respect in Alexandria as a teacher and a paragon of probity and also as a wise counsellor in civil affairs. But, unfortunately for her, she was hated by the local bishop – later canonized as St Cyril – whose men dragged her into a church, scraped off her skin and cut her into pieces. Because Hypatia was not a Christian, because she had scientific interests, and because she lived towards the very end of ancient civilization, she has been portrayed as a defender of science against religion, as a doomed representative of the values of pre-Christian antiquity and as the last candle of free inquiry to be snuffed out before the long night of clerical scholasticism. In his *History of Western Philosophy*, Bertrand Russell wrote of 'the lynching of Hypatia, a distinguished lady who, in an age of bigotry, adhered to the Neoplatonic philosophy and devoted her talents to mathematics ... After this Alexandria was no longer troubled by philosophers.'

In fact, Hypatia was not the end of anything. Philosophy and science continued in Alexandria a full century after her death (most notably in the person of John Philoponus, to whom we shall come in a moment). Nor, it seems, was Hypatia a martyr to paganism. Although she was certainly no believer in Christianity, she did not attend pagan temples either, or join those who opposed their conversion into churches. Some of her pupils were Christians, two of whom later became bishops. It appears that Hypatia was in fact assassinated for political reasons. She was caught in the middle of a struggle for power between Bishop Cyril and Orestes, the imperial prefect of Alexandria, with whom she was friendly. Cyril feared that such a powerful supporter made Orestes unbeatable, so he encouraged rumours that she was a witch and a troublemaker. A gang of thugs employed by Cyril apparently took matters into their own hands and decided to get her out of the way. In short, Hypatia was simply in the wrong place at the wrong time with the wrong friends.

Alexandria's most remarkable philosopher of the next century, John Philoponus (AD *c*.490–*c*.530), was a Christian writer on physics and philosophy who was so ahead of his time that he tends to be left out of history in order to keep the story simple. He argued brilliantly against Aristotle's world-picture and on several important matters in physics he took up positions which are commonly thought not to have been espoused until Galileo's day. For example, Philoponus attacked Aristotle's theory that the earth and the heavens are separate realms which need radically different physical principles to explain them. Philoponus denied that the stars were eternal and unchangeable and thus rejected the whole basis of what was to become standard medieval cosmology. He carefully demolished Aristotle's arguments, showing that they did not make sense in themselves and moreover that they contradicted other things which Aristotle had said. Most significantly, Philoponus made extensive use of personal observation and even experiment to support his own physical theories. Consider, for example, what he had to say about Aristotle's assertion that unsupported bodies fall towards the earth with a speed that is proportional to their weight – i.e., that heavy things fall faster than light ones:

But this is completely erroneous, and our view may be corroborated by actual observation more effectively than by any sort of verbal argument. For if you let fall from the same height two weights of which one is many times as heavy as the other, you will see that the ratio of the times required for the motion does not depend on the ratio of the weights, but that the difference in time is a very small one.

Philoponus' own theory of falling bodies was not quite right, but the experiment he describes here (which does at least refute Aristotle's view) was heralded as a momentous scientific breakthrough when it was repeated in the seventeenth century. Nowadays the experiment is traditionally credited to Galileo, who lived more than 1,000 years later than Philoponus (and who knew his works well). Attributing it to Galileo is neater because he is not thought of as a philosopher, whereas Philoponus is, and this is supposed to be a 'scientific' discovery rather than a 'philosophical' one.

Philoponus was the last of his kind: as far as one can tell, nobody in Western Europe practised his sort of analysis of nature again until the fourteenth century. The Greek tradition of inquiry had passed instead to the Arab world. Greek medical, scientific, mathematical and philosophical learning spread to Arab lands from around the middle of the eighth century and stayed there until Latin translations were made from the texts in Arab hands 300–400 years later. Until the end of the twelfth century, Arab civilization had a clear lead in all these fields. The West had nobody to compare with great polymaths like Al-Kindi (AD *c*.812–*c*.873), Al-Farabi (AD *c*.870–*c*.950) and Ibn Sina (later known in the west as Avicenna, AD *c*.980–*c*.1037), or the many specialist doctors, physicists and especially mathematicians whose works were so eagerly studied in the West when they eventually became available. Arab scholars were familiar with the writings of Hippocrates, Galen, Euclid, Ptolemy and Archimedes, as well as those of Plato and Aristotle. They also did important original research, developing among many other things a sophisticated theory of optics in the eleventh century. We have already looked at some of the reasons why the spirit of inquiry declined so drastically in the West. Exactly why it flourished, for a while, in the Arab world is too large a subject to be addressed here.

While Philoponus was more or less ignored for a long time, one of his contemporaries turned out to have quite an effect on the course of Western philosophy. Boethius (AD *c*.475–524) was a Christian philosopher and theologian from an aristocratic Roman family who worked as principal minister to Theodoric the Ostrogoth, the ruler of Italy from 493 to 526. Boethius was depressed by the rapid degeneration of intellectual life and by the fact that few people in the West could read the Greek classics any more. He set out to translate all of Plato's and Aristotle's works into Latin so that they would not be lost to future generations. Unfortunately he was executed for treason before this ambitious project could get very far. Its only surviving fruits are Latin versions of Aristotle's logical writings, which may help to explain why early medieval philosophers were so obsessed with old logic. They had little else to study. It is intriguing to speculate how much better informed the Latin world might have been if only the labours of Boethius had not been cruelly cut short. On the other hand, his indictment on what were probably trumped-up charges did have one happy result, though not for him. It was while he was in prison under sentence of death that Boethius wrote his impassioned *The Consolation of Philosophy*. Impending extinction concentrated his mind wonderfully: this masterpiece became one of the most widely read books of medieval times. King Alfred the Great, Chaucer and

Queen Elizabeth I were among those who made English translations of it. It might never have been written had Boethius lived to a ripe, uneventful and scholarly old age instead of getting caught up in Italian politics.

The *Consolation* takes the form of a dialogue between Boethius, who speaks in prose, and Lady Philosophy, who replies mostly in verse. Lady Philosophy answers Boethius' despondent meditations about the miseries and injustice of life with a mixture of Stoic and Platonic wisdom. Adversity in general and evil rulers in particular are powerless to harm a good man, she says, because a good soul will remain untouched by 'slippery Fortune', and besides divine Providence oversees everything. Lady Philosophy steers him away from the many false roads to happiness and tries to guide him instead towards the contemplation of all that is good – which is to say, God:

> Grant, Father, that our minds Thy august seat may scan,
> Grant us the sight of true good's source, and grant us light
> That we may fix on Thee our mind's unblinded eye.
> Disperse the clouds of earthly matter's cloying weight;
> Shine out in all Thy glory; for Thou art rest and peace
> To those who worship Thee; to see Thee is our end,
> Who art our source and maker, lord and path and goal.

The book never explicitly mentions Christianity. But it manages to address, in a non-technical manner, many of the philosophical problems that are likely to intrigue a believer. For example, it includes a solution to the puzzle of how man can be said to have any real choice in his actions if an omniscient God always knows beforehand what he is going to do. Boethius' answer starts from the idea that there is no difference between past, present and future from God's point of view. For God, all of eternity is like the present. So when God foresees what I will do, my freedom is no more curtailed by this fact than it would be by somebody observing what I am doing while I am doing it. Essentially the same solution was adopted by St Thomas Aquinas and some other late-medieval theologians.

*The Consolation of Philosophy* set the pattern for popular philosophizing. It showed Philosophy as a soothing balm to heal life's wounds and as a source of perennial wisdom that could illuminate religious questions. It also served to broadcast the Platonic world-picture to a civilization that knew virtually none of the writings of 'my servant Plato', as Lady Philosophy called him. Many of the themes and images in medieval literature that derive ultimately from Plato or Aristotle made a vivid early appearance in Boethius' *Consolation*.

The influence of Boethius was not by any means confined to popular philosophy and literature. By inventing and adapting Latin words to express some of Aristotle's concepts, Boethius made just as much of an impact on technical philosophy and theology. His new jargon was pounced on and used by the scholar-monks of the early Middle Ages and later by the teachers in the first universities. They used this technical terminology to analyse the Trinity and other intricate subjects – no doubt under the impression that they were thereby clarifying matters, though sometimes they achieved precisely the opposite.

Boethius also posed a logical problem that obsessed philosophers for centuries afterwards. It came to be known as the problem of universals, and it was first mentioned in a text by Porphyry that was much studied after Boethius translated it into Latin. The problem concerns general terms or concepts that can be applied to many things at once, such as 'red' or 'beautiful' or 'square'. The question is what sort of existence such general qualities as redness, beauty or squareness may be said to have. Do they exist only in the mind, or only in language, or do they have some sort of objective and external existence, like the physical things to which they apply? Obviously, square things exist; but does squareness itself exist? Porphyry had laid this question aside as too difficult, but Boethius discussed it at length and thereby established it as the major philosophical problem for all who were interested in abstract logical questions. By the twelfth century, there were reckoned to be no fewer than thirteen distinct shades of opinion on the matter.

Boethius' interest in logic reflected his concern for the state of the seven 'liberal arts' – so-called because the Romans regarded them as suitable studies for a free man. These seven respectable subjects were grammar, rhetoric, logic, arithmetic, geometry, astronomy and music. Boethius thought that there was room for improvement in most parts of this standard curriculum. He was fairly satisfied with the available

Latin works on grammar, rhetoric and elementary logic, but he proposed to write new ones for the other four subjects and to provide better treatments of advanced topics in logic, such as the problem of universals. It is not clear whether Boethius ever got round to writing his textbooks on geometry or astronomy; if he did, they did not survive. But his works on arithmetic, music and logic were widely used for centuries. Seven hundred years later, when the first university undergraduates began their studies in the thirteenth century, the liberal arts still comprised the basic curriculum. And some of the works of Boethius were still set texts.

It is hardly surprising that the substance of education had changed so little in the intervening years. Education was not exactly a thriving industry in the Dark Ages. For about 300 years after Boethius' time, scholarly activity was largely confined to monasteries and almost entirely devoted to theological and ecclesiastical matters. There were no changes for the better in the intellectual world until the reforms of Charlemagne at the end of the eighth century, and there were many changes for the worse. After the death of Boethius, which had come in the same decade as the death of Philoponus and the closing of the Athenian schools, there was certainly nothing that could be described as philosophy in Europe until the time of Charlemagne.

Charlemagne began as king of the Franks and ended up ruling most of France, Belgium, Holland, Switzerland and Italy plus substantial parts of modern Germany and Austria. His Christian empire was almost as large as the western part of the old Roman one, and he wanted educated men to run it. First he set up a palace school to educate the royal family, future bishops and civil servants, then he set up schools attached to monasteries and cathedrals throughout his realm. This network of church schools, which taught the old liberal arts, led to a greater spread of education than the Latin West had seen since Roman times. It was aimed only at the clergy and it did not produce any great works of scholarship or research, but it was at least a start.

Of the scholars who came to take part in this minor renaissance in the ninth and tenth centuries, the only one with evident philosophical gifts was John Scotus Eriugena, the Irishman who translated the bogus works of Pseudo-Dionysius (see page 374). He joined the court of Charles the Bald, Charlemagne's grandson, who asked him to translate various Greek theological books. Eriugena produced a relatively sophisticated theory of nature based on Christian principles, an attempted reconciliation of Neoplatonism and orthodox theology, and contributions to several of the liberal arts. He quickly became famous as the leading intellectual of his day, famous enough to generate the sort of stories which eminent philosophers often attract – in his case a tale that he was summoned to England by Alfred the Great, where he was stabbed to death by the pens of his students.

Eriugena died in around the late 870s (nobody knows where or how), by which time political chaos and ecclesiastical weakness had put the civilizing reforms of Charlemagne and his successors under heavy strain. Invading Vikings, Magyars and Saracens disrupted civil life, and the Church disrupted itself by falling prey to corruption that reached as high as the Pope. Learning retreated once more into the monasteries. In the tenth century, some Benedictines made serious studies of logic and debated Boethius' problem of universals. But medieval philosophy did not really begin to make progress until Europe itself did. From around the middle of the eleventh century, European civilization started to reap the benefits of political stability, economic and technological development (particularly in agriculture), and the urbanization of the populace.

The population of Europe probably doubled and may even have quadrupled between 1000 and 1200. As trade and commerce grew, large numbers of people moved to the towns and cities. One effect of these new concentrations of wealth was an increase in the demand for education and a surge of intellectual activity. Not only did the ecclesiastical schools multiply, secular ones sprang up outside the Church system to provide an education for anyone who could afford it. Sometimes 'schools' would move from place to place as students followed a gifted master on his travels, like the itinerant Greek Sophists of the fifth century BC. In addition to the traditional curriculum of the liberal arts and training in theology, preparation for a career in law or medicine now became available. The new students needed something to study, so determined attempts were made to recover mastery of the Latin classics. The works of Latin encyclopediasts and translations of parts of Plato's *Timaeus* served as source books in cosmology and natural philosophy; a few translations of mathematical and medical texts from the Arabs trickled into circulation. And Boethius' translations of and commentaries on Aristotle's logic were intensely scrutinized. Most significantly for the development of philosophy, some intellectual adventurers tried to apply the rational methods of logic to problems in theology. Mixing faith and reason could be a controversial and even dangerous business, but it was becoming inevitable.

The most famous fusion of faith and reason from those times is the so-called 'ontological' proof of the existence of God, which was formulated by St Anselm (1033–1109), an Italian who joined the Benedictine order in Normandy and ended up as Archbishop of Canterbury. Anselm had long wanted to find 'a single argument, needing no proof beyond itself' which would reveal the nature and existence of God. After a long search, he almost gave up this theological holy grail in despair. But then suddenly, during morning prayers one day, it came to him. We believe, he says, that God is 'something than which nothing greater can be conceived', and he thought that he could conjure God's existence out of this mere definition. Given the fact that such a greatest conceivable being does at least exist in people's minds, Anselm argued, the only question is whether it exists in reality as well. It must do, he says, for the following reason. If God existed only in the mind, then He would not be the greatest conceivable being after all, since it would be possible to conceive of something even greater – namely a God who existed in reality. So if God is defined as 'something than which nothing greater can be conceived', it follows that He exists.

Plenty of other things followed too, or so it seemed to Anselm. But it is only this first stage of his argument, the part that seeks to demonstrate God's existence, which caught the attention of later thinkers. This ingenious but fallacious proof has been knocked down and then propped up again many times in the history of philosophy. A contemporary of Anselm pointed out that the same reasoning implies that somewhere in the world's oceans there exists a greatest conceivable island, which is absurd. Anselm replied to this critic, but not convincingly. In the thirteenth century, St Thomas Aquinas dismissed Anselm's proof, after which it was not much discussed during the Middle Ages. But four centuries later, Descartes revived it in a slightly different form, as did Spinoza and Leibniz. Hume and Kant attacked the argument once more in the eighteenth century, whereupon Hegel tried to reinstate it yet again. Bertrand Russell demolished it at the beginning of the twentieth century, but even that was not quite the end of the matter. A handful of people have attempted to resurrect it since, including Kurt Gödel, one of the century's greatest mathematicians – whose opinions were often a little strange. Several twentieth-century theologians mused on it approvingly.

Anselm did not produce his proof in order to convince unbelievers, least of all himself. He constructed this chain of reasoning (which is presented in the form of a prayer or meditation) because he wanted to reach a deeper intellectual understanding of God. 'It is not your sublimity, O Lord, I seek to penetrate, for my mind is no match for it, but I do desire to understand something of your truth.' Anselm brought logical techniques to bear on religious questions whenever he thought it was useful to do so. For this reason he is sometimes described as the father of scholasticism. But although he did reflect on the relationship between thought, language and reality, he usually pursued such themes only insofar as a clear view of Christian dogma seemed to call for such explorations. Like most of his contemporaries, he had little interest in philosophical topics for their own sake, and was certainly never tempted to stretch a doctrinal point in order to make better sense of it. Unlike Peter Abelard (1079–1142), the first important medieval philosopher and a very different sort of man, logic never got Anselm into trouble.

Abelard called his autobiography 'the history of my misfortunes'. The most famous of these misfortunes was his castration by the enraged relatives of his lover, Héloïse. Even this unhappy event was indirectly brought about by his scholarly prowess and his passionate involvement with logic:

Since I preferred the armor of logic to all the teaching of philosophy, I exchanged all other arms for it and chose the contests of disputation above the trophies of warfare. And so, practising logic I wandered about the various provinces wherever I heard the pursuit of this art was vigorous.

Soon he became very successful as a lecturer in Paris, and it went to his head:

success always puffs up fools and worldly repose weakens the strength of one's mind and readily loosens its fiber through carnal allurement. At a time when I considered I was the one philosopher in the world and had nothing to fear from others, I began to relax the reins on my passions.

At this time he came across Héloïse, a girl 'of no mean appearance' with striking literary gifts and a philosophical bent that was regarded as most unusual for a female.

I then enjoyed such renown and was so outstanding for my charm of youth that I feared no repulse by any woman whom I should deign to favour with my love. I felt that this maiden would all the more readily yield to me as I knew she possessed and cherished a knowledge of letters.

He inveigled himself into the house of Héloïse's uncle and arranged to become her teacher. Abelard could not believe his luck: 'He put his niece entirely under my control . . . I was astonished at his simplicity in this matter and would have been no more astounded if he had been giving over a tender lamb to a ravenous wolf.'

The result was a child they named Astralabe. Héloïse became a nun and later the head of a community of nuns in an oratory which Abelard built. Héloïse and Abelard remained more than devoted to one another and exchanged many letters, as a result of which their story became one of the most famous of the Middle Ages.

Abélard's precocious ability caused him problems throughout his career. He humiliated his first teacher three times in disputations, mainly in arguments over the problem of universals (see page 389). He was apt to describe the views of more eminent colleagues as 'mad' and he quarrelled with more or less everyone. The more students he won away from older and more distinguished Churchmen, the more envy and rivalry he attracted. At one stage he was elected abbot of a monastery in a barbarous part of Brittany where the monks were forever plotting against him and even tried to poison him. He was twice censured by Church councils, and his enemies conspired to have the Pope condemn him as a heretic, excommunicate his followers and order his books to be burned (the sentence was later lifted). One may sometimes sympathize with the annoyance of Abelard's persecutors at an upstart's arrogance, but on the whole they were less sympathetic characters than he was. His chief enemy, St Bernard of Clairvaux, was one of the most virulent and rabble-rousing anti-Semites of the day, whose intolerance and narrow-mindedness contrast unfavourably with the respectful portrayal of the Jew in Abelard's *Dialogue between a Philosopher, a Jew, and a Christian.*

Much of Abelard's best work was devoted to logic, which in those days covered not only the study of reasoning but also questions about language and meaning, such as the problem of universals. Even such apparently anodyne subjects could generate hot controversy in those days, not just because they happened to be the most convenient battle-ground for intellectual display, but because theories about logic could have religious implications (for example, about the Trinity). Abelard's intellectual curiosity and his prowess in such matters spilled over into theology and led to one of the most influential of his writings, *Sic et non* ('For and Against'). This was a collection of 158 apparent contradictions from Scripture and from the works of the Church Fathers, together with a set of methods for weighing up the arguments in such conflicts and thus resolving them. Such exercises in dialectic came to serve as a model for the scholastic procedures used in university teaching.

Others of his writings mark out Abelard as the first serious moral philosopher of medieval times. He went beyond the established traditions of pious moralizing, which usually involved little more than quoting Scripture or other religious authorities, and tried to apply rational analysis to the nature of moral goodness. In order to discover exactly what sin and virtue amounted to, he started by distinguishing the different senses in which something may be said to be good or bad. There are some uses of 'good' in which the word is plainly not intended in a moral sense: 'a good day for fishing', for instance, or 'a good knife'. And there are other uses of 'good' that appear to be moral but which Abelard argued are not quite what they seem. 'It is good that such-and-such happened' is a case in point. According to Abelard, when we say that it is a good thing that a certain event came about, we are really just saying that this event played some part in the divine plan. We are not passing moral judgement on it, because to do so would be to pass judgement on God. After all, absolutely everything that happens is ordained by a provident God and is therefore in some sense good. What follows from this, he reasoned, is that the difference between a morally good action and a morally bad one cannot lie merely in the consequences of the actions, for every action has an outcome that is ultimately good from God's all-seeing point of view.

Abelard concluded that moral goodness must rather be a matter of having the right intentions. Intentions are the only things which God will consider when he comes to weigh people in the balance on the Day of Judgement (though down here on earth it is necessary for us to be more rough and ready in our moral judgements, since we cannot always look into people's hearts to discover their intentions, and we need to encourage certain sorts of behaviour and to deter others). As for the question of what makes an intention good or bad, Abelard's answer is straightforwardly theological: the difference lies in God's wishes, or rather in what His wishes are believed to be. A man sins when he scorns what he takes to be God's wishes and acts well when he seeks to embrace them. Thus Abelard's moral philosophy is by no means entirely independent of his religion; in some places he relies just as much on Scriptural authority as his less philosophically minded predecessors and contemporaries did. Still, he took many opportunities to refine Christian moral thinking by drawing out the theological consequences of his focus on intention as the key to sin. For example, he argued that the Jews who persecuted Christ were not in fact sinning if they believed that they were thereby fulfilling God's will, which they apparently did. This was a brave and dangerous thing to say in twelfth century northern Europe. But it followed inescapably from Abelard's carefully argued premises, so he said it.

Abelard's analysis of moral concepts was far less sophisticated than Aristotle's, but it was a striking enough achievement in those days even to approach ancient standards of philosophizing. With so little left to go on, the intellectuals of Abelard's world were struggling to rediscover what others had learned long ago. This painful break in the West's intellectual tradition was, however, about to be mended. Abelard died just too soon. If he had lived one century later, he would have had access to a vastly greater store of ancient learning. It was round about the time he died, in the middle of the twelfth century, that translations of Greek, Arabic and Jewish works of ethics, logic, medicine, astrology, alchemy, mathematics and natural science began to flood into northern Europe. This considerably raised the standards of debate in many subjects. Although the Latin West was still some centuries away from the point where it could claim to have overtaken the achievements of the ancients, progress of a sort was at last being made.

The new influx of translations was prompted by several things. The Christian reconquest of Arab-occupied Spain was one of the most important: it allowed easier access to Moslem culture and to the Greek flame which that culture still tried to guard. Many Christian scholars travelled to Spain to learn Arabic, find books and translate them into Latin. Some of these books were Arabic originals, others were Syriac or Arabic versions of Greek works. One man, Gerard of Cremona, went to Spain and translated seventeen works on mathematics and optics, twelve or more on astronomy, fourteen on logic and physics and twenty-four medical treatises. Some books, mainly from Sicily and Constantinople, were rendered directly from Greek by the handful of Latin scholars who still had a mastery of the language. A rapid growth in the number and size of schools – and the birth of the first universities in Paris and Oxford in the first quarter of the thirteenth century – increased the incentives to search out, translate and circulate such works.

By the time the university of Paris received its charter in 1210, Western intellectuals faced a type of challenge that was entirely unfamiliar to them. Instead of struggling to retrieve a few fragments of learning, the task now was to cope with a deluge of it. Most of the newly available scientific works – such as Euclid's *Elements*, Ptolemy's *Alamagest*, Avicenna's *Canon of Medicine* and al-Khwarizmi's *Algebra* – presented no particular ideological problem. But some of Aristotle's books did. As we have seen, his doctrines were sometimes hard to reconcile with Christian theology (see page 352). The writings of his greatest Arabic commentator, Averroes (1126–98), were even more problematic. But although parts of the Aristotelian corpus were at first banned in some places, such an attitude obviously amounted to intellectual suicide and could not be sustained. Thinkers such as St Thomas Aquinas set about the daunting but necessary project of trying to combine Christianity with the latest developments – that is, with Aristotelianism. Even such well-intentioned and eminently pious efforts were censured in some quarters in the early days, though the teachings of Aquinas were upheld by the important theological Council of Lyons in 1274. Thomism, as Aquinas' synthesis came to be known, was clearly the crowning achievement of Christian philosophizing, and was somewhat belatedly recognized as such when this modified version of Aristotelianism became the official philosophy of the Roman Catholic Church by papal appointment in 1879. (This was the year of Einstein's birth; the Church does not act hastily in philosophical matters.)

Most of what would now be called philosophy was in medieval times taught under the headings of logic, theology or 'natural philosophy' (i.e., science). Because there was little opportunity for philosophical activity outside the confines of such Church-controlled university courses, any scholar who was tempted to side with the ancients or with the Arabs on some controversial matter soon found himself in a difficult position. Not everyone could strike Aquinas' happy note of harmony when trying to reconcile reason and revelation. Independent-minded thinkers could not openly teach anything which directly contradicted the faith, so they took refuge in evasive ambiguities. They put forward their rational arguments on the one hand while quickly adding on the other that the heretical conclusions of such trains of thought were of course trumped by Christian revelation. Philosophy demonstrates so-and-so, but philosophy is naturally not the whole truth. This was sometimes argued, for example, with respect to the creation of the world. Aristotelianism shows that the world must always have existed. Christianity shows that it was created out of nothing at a particular point in time. Therefore we must believe that it was created, even if we can apparently demonstrate that it was not. Sometimes this sort of double-edged presentation may simply have been a subterfuge to smuggle unorthodox beliefs on to the curriculum; sometimes it was undoubtedly a sincere expression of perplexity; but always it was confused. The Church rightly condemned any attempt to suggest that there could be two sorts of truth, one theological and one philosophical. Either the world was created or it was not, and there was no room for two truths about this or any other matter.

At the end of the thirteenth century, conservatives in the Church fired a warning shot at Greek-style rationalist philosophizing. The use of man's natural faculty of reason was, they said, all very well, but only if it came to the right conclusions. In 1277 the bishop of Paris listed 219 conclusions it was not allowed to come to, and hoped that this would solve the problem. Yet natural reason could not easily be confined within such artificial boundaries. Some thinkers who were secretly dissatisfied with the attempts to set arbitrary limits to their thinking reacted by expressing themselves in a rather jokey way. After expounding arguments which seemed to show that a biblical creation was impossible, one French philosopher in the fourteenth century reluctantly agreed that there had nevertheless been one, but papered over this yawning logical gap by remarking: 'Let it be added, that creation very seldom happens; there has never been but one, and that was a very long time ago.'

The uneasy compromise between faith and reason prompted more than just jokes. The condemnations of 1277 contributed to the eventual collapse of the neo-Aristotelian world-picture and the birth of a new and less book-bound approach to the investigation of nature. This was a long time coming, for bookish scholasticism was still in its heyday and it was three centuries before a new world-picture was comfortably in place. It was also accidental, because the condemners had merely intended to attack religious heresy and those few parts of Aristotelianism which seemed to lead to it. Nevertheless, the conflict between faith and reason at the end of the thirteenth century generated ideas that eventually helped to undermine the whole medieval approach to knowledge.

The main target of the condemnations was 'Averroism', named after the twelfth-century Arab commentator on Aristotle. Averroes regarded philosophy as the sole provider of literal truth, and theology as a collection of largely metaphorical sayings. The Averroist approach was to examine each topic by the light of natural reason, as Aristotle had done, and then to try and work out how God could be fitted into the picture. It was important not to proceed the other way round and put religion first: alleged religious revelations could not be allowed to overthrow what one had painstakingly managed to work out about the world. Thus the 147th Averroist proposition condemned by the bishop said that if something had been established as contrary to nature, then not even God could bring it about. Against this, the biblical conservatives insisted that there were no such limits to God's freedom. It was this emphasis on God's absolute power which turned out to have far-reaching consequences.

According to the old Greek conception of God, He is a part of nature and therefore subject to its laws. Plato's Master-Craftsman did not have an entirely free hand when he assembled the world: He had to work with materials whose properties were already fixed. Not even He could make fire cold or create rivers out of air. Aristotle's God was similarly obliged to observe the principles of physics. But the biblical God wrote the laws of nature Himself and so could create whatever He wanted. If He had wished to make rocks lighter than air, or make chick-embryos grow into cows, or make the moon the centre of the universe, then there was nothing to stop Him. The main effect of this disconcerting but ultimately liberating affirmation of God's freedom was to make people question how much it was possible to work out about the world. One might reason that nature had to proceed in a certain fashion, but maybe God had different ideas. Aristotle might argue that such-and-such was the simplest explanation for some phenomenon – but what if God preferred to do things the complicated way? The most plausible theories might thus turn out to be wrong. Emboldened by this thought, some thinkers in the fourteenth century began to explore possibilities that had been rejected by Aristotle. These included the possibility that the stars are not eternal and unchanging, that the earth rotates, and even that there might be many other worlds like ours.

Among the best philosophers to ponder the implications of God's freedom was William of Ockham (*c.*1285–1349), who lectured on theology at Oxford, wrote an enormous amount about logic and was excommunicated in 1326 over an issue in Church politics. Ockham argued that God can do absolutely anything that does not involve a contradiction in terms. (God cannot make a married bachelor, because all bachelors must by definition be unmarried, but Ockham reasoned that such purely verbal necessities do not count as a limitation of His powers.) It follows, Ockham pointed out, that whenever there is no contradiction in supposing two things to exist apart from one another, they can actually be separated by God. God could, for instance, produce a cause without producing its usual concomitant effect. He could make the sun rise tomorrow and never set again, because a sun that rises without setting may be very odd but it is not actually a contradiction in terms. Ockham realized that one consequence of this is that science can tell us only what does happen, not what must happen. There is nothing which must happen, because God can always intervene.

This idea undermined a key element of the scholastic approach to science. According to the medieval consensus about knowledge, science worked by uncovering 'natural necessities' or essences. Scientific research – i.e., for a busy thirteenth-century teacher, reading very old books – told one the essential properties of a thing, and from these essences one could deduce why it must behave in the way that it does. For example, it is of the essence of stars to rotate in perfect circles, ergo this star must rotate in a perfect circle. That was science. But Ockham argued that talk of such essences is superfluous. It does not add anything to our understanding of the phenomena concerned and it misleads us into thinking that we can prove things which in fact we cannot. God is not obliged to take notice of any 'natural necessities' when He decides how the world will be, so why should we be concerned with them?

This dismissive criticism was typical of Ockham. He regarded physics and indeed philosophy as a whole as full of abstractions that could and should be dispensed with. 'Natural necessities' were one instance of such bogus concepts, and there were many more. To shave them away he applied what came to be known as 'Ockham's Razor', which is usually stated as the principle that 'entities are not to be multiplied beyond necessity'. This quotable maxim does not in fact occur in Ockham's published writings, but it does accurately reflect his economical approach. He held that theories should be as simple as possible and should invoke as few things as they can. It is all too easy, he said, to be misled by the vagaries of language into thinking that the world is more complicated than it in fact is. Philosophers fail to realize, for example, that abstract nouns often exist merely 'for the sake of brevity of speech or ornamentation of language' and do not necessarily correspond to anything in reality. So we need to be always on our guard and ready with the Razor in case a bogus abstraction should wander by. Ockham sought to demonstrate that many of the concepts used in scholastic arguments were indeed little more than ornamentation – and not very attractive ornamentation at that.

He could perhaps have been more assiduous in using his Razor on himself, for his own writings are a labyrinth of arcane and often unnecessary technicalities. But his critique of his predecessors was powerful and disconcerting, particularly in religious matters. He carefully dismantled each of the five standard proofs for the existence of God that had been formulated by Aquinas. It is impossible, Ockham concluded, to demonstrate that there is one infinite, supreme and perfect being. God's existence can be known by faith, but it cannot be proved by reason. He similarly attacked the traditional arguments for the immortality of the soul. Ockham pointed out that because God is entirely free in His actions, He can choose to grant eternal life to whomever He wants and is certainly not obliged to give it to every good Christian. In general, there was not much one could prove about what God must be like or what His plans are. Thus the emphasis on God's freedom that had been underlined by the condemnations of 1277 turned out in Ockham's hands to raise all sorts of unsettling possibilities, not only in physics but in theology too.

Ockham's achievements also included several advances in logic, which was one of the most intensively studied branches of philosophy in the fourteenth century. He and his successors studied several types of inference that had been neglected by Aristotle and investigated many paradoxes in a new and sophisticated way. But this work made no lasting impact because by the middle of the next century most important thinkers were thoroughly sick of the subject. Logic had been the backbone of higher education for a long time, and the intellectual reformers of the Renaissance decided that enough was enough. Ockham's 1,368 new syllogisms were therefore consigned to the same bin as Aristotle's 192 old ones.

Although fourteenth-century logic turned out to be a dead-end, physics was a different story. Some thinkers took the unusual step of introducing measurement and calculation into the discussion of nature; this was a new approach for medieval philosophy and it laid the foundations for some of Galileo's ideas. A group of philosophers based at Merton College, Oxford, who became known as the 'Oxford Calculators', toyed with a mathematical analysis of motion and produced more or less the modern concept of velocity. This proved to be such a fascinating exercise that they got carried away and tried to perform precise measurements of such imponderables as sin and grace as well. (One of the Calculators subsequently became Archbishop of Canterbury, though not because of this misconceived feat.) In less fanciful work the Calculators distinguished between the intensity and the volume of heat, thus anticipating the modern distinction between heat and temperature; but they did not really know how to measure either of these things. In general, their efforts suffered from the fact that they were more interested in the art of logical disputation than in the investigation of nature. They treated physical problems as if they were abstract logical paradoxes, and were more intrigued by theoretical puzzles about infinity than by the practical challenges of predicting and controlling natural phenomena. Nevertheless, they were stumbling along the right lines, and their work proved to be anything but a dead-end.

Nicholas Oresme (*c.*1325–82), a Parisian philosopher and bishop, pursued similar investigations with a consistently clearer head. He invented a way to represent some of the Calculators' ideas in geometrical form, which enabled him to produce proofs of several important theorems about acceleration and velocity (his diagrams are the ancestors of modern graphs). Oresme also offered sympathetic accounts of outlandish, anti-Aristotelian theses, such as that the earth rotates and that it might not be the only world of its kind. The scientific thought of Oresme was thus ahead of its time in two ways. It gave mathematical techniques greater prominence than they had generally enjoyed in medieval physics; and it questioned – at least in theory – some of the central dogmas of the Aristotelian world-picture.

But only in theory. Oresme's explorations of the alternatives to received wisdom nearly always pulled back from the brink at the last moment. He was not alone in this. On the whole, fourteenth-century thinkers continued to believe that the stars were eternal, that the earth remained still, that there were no other worlds, and indeed most of the rest of their Aristotelian inheritance. They were fascinated by the rival possibilities, but they did not actually endorse them. Oresme may have refuted the arguments that had traditionally been used to prove that the earth does not move, but he ended up defending the traditional view anyway. To help decide the issue, he approvingly cited the 93rd Psalm: 'For God hath established the world, which shall not be moved.'

It was not simply religion that held back Oresme and those like him. Thinkers in the fourteenth century had the ability and the inclination to tinker with Aristotle's theories, but they did not have anything comparably systematic to put in their place. Aristotle had explained more or less everything, so why upset the apple-cart? It seemed point-less to deny received views without being able to articulate an equally comprehensive alternative, especially when those views had received the sanction of the educational authorities (i.e., the Church) and even sometimes apparently of Scripture. It was, however, acceptable to explore alternatives purely as an intellectual exercise, and this is largely what men like Oresme were doing.

The condemnations of 1277 had in fact both stimulated and retarded the investigation of nature, for their emphasis on God's freedom brought stultifying implications for science as well as encouraging ones. On the one hand, since God could have done anything He wanted when arranging the world, the only way to find out what He actually did would be to examine the facts. This seemed to be an inducement to active and open-minded scientific research because it implied that even the most plausible-sounding theories required confirmation. On the other hand, since God could have made things very complicated and obscure, what hope was there of ever getting at the truth? The evidence on some questions may seem to point firmly in a certain direction – for example, to the conclusion that the earth rotates – but what does that prove? God could easily have made the earth stand still and yet have made it appear not to. He was utterly free to be utterly ingenious. So no apparent confirmation would be quite good enough to assure us that we had grasped God's mysterious ways. Thus science became something of a game. One could entertain all sorts of theories, work out their consequences and test them against one's observations. But discovering God's truth was quite another matter. This humbling thought made men like Oresme think twice about claiming to have got to the bottom of anything.

The sixteenth-century precursors of the scientific revolution had no such qualms. In 1543, when Copernicus published his account of the earth rotating on its axis and circling the sun, one of the most revolutionary things about his work was his claim that it was actually true. He proposed his new astronomy not as a hypothetical exercise in planetary calculations but as an account of the way the solar system really was. Some of his friends wanted to disguise this shocking fact: his *De Revolutionibus* first appeared with an anonymous preface which claimed in effect that Copernicus did not really mean it. According to the preface, which was inserted by a nervous friend who saw the dying author's work through the press, Copernicus did not intend to imply anything about the actual positions and movements of the heavenly bodies. The book merely illustrated how its alternative model of the heavens could provide a useful basis for calculations.

The disarming preface did not fool anyone. Copernicus' ideas had been circulating for some years before the publication of *De Revolutionibus* and were immediately attacked by the Protestant reformers as unacceptable deviations from Scripture. Martin Luther (1483–1546), who insisted on a strictly literal reading of the Bible – a return, as he saw it, to original Christianity – called Copernicus a fool and an upstart astrologer. The Catholic Church was less committed to biblical fundamentalism and slower to come out with its official condemnation. But by the end of the sixteenth century the growth of the Protestant threat had made the Catholic hierarchy more sensitive to challenges to its intellectual authority. Copernicanism was becoming such a challenge and therefore had to be stamped on. As a result, in 1610 Catholics were forbidden to read Copernicus (in fact the Catholic Church pointlessly and impotently refused to authorize the printing of any Copernican works until 1822). By the 1630s most competent men of science agreed that the earth went round the sun; but this consensus just made the Catholic Church even more aggressive in asserting its right to determine what people should believe. In 1633 the Inquisition famously pressed Galileo to retract his support for Copernicus, which he infamously did.

One reason why Copernicanism escaped earlier censure by the Catholic Church was that its implications took time to sink in. Only when the new astronomy had been adopted by some outspoken thinkers did it become clear how unsettling it could be. Perhaps the most disturbing example was that of Giordano Bruno, a remarkable friar who was burned at the stake in 1600. So heinous were his views that he was refused the usual courtesy of being garrotted before the fires were lit. If anyone doubted that mere astronomical theories could have grave religious consequences, they had only to look at all the occult nonsense which Bruno believed in.

Copernicanism certainly seemed to thrive in bad company. The documents of Bruno's trial have been lost, so nobody knows exactly which of his heresies were singled out by the Inquisition. His wide-ranging works offer many brands of unorthodoxy to choose from. He lectured on theology, natural philosophy, an eccentric form of logic and the art of memorization, among other things. He wrote treatises on magic, diatribes against Aristotle, criticisms of the Bible, cosmological poems, and philosophical dialogues in which he openly cast doubt on Christian doctrines. Sometimes he announced himself to be a Lutheran, sometimes a Calvinist, but his real denomination was barely Christian at all. He was fascinated by magic, obsessed with all manner of occult fantasies and especially keen on ancient Egyptian religions. It was partly the influence of esoteric sun-worshipping creeds that led Bruno to endorse Copernicus' picture of the cosmos.

And it was partly his enthusiasm for the little-known ideas of Lucretius and the Greek atomists that made him go one step further and put Copernicus' reorganized solar system inside an infinite universe:

There is a . . . single vast immensity which we may freely call Void: in it are innumerable globes like this on which we live and grow; this space we declare to be infinite. For there is no reason, nor defect of nature's gifts . . . to hinder the existence of other worlds throughout space.

As we have seen, some fourteenth-century thinkers toyed with the idea of a plurality of worlds without going so far as to believe in them. But Bruno enthusiastically endorsed this crowded cosmology as a wonderful discovery, one of many surprising truths that were being uncovered in his time. He argued that a richly populated universe was the most fitting manifestation of God's immeasurable greatness. God is glorified, he wrote, 'not in one, but in countless suns; not in a single earth, but in a thousand, I say, in an infinity of worlds'.

This was an extremely upsetting idea. A universe of many worlds may glorify God, but where does it leave man? His home is no longer the centre of the universe but just another speck in the void. Can he really then be the centrepiece of creation? And where, incidentally, is heaven in this new scheme of things? Bruno does not quite count as one of the new generation of men of science like Galileo; he was more likely to cite bogus scriptures or Neoplatonic ramblings than any experiments, calculations or observations in support of his theories. But some of his ideas were similar to those of the Galileans and were expressed in an even more disconcerting way. The universe which he and the scientists described had little in common with the one that medieval man had been assured he lived in.

The poet Donne spoke for puzzled laymen as much as for embattled theologians when he wrote of the uncertainties that were crowding into the world of the early 1600s:

> . . . new Philosophy calls all in doubt,
> . . .
> The Sun is lost, and th'earth, and no man's wit
> Can well direct him where to look for it.
> And freely men confess that this world's spent,
> When in the Planets, and the Firmament
> They seek so many new . . .
> Tis all in pieces, all coherence gone

Of course, the sun and earth had not been lost at all. They had at last been found, thanks to the wit of Copernicus. Just as people had long mistaken the sun's apparent movement for a real motion, so conservatives in the seventeenth century were now mistaking a sunrise for a sunset. Coherence was dawning, not disappearing, as a new world-picture began to form. Perhaps one reason why it did not seem like it at the time was that too much was changing too clamorously and at once for anyone to see clearly what was happening.

The time when Copernicus was born, in the second half of the fifteenth century, had in many ways been a quieter one. Scientific study was not yet a theological battleground. The spread of printed books and the uncontrollable proliferation of ideas that this eventually brought had only just started. Perhaps most importantly, the disputes of the learned world had not yet been caught up in the bloody wars between Protestants and Catholics. Nevertheless, several areas of intellectual life were in a state of creative upheaval. Europeans were already beginning to explore new worlds. These were not new planets or new cosmologies, but new continents, new skills, new attitudes to nature and to education, and the worlds of new – or rather, long-forgotten – authors.

The neglected study of Greek and other ancient languages began to revive, thus reopening a passage to the past that had been closed for almost 1,000 years. Not only did scholars begin to demand better texts and translations of the classical works that their medieval predecessors already knew (or thought they knew), they also set out to reclaim those parts of their intellectual heritage which had been ignored in the great wave of scientific and philosophical translations of the twelfth and early thirteenth centuries. There was a rebirth of interest in literary, political, ethical, historical and other ancient books for which there had been little room in the narrow medieval curriculum. First in Italy and later in northern Europe, a new model of intellectual excellence emphasized literary studies, philology, oratory, poetry and history. This *studia humanitatis* – or study of the 'humanities' as they are now known – developed partly to prepare men for work in the councils of princes and republics, the chanceries of cities and states, and in papal offices. The new class of secretaries and secular scholars wanted to know how to write well rather than how to conduct theological disputations. They wanted to be able to compose elegantly persuasive letters, not resolve logical conundrums. Such intellectual developments outside the universities influenced what went on inside them too.

One effect which this 'humanist' movement had on philosophy was to increase interest in the fields of ethics and politics. Aristotle's moral treatises and his *Poetics* were widely studied. Plato's works, with their incomparably superior literary qualities, were also popular. Another consequence of humanist attitudes was an outspoken hostility to the barbarous language and formalistic methods of scholastic argument. One Italian thinker, Lorenzo Valla, vented his frustration with medieval logic thus:

'No man is a stone; some man is an animal; therefore some animal is not a stone.' I can hardly keep myself from screaming, Have you ever heard anyone arguing like this, you nation of madmen?

Valla and other humanists were understandably more interested in the methods of effective rhetoricians than in the abstract and artificial syllogisms of Aristotle. Old Latin authors such as Cicero were now enthusiastically read for the stylistic skills that had been painfully absent from the Latin of scholastic commentaries; the fact that Cicero had almost nothing original to say was of little significance given how beautifully he said it. The humanists regarded his oratory as a model of how to present a case, and enjoyed his philosophical works as readable source books for the Hellenistic philosophies of life that had been virtually unknown to teachers in the medieval universities.

The most influential of the humanist scholars was Erasmus of Rotterdam (1469–1536), whose critique of university philosophers in his *In Praise of Folly* recalls Plato's attack on the allegedly pettifogging Sophists of Periclean Athens. Erasmus made scholasticism seem absurd and petty. He had an easy task convincing his readers that the theologians of the day were ignorant and corrupt buffoons, as did François Rabelais, who made fun of the same targets in his rumbustious novel, *Gargantua*, in 1534. Erasmus was probably right when he said that many clerics barely understood the texts they claimed to teach. The Black Death had severely diminished the pool from which the Church drew its intellectual talent. Erasmus' attacks on the opulent but spiritually impoverished Church establishment paved the way for the Protestant Reformers, Luther and Calvin. The literary skills of an expert humanist turned out to be powerful weapons in this battle, for Erasmus' scholarly work on the Scriptures and early Christian writings helped him to show how far the contemporary Church was from original Christianity.

An Italian contemporary of Erasmus, Niccolò Machiavelli (1469–1527), undermined the authority of theologians in a different manner. He developed a new way to write about politics that simply bypassed religious issues. Instead of giving theological justifications for political institutions and practices, he offered a realistic guide to getting and exercising power. One brief work of his, *The Prince*, is famous for its portrait of the successful ruler as a man who knows when to ignore his moral scruples and press ruthlessly on. Machiavelli's main work, the *Discourses*, is less shocking but far longer and therefore not so well known. Partly because of *The Prince*, Machiavelli has a reputation as an exponent of calculating callousness, but on the whole his writings are not so much cynical as sociological. They set out to describe how politics is played in the real world. The result was a novel type of social study that would have been out of place in the Church-dominated medieval curriculum.

The investigation of nature was also taking on a new aspect in Renaissance times. It was becoming, in a word, more practical. This was most evident at first in Italian universities, where natural philosophy had long been studied in conjunction with medicine instead of being subordinated to theology as it was at Paris and Oxford. Many of the most interesting scientific works of the Renaissance now came from this more pragmatic and experimental medical tradition (Copernicus, for one, was a trained doctor and better known in his own lifetime for his medicine than for his astronomy). The new practical approach to nature could also be seen in the work of Renaissance painters. They began to take an interest in the art of observation in order to make their creations more realistic. Leonardo da Vinci (1452–1519) has a notable place in the history of science and technology not only for his famously sketchy inventions, which ranged from helicopters to rapid-firing guns, but also for his advice to fellow artists along these lines. They should, he said, make sure to study the weather for the sake of their landscapes; they should study mathematics for the sake of visual perspective – the laws of which had recently been discovered by an architect and polymath, Leon Battista Alberti; and they should study physiology in order to represent the human body correctly. Above all, they should take care to observe and study not books but the world, striving to make discoveries for themselves and not rely on second-hand accounts. Just as the new scholars of the humanities urged a return to original texts in order to behold ancient learning without its medieval encrustations, so Leonardo argued that

it is safer to go direct to the works of nature than to those which have been imitated from her originals with great deterioration and thereby to acquire a bad method, for he who has access to the fountain does not go to the water-pot.

Similar advice was offered by Luis Vives (1492–1540), a Spanish humanist who was an outspoken critic of the scholastic tradition in science. But he directed it at philosophers rather than artists. He stressed the importance of relying on one's own careful observations and said that the way forward for natural philosophy lay in the study of crafts and practical techniques. His point was not that philosophers should lay down their pens and become mechanics instead. Rather he was suggesting that they had much to learn from artists, engineers, architects and from the instrument-makers who supplied astronomers, musicians and navigators – that is, from the men of the Renaissance who had made it their business to observe, record, analyse and where possible to manipulate natural phenomena. The practical ways of professionals in the street were, he argued, a surer path to the know-ledge of nature than were the ways of traditional scholars in the universities.

One striking fact about nature in the Renaissance is that there was a lot more of it about. The fifteenth century was a time of audacious voyages of discovery, mostly originating from Spain and Portugal, which brought back news of unknown species and other unfamiliar sights. Nothing in the works of the ancients could account for what the explorers were now seeing for themselves. After visiting the continent which was later named after him, Amerigo Vespucci said that Pliny's *Natural History* – still a standard work after 1,400 years – had not managed to cover even one-thousandth of the creatures that were to be observed there. The immense diversity of creation, 'unknown to the ancients, but known to us', was beginning to be apparent.

'In that hemisphere', wrote Vespucci in his widely read *Letter on the New World* in 1503, 'I saw things incompatible with the opinions of philosophers.' He was struck not only by the novel varieties of flora and fauna, meteorological phenomena and other natural wonders, but also by the extraordinary habits and attitudes of the natives. It seemed that even human nature was different in the New World. The people have no religion, Vespucci wrote, and live unconstrained like animals. They are perfectly happy without the trappings of civilization and seem to be 'Epicureans' rather than 'Stoics', by which he apparently meant that they were more interested in pleasing themselves than in doing their duty. No doubt Vespucci misinterpreted and embroidered much of what he saw. He claimed, for example, that these free spirits commonly lived to the age of 150. But one evident truth shone through the questionable details of his and other explorers' discoveries, namely that what had passed in medieval Europe for knowledge of the world was at best incomplete and at worst plain wrong. It was therefore necessary to discard many ancient prejudices and to start afresh – to return to the fountain of nature itself, as Leonardo had urged, and not rely any more on the stagnating contents of ancient water-pots.

It was in this spirit that many sixteenth-century thinkers demonstrated their contempt for ancient men of science, sometimes in theatrical ways. Philippus Aureolus Theophrastus Bombastus von Hohenheim, commonly known as Paracelsus (1493–1541), sometimes began his lectures on medicine by burning copies of the works of Galen and Avicenna. This flamboyant gesture presumably made its point. Petrus Ramus (1515–72), a Parisian philosopher, is said to have publicly defended the thesis that 'everything Aristotle said is fabrication'. Even if he did not actually say this, many others certainly thought it. (Ramus was caught up and killed in the St Bartholomew's Day Massacre in 1572, an event somewhat fancifully described in a tragedy by Christopher Marlowe: 'Was it you who scoffed at Aristotle?' a soldier asks Ramus in the play. 'Yes,' Ramus replies. 'Kill him,' orders the soldier.)

The book-burning Paracelsus yielded to the authority of no text except the Bible, or so he claimed. He made much of preferring his own experience and experiments to the hand-me-down wisdom of the ancients. But in fact he depended on old sources and traditions more than he cared to admit. They were just not the usual sources and traditions. Paracelsus may have rejected Greek chemistry with its four elements and Greek medicine with its four humours, but his own ideas about chemical medicine (in which the noxious trio of mercury, sulphur and salt played the leading parts) owed much to Arab alchemists from 800 years earlier. In addition to alchemy, Paracelsus was passionately interested in astrology and in the Jewish Cabala, among other occult topics. This eclectic supernaturalism was typical of the times. Many Renaissance thinkers saw no great divide between what we call science and what we call magic. Indeed, the development of early modern science owes some of its impetus to Renaissance magic.

It is not just that alchemy and astrology sometimes acted as nurse-maids to chemistry and astronomy, developing techniques that found their way into more mature scientific work. It is not just that Pythagorean and Cabalistic number-mysticism were partly responsible for inspiring men like Kepler to seek mathematical keys to nature. The relationship between science and magic went deeper than such occasional meetings might suggest. The fact is that it was essentially the spirit of the magician which animated the first Renaissance investigators of nature. A magician, in those days, was one who aimed to harness the hidden powers in things and exploit these powers in order to perform wonders. He wanted the elusive sort of knowledge that could be turned to practical effect, and was typically so eager to find it that he searched in what now seem to be some of the unlikeliest places – such as the numerological conjuring of the Cabala or the whispering world of spirits.

We have already seen that the most important difference between Aristotle's approach to scientific knowledge and that of a man like Francis Bacon, the prophet of modern science, lay in their hopes for its practical application (see page 226). Aristotle had virtually no such hopes; Bacon was obsessed by them. 'Human knowledge and human power come to the same thing,' Bacon wrote, 'for where the cause is not known the effect cannot be produced.' In the 1620s he advocated the founding of a club of investigators whose goal would be 'the knowledge of Causes, and secret motions of things; and the enlarging of the bounds of Human Empire, to the effecting of all things possible'. Some forty years later, Bacon's proposal led to the establishment of the Royal Society, whose members included Robert Boyle and Isaac Newton. Such men were in part the heirs of the Renaissance magicians who had wanted to turn the passive study of nature into the active management of its powers. The members of the Royal Society made the magicians' dreams a reality, or at least tried their best to do so.

Bacon had harsh words for some of the Renaissance dabblers in the occult, though his main complaint was not that their magic did not work but rather that it worked too effortlessly. It was a lazy art, he thought, too casual and underdeveloped, but by no means altogether along the wrong lines. Bacon's reservations did not prevent him from endorsing a basically magical or spiritualistic view of the world. He acknowledged, for example, the efficacy of mystic talismans: 'many things . . . work upon the spirits of man by secret sympathy and antipathy . . . [*as in*] the virtues of precious stones . . . [*that*] have in them fine spirits'. On the whole, Bacon wanted to build on astrology, alchemy and magic, not abolish them, because he regarded their goal of knowledge married to power as a good one to aim at. (So did Newton, who was something of an occultist crank by modern standards. He wrote more than a million words of alchemical gibberish. But by the latter half of the seventeenth century, when Newton lived, such interests had become unusual for a scientist and he kept his occult activities largely to himself.)

Renaissance thinkers drew a clear dividing line between so-called 'natural magic' and demonic magic. The former, but not the latter, was deemed to be largely consistent with Christianity and well worth cultivating. Even St Thomas Aquinas had devoted a treatise to such practices as the harmless but in his view effective use of astrological talismans. While demonic magic involved Faustian attempts to invoke forbidden forces and communicate illicitly with the dead, natural magic sought to exploit invisible and intangible yet entirely natural phenomena:

nature is a magician everywhere baiting traps with particular foods for particular objects. The farmer prepares his field and seeds for gifts from heaven . . . The philosopher who is learned in natural and astronomical matters and whom we are wont rightly to call a magician, likewise implants heavenly things in earthly objects by means of certain alluring charms used at the right moment.

So wrote Marsilio Ficino (1433–99), a Florentine scholar and thinker who was responsible for producing Latin translations of what became the most influential occult texts of the Renaissance. These were the so-called 'Hermetic' writings, a set of books by unknown Greek authors some time between AD 100 and 300 but believed in Ficino's day to be the work of Hermes Trismegistus, a mythical Egyptian seer from just after the time of Moses. The 'natural magic' advocated by Ficino and others in the late fifteenth century managed to combine elements of diverse occult traditions with orthodox religion. Indeed, occultism and Christianity were seen as complementary: 'there is no department of knowledge that gives us more certainty of Christ's divinity than magic and cabala', wrote Giovanni Pico della Mirandola, a like-minded colleague of Ficino, in 1486.

By the mid-sixteenth century, the esoteric ideas of natural magic were turning into a whole new philosophy of nature. Men such as Paracelsus and Bruno described an enchanted world of hidden symmetries and spiritual sympathies that could be manipulated by the right spells. This seemed a more colourful and energetic world than the one described in Aristotelian university texts. It suited the vivacity of the times. The magical point of view saw nature as ripe for exploitation, which was an enticing prospect to the resourceful and optimistic men of the Renaissance. Although there were some men of science who had little or no interest in the occult, they were exceptional and their books were not so widely read as those of the magicians or part-magicians. For the most part in sixteenth-century natural philosophy, 'one scarcely knows where science begins and the seance ends', as one modern history puts it.

The blending of science and magic in the creative confusions of the Renaissance is nicely illustrated by the case of John Dee (1527–1608), who may well have been the model for Shakespeare's Prospero in *The Tempest*. Dee was one of the leading mathematicians in Elizabethan England. He conducted geographical and hydrographical surveys of newly discovered lands for the Queen and did important work on trigonometry, navigation and the reform of the calendar. But he also devoted much of his time to communicating with angels, using prayers, crystals, mirrors, mystic numbers and other magical equipment to do so. These attempts did not succeed as often as he would have liked, but the angels did apparently dictate various books to him via his allegedly psychic associate. It is a telling fact that it was not these efforts to communicate with the spiritual realm, nor his keen involvement in astrology, alchemy and Cabala, which earned Dee his reputation as a mighty magician. Rather it was some purely mechanical stage-effects that he produced in the course of a performance of a Greek comedy at Trinity College, Cambridge, in 1546. Clever machines – in this case, a huge artificial flying beetle – were evidently regarded as more 'supernatural', because less familiar, than good-luck charms or talking angels.

The inventions of Renaissance conjurors and engineers may sometimes have been genuinely new, but their enthusiasm for magic had very old roots. While the outdated texts of Greece and Rome were often scorned when it came to natural history or physics, there were some areas of knowledge in which the ancients set an example to be followed. The occult, like the humanities, was one of them. The natural magicians of the fifteenth and sixteenth centuries were in effect returning to the rampant supernaturalism and eclectic religiosity of the Greek world of late antiquity. Marsilio Ficino's many translations included works by occultist Neoplatonists such as Iamblichus, Porphyry, Proclus and also the *Chaldean Oracles* which inspired these men to some of their more esoteric fantasies (see pages 370–72). Of all the strands in Ficino's thought, the mystical Platonism of Plotinus and his followers was perhaps the most prominent. Ficino's influential conception of the religious life as a step-by-step ascent to a purified spiritual realm owed more to this ancient tradition than to anything else.

It was Ficino who brought Plato back into circulation. He produced the first complete translation of his works to be made in the West, thus making them accessible to all learned people and not just the small but increasing number who knew Greek as well as Latin. Because the name of Plato had always been on people's lips, it is easily forgotten how little was known until the late fifteenth century of what he actually said. Very few Europeans since the beginning of the Middle Ages had been familiar with more than a smattering of Plato, usually just the creation-story of the *Timaeus* plus a few rumours about a higher plane of reality, abstract and mathematical in its perfection, that lurked beyond the material world. Now Plato's ideas as well as his name were on people's lips. Ficino's edition was an immediate best-seller, though his accompanying commentaries gave readers the impression that Plato's philosophy was more homogeneous, consistent and dogmatic than it in fact was. Supported by his patron, Cosimo de' Medici, Ficino even founded some sort of Platonic Academy in Florence, modelled on the Athenian original, though the only known fact about its activities is that it celebrated Plato's birthday with banquets.

Like St Augustine, Ficino believed that Platonism contained important anticipations of Christianity. But Ficino went further. He regarded

Plato's writings as no less authoritative than the Bible. Philosophy could be as divinely inspired as Scripture, and Plato's definitely was, or so Ficino believed. He argued that what Plato had called the mind's contact with 'goodness itself' (or the Form of the Good) was the same as what Christians called the knowledge of God. By marrying Platonism to Christianity, Ficino both raised the faith to the heights of philosophy and brought philosophy down to earth. He maintained that the mystical union with the supreme 'being beyond being' that the Neoplatonists talked about was achievable during mortal life if one practised the gospel of love. This gospel could of course be found in the Bible, but it could also be found in Diotima's speech in Plato's *Symposium* with its famous image of the soul's ascent to the heavenly world of Forms (see page 172). Ficino wrote an influential commentary on the *Symposium* which popularized the idea of 'Platonic love'. The true love of a person, he argued, is a sort of preparation for the love of God. If the feeling is mutual, and if the lover has learned to transcend merely bodily desires to focus on the soul, then it becomes a form of religious devotion. The idea of Platonic love became a favourite topic for poets and essayists, long outliving the Renaissance philosophical literature in which it was born. Some critics trace its influence as far as twentieth-century poets including Yeats, Rilke and Wallace Stevens. Nowadays, though, the term itself has come to connote little more than celibacy.

The shadow of Plato hung over the science of the Renaissance as well as its poetry. Although the theories of natural philosophy taught in the universities were essentially those of Aristotle and consequently attached little significance to quantities and their measurement, the work of many practical men and freelance investigators of nature was marked by an obsession with mathematics. This not only recalled Plato and the Pythagoreans but often stemmed directly from their writings. The painters who studied the laws of perspective, the craftsmen who calculated busily away, and even the magicians with their codes of mystic numbers were all in effect pursuing Plato's goal of using mathematics as a key to unlock the secrets of nature. The would-be mathematizers often tried to run long before they could walk; Nicholas of Cusa (1401–64), an early advocate of mathematical methods and a Platonist of sorts, said that it was possible to predict the size of a harvest by carefully weighing water and grains of corn in March. Yet this stumbling enthusiasm for numbers and their applications paved the way for the successes of Galilean science. Copernicus, Galileo and Kepler were all deeply influenced by the revived Platonic tradition. 'Was not Plato perfectly right', said Galileo, 'when he wished that his pupils should be first of all well grounded in mathematics?'

One lesser feature of Renaissance Platonism that helped by chance to prepare the ground for developments in the seventeenth century was its veneration of the sun. Plato's comparison of the sun to 'goodness itself' led Renaissance Platonists to describe it in ways that made Copernicanism later sound almost natural. Ficino, for example, wrote that

Nothing reveals the nature of the Good more fully than the light [*of the sun*]. First, light is the most brilliant and clearest of sensible objects. Second, there is nothing which spreads out so easily, broadly, or rapidly as light. Third, like a caress, it penetrates all things harmlessly and most gently. Fourth, the heat which accompanies it fosters and nourishes all things and is the universal generator and mover. Just look at the skies, I pray you. The sun can signify God himself to you . . .

Ficino had no interest in the development of astronomy as a science, but his idea that the sun is god-like made it seem fitting that it should sit at the centre of things. Copernicus himself drew on this Platonic comparison between God and the sun to support his revolutionary doctrine: 'In the middle of all sits Sun enthroned. In this most beautiful temple could we place this luminary in any better position from which he can illuminate the whole at once?' The Sun, he said, 'sits as upon a royal throne ruling his children the planets which circle around him'. Johannes Kepler, who improved Copernican astronomy by (among other things) working out that the planets' orbits were not in fact circular but elliptical, also exploited the idea that the centre of the universe was an appropriate home for a divine entity.

Ficino's great labour in translating Plato's works could not have made the impact it did if his career had not coincided with a remarkable development. When Ficino was born, the number of manuscript books in Europe could be numbered in the thousands, and access to these rarities was still relatively hard to come by. The volumes in libraries were often secured to their shelves with chains. But by the time Ficino died in 1499, presses were running at 200–300 sites in Europe and there were at least 10 million books in circulation. A private collector could easily own several thousand titles. Gutenberg had produced his famous bible from the first press with movable and interchangeable type in 1454 when Ficino was a young man. The result of this new technology was not only a deluge of books but the beginnings of mass literacy. Gutenberg and his fellow printers had literally freed the book from its chains.

At the start of the sixteenth century, the reading public was not only more numerous but also more diverse than it had been in the days when intellectual life was the province of the Church. The broadening horizons of Renaissance Europe and the patronage of businessmen, statesmen and wealthy ruling families had led to the formation of a more secular intelligentsia. A wide range of publications was churned out to satisfy every kind of literary appetite, from undemanding works like Aesop's fables and Boccaccio's steamy stories to scholarly editions of Greek mathematical works. Scientific and philosophical literature strayed away from the models that had served medieval monks and teachers and evolved new forms to meet the needs of a broader readership. Increasing numbers of works were written in vernacular languages rather than in Latin, and by the end of the sixteenth century the treatise and the essay were beginning to supplant the traditional academic format of the commentary. Modern philosophical literature – the writings of Hobbes and Descartes that are read today, for example – was just around the corner.

Aristotle and his commentators also benefited from Gutenberg's revolution; Aristotelian works were much reprinted in the early sixteenth century and may have reached a larger audience than ever before. But it was too late. Although Aristotelianism was far from dead in many university faculties and religious institutions, history was already leaving it behind. The main impetus for what was coming to be known as the 'new philosophy' derived largely from Scepticism and Epicureanism, two of the old rivals of Aristotelian thinking that had been submerged for more than a millennium. Few intellectuals of the sixteenth and seventeenth centuries called themselves Epicureans or Sceptics. Yet it was these old Hellenistic philosophies, now widely available, that were pointing them in new directions.

Among the old works recovered in the late sixteenth century and translated into Latin were Diogenes Laertius' *Lives of the Philosophers*, which included his biography of the first great Sceptic, Pyrrho, and books by Cicero that defended the milder form of scepticism once practised in the Athenian Academy. From such works people learned of philosophers who enigmatically and annoyingly refused to commit themselves one way or another. Such a philosophy naturally attracted some ridicule. In the 1530s, Rabelais jokily portrayed a fictitious 'Pyrrhonian' philosopher, Trouillogan, in his *Gargantua and Pantagruel*. Rabelais' hero could not get a straight answer out of Trouillogan about whether or not he ought to get married, nor could he even find out whether this 'philosopher' was happily married himself:

Are you married?
I think so.
You were also married before you had this Wife.
It is possible.
Had you good Luck in your first Marriage?
It is not impossible.
How thrive you with this Second Wife of yours?
Even as it pleaseth my Fatal Destiny.
But what in good earnest? tell me: Do you prosper well with her?
It is likely.
But on, in the name of God: I vow, by the Burthen of Saint *Christopher*, that I had rather undertake the fetching of a Fart forth of the Belly of a dead Ass, than to draw out of you a positive and determinate Resolution.

It may have been funny when taken too far, but ancient Scepticism began to strike a sympathetic chord in the sixteenth century. There were, after all, bigger questions at issue in those days than the desirability of marriage, and a sceptical suspension of judgement did seem an appropriate response to some of them. All sorts of conventional certainties were being called into doubt by new discoveries in astronomy, geography, anatomy and other subjects. These doubts bred more doubts. With so many old ideas coming under attack, an intelligent person had to wonder how secure the new ones were. As the essayist Montaigne (1533–92) later put it: 'Since Ptolemy was once mistaken over his basic tenets, would it not be foolish to trust what moderns are saying now?'

Faced with a profusion of new theories, a few defeatists claimed to reject all attempts to understand the world. One anti-intellectual diatribe published in 1526 went so far as to pronounce knowledge 'the very pestilence, that putteth all mankind to ruine and hath made us subjecte to so many kindes of sinne'. Better, wrote the author, 'to be Idiotes, and knowe nothinge' than to have one's head filled with pernicious ideas. But although such thoroughgoing scepticism was an understandable reaction to the plethora of 'knowledge' then on offer, it was a hard philosophy to stick to and nobody really did stick to it. (Even the author of this polemic later found all sorts of doctrines he could believe in.) It was more usual and more plausible to employ the weapons of Scepticism in a strictly limited way. Sceptical arguments were generally used to undermine outdated or overambitious claims to knowledge, not to attack all intellectual activity.

Erasmus, for instance, invoked the ancient Sceptics to puncture the pretensions of dogmatic theologians and to defend a more cautious approach to the controversies of the day. He warned that 'human affairs are so complex and obscure that nothing can be known of them for certain, as has been rightly stated by my Academicians [*i.e. the Sceptics described by Cicero*]'. Man's mind, Erasmus wrote, 'is so formed that it is far more susceptible to falsehood than to truth', so it is often wiser to admit that one can reach no conclusion than to plunge in and make a fool of oneself. The theological debate about man's free-will was a case in point. Erasmus was doubtful of some recent attempts by Luther to solve this old problem, noting that it was an issue of great complexity about which learned theologians had disagreed for centuries. Was it really plausible to suppose that Luther had now stumbled upon the truth that had escaped his predecessors for so long? Surely it was more sensible, Erasmus argued, to follow the example of the ancient Sceptics and suspend judgement on the matter. This noncommittal stance enraged Luther, who warned Erasmus that the Holy Ghost was certainly not a Sceptic and that He would take a dim view of such feeble indecision when the Day of Judgement came.

Luther insisted that Christians could not afford the perverse luxury of scepticism. They had to make definite commitments one way or the other and were not allowed to sit on the fence: 'Nothing is more characteristic among Christians than assertion. Take away assertions, and you take away Christianity.' Yet, ironically, it was Luther and the other Protestant reformers who did more than anyone to unleash a plague of scepticism. For it was they who outrageously challenged the credentials of religious authorities and thereby made the question 'How do you know?' the most pressing question of the age. Luther refused to accept that the Church establishment was always right: 'I put no trust in the unsupported authority of Pope or [*Church*] councils, since it is plain that they have often erred and often contradicted themselves.' Instead he upheld individual conscience as the arbiter of truth in religious matters. A good Christian should look to the Scriptures, interpreted in the light of his conscience and his own religious experience, in order to find out what to believe. This was the essence of Protestantism. But Luther's challenge to the Church raised an inescapable question. In a world of fierce disagreements, exactly whose conscience was it that was to be the guide? Whom could you trust if you could not trust the Pope?

The defenders of Catholic orthodoxy were quick to turn Luther's own challenges against him. If he could ask embarrassing questions about 'unsupported authority', then so could they. It is all very well to attack the credentials of the Pope and his hierarchy, they argued, but if you are going to abandon tradition then you will need something to put in its place, and whatever you choose is bound to be even more questionable. If the Pope's judgement can be doubted, so can yours. Thus traditionalists found that when attacks on authority were taken to their logical conclusion, they could be used to support traditionalism. By raising the stakes in the game which Luther had started, the claims of dissenters could be undermined, thus (in theory) throwing bewildered souls back into the reassuring arms of the Church. Scepticism could make men 'conscious of the darkness they are in, so that they will implore help from on high and submit to the authority of the faith'.

Naturally the Protestant reformers were not prepared to submit so easily. Even if we have no choice but to yield to authority, they replied, how do we know that the authority of today's Church is the right one to yield to? How do we even know who the rightful Pope is? There have, after all, been rival claimants to the papacy in the past: in 1409 there were no fewer than three would-be popes at the same time. Thus each side, Protestant and Catholic, could play the sceptic against the other. The result was deadlock. Once Luther had questioned the basis of religious knowledge, there could be no simple answer to the puzzle of where to turn in order to support one's views.

Yet the traditionalists could at least claim to be following more faithfully in the footsteps of the ancient Sceptics than the Protestants were. Both Pyrrho and Sextus Empiricus had said that one should go along with the generally accepted customs of the day; they counselled conservativism on the grounds that no case for change could ever be made sufficiently convincing. This favoured the Catholic side in the battle of faiths, for there was no doubt that the Pope, even if he could not be proved to be the 'rightful' Pope, was nevertheless the generally accepted one. Because ancient Scepticism thus endorsed a docile acceptance of the *status quo*, it was Catholic thinkers who made the most enthusiastic use of its ideas in the theological wars that raged through the sixteenth and seventeenth centuries.

The irresistible and unanswerable question 'How do you know?' quickly spread beyond the confines of theology. When the works of Sextus Empiricus were published in Latin in the 1560s, a whole armoury of sceptical arguments designed to show the weakness of human reason, the unreliability of perception and the apparently relative nature of human values and ideas was put at the disposal of philosophers. Shortly afterwards, Montaigne's essays (written in French) drew these arguments to the attentions of a wider public. Montaigne's work powerfully brought home the limited and biased nature of human experience and the uncertainties that dogged all efforts to find the truth. Bacon and Descartes were among those who read him and resolved to try and put human knowledge on a firmer footing.

Francisco Sanchez (1552–1623), a distant cousin of Montaigne who taught medicine and philosophy at Toulouse University, also played a key part in bringing scepticism to philosophical prominence. While Montaigne sought only to show that one should suspend judgement on some matters and that reason needed to be supplemented by faith, his cousin drew a more positive and far-reaching moral. Sanchez aimed to demonstrate that there were definite limits to human knowledge and that the nature of these limits required a comprehensive change in the conception of science. The best that man can do to understand the natural world, he argued in his treatise *Why Nothing Can be Known* (1581), is to make limited claims about the appearances of things, based on observation and experience. He referred to this cautious and empirical approach as 'scientific method' – apparently the first use of this now-familiar term. Unqualified knowledge of the intrinsic nature of things was, he maintained, available only to God. It was certainly not available to Aristotle, whose ambitiously all-encompassing theories were still the staple diet of scientific education in most universities.

If Sanchez's scepticism depressingly implied that full-blown know-ledge was beyond man's reach, it had a bright side too. The idea that scientific studies could provide a provisional account of things that would serve as a guide to everyday life suited the practical and experi-mental approach to nature which some Renaissance men had preached and which Galileo, among others, was now pursuing. A sceptically oriented conception of 'scientific method' helped the new science in at least two ways. First, sceptical arguments were a useful stick with which to beat old ideas and thereby to clear a path for new ones. Sanchez himself produced powerful attacks on Aristotelianism and occultism. Second, scepticism seemed in some ways positively to sup-port the new physics (or, as it was commonly then called, the 'new philosophy') of Galileanism. To see how, we must look more closely at the Galilean world-picture – which is essentially the modern world-picture.

Nowadays Galileo is remembered for the astronomical heresies that brought him into conflict with the Inquisition, namely his Copernican belief that the earth goes round the sun and his un-Aristotelian belief that the heavens are subject to the same physical laws as the earth. These are the shocking truths which Galileo's telescope confirmed and which made some conservatives famously refuse to look through that infernal instrument. But there was something else unacceptable in Galileo's writings which played at least as important a part in getting him condemned. This was his espousal of the atomistic physics of Democritus, Epicurus and Lucretius, according to which the physical world is ultimately to be understood in terms of the mechanical inter-actions of tiny particles. These particles were held to possess measur-able properties such as size, position and weight but none of the sensory or 'secondary' qualities such as colour, texture and taste. In the opinion of Democritus, and of Galileo, these latter qualities are entirely subjective and are to be explained merely as the effects of atoms on our sense-organs. 'Natural philosophy' was henceforth to be concerned primarily with the mechanical and mathematical aspects of nature. That was the premise of the science pioneered by Galileo, Descartes and Boyle and brought more or less to fruition by Isaac Newton.

There were several things wrong with this from the Church's point of view. First, atomism came from a highly suspect background. There did not seem to be much room for God in Democritus' universe, none at all in the universe of Lucretius, and Epicurus had the reputation of being not exactly a pious and upstanding fellow. Secondly, theologians argued that the atomistic theory of matter was inconsistent with the doctrine of the Eucharist, which was no small issue.

According to this doctrine, when bread and wine are consecrated by a priest in the appropriate ritual formula they become 'transubstan-tiated' so that they take on the substance of Christ's body and blood. Although they evidently retain the appearance of bread and wine (they keep, for example, its texture, colour and taste – what atomists called its subjective 'secondary' qualities), it was held that they somehow lose the intrinsic nature of bread and wine. In other words, they are not really bread and wine any more. But this is impossible according to atomism. On the atomistic way of looking at things, the appearance of a piece of matter cannot be separated from its substance in this fashion. The substance of the bread, that is, its intrinsic nature, consists in the type and arrangement of its minute particles, and its appearance is simply the effect of these particles on our senses. How, then, can the bread change its substance without thereby changing its appearance? If the bread really consisted of atoms of Christ's body, then it would have to have the appearance of Christ's body. And if it had the appearance of bread, which it plainly does, then this could only be because it in fact consisted of particles of bread. Theologians therefore concluded that from Galileo's doctrines 'it follows that in the Sacrament there are substantial parts of bread or wine, which is the error condemned by the Sacred Tridentine Council, Session 13, Canon 2'.

Galileo's atomistic physics did not only have awkward theological implications. It amounted to a comprehensive rejection of traditional natural philosophy. Perhaps because of Aristotle's passion for biology, medieval science had inherited an essentially organic model of the world. Aristotle tended to see the part in terms of the whole, and the whole as resembling something alive: even the behaviour of inanimate objects was explained almost as if it were the activity of living creatures. For example, although Aristotle did not think that a falling stone literally 'wanted' to reach the earth as it plummeted towards it, he described this motion as a return to the stone's 'natural place' or home, almost as if it were a rabbit heading for its warren. Such semi-biological modes of explanation were now replaced by rigidly mechanical ones. Thus Boyle, following Galileo and the Greek atomists, described the world as a 'great *automaton*', and compared it to a watch or clock.

Yet the world did not seem, on the surface of things, to be like a clock. The working parts of this alleged mechanism, that is, the particles or atoms which are the focus of Galilean science, are not directly observable because they are too small to be seen. Galilean science treated matter in an abstract, mathematical way that seemed far removed from untutored common sense. It thus chose to ignore some of what our eyes and ears tell us about everyday objects, and it was in this respect that it echoed scepticism to some extent. The Greek Sceptics had insisted that sense-perception was unreliable and subjective; modern atomistic science now seemed to agree. What the senses tell us was indeed not the whole truth about the world. Galilean atomism thus replaced the great divide between earth and heavens that had marked Aristotelian science with a quite different and even more radical sort of divide. It separated the everyday world of colours, tastes and smells from the geometrical world of invisible particles which serious investigators of nature were henceforth to focus on.

Explaining how an updated form of Epicurean atomism could be the heart of a practical 'scientific method' was the life's work of Pierre Gassendi (1592–1655), a French professor of mathematics and philosophy who was an active researcher in astronomy, anatomy and the physics of motion. Gassendi was also a Catholic priest, and his first task was to make room for God and immortal souls in the mechanical universe of ancient atomism. Gassendi sought to Christianize Epicurus, much as Aquinas had sought to Christianize Aristotle. He was never as famous as Aquinas had been – for one thing, his works were far too long-winded – but it was largely thanks to Gassendi that by the end of the seventeenth century the 'mechanical philosophy' was sufficiently purged of the suspicion of atheism to be acceptable to all men of science. Gassendi and his friend Marin Mersenne (1588–1648), who was also a priest, were at the centre of a circle of avant-garde mathematicians and thinkers, which included Galileo, Kepler, Descartes and Hobbes, who were developing and interpreting the ideas of the new mechanical science.

According to Gassendi's modified atomism, the atoms which comprise the universe are not eternal and infinite but are limited in number and were created by God. Their motions are not wholly random, as Democritus and Epicurus held, but were initiated by and can sometimes be directed by God. Everything physical was to be explained by the mechanics of divinely guided atoms – even human thought could be explained in terms of physical distortions of the material of the brain – or so Gassendi claimed. But in addition to the physical world, there was also a spiritual world which contained God and immortal human souls. Thus Gassendi revamped Epicurus' picture of the universe to produce something more conformable to biblical ideas. This Christian atomism provided the framework which Boyle and Newton subsequently adopted.

It was not only in physics that Gassendi drew inspiration from Epicurus. He accepted Epicurus' doctrine that tranquillity of soul was the highest moral good, and he tried to give that idea a Christian slant too. (Hobbes, who was deeply influenced by Gassendi, seems to have derived his emphasis on the supreme importance of peace from Gassendi's Epicurean ethics.) Gassendi also echoed Epicurus' empiricism: 'experience is the balance in which the truth of any matter is to be weighed', he wrote. A genuine science must pay far more attention to observation than to theory, and in this respect Galilean science performed far better than its Aristotelian predecessors. However, Gassendi believed that the scope of human knowledge was severely limited. Observation and experiment may provide us with all the genuine information that we have about the physical world, but that is not actually very much. The best that science can do is give us some provisional knowledge about appearances, not about how things really are: 'no proposition that makes assertions about the nature of a thing according to itself can be affirmed with confidence'.

Both Gassendi and Mersenne were awed by the challenge of Pyrrhonist Scepticism and neither of them could see how to answer it directly. On the other hand they were also convinced that Galilean science was along the right lines. It certainly seemed to work as a 'scientific method' for predicting and manipulating phenomena. So they espoused what they called a mitigated or constructive type of scepticism, according to which atomism was to be treated as a sort of working assumption or model. The new science was a useful tool, indeed the most useful one yet developed for practical investigators of nature, but it was not necessarily any more than that. Because of the weakness of the human mind that the relentless questioning of the sceptics had revealed, only God could know for certain whether mechanistic atomism was actually true.

All the best thinkers of the seventeenth century struggled with the questions raised by the new science. How is mental activity to be analysed in terms of particles of matter? What is the place of man in a mechanistic universe, and what is the place of God? What sort of information do physics and mathematics give us? If atomism is right in saying that many of our perceptions are subjective, how much of the truth about the world can be inferred from the evidence of our senses? And how does one prevent the cautious approach which is distinctive of a 'scientific method' from degenerating into extreme scepticism? These issues have in one way or another motivated philosophy ever since. It is by virtue of its engagement with the special problems posed by modern science that modern philosophy is distinguished from pre-modern philosophy.

Thomas Hobbes (1588–1679) was one of the first to attempt a

comprehensive theory of man and the universe in the light of the new science. When he was in his early forties, he had a sudden awakening and turned from literary pursuits to mathematics, physics and thence to general philosophy. He developed a passionate interest in geometry; he joined his employer, the Earl of Newcastle, in conducting experiments in optics; and he made a pilgrimage to see Galileo. Unfortunately, his enthusiasm for scientific subjects far outstripped his ability in them: he would not stop trying to square the circle, for example, even when this had been demonstrated to be a geometrical impossibility. But he made his mark by trying to apply to man the mechanical and mathematical approach to nature that he learned from Kepler and Galileo. As we have seen (page 258), Hobbes formulated the revolutionary theory that thinking is a type of computation, i.e., a mechanical process just like the ones which physicists were trying to describe in the workings of nature as a whole. So eagerly did Hobbes embrace and generalize the mechanical view of the world that his philosophy was roundly condemned as dangerously irreligious. Some bishops stated in parliament that his doctrines were a likely cause of the Great Fire of London in 1666.

In the political writings for which he is now remembered, most famously *Leviathan* (1651), Hobbes presented a view of society that was inspired not only by mechanistic science but also by the challenge of scepticism. It echoed mechanism in the way it presented human psychology as a matter of desires and aversions pushing and pulling men along. And it sought to satisfy sceptics by proposing practical principles that even someone who was doubtful of discovering the truth might regard it as reasonable to live by. According to Hobbes, it is plain that the basic motive of human activity is self-preservation. Since nobody can easily preserve himself in solitude – for such an existence would tend to be 'poor, nasty, brutish, and short', as Hobbes famously wrote – men seek to live in the society of others. Yet this exposes them to the hazards of other people's attempts at self-preservation, which are likely to conflict with their own. It follows, Hobbes argued, that it is in everyone's best interests to submit to an all-powerful monarch whose absolute authority will protect each man against his neighbour. Even the Church would have to take its instructions from the sovereign, who was to have the power to resolve theological disputes by royal pronouncement and thus to determine what people ought to believe. God Himself was a material being, as everything was, though Hobbes did at least concede that He was invisible. No wonder the bishops spoke out.

Hobbes's unusual political and theological conclusions were, he believed, inevitable consequences of the 'new philosophy' of Galileo. He could not see how a science of man could proceed except on the basis of principles that were as rigid and mechanical as those invoked by the science of motion. He wanted a mathematics of the state, and an absolute dictatorship was the only way to ensure that all the sums would come out right. It also provided a sort of solution to some of the uncertainties that fed contemporary scepticism, for it removed the need to answer various difficult questions by dumping them at the feet of the King for him to resolve by decree. There were other and more impressive aspects to Hobbes's philosophy: he was a link in the notable chain of British 'empiricist' thought that runs from William of Ockham through Locke, Hume and Russell to the present day. But Hobbes's main ambition was to produce a widely acceptable general philosophy that would be consonant with the new science, and in this he failed.

René Descartes (1596–1650) was more successful. His striking answers to the issues raised by the new world-picture captured the imagination of his times, at least for a while. Descartes also enjoyed much greater authority among learned men, because far from being a somewhat eccentric amateur like Hobbes, Descartes was a mathematician and man of science whose importance was quickly recognized to be second only to that of Galileo. In addition, he was more orthodox in his religion than Hobbes, and wisely silent on inflammatory issues of politics.

Descartes felt the urgency of the question that had been neatly put by Montaigne: if so many old views are mistaken, how can we be certain of the new ones? Like Francis Bacon before him, Descartes believed that nothing less than a complete overhaul of the principles of inquiry was required in order to establish confidence in the new ways of thinking. Bacon's own contribution, namely his rules for assembling and collating empirical results, were largely sound, but they did not go far enough. For one thing, they did not address the problem of radical scepticism. How would one defend the new science, or indeed anything at all, against a determined critic who questioned absolutely everything? Only if one could find a way to satisfy such an imaginary opponent, Descartes believed, could the new science be placed on a satisfactory footing. Galileo's system was an impressive structure, and Descartes himself had no doubt that it was correct, but he felt that '[*Galileo's*] building lacks a foundation', and he aimed to provide one.

Bacon had written that 'If a man will begin with certainties, he shall end in doubts; but if he will be content to begin with doubts, he shall end in certainties.' Descartes devised a way to make this aphorism come true, or so he believed. By confronting the most extreme sort of scepticism while also ingeniously exploiting some of its good points, he sought to establish the truth of the new science once and for all. He also tried to show that far from conflicting with religion, the new science actually depended on it. In Descartes' engaging writings, elements of the two Hellenistic philosophies of Pyrrhonian scepticism and Epicurean mechanism came together to provide a novel elaboration of the scientific world-picture. Thus it came about that Western thought regained the vigour that it had lost at the end of antiquity, when philosophy took refuge in the haven of piety.

# Notes

Abbreviations of frequently cited translations:

ATH:  *The Art and Thought of Heraclitus*, edited and translated by C. H. Kahn, Cambridge University Press, 1979.

CDP:  *The Collected Dialogues of Plato*, edited by Edith Hamilton and Huntington Cairns, Princeton University Press, 1963.

CWA:  *The Complete Works of Aristotle*, edited by Jonathan Barnes, Princeton University Press, 1984.

KRS:  *The Presocratic Philosophers*, edited and translated by G. S. Kirk, J. E. Raven and M. Schofield, Cambridge University Press, 2nd edition, 1983.

LOP:  *Lives of the Philosophers*, by Diogenes Laertius, translated by R. D. Hicks, Loeb Classical Library, 1972.

PWD:  *The Philosophical Writings of Descartes*, edited and translated by J. Cottingham, R. Stoothoff, D. Murdoch and A. Kenny, Cambridge University Press, vol. 1 (1984), vol. 2 (1985), vol. 3 (1991).

THP:  *The Hellenistic Philosophers*, edited by A. A. Long and D. N. Sedley, Cambridge University Press, 1987.

References to Presocratic fragments use the standard numbering of H. Diels, *Die Fragmente der Vorsokratiker*, 6th edition (except in the case of Heraclitus, where ATH's numbering is used). References to the works of Plato and Aristotle use the standard pagination of Stephanus and Bekker respectively, followed by the page number in CDP or CWA.

## 1 The Archetypes: *the Milesians*

p. 3 *Seven and sixty years* . . . Diogenes Laertius, *Lives of the Philosophers*, IX, 18 (LOP, vol. 2, p. 427).

p. 3 Nietzsche: *Philosophy in the Tragic Age of the Greeks*, trans. Marianne Cowan, Gateway Editions, 1962, p. 31.

p. 7 *because it floated* . . . Aristotle, *On the heavens*, 294a28 (CWA, p. 484).

p. 8 *It is said that once* . . . Diogenes Laertius, *op. cit.*, I, 34 (LOP, vol. 1 p. 35).

p. 9 *pay penalty* . . . quoted in Simplicius, *On Aristotle's Physics*, 24, 13 (KRS, p. 107).

p. 10 *Hot, Cold, Moist* . . . Milton, *Paradise Lost*, II, 898.

p. 11 *For it behoves* . . . Aristotle, *On the heavens*, 295b10 (KRS p. 133).

p. 15 He says that the heavenly bodies do not move . . . Hippolytus, *Refutatio Omnium Haeresium*, 1, 7, 6 (KRS, p. 154).

p. 16 *Then what is the thunderbolt?* . . . Aristophanes, *Clouds*, 403 (trans. T. G. West and S. T. West in *Four Texts on Socrates*, Cornell University Press, 1984).

p. 16 *loud-crashing Earth-Shaker.* Hesiod, *Theogony*, 441 (Loeb Classical Library edition, trans. H. G. Evelyn-White, p. 111).

p. 16 *the earth, through being drenched* . . . Aristotle, *Meteorology*, 365b6 (KRS, p. 158).

p. 18 *This disease styled sacred* . . . Hippocrates, *The Sacred Disease*, XXI, 1 (Loeb Classical Library edition, trans. W. H. S. Jones, vol. 2).

p. 19 Herodotus: *Histories*, VI, 98.

p. 19 *Any power, any force* . . . G. M. A. Grube, *Plato's Thought*, Methuen, 1935, p. 150.

p. 20 *The power of speech* . . . Aristotle, *Politics*, 1253a14 (CWA, p. 1, 988).

# 2 The Harmony of the World: *the Pythagoreans*

p. 21 *What is the opinion of Pythagoras* . . . Shakespeare, *Twelfth Night*, IV, 2.

p. 22 *of which the main tenets* . . . Bertrand Russell, *History of Western Philosophy*, Allen & Unwin, 1961, p. 29.

p. 22 *Intellectually one of the most important* . . . ibid., p. 49.

p. 22 *Above all, he forbade as food* . . . Diogenes Laertius, *Lives of the Philosophers*, VIII, 19 (LOP, vol. 2, p. 337).

p. 23 *the irritation felt by the plain man* . . . J. Burnet, *Early Greek Philosophy*, Black, 1892, p. 98.

p. 24 *in most respects* . . . Aristotle, *Metaphysics*, 987a30 (CWA, p. 1561).

p. 26 *So, now flaunt your purity!* . . . Euripides, *Hippolytus*, 952 (Penguin, 1953, trans. Philip Vellacott).

p. 26 *practised inquiry* . . . Heraclitus, fragment XXV in ATH.

p. 27 *Leon . . . asked him to name the art* . . . Cicero, *Tusculan Disputations*, V, 3, 8 (Loeb Classical Library Edition, trans. J. E. King, p. 433).

p. 27 *Herein I emulate the Pythagoreans* . . . Proclus, *In Euclidem* (quoted in Sir Thomas Heath, *A History of Greek Mathematics*, Dover Publications, 1981, p. 141).

p. 28 *For surely, Adeimantus* . . . Plato, *Republic*, 500c (CDP, p. 735).

p. 28 *above all because* . . . Bertrand Russell, *The Problems of Philosophy*, Oxford, 1912, p. 94.

p. 29 *he who has been earnest* . . . Plato, *Timaeus*, 90b (CDP, p. 1,209).

p. 29 *through the infinity of the universe* . . . Bertrand Russell, *op. cit.*, p. 92.

p. 31 *the Pythagoreans* . . . Aristotle, *On the heavens*, 300a15 (CWA, p. 492).

p. 33 *The men of old* . . . Plato, *Philebus*, 16d (CDP, p. 1,092).

p. 35 *the one major case* ... G. E. R. Lloyd, *Magic, Reason and Experience,* Cambridge, 1979, p. 146.

p. 35 *Sit, Jessica* ... Shakespeare, *Merchant of Venice,* V, 1.

p. 36 *What happens to men* ... Aristotle, *On the heavens,* 290b27 (CWA, p. 479).

p. 36 *melodious and poetical* ... Aristotle, *On the heavens,* 290b30 (CWA, p. 479).

p. 38 *they were the first* ... Aristotle, *Metaphysics,* 985b24 (CWA, p. 1,559)

p. 39 *theologians would not have sought* ... Bertrand Russell, *History of Western Philosophy,* p. 56.

p. 39 *Their houses* ... Jonathan Swift, *Gulliver's Travels* (1726), III, 2.

p. 40 *the feeling that intellect* ... Bertrand Russell, *My Philosophical Development,* Allen & Unwin, 1959, p. 158.


## 3 The Man Who Searched for Himself: *Heraclitus*

p. 41 *the part I understand* ... Socrates in Diogenes Laertius, *Lives of the Philosophers,* II, 22 (LOP, vol. 1, p. 153).

p. 41 *Death is all things* ... Fr. LXXXIX in ATH.

p. 41 *Lifetime is a child* ... Fr. XCIV in ATH.

p. 41 *the absence of anything enigmatic* ... Charles Kahn in ATH, p. 26.

p. 41 *Nature loves to hide.* Fr. X in ATH.

p. 42 *the prince of impostors.* Fr. XXVI in ATH.

p. 42 *neither declares or conceals* ... Fr. XXXIII in ATH.

p. 43 *I went in search of myself.* Fr. XXVIII in ATH.

p. 43 *You will not find out the limits* ... Fr. XXXV in ATH.

p. 43 *Man's character* ... Fr. CXIV in ATH.

p. 43 *Whatever comes from sight* ... Fr. XIV in ATH.

p. 43 *things unknown.* Fr. XII in ATH.

p. 43 *much learning, artful knavery.* Fr. XXV in ATH.

p. 44 *Men are deceived* ... Fr. XXII in ATH.

p. 44 *men ever fail to comprehend* ... Fr. I in ATH.

p. 44 *All things come to pass* ... Fr. LXXXII in ATH.

p. 44 *All things are one.* Fr. XXXVI in ATH.

p. 44 *Even the potion* ... Fr. LXXVII in ATH.

p. 45 *As they step into the same rivers* ... Fr. L in ATH.

p. 45 *War is father of all* ... Fr. LXXXIII in ATH.

p. 45 *Homer was wrong* ... Fr. LXXXI in ATH.

p. 45 *The death of fire* ... Fr. XLI in ATH.

p. 46 *fire everliving* ... Fr. XXXVII in ATH.

p. 46 *all things are requital* ... Fr. XL in ATH.

p. 47 *Cold warms up* ... Fr. XLIX in ATH.

p. 47 *For souls it is death* ... Fr. CII in ATH.

p. 47 *they are one.* Fr. XIX in ATH.

p. 47 Flann O'Brien: *The Third Policeman*, MacGibbon and Kee Ltd, 1967, chapter 8.

p. 47 *The way up and down* . . . Fr. CIII in ATH.

p. 47 *The same* . . . Fr. XCIII in ATH.

p. 47 *It is disease* . . . Fr. LXVII in ATH.

p. 47 *The sea is the purest* . . . Fr. LXX in ATH.

p. 49 *the views . . . of the professed Heracliteans* . . . Aristotle, *Metaphysics*, 1010a10 (CWA, p. 1,594).

p. 49 *many of our modern philosophers* . . . Plato, *Cratylus*, 411c (CDP, p. 447).

p. 50 *there is no discussing these principles* . . . Plato, *Theaetetus*, 179e (CDP, p. 884).

p. 50 *One cannot step twice* . . . Fr. LI in ATH.

p. 50 *there is nothing stable or permanent* . . . Plato, *Cratylus*, 411c (CDP, p. 447).

p. 51 *persuaded of the truth* . . . Aristotle, *Metaphysics*, 1078b12 (CWA, p. 1,705).

## 4 The Truth About Nothing: *Parmenides*

p. 52 *And the goddess greeted me* . . . Fr. 1, 22 (KRS, p. 242).

p. 53 *Who did you pass* . . . Lewis Carroll, *Through the Looking-Glass*, chapter VII.

p. 54 *We know how to speak many false things* . . . Hesiod, *Theogony*, 27 (Loeb Classical Library edition, trans. H. G. Evelyn-White, p. 81).

p. 54 *both the unshaken heart* . . . Fr. 1, 29 (KRS, p. 242).

p. 56 *what need would have driven it* . . . Fr. 8, 9 (KRS, p. 250).

p. 56 *whole and of a single kind* . . . Fr. 8, 3 (KRS, p. 248).

p. 56 *equally balanced* . . . Fr. 8, 43 (KRS, p. 252).

p. 56 *although these opinions* . . . Aristotle, *On generation and corruption*, 325a18 (CWA, p. 531).

p. 57 *you must hold back your thought* . . . Fr. 7 (adapted from KRS, p. 248).

p. 59 Plato on Parmenides: Plato, *Sophist*, 256c–268c.

p. 59 *His assumption* . . . Aristotle, *Physics*, 186a24 (CWA, p. 318).

p. 59 *look upon thinking* . . . Aristotle, *On the soul*, 427a22 (CWA, p. 679).

p. 59 *there is one being whom I respect above all* . . . Plato, *Theaetetus*, 183e (CDP, p. 888).

p. 62 *said much about the earth* . . . Plutarch, *Adv. Colotem*, III4B (KRS, p. 257).

p. 62 *no thought of mortal men* . . . Fr. 8, 61 (KRS, p. 258).

p. 63 *Parmenides began Philosophy proper.* Hegel, *Lectures on the History of Philosophy*, trans. E. S. Haldane, Kegan Paul, 1892, vol. 1, p. 254.

p. 63 *the transient has no truth.* Hegel, *loc. cit.*

p. 63 *cold bath* . . . Nietzsche, *Philosophy in the Tragic Age of the Greeks*, trans. Marianne Cowan, Gateway Editions, 1962, p. 78.

p. 63 Xenophanes on God: KRS, pp. 169–72.

p. 63 Nietzsche on Xenophanes: *loc. cit.*, p. 69ff.

# 5 The Ways of Paradox: *Zeno*

p. 65 *is in fact a sort of defence* . . . Parmenides, 128c (CDP, p. 922).

p. 66 on the racetrack paradox: see Aristotle, *Physics*, 239b11 (CWA, p. 404); 233a21 (CWA, p. 393); 263a4 (CWA, p. 439).

p. 66 *a pupil of Zeno* . . . Plutarch's *Lives* (Loeb Classical Library edition, trans. Bernadotte Perrin, vol. 3, p. 11).

p. 66 *inventor of dialectic.* Diogenes Laertius, *Lives of the Philosophers*, IX, 25 (LOP, vol. 2, p. 435).

p. 67 *to be refuted in every century* . . . 'Process and Reality' (1932), reprinted in *Essays in Science and Philosophy*, Rider, 1948, p. 87.

p. 67 Russell's treatment: *The Principles of Mathematics*, Unwin, 1903, chapters XLII, LIV; *Our Knowledge of the External World*, Open Court, 1914, lecture VI, 'Mathematics and the Metaphysicians', reprinted in *Mysticism and Logic*, Unwin, 1917.

p. 67 Tolstoy: *War and Peace*, book XI, chapter 1.

p. 67 farce: *Jumpers* by Tom Stoppard, Faber, 1972, pp. 27–8.

p. 68 contemporary physics: *The Natural Philosophy of Time*, by G. J. Whitrow, Oxford, 2nd edition, 1980, pp. 200–5; *Time, Space and Philosophy*, by Christopher Ray, Routledge, 1991, pp. 5–6; *Modern Science and Zeno's Paradoxes*, by Adolf Grunbaum, Wesleyan University Press, 1967.

p. 68 modern commentator: Gregory Vlastos, 'Zeno of Elea', in *The Encyclopaedia of Philosophy*, ed. Paul Edwards, Macmillan, 1967, vol. 8, p. 373.

p. 69 Cantor on infinity: see the works by Russell mentioned above; or 'Infinity' by Hans Hahn, reprinted in *The World of Mathematics*, vol. 3, ed. James Newman, Simon & Schuster, 1956.

p. 69 *the ghosts of departed quantities.* George Berkeley, *The Analyst*, section 35 (reprinted in *A Source Book in Mathematics*, ed. D. E. Smith, New York, 1959, p. 633).

p. 69 arrow paradox: KRS, p. 272–4.

p. 70 Another of his paradoxes: KRS, p. 274–6.

# 6 Love and Strife: *Empedocles*

p. 73 comparison to Faust: E. Zeller, *Outlines of the History of Greek Philosophy*, trans. L. R. Palmer, Meridian Books, 1955, p. 71.

p. 73 *Go forward, Faustus* . . . Marlowe, *The Tragical History of Dr Faustus* (1604), I, 1.

p. 74 Diogenes Laertius, VIII, 68 (LOP, vol. 2, p. 383); Milton, *Paradise Lost*, III, 470; Arnold, *Hymn to Empedocles*.

p. 74 *I go about honoured by all* . . . Fr. 112 (KRS, p. 313).

p. 74 *Fools!* Fr. 11 (KRS, p. 291).

p. 75 *already been once a boy* . . . Fr. 117 (KRS, p. 319).

p. 75 father of rhetoric: Quoted in Diogenes Laertius, IX, 25 (LOP, vol. 2, p. 435).

p. 75 *of all mortal things* . . . Fr. 8 (KRS, p. 291).

p. 75 *comply with custom.* Fr. 9 (KRS, p. 291).

p. 76 *men . . . seize pigments* . . . Fr. 23 (KRS, p. 293).

p. 79 *Here sprang up many faces* . . . Fr. 57 (KRS, p. 303).

p. 80 *Most of the parts of animals* . . . Aristotle, *Physics*, 196a23 (CWA, p. 335).

p. 80 *survived, being organized spontaneously* . . . Aristotle, *Physics*, 198b30 (CWA, p. 339).

p. 80 *We here see* . . . Charles Darwin, 'An Historical Sketch of the Progress of Opinion on the Origin of Species, previously to the Publication of This Work', appended to 6th edition of *The Origin of Species* (1872), fn1.

p. 80 *nothing to say.* Aristotle, *Rhetoric*, 1407a34 (CWA, p. 2,244).

p. 80 *colour is an effluence* . . . Plato, *Meno* 76d (CDP, p. 359).

p. 81 *for thrice ten thousand years* . . . Fr. 115 (KRS, p. 315).

p. 82 *For nine years* . . . Hesiod, *Theogony*, 801 (Loeb Classical Library edition, trans. H. G. Evelyn-White, p. 137).

p. 82 *an exile from the gods* . . . Fr. 115 (KRS, p. 315).

p. 82 *Alas that the pitiless day* . . . Fr. 139 (KRS, p. 319).

p. 82 *in an alien garment* . . . Fr. 126 (KRS, p. 316).

p. 82 *Among them was no war-god* . . . Fr. 128 (KRS, p. 318).

p. 82 *All things were tame and gentle* . . . Fr. 130 (KRS, p. 318).

p. 83 *But at the end they come* . . . Frs. 146, 147 (KRS, p. 317).

p. 83 *Come now, observe with all your powers* . . . Fr. 3 (KRS, p. 285).

# 7 Mind and Matter: *Anaxagoras*

p. 84 *I do not believe* . . . Plato, *Apology*, 26d (CDP, p. 12).

p. 85 *filled full of the so-called* . . . Plutarch, *Life of Pericles*, V (Loeb Classical Library edition, trans. Bernadotte Perrin, p. 13).

p. 85 Socrates on the rhetorical powers of Pericles: Plato, *Phaedrus*, 269 (CDP, p. 515).

p. 86 *from the ancient days* . . . Cicero, *Tusculan Disputations*, V, IV, 10 (Loeb Classical Library edition, trans J. E. King, p. 435).

p. 87 *When I was young* . . . Plato, *Phaedo*, 96a (CDP, p. 78).

p. 88 *How could hair* . . . Fr. 10 (KRS, p. 369).

p. 89 *things . . . appear different* . . . Aristotle, *Physics*, 187b3 (CWA, p. 320).

p. 89 *corn also, when it is being ground* . . . Lucretius, *On the Nature of Things*, 1, 880 (Loeb Classical Library edition, trans. W. H. D. Rouse and M. F. Smith, p. 73).

p. 90 *parts which only reason* . . . Aetius, *Placita*, I, 3, 5 (KRS, p. 375).

p. 90 *Appearances are a glimpse* . . . Fr. 21 (KRS, p. 383).

p. 90 *Neither is there a smallest* . . . Fr. 3 (trans. after Zeller; cf. KRS, p. 360).

p. 91 *And it began to rotate* . . . Fr. 12 (KRS, p. 363).

p. 91 *there are some things in which* . . . Fr. 11 (KRS, p. 366).

p. 91 *all knowledge about everything* . . . Fr. 12 (KRS, p. 363).

p. 93 *I knew that my children* . . . Diogenes Laertius, *Lives of the Philosophers*, II, 13 (LOP, vol. 1, p. 143).

p. 93 *Have you no concern* . . . Diogenes Laertius, *ibid.*, II, 7 (LOP, vol. 1, p. 137).

# 8  He Who Laughs Last: *Democritus*

p. 94 *Do not be suspicious* . . . [etc.] Frs. 91, 43, 61 (trans. J. M. Robinson in *An Introduction to Early Greek Philosophy*, Boston, 1968, pp. 227, 235).

p. 96 *When man's life* . . . *On the Nature of Things*, 1.62 (Loeb Classical Library edition, trans. W. H. D. Rouse and Martin Smith, p. 8).

p. 96 *on the King of Persia:* Fr. 118.

p. 97 *these atoms move* . . . Simplicius, *De caelo*, 242 (KRS, p. 426).

p. 97 *creatures . . . flock together* . . . Fr. 164 (KRS, p. 420).

p. 98 *On sweet things, etc.:* Theophrastus, *De causis plantarum*, 6, 1, 6.

p. 98 *On thunder:* Aetius, *Placita*, III, 3, 1 (trans. C. Bailey in *The Greek Atomists and Epicurus*, Oxford, 1928, p. 153).

p. 99 *the motes in the air* . . . Aristotle, *On the soul*, 404a2 (CWA, p. 644).

p. 99 *The hidden nature of a thing* . . . Lamery, *Cours de Chymie* (1675), quoted in F. M. Cornford, *Before and after Socrates*, Cambridge, 1932, p. 26.

p. 100 *Melissus:* Fr. 8 (KRS, p. 399).

p. 101 *The same thing* . . . *Metaphysics*, 1009b3 (CWA, p. 1,593).

p. 101 *By convention sweet* . . . Fr. 9 (KRS, p. 410).

p. 101 *colours as names:* Parmenides, Fr. 8 (KRS, p. 252).

p. 102 *He expressly declares* . . . Sextus Empiricus, *Adversus Mathematicos*, VII, 139 (Loeb Classical Library edition, trans. R. G. Bury, vol. 2, p. 77).

p. 102 *Whenever I conceive* . . . Galileo, *Il Saggiatore* (1623), quoted in *Discoveries and Opinions of Galileo*, trans. Stillman Drake, Anchor Books, 1957, p. 274.

p. 102 *an atomical philosophy* . . . cited in Charles Singer, *A Short History of Scientific Ideas to 1900*, Oxford, 1959, p. 273.

p. 103 *nothing in the Objects* . . . *An Essay concerning Human Understanding* (1690), II, 8, 10.

p. 104 *elementary particles of various types* . . . Steven Weinberg, *The Discovery of Subatomic Particles*, Penguin, 1993.

p. 105 *In some worlds there is* . . . Hippolytus, *Refutatio Omnium Haeresium*, 1, 13, 2 (KRS, p. 418).

p. 105 *from infinite time* . . . *On the Nature of Things*, V, 422 (Loeb Classical Library edition, trans. W. H. D. Rouse and Martin Smith, p. 409).

p. 105 *The Selfish Gene*, Oxford, 2nd edition, 1989, pp. 1, 2, 13.

p. 106 *emerged from the ground* ... Lactantius, *Institutiones divinae*, VII.7.9, (trans. J. M. Robinson, *op.cit.*, p. 216).

p. 106 pupils of animals: Fr. 154.

p. 107 indulgence in education: Fr. 178.

p. 107 *A man who wants children* ... Fr. 277 (trans. J. M. Robinson, *op. cit.*, p. 227).

p. 108 *a sophistical rhetorician* ... Benjamin Disraeli in *The Times*, 29 July 1878.

## 9 Opening Pandora's Box: *the Sophists*

p. 109 *Mighty indeed* ... Thucydides, *The Peloponnesian War*, II, 41 (trans. Rex Warner, Penguin, 1954, p. 148).

p. 109 *Our constitution* ... ibid., II, 37 (p. 145).

p. 110 *We Athenians* ... ibid., II, 40 (p. 147).

p. 110 *And here we have a map of the world* ... Aristophanes, *Clouds*, 206.

p. 111 *The proper care* ... Plato, *Protagoras*, 318e (CDP, p. 317).

p. 112 Hippias at the Games: Plato, *Lesser Hippias*, 368b.

p. 113 *I have never found* ... ibid., 364a (CDP, p. 201).

p. 113 *The whole of life* ... Antiphon, Fr. 51 (trans. Kathleen Freeman, *Ancilla to the Pre-Socratic Philosophers*, Harvard, 1948, p. 150).

p. 113 *Life is like* ... Fr. 50 (*loc. cit.*).

p. 113 *the art of the sophist* ... Aristotle, *Topics*, 165a (CWA, p. 279).

p. 114 *Gorgias said that you should* ... Aristotle, *Rhetoric*, 1419b2 (CWA, p. 2,268).

p. 114 *we must be able to employ persuasion* ... ibid., 1355a29 (CWA, p. 2,154).

p. 114 One associate of Socrates: Xenophon, *Memorabilia*, 1, VI, 13.

p. 114 *makes the weaker argument defeat* ... Plato, *Apology*, 19b (CDP, p. 5).

p. 115 *Has one of the Sophists* ... Plato, *Meno*, 92b (CDP, p. 376).

p. 115 *I loathe that* ... Eupolis (in *Socrates: A source book*, compiled by John Ferguson, Macmillan, 1970, p. 173).

p. 115 *You have seen it for yourself* ... Plato, *Apology*, 18b (CDP, p. 5).

p. 116 *I must try* ... ibid., 19a (CDP, p. 5).

p. 116 *I have never countenanced* ... ibid., 33a (CDP, p. 18).

p. 116 *lads when they first get a taste* ... Plato, *Republic*, 539b (CDP, p. 771).

p. 118 Gorgias on communication: Fr. 3 (trans. Kathleen Freeman, *op. cit.*, p. 129).

p. 118 *the power of speech* ... Gorgias, Fr. 11 (14) (*loc. cit.*, p. 133).

p. 118 *persuasion, when added to speech* ... Gorgias, Fr. 11 (13) (*loc. cit.*, p. 132).

p. 119 *Man is the measure of all things.* Protagoras, Fr. 1 (KRS, p. 411, n1).

p. 120 *is to me such as it appears* ... Plato, *Theaetetus*, 152a (CDP, p. 856).

p. 120 *Sometimes, when the same wind* ... ibid., 152b (CDP, p. 857).

p. 121 *There remains the question of dreams* ... ibid., 157e (CDP, p. 862).

p. 121 *if Protagoras is right* ... Plato, *Cratylus*, 386c (CDP, p. 424).

p. 122 *The true is the name* ... William James, *Pragmatism* (1907), Lecture II (Harvard University Press edition, 1975, p. 42).

p. 122 *wise and honest public speakers* ... Plato, *Theaetetus*, 167c (CDP, p. 873).

p. 124 *if anyone were to propose* ... Herodotus, *Histories*, III, 38 (trans. H. Carter, Oxford, 1962, p. 182).

p. 125 Locke and Rousseau: John Locke, *Second Treatise on Civil Government* (1690); Jean-Jacques Rousseau, *Du Contrat social* (1762).

p. 125 *the laws of men* ... Antiphon, Fr. 44 (trans. J. M. Robinson, *An Introduction to Early Greek Philosophy*, Boston, 1968, p. 251).

p. 125 *most of the things* ... Antiphon, *loc. cit.*

p. 125 *custom, the tyrant* ... Plato, *Protagoras*, 337d (CDP, p. 331).

p. 125 *if the case* ... Antiphon, *loc. cit.* (p. 252).

p. 127 *The eye of Zeus* ... Hesiod, *Works and Days*, 264 (trans. D. Wender, Penguin, 1973, p. 67).

p. 128 *About the gods* ... Protagoras, Fr. 4 (trans. K. Freeman, *op. cit.*, p. 126).

## 10  Philosophy's Martyr: *Socrates and the Socratics*

p. 131 *[y]ou are mistaken* ... Plato, *Apology*, 28b (CDP, p. 14).

p. 131 *started wrestling* ... Plato, *Symposium*, 220c (CDP, p. 571).

p. 132 *fell into a fit* ... ibid., 174d, 175b (CDP, pp. 529–30).

p. 132 *I have never lived* ... Plato, *Apology*, 36b (CDP, p. 21).

p. 132 *anyone who is close* ... Plato, *Laches*, 187e (CDP, p. 131).

p. 133 *who had only to put his flute* ... Plato, *Symposium*, 215b (CDP, p. 566).

p. 133 *speaking for myself* ... ibid., 215d (CDP, p. 567).

p. 134 *I've been bitten* ... ibid., 218a (CDP, p. 569).

p. 134 *The first step, then* ... Xenophon, *The Banquet*, V (trans. adapted from E. C. Marchant and O. J. Todd, *Xenophon*, Loeb Classical Library edition, vol. 4, p. 599).

p. 139 *After puzzling about it* ... Plato, *Apology*, 21b (CDP, p. 7).

p. 139 *I reflected as I walked away* ... ibid. 21d (CDP, p. 7).

p. 139 *whenever I succeed* ... ibid., 23a (CDP, p. 9).

p. 140 *the arguments never* ... Plato, *Theaetetus*, 161a (CDP, p. 866).

p. 140 *If I say that this* ... Plato, *Apology*, 37e (CDP, p. 23).

p. 140 *it has always been* ... Plato, *Crito*, 46b (CDP, p. 31).

p. 141 *in obedience to God's commands* ... Plato, *Apology*, 33c (CDP, p. 19).

p. 141 *I want you to think* ... ibid., 22a (CDP, p. 8).

p. 141 *when it comes* ... ibid., 31d (CDP, p. 17).

p. 142 *I spend all my time* ... ibid., 30a (CDP, p. 16).

p. 142 *ashamed that you give* ... ibid., 29e (CDP, p. 22).

p. 142 *these people give you* ... ibid., 36e (CDP, p. 22).

p. 142 Apollodorus: Xenophon, *Socrates' Defence*, 28.

p. 143 *to be afraid of death* ... Plato, *Apology*, 29a (CDP, p. 15).

p. 143  *heroes of the old days* . . . ibid., 41b (CDP, p. 25).

p. 143  *the work of* . . . Plato, *2nd Letter*, 314c (CDP, p. 1, 567).

p. 144  *All his private conduct* . . . Xenophon, *Memoirs of Socrates*, IV (trans. E. C. Marchant, Loeb Classical Library edition, p. 309).

p. 144  *that stuffy old prig.* Jonathan Barnes, *The Presocratic Philosophers*, Routledge, 1982, p. 448.

p. 145  modern scholars: particularly Gregory Vlastos, *Socrates: Ironist and Moral Philosopher*, Cambridge, 1991; *Socratic Studies*, Cambridge, 1994.

p. 146  *purified* . . . Plato, *Phaedo*, 67c–d (CDP, p. 50).

p. 147  *mathematics has come to be* . . . Aristotle, *Metaphysics*, 992a32 (CWA, p. 1,568).

p. 147  *our birth is but a sleep* . . . Wordsworth, 'Intimations of Immortality' (1807) V.

p. 148  *we have helped him* . . . Plato, *Meno*, 84b (CDP, p. 368).

p. 149  *At present these opinions* . . . ibid., 85c (CDP, p. 370).

p. 149  *I shall question him* . . . Plato, *Apology*, 29e (CDP, p. 370).

p. 149  *sometimes, however* . . . Plato, *Lesser Hippias*, 372d (CDP, p. 209).

p. 150  *I am full of defects* . . . ibid., 372b (CDP, p. 209).

p. 151  *an accurate knowledge of all that.* Plato, *Euthyphro*, 5a (CDP, p. 172).

p. 151  *Is what is holy* . . . ibid., 10a (CDP, p. 178).

p. 151  *Those who believe that God* . . . Leibniz, *Theodicy* (1710), 176 (trans. E.M. Huggard, Open Court, 1985, p. 236).

p. 152  *We must not limit our inquiry* . . . Aristotle, *Magna Moralia*, 1182a4 (CWA, p. 1,868).

p. 152  *he thought all the virtues* . . . ibid., 1216b2 (adapted from CWA, p. 1,925).

p. 153  *he is doing away with* . . . ibid., 1182a21 (CWA, p. 1,868).

p. 153  *No one, he said, acts* . . . Aristotle, *Nicomachean Ethics*, 1145b27 (CWA, p. 1,810).

p. 154  *in the strength of his character* . . . K. Joel (quoted in W. K. C. Guthrie, *Socrates*, Cambridge, 1971, p. 138).

p. 154  *Evil, be thou my Good.* Milton, *Paradise Lost*, IV.110.

p. 154  *no one would choose evil* . . . Aristotle, *Magna Moralia*, 1200b26 (CWA, p. 1,900).

p. 154  *divine naïveté* . . . Nietzsche, *The Birth of Tragedy* (1872), 13 (trans. W. Kaufmann, Random House, 1967, p. 88).

p. 154  *wisdom full of pranks.* Nietzsche, *Der Wanderer und sein Schatten* (1880), 86.

p. 155  *This was Socrates' Muse* . . . Galen, *On the Use of the Parts of the Body*, I, 9.

p. 155  *mutilated by* . . . Plato, *Crito*, 47e (CDP, p. 33).

p. 155  *nothing can harm* . . . Plato, *Apology*, 41d (CDP, p. 25).

p. 155  *the difficulty is not* . . . ibid., 39b (CDP, p. 24).

p. 156  *to live well means* . . . Plato, *Crito*, 48b (CDP, p. 33).

p. 156 *the just [man] is happy* . . . Plato, *Republic*, 354a (CDP, p. 604).

p. 158 *So there is every* . . . Plato, *Gorgias*, 507b (CDP, p. 289).

p. 158 *Those who say that the victim* . . . Aristotle, *Nicomachean Ethics*, 1153b19 (CWA, p. 1,823).

p. 158 *if you are serious* . . . Plato, *Gorgias*, 481c (CDP, p. 265).

p. 158 *it is no ordinary matter* . . . Plato, *Republic*, 352d.

p. 162 *A Socrates gone mad.* Diogenes Laertius, *op. cit.*, VI, 54 (LOP, vol. 2, p. 55).

p. 164 *travelled around with her husband* . . . *ibid.* VI, 96 (as trans. J. M. Rist in *Stoic Philosophy*, Cambridge, 1969, p. 61).

p. 165 *wrangling Euclides* . . . Timon of Phlius, in Diogenes Laertius, *op.cit.*, II, 107 (LOP, vol. 1, p. 237).

p. 165 *O Stranger* . . . Athenaeus, *Deipnosophistai*, IX, 410E (trans. St George Stock in *Stoicism*, London, 1908, p. 36).

p. 165 Gödel's Theorem: see *Gödel's Proof*, by E. Nagel & J. R. Newman, London, 1959.

p. 167 *I know how to produce* . . . Plato, *Gorgias*, 474a (CDP, p. 256).

p. 168 *If you put me to death* . . . Plato, *Apology*, 30e (CDP, p. 16).


## 11 The Republic of Reason: *Plato*

p. 169 *one who feels no* . . . (etc.) Plato, *Republic*, 475c–e (CDP, p. 714–5).

p. 169 *delight in beautiful* . . . (etc.) *ibid.*, 476b–c (CDP, p. 715).

p. 170 *I imagine that whenever the mind* . . . Roger Penrose, *The Emperor's New Mind*, Oxford, 1989, p. 428.

p. 170 *the workings of the actual* . . . *ibid.*, p. 159.

p. 171 *things are not* . . . Plato, *Cratylus*, 386c (CDP, p. 424).

p. 172 *must set himself to be* . . . (etc.) Plato, *Symposium*, 210b–d (CDP, p. 562).

p. 172 *And now, Socrates* . . . *ibid.*, 210e (CDP, p. 562).

p. 172 Mystical philosophers and early Christian writers: Plotinus, *Enneads*, 1, 6, 8–9. Origen: *De Principis*, II, xi, 7. St Augustine: *Confessions*, 9, 10.

p. 174 *when names, definitions* . . . Plato, *7th Letter*, 344b (as trans. W. K. C. Guthrie, *A History of Greek Philosophy*, Cambridge, 1978, vol. 5, p. 410).

p. 175 *withdrew in disgust* . . . *ibid.*, 325a (CDP, p. 1,575).

p. 176 *the justest man* . . . *ibid.*, 324e (CDP, p. 1,575).

p. 176 *some of those in control.* *ibid.*, 325b (CDP, p. 1,575).

p. 176 *finally saw clearly* . . . *ibid.*, 326a (CDP, p. 1,576).

p. 176 *I found myself utterly at odds* . . . (etc.) *ibid.*, 326b–d (CDP, p. 1,576).

p. 177 *liberty for the Syracusans* . . . *ibid.*, 324b (CDP, p. 1,574).

p. 177 *set before him* . . . (etc.) *ibid.*, 327a–b (CDP, p. 1,576).

p. 177 *a regimen that counts* . . . Plutarch, *Life of Dion*, IV, 6 (trans. Bernadotte Perrin, Loeb Classical Library edition, p. 9).

p. 178 *how many subjects* . . . Plato, *7th Letter*, 340d (CDP, p. 1,588).

p. 179 *I feared to see myself* . . . ibid., 328c (CDP, p. 1,578).

p. 179 *forsook my own pursuits* . . . ibid., 329b (CDP, p. 1,578).

p. 179 *The young king once* . . . Plutarch, *Life of Dion*, VII, 7 (Loeb Classical Library edition, p. 17).

p. 180 *It makes no difference* . . . (etc.) Plato, *Republic*, 592b (CDP, p. 819).

p. 181 *you must look at the matter* . . . Plato, *Republic*, 343c (CDP, p. 593).

p. 181 *no one could be found* . . . ibid., 360b (CDP, p. 607).

p. 182 *what it is that* . . . ibid., 367e (CDP, p. 614).

p. 183 *a change to a new type of music* . . . ibid., 424c (CDP, p. 666).

p. 183 Allan Bloom: *The Closing of the American Mind*, Simon & Schuster, 1987.

p. 184 *to represent the evil* . . . Plato, *Republic*, 401b (CDP, p. 646).

p. 184 *the multitude* . . . (etc.) ibid., 431d (CDP, p. 673).

p. 185 *was not impracticable* . . . ibid., 456c (CDP, p. 695).

p. 186 *certain ingenious lots* . . . ibid., 460a (CDP, p. 699).

p. 186 *the offspring of the good* . . . ibid., 460c (CDP, p. 699).

p. 186 *distasteful topic.* ibid., 502d (CDP, p. 738).

p. 186 *from fathers* . . . ibid., 461a (CDP, p. 700).

p. 187 *our purpose was not* . . . ibid., 472c (CDP, p. 711).

p. 187 *Do you think* . . . ibid., 472d (CDP, p. 711).

p. 187 *the smallest change* . . . ibid., 473b (CDP, p. 712).

p. 187 *those whom we now call* . . . ibid., 473d (CDP, p. 712).

p. 188 *altogether the best* . . . ibid., 540a (CDP, p. 771).

p. 188 *do not fall short of* . . . ibid., 484d (CDP, p. 721).

p. 188 *a mind habituated* . . . ibid., 486a (CDP, p. 722).

p. 188 *a cowardly and illiberal spirit* . . . ibid., 486b (CDP, p. 722).

p. 188 *strivers after truth* . . . ibid., 485d (CDP, p. 722).

p. 189 *when they have thus beheld* . . . ibid., 540a (CDP, p. 771).

p. 190 *And if* . . . *one should* . . . ibid., 515d (CDP, p. 748).

p. 190 *at this point he* . . . ibid., 516b (CDP, p. 749).

p. 191 *what passed for wisdom there.* ibid., 516c (CDP, p. 749).

p. 191 *provoke laughter* . . . (etc.) ibid., 517a (CDP, p. 749).

p. 192 *uneducated and inexperienced* . . . ibid., 519c (CDP, p. 751).

p. 192 *linger there* . . . ibid., 519d (CDP, p. 752).

p. 192 *the law is not* . . . ibid., 519e (CDP, p. 752).

p. 192 *Down you must go* . . . ibid., 520c (CDP, p. 752).

p. 192 *the fourth and final* . . . ibid., 544c (CDP, p. 773).

p. 192 *hereditary principalities* . . . ibid., 544d (CDP, p. 774).

p. 194 *high-spirited* . . . (etc.) ibid., 548c (CDP, p. 777).

p. 194 *from being lovers* . . . ibid., 551a (CDP, p. 779).

p. 194 *Suppose men* . . . ibid., 551c (CDP, p. 780).

p. 194 *chock-full* . . . (etc.) ibid., 557b (CDP, p. 785).

p. 194 *a garment* . . . ibid., 557d (CDP, p. 786).

p. 195 *the tolerance* . . . ibid., 558a (CDP, p. 786).

p. 195 *he establishes . . . ibid.*, 561b (CDP, p. 789).

p. 195 *a kind of equality . . . ibid.*, 558c (CDP, p. 786).

p. 196 *day by day . . . ibid.*, 561c (CDP, p. 789).

p. 196 *so sensitive . . . ibid.*, 563d (CDP, p. 791).

p. 196 *the father . . . ibid.*, 562e (CDP, p. 791).

p. 196 *the horses and asses . . . ibid.*, 563c (CDP, p. 791).

p. 196 *the exploited group . . .* (etc.) Peter Singer, *Animal Liberation*, Thorsons, 1983, p. xii.

p. 197 *finally pay no heed . . .* Plato, *Republic*, 563d (CDP, p. 792).

p. 197 *devise that famous . . . ibid.*, 566b (CDP, p. 794).

p. 197 *trying to escape . . . ibid.*, 569b (CDP, p. 797).

p. 198 *Our dreams . . . ibid.*, 572b (as trans. C. M. A. Grube and C. D. C. Reeve, Hackett, 1992, p. 242).

p. 198 *are awakened in sleep . . . ibid.*, 571c (CDP, p. 798).

p. 198 *either his nature . . . ibid.*, 573c (trans. Grube and Reeve, p. 243).

p. 198 *full of slavery . . . ibid.*, 577d (trans. Grube and Reeve, p. 248).

p. 198 *so far from finding . . . ibid.*, 579e (CDP, p. 806).

p. 199 *ill-governed in his own soul. ibid.*, 579c (CDP, p. 806).

p. 200 *pleasures mixed . . . ibid.*, 586b (trans. Grube and Reeve, p. 257).

p. 200 *those who have no experience . . . ibid.*, 586a (trans. Grube and Reeve, p. 257).

p. 200 twentieth-century critics: Sir Karl Popper, *The Open Society and its Enemies*, Routledge, 1945, vol. 1.

p. 201 *preferably indwelling . . .* Plato, *Republic*, 590d (CDP, p. 818).

p. 201 *we don't allow . . . ibid.*, 590e (adapted from Grube and Reeve, p. 262).

p. 202 *expert craftsmen . . . ibid.*, 395c (CDP, p. 640).

p. 202 *unity is the greatest . . . ibid.*, 464b (CDP, p. 703).

p. 202 *There comes a point . . .* Aristotle, *Politics*, 1263b (as trans. T. A. Sinclair, Penguin, 1962, p. 65).

p. 202 *when they meet . . . ibid.*, 1281b (CWA, p. 2,033).

p. 203 *there are some arts . . . ibid.*, 1282a (CWA, p. 2,034).

p. 204 *the world is . . .* Plato, *Timaeus*, 29a (CDP, p. 1,162).

p. 205 *it is not to be conceived . . . Principia* (2nd edition, 1713), General Scholium to Book III (in *Newton's Philosophy of Nature*, Hafner, 1953, p. 42).

p. 205 Kant: *Theory of the Heavens* (1755) and *The Only Possible Ground for a Proof of the Existence of God* (1763). See also *Kant and The Exact Sciences*, by Michael Friedman, Harvard, 1992, pp. 11–13.

p. 205 Hume: *Dialogues Concerning Natural Religion* (1779).

p. 207 *that in man . . .* R. L. Nettleship, *Lectures on the Republic of Plato*, Macmillan, 1901, p. 220.

p. 208 *craftsmen do not . . .* Plato, *Gorgias*, 503e (CDP, p. 286).

p. 209 *Where the Christian says . . .* G. M. A. Grube, *Plato's Thought*, Methuen, 1935, p. 150.

p. 210 *Enough if we adduce . . . Timaeus*, 29c (CDP, p. 1,162).

p. 211 *a figure that . . . ibid.*, 33c (as trans. by D. Lee, *Timaeus and Critias*, Penguin, 1971, p. 45).

p. 211 *a moving image of eternity. ibid.*, 37d (CDP, p. 1,167).

p. 212 *Mind, the ruling power . . . ibid.*, 48a (CDP, p. 1,175).

p. 213 *if they were created . . . ibid.*, 41c (CDP, p. 1,170).

p. 213 *who were cowards . . .* (etc.) *ibid.*, 91–2 (CDP, pp. 1,210–11).

p. 214 *on the joints of the bones . . . ibid.*, 74e (CDP, p. 1,197).

p. 214 *thus producing insatiable . . . ibid.*, 73a (CDP, p. 1,195).

p. 215 *no man is voluntarily bad . . . ibid.*, 86e (CDP, p. 1,206).

p. 215 *the influence of . . .* (etc.) George Sarton, *Ancient Science Through the Golden Age of Greece*, 1952 (Dover edition, 1993, pp. 423 and 430).

p. 216 *Linnaeus and Cuvier . . .* Charles Darwin, Letter to William Ogle, 1882 (*Darwin's Life and Letters*, ed. F. Darwin, 1887, London, vol. 3 p. 252).

p. 216 *There is a fault . . .* Lucretius, *On the Nature of Things*, IV, 823 (adapted from the Loeb Classical Library edition trans. W. H. D. Rouse and M. F. Smith, p. 341).

p. 217 *he answered me . . .* Robert Boyle, *Disquisition about the Final Causes of Natural Things* (1688) (quoted in *A History of Embryology*, by Joseph Needham, Cambridge, 2nd edition, 1959, p. 59, n1. Spelling and punctuation modernized).

p. 217 Heisenberg: see *The Advancement of Science and its Burdens*, by Gerald Holton, Cambridge, 1986, pp. 122, 144, 151, 162.

p. 218 Popper: *Conjectures and Refutations*, Routledge, 5th edition, 1974, p. 89.

p. 218 *A man may sometimes . . .* Plato, *Timaeus*, 59c (CDP, p. 1,184).

p. 219 *natural, or no less real . . .* Plato, *Laws*, 890d (CDP, p. 1,446).


# 12 The Master of Those Who Know: Aristotle

p. 221 *nature does not give weapons . . .* Aristotle, *Generation of Animals*, 759b (CWA, p. 1,176).

p. 221 history of embryology: Joseph Needham, *A History of Embryology*, Cambridge, 2nd edition, 1959, p. 56.

p. 222 *speculations apparently . . .* John Herschel, *A Preliminary Discourse on the Study of Natural Philosophy* (1830), Chicago, 1987, p. 11.

p. 222 *master of those who know.* Dante, *Inferno*, IV, 131.

p. 000 *How fortunate that man was . . .* Descartes, Letter to Plempius, 15 February 1638 (PWD, vol. 3, p. 79).

p. 223 *I may tell you . . .* Descartes, Letter to Mersenne, 28 January 1641 (PWD, vol. 3, p. 173).

p. 223 *The longest tyranny . . .* John Dryden, 'To Dr Charleton' (1662).

p. 224 *Such appears to be the truth . . .* Aristotle, *Generation of Animals*, 760b (CWA, p. 1,178).

p. 224 *We must survey* . . . Aristotle, *Nicomachean Ethics*, 1179a (CWA, p. 1,863).

p. 224 *not only admitted experience* . . . Galileo, *Letters on Sunspots* (1613), trans. Stillman Drake, *Discoveries and Opinions of Galileo*, Doubleday, 1957, p. 118.

p. 225 *in the whole range of times past* . . . Aristotle, *On the heavens*, 270b (CWA, p. 451).

p. 225 *his knowledge had included* . . . Galileo, *op. cit.*, p. 118.

p. 226 seventeenth-century Italian critic: Lodovico Castelvetro (1505–71).

p. 226 layman's guide to science: Bryan Appleyard, *Understanding the Present*, Pan, 1992, p. 27.

p. 226 *moved more jubilantly* . . . Herbert Butterfield, *The Origins of Modern Science*, Bell & Hyman, 2nd edition, 1957, p. 6.

p. 227 *Plato is dear to me* . . . traditional attribution (perhaps based on *Nicomachean Ethics*, 1096a).

p. 227 *Orders were given* . . . Pliny the Elder, *Natural History*, VII.44 (trans. J. Healy, Penguin, 1991, p. 114).

p. 228 *sin twice against philosophy*. *Life of Aristotle* (5th century AD), attributed to Ammonius Hermiae or John Philoponus.

p. 228 *All men by nature* . . . Aristotle, *Metaphysics*, 980a (CWA, p. 1,552).

p. 228 *a natural instinct* . . . Aristotle, *Rhetoric*, 1355a (CWA, p. 2,154).

p. 230 *is beautiful because* . . . Plato, *Phaedo*, 100c (CDP, p. 81).

p. 230 *to speak abstractly and idly*. Aristotle, *Eudemian Ethics*, 1217b (CWA, p. 1,927).

p. 231 *we can dismiss* . . . Aristotle, *On the Soul*, 412b (CWA, p. 657).

p. 231 *the loftier interest* . . . Aristotle, *Parts of Animals*, 645a (CWA, p. 1,004).

p. 233 *Of substances constituted* . . . *loc. cit.*, 644b (CWA, p. 1,003).

p. 233 *for each and all* . . . (etc.) *loc. cit.*, 645a (CWA, p. 1,004).

p. 234 *why shouldn't nature work* . . . Aristotle, *Physics*, 198b (trans. after J. L. A. Ackrill, *Aristotle the Philosopher*, Oxford, 1981, p. 41).

p. 234 *For teeth and all* . . . *loc. cit.*, 198b (CWA, p. 339).

p. 237 British clergyman: William Buckland, *Geology and Mineralogy Considered with Reference to Natural Theology*, London, 1836.

p. 237 *exist for the sake of* . . . Aristotle, *Politics*, 1256b (CWA p. 1,993).

p. 237 *I consider the customary search* . . . Descartes, *Meditations*, IV (PWD, vol. 2, p. 39).

p. 238 *the love that moves* . . . Dante, *Paradiso*, Canto XXXIII.

p. 246 *We assume the gods* . . . Aristotle, *Nicomachean Ethics*, 1178b (CWA, p. 1,862).

p. 249 *hold good for everything that is* . . . Aristotle, *Metaphysics*, 1005a (CWA, p. 1,587).

p. 251 *above the natural philosopher* . . . (etc.). *loc. cit.*, 1005a (CWA, p. 1,587).

p. 251 *must inquire also* . . . *loc. cit.*, 1005b (CWA, p. 1,587).

p. 251 *certain things being stated* . . . Aristotle, *Prior Analytics*, 24b (CWA, p. 40).

p. 152 *That some deductions* . . . Aristotle, *Sophistical Refutations*, 164a (CWA, p. 278).

p. 253 *See how the Fates* . . . Gilbert and Sullivan, *The Mikado*.

p. 255 *Barbara celarent* . . . from the *Introductiones in Logicam* by William of Shyreswood (thirteenth century), quoted in William and Martha Kneale, *The Development of Logic*, Oxford, 1962, p. 232.

p. 255 *to all appearances* . . . Immanuel Kant, *Critique of Pure Reason* (1787), trans. Norman Kemp Smith, Macmillan, 1929, p. 17.

p. 255 *the form to which* . . . Richard Whately, *Elements of Logic* (1826), 9th edition, p. 13.

p. 255 *the universal types* . . . J. S. Mill, *System of Logic* (1843), II, 2, 1.

p. 255 Augustus de Morgan: see his *On the Syllogism & Other Logical Writings* (1846–68), Routledge, 1966.

p. 256 Stoic logic: see Benson Mates, *Stoic Logic*, University of California Press, 1961.

p. 256 Galen: see ' "A third sort of syllogism": Galen and the logic of relations', by Jonathan Barnes, in *Modern Thinkers & Ancient Thinkers*, ed. R. W. Sharples, London, 1993.

p. 257 *a kind of universal mathematics* . . . Leibniz, *New Essays on Human Understanding* (1703–5), IV, 7 (trans. P. Remnant and J. Bennett, Cambridge, 1981, p. 478).

p. 257 *The only way to rectify* . . . Leibniz, 'The Art of Discovery' (1685), trans. P. Wiener in *Leibniz Selections*, Scribners, 1951, pp. 51–2.

p. 257 *a language whose signs* . . . Leibniz, 'Towards a Universal Characteristic' (1677), trans. P. Wiener (*op. cit.*, p. 18).

p. 258 Lull: see Martin Gardner, *Logic Machines and Diagrams*, Harvester, 1983, chapter 1.

p. 258 *By ratiocination I mean* . . . Hobbes, *Elements of Philosophy* (1656), 1, 2.

p. 258 Boole: *The Mathematical Analysis of Logic* (1847).

p. 259 Peirce: *Reasoning and the Logic of Things* (1898) (ed. K. L. Ketner, Harvard, 1992).

p. 259 Frege: *Begriffschrift* (1879) (trans. and ed. T. W. Bynum, Oxford, 1972).

p. 259 recent scholarship: H. Putnam, 'Peirce the Logician', in his *Realism with a Human Face*, Harvard, 1990; W. Quine, 'Peirce's Logic' (1989), in his *Selected Logic Papers*, enlarged edition, Harvard, 1995; W. Goldfarb, 'Logic in the 20s', in *Journal of Symbolic Logic*, 49 (1979), pp. 351–368.

p. 259 logic and computers: see Martin Davis, 'Mathematical Logic and the Origin of Modern Computing' and 'Influences of Mathematical Logic on Computer Science', both in *The Universal Turing Machine*, ed. R. Herken, Oxford, 1988.

p. 262 *It is the mark of an educated man* . . . Aristotle, *Nicomachean Ethics*, 1094b (CWA, p. 1,730).

p. 263 *the whole account* . . . *ibid.*, 1104a (CWA, p. 1,743).

p. 265 *old customs* . . . (etc.) Aristotle, *Politics*, 1268b (CWA, p. 2,013).

p. 265 *superior refinement and active disposition* . . . Aristotle, *Nicomachean Ethics*, 1095b (CWA, p. 1,731).

p. 266 *just as for a flute-player* . . . ibid., 1097b (CWA, p. 1,735).

p. 267 *in accordance with* . . . ibid., 1098a (CWA, p. 1,735).

p. 267 *for one swallow* . . . ibid., 1098a (CWA, p. 1,735).

p. 267 *sufficiently equipped with external goods.* ibid., 1101a (CWA, p. 1,739).

p. 268 *fall short of or exceed* . . . ibid., 1107a (CWA, p.1,748).

p. 268 *moral excellence is concerned* . . . ibid., 1106b (CWA, p. 1,747).

p. 269 *Aristotle's works are full of platitudes* . . . J. O. Urmson, *Aristotle's Ethics*, Blackwell, 1988, p. 71.

p. 270 *the life according to intellect* . . . Aristotle, *Nicomachean Ethics*, 1178a (CWA, p. 1,862).

p. 270 *best thing in us* . . . (etc.) ibid., 1177a (CWA, pp. 1,860–61).

p. 272 *we must not follow* . . . (etc) ibid., 1177b (CWA, p. 1,861).

p. 272 *in a secondary degree* . . . (etc.) ibid., 1178a (CWA, p.1,862).

p. 272 *shall we not* . . . ibid., 1094a (CWA, p. 1,729).

p. 272 *we are inquiring* . . . ibid., 1103b (CWA, p. 1,743).

p. 272 *master art.* ibid., 1094a (CWA, p. 1,729).

p. 272 *It makes no small difference* . . . (etc.). ibid., 1103b (CWA, p. 1,743).

p. 273 *it is through laws* . . . ibid., 1180b (CWA, p. 1,866).

p. 273 *that which is always* . . . Aristotle, *Metaphysics*, 1027a (CWA, p. 1,622).

p. 274 *poetry is something* . . . Aristotle, *Poetics*, 1451a (trans. after T. S. Dorsch, *Classical Literary Criticism*, Penguin, 1965, pp. 43–4).

p. 274 *consists in rejoicing* . . . (etc.). Aristotle, *Politics*, 1340a (CWA, p. 2,126).

p. 275 *hymns to the gods* . . . Plato, *Republic*, 607a (CDP, p. 832).

p. 275 *Tragedy is* . . . Aristotle, *Poetics*, 1449b (CWA p. 2,320).

p. 276 *like ourselves* (etc.). ibid. 1453a–1454a (CWA, p. 2,325):

p. 277 *might lead a timorous man* . . . R. Janko, 'From Catharsis to the Aristotelian Mean', in *Essays on Aristotle's Poetics*, edited by A. O. Rorty, Princeton, 1992, p. 352.

p. 278 *in inspiring the pleasure of the ridiculous* . . . (etc.). Umberto Eco, *The Name of the Rose* (trans. Warren Weaver, Picador, 1985, p. 468).

p. 278 *if one day* . . . loc. cit. pp. 476–8.

p. 279 *Because it was by the Philosopher* . . . loc. cit., p. 473.

# 13 Three Roads to Tranquillity: *Epicureans, Stoics and Sceptics*

p. 283 *Empty are the words* . . . quoted in Porphyry's *To Marcella*, 31 (THP, p. 155).

p. 284 *so easily grasped* . . . Cicero, *Tusculan Disputations*, IV, 3 (Loeb Classical Library edition, trans. J. E. King, p. 335).

p. 286 *in accordance with nature*. Stobaeus, *Anthologium*, II, 75 (THP, p. 394).

p. 291 *notorious midnight philosophizings*. Diogenes Laertius, *Lives of the Philosophers*, X, 7 (LOP, vol. 2, p. 585).

p. 291 *the world is filled* ... John of Salisbury, *Policraticus* (1159), VIII, 24 (trans. H. Jones, in his *The Epicurean Tradition*, Routledge, 1989, p. 140).

p. 291 *Serenely full* ... Sydney Smith, 'Recipe for A Salad'.

p. 292 *sex is never* ... Epicurus, *Vatican Sayings*, 51 (THP, p. 116).

p. 292 *Roman vice* ... W. E. H. Lecky, *History of European Morals*, Longmans, 1882, vol. 1, p. 231.

p. 292 *when we say that pleasure* ... Epicurus, *Letter to Menoeceus*, 131 (THP, p. 114).

p. 293 *the impossibility* ... Epicurus, *ibid.*, 132 (THP, p. 114).

p. 293 *the just life* ... Epicurus, *Key Doctrines*, 17 (THP, p. 125).

p. 294 *immortal*. Epicurus, *Vatican Sayings*, 78 (THP, p. 126)

p. 294 *It is more pleasurable* ... Plutarch, *Against Epicurean Happiness*, 1097A (THP, p. 126).

p. 294 *the undisturbed man* ... Epicurus, *Vatican Sayings*, 79 (THP, p. 126).

p. 294 *Nature has placed* ... Bentham, *Introduction to the Principles of Morals and Legislation* (1789), I, 1.

p. 294 *the greatest happiness* ... Bentham, *Deontology* (1834), vol. 1, p. 300.

p. 294 *calculation and survey* ... Epicurus, *Letter to Menoeceus*, 130 (THP, p. 114).

p. 295 *We must liberate ourselves* ... Epicurus, *Vatican Sayings*, 58 (THP, p. 126).

p. 295 *an activity* ... Sextus Empiricus, *Adversus Mathematicos*, II, 169 (THP, p. 156).

p. 295 *What is insatiable* ... Epicurus, *Vatican Sayings*, 59 (THP, p. 116).

p. 295 *fears concerning* ... Epicurus, *Key Doctrines*, 10 (THP, p. 115).

p. 295 *mind and spirit* ... (etc.) Lucretius, *On the Nature of Things*, III, 161–176 (trans. R. Latham, Penguin, 1951, p. 101).

p. 296 *seeing that when we* ... Epicurus, *Letter to Menoeceus*, 125 (THP, p. 150).

p. 296 *a correct understanding* ... (etc.). Epicurus, *ibid.*, 124–126 (THP, pp. 149–50).

p. 297 *they are delicate* ... Lucretius, *op. cit.*, IV, 726 (THP, 74).

p. 297 *opinions, on the other hand* ... (etc.). Sextus Empiricus, *Adversus Mathematicos*, VII, 210 (THP p. 81).

p. 299 *If you fight* ... Epicurus, *Key Doctrines*, 23 (THP, p. 80).

p. 300 *do not trump up* ... Lucretius, *ibid.*, IV, 386 (THP, p. 82).

p. 301 *storm-tossed* ... Lucretius, *ibid.*, IV, 1076 (Penguin, p. 163).

p. 301 *you assure yourself* ... Lucretius, *ibid.*, IV, 1066 (p. 163).

p. 301 *Body clings greedily* ... Lucretius, *ibid.*, IV, 1108 (p. 164).

p. 302 *sprite* (etc.) Lucretius, *ibid.*, IV, 1162–1167 (p. 166).

p. 302 *in her physical nature* ... Lucretius, *ibid.*, IV, 1174 (p. 167).

p. 302 *Vent the seed* ... Lucretius, *ibid.*, IV, 1065 (p. 163).

p. 302 *an alluring face* ... Lucretius, *ibid.*, IV, 1033 (p. 162).

p. 302 *Food and fluid* . . . Lucretius, *ibid.*, IV, 1091 (p. 164).

p. 303 *no collision* . . . Lucretius, *ibid.*, II, 222 (p. 66).

p. 303 *a piece of childish fancy.* Cicero, *De finibus*, I, 6 (Loeb Classical Library edition, trans. H. Rackham, p. 23).

p. 304 *it would be better* . . . Epicurus, *Letter to Menoeceus* (THP, p. 102).

p. 304 *if all movement* . . . Lucretius, *op. cit.*, II, 251 (Penguin, p. 67).

p. 305 *science thereby withdraws,* . . . A. S. Eddington, *The Nature of the Physical World* (1928), Everyman's Library edition, 1935, p. 284.

p. 305 *if it is a matter* . . . A. J. Ayer, 'Freedom and Necessity', in his *Philosophical Essays*, Macmillan, 1954, p. 275.

p. 306 *for a comprehensive view* . . . Epicurus, *Letter to Herodotus*, 35 (LOP, vol. 2, p. 567).

p. 306 *we must grasp* . . . Epicurus, *ibid.*, 37 (THP, p. 87).

p. 306 *keep thought always* . . . C. Bailey, *The Greek Atomists and Epicurus*, Oxford, 1928, p. 235.

p. 306 *all our notions* . . . Diogenes Laertius, *Lives of the Philosophers*, X, 32 (LOP, vol. 2, p. 561).

p. 307 *When the winds* . . . Lucretius, *op. cit.*, II, 1 (trans. A. A. Long in his *Hellenistic Philosophy*, University of California Press, 1974, p. 74).

p. 308 *You, who out of black darkness* . . . Lucretius, *op. cit.*, III, 1 (Penguin, p. 96).

p. 308 *Do not seek* . . . Epictetus, *Encheiridion*, 8 (Loeb Classical Library edition of Epictetus, trans. W. Oldfather, vol. 2, p. 491).

p. 308 *It is not the things* . . . Epictetus, *ibid.*, 5 (p. 489).

p. 312 *Under all forms* . . . B. Ward and R. Dubos, *Only One Earth* (Penguin, 1972, p. 83). Quoted in A. A. Long, *op. cit.*, p. 158.

p. 313 *Never say about anything* . . . Epictetus, *op. cit.*, 11 (p. 491).

p. 314 *no one will ever* . . . Epictetus, *ibid.*, 1 (p. 483).

p. 314 *Withdraw into yourself.* Marcus Aurelius, *Meditations*, VII, 28 (trans. A. S. L. Farquharson, Everyman, 1992, p. 47).

p. 314 *The happy man* . . . Seneca, *On Sophistical Argumentation*, 9 (trans. R. M. Gummere, *Epistulae Morales*, Loeb Classical Library edition, vol. 1, p. 295).

p. 314 *I deny that riches* . . . Seneca, *On the Happy Life*, 24 (trans. J. W. Basore, *Moral Essays*, Loeb Classical Library edition, vol. 2, p. 165).

p. 315 *be not troubled* . . . Marcus Aurelius, *Meditations*, VIII, 5 (p. 53).

p. 317 *a certain imperious* . . . Aulus Gellius, *Attic Nights*, VII, 2 (trans. J. B. Gould in his *The Philosophy of Chrysippus*, SUNY Press, 1970, p. 148).

p. 317 *The story goes* . . . Diogenes Laertius, *Lives of the Philosophers*, VII, 23 (THP, p. 389).

p. 320 *the doer and source of all* (etc.) Aeschylus, *Agamemnon*, 1,485 (trans. P. Vellacott, Penguin, 1956, p. 94).

p. 320 *Why is it that God* . . . Seneca, *On Providence*, IV (trans. J. W. Basore, *Moral Essays*, Loeb Classical Library edition, vol. 1, p. 29).

p. 321 *Evil of every sort* . . . Seneca, *op. cit.*, VI (p. 43).

p. 322 *Nature made us relatives* . . . Seneca, *Epistle* XCV.

p. 322 Epictetus on self-interest: *Discourses*, II, 10.

p. 322 *Her husband is lucky.* Epictetus, *op. cit.*, II, 18.

p. 323 *There have ever been stern* . . . W. E. H. Lecky, *op. cit.*, vol. 1, p. 172.

p. 324 *Place me in the midst* . . . (etc.) Seneca, *On the Happy Life*, 25 (trans. J. W. Basore, *Moral Essays*, Loeb Classical Library edition, vol. 2, p. 165).

p. 325 *He was always in the same mental state* . . . Diogenes Laertius, *Lives of the Philosophers*, IX, 63 (THP, p. 13).

p. 325 *avoiding nothing* . . . Diogenes Laertius, *ibid.*, IX, 62 (THP, p. 13).

p. 325 *often* . . . *he would leave* . . . Diogenes Laertius, *ibid.*, IX, 63 (LOP, vol. 2, p. 477).

p. 325 *although he practised philosophy* . . . Diogenes Laertius, *ibid.*, IX, 62 (THP, p. 13).

p. 326 *unloosed the shackles* . . . Timon, Fr. 822 (THP, p. 18).

p. 327 *neither our sensations* . . . Aristocles, quoted in Eusebius, *Praeparatio evangelica*, 14, 18 (THP, p. 15).

p. 327 *Nobody knows* . . . Xenophanes, Fr. 34 (KRS, p. 179).

p. 327 *The Ethiopians* . . . Xenophanes, Fr. 16 (KRS, p. 169).

p. 328 *less intelligent than a banjo.* Timon, Fr. 812 (LOP, vol. 2, p. 127).

p. 329 *nothing is honourable* . . . Diogenes Laertius, *op. cit.*, IX, 61 (adapted from THP, p. 13).

p. 330 *Sceptics are philanthropic* . . . Sextus Empiricus, *Outlines of Pyrrhonism*, III, 280 (trans. J. Annas and J. Barnes as *Outlines of Scepticism*, Cambridge, 1994, p. 61).

p. 330 *no impression* . . . Cicero, *Academica*, II, 78 (THP, p. 243).

p. 332 *in persuasiveness* . . . Diogenes Laertius, *op. cit.*, IV, 37 (LOP, vol. 1, p. 415).

p. 332 *a Pyrrhonian* . . . David Hume, *An Enquiry Concerning Human Understanding* (1748), XII.

p. 332 *how is it that* . . . Plutarch, *Adversus Colotem*, 1122e (THP, p. 450).

p. 333 *That honey is sweet* . . . Timon, quoted in Diogenes Laertius, *op. cit.*, IX, 105 (THP, p. 15).

p. 333 *laws and customs* . . . Sextus Empiricus, *op. cit.*, I, 231 (*loc. cit.*, p. 61).

p. 334 *adopted the practice* . . . Eusebius, *Praeparatio Evangelica*, 14, 7, 15 (trans. J. Hankinson, in his *The Sceptics*, Routledge, 1995, p. 95).

p. 335 *When they suspended* . . . Sextus Empiricus, *op. cit.* I, 29 (p. 11).

p. 336 *make firm assertions* . . . Sextus Empiricus, *ibid.*, I, 208 (p. 53).

p. 337 *When we say that Sceptics* . . . Sextus Empiricus, *ibid.*, I, 13 (p. 6).

p. 337 *go along with.* Sextus Empiricus, *ibid.*, 230 (p. 61).

p. 338 *everyday observances.* Sextus Empiricus, *ibid.*, I, 23 (p. 9).

p. 338 *in conformity with his ancestral customs* . . . Sextus Empiricus, *Adversus Mathematicos*, IX, Loeb Classical Library (edition of Sextus, trans. R. G. Bury, vol. 3, p. 29).

p. 338 *from an everyday point of view.* Sextus Empiricus, *Outlines of Pyrrhonism*, I, 24 (*op. cit.*, p. 9).

p. 338 *depend on passive* . . . Sextus Empiricus, *ibid.*, I, 22 (p. 9).

p. 338 *for this, like Agriculture and Navigation* . . . Sextus Empiricus, *Adversus Mathematicos*, V, 2 (*op. cit.*, vol. 4, p. 323).

p. 341 *Sceptics . . . employ weighty arguments* . . . Sextus Empiricus, *Outlines of Pyrrhonism*, III, 280 (p. 216).

p. 341 *an ability to set out* . . . Sextus Empiricus, *ibid.*, I, 8 (p. 4).

p. 341 *it is no doubt easy* . . . Sextus Empiricus, *ibid.*, I, 112 (p. 29).

p. 342 *profess to hunt down* . . . Philo of Alexandria (c. 30 BC–AD 45), *On drunkenness*, 198 (trans. J. Annas and J. Barnes in their *The Modes of Scepticism*, Cambridge, 1985, p. 155).

p. 342 *there have been countless inquiries* . . . Philo of Alexandria, *op. cit.*, 202 (p. 156).

p. 343 *All his life* . . . Pierre Bayle, *Historical and Critical Dictionary* (1697), 'Pyrrho' (trans. R. Popkin, Hackett, 1991, p. 194).

p. 344 *perpetually troubled* . . . (etc.) Sextus Empiricus, *Outlines of Pyrrhonism*, I, 27 (p. 10).

p. 344 *we agree that* . . . (etc.) Sextus Empiricus, *ibid.*, I, 29 (p. 11).

## 14 The Haven of Piety: *From Late Antiquity to the Renaissance*

p. 346 *And so let me anchor* . . . Proclus, *Hymns* (quoted in *Outlines of the History of Greek Philosophy*, by Eduard Zeller, trans. L. Palmer, New York, 1957, p. 337).

p. 347 *hath no otherwise place* . . . Hobbes, *Leviathan* (1651), IV, 46 (punctuation modernized).

p. 347 *the kind of degenerate learning* . . . Francis Bacon, *The Advancement of Learning* (1605), L, iv, 5.

p. 351 *the lust of the eyes* . . . (etc.) St Augustine, *Confessions*, X, xxxv (trans. H. Chadwick, Oxford, 1991, p. 211).

p. 353 *a literate man* . . . C. S. Lewis, 'Imagination and thought in the Middle Ages' (1956) in his *Studies in Medieval and Renaissance Literature*, Cambridge, 1966, p. 43.

p. 358 Scotus on angels and space: see Helen Lang's *Aristotle's Physics and its Medieval Varieties*, SUNY Press, 1992, chapter 8.

p. 360 *fashioned by God* . . . Alcinous, *Didaskalikos*, 12 (trans. J. Reedy as *The Platonic Doctrines of Albinus*, Phanes Press, 1991, p. 42).

p. 360 *without motion himself* . . . Alcinous, *ibid.*, 10 (p. 38).

p. 360 *contemplate eternally* . . . Alcinous, *loc. cit.* (p. 39).

p. 360 *most marvellous providence.* Alcinous, *ibid.*, 12 (p. 42).

p. 360 *one contemplates first* . . . Alcinous, *ibid.*, 12 (p. 40).

p. 361 *the heavenly ladder* . . . (etc.) Plato, *Symposium*, 211c–d (CDP, p. 563).

p. 361 Numenius on Plato: quoted in Clement of Alexandria, *Stromateis*, 1.21.

p. 361 *a summary of Plato's principal teachings* . . . Alcinous, *op. cit.*, 1 (p. 21).

p. 362 *learning to know* . . . Hermes Trismegistus, *Asclepius*, 12 (trans. E. R. Dodds in his *Pagan and Christian in an Age of Anxiety*, Cambridge, 1965, p. 92).

p. 364 *some 20,000 facts* . . . Pliny, *Natural History*, preface (trans. J. Healy, Penguin, 1991, p. 5).

p. 364 *A surprising fact* . . . Pliny, *ibid.*, XXVIII, 36 (p. 255).

p. 364 *The most carefully researched authorities* . . . Pliny, *ibid.*, XXXVI, 109 (p. 356).

p. 364 *For what reason our forefathers* . . . Aulus Gellius, *Attic Nights* (trans. J. C. Rolfc, Locb Classical Library edition).

p. 366 *seemed ashamed* . . . Porphyry, *Life of Plotinus*, 1 (trans. A. H. Armstrong in the Loeb Classical Library edition of Plotinus, vol. 1, p. 3).

p. 366 *nothing can be affirmed of it* . . . Plotinus, *Enneads*, III, 8, 10 (trans. S. MacKenna, Penguin, 1991, p. 246).

p. 367 *supremely adequate* . . . Plotinus, *ibid.*, VI, 9, 6 (p. 542).

p. 368 *beauty beyond beauty.* Plotinus, *ibid.*, VI, 7, 32 (p. 501).

p. 368 *the soul looks upon the wellspring of life* . . . Plotinus, *ibid.*, VI, 9, 8–9 (p. 545).

p. 368 *When the soul begins* . . . Plotinus, *ibid.*, VI, 9, 11 (p. 548).

p. 369 *is apt to prove wearisome.* Hegel, *Lectures on the History of Philosophy*, I, 3, C, 2 (trans. E. S. Haldane, Kegan Paul, 1892, vol. 2, p. 407).

p. 370 *our way then takes us beyond knowing.* Plotinus, *op. cit.*, VI, 9, 4 (p. 540).

p. 370 *proof . . . evidence* . . . (etc.) Plotinus, *ibid.*, VI, 9, 10 (p. 547).

p. 371 *by the efficacy* . . . Iamblichus, *De mysteriis*, 96, 13 (trans. E. R. Dodds, in *The Greeks and the Irrational*, California, 1951, p. 287).

p. 372 *a power higher* . . . Proclus, *Platonic Theology* (trans. E. R. Dodds, *ibid.*, p. 291).

p. 372 *attack mathematically everything in nature.* Iamblichus, *On the Common Mathematical Science*, 32 (trans. G. E. R. Lloyd in his *Greek Science After Aristotle*, Norton, 1973, p. 156).

p. 374 *would not have been created* . . . A. C. Lloyd in *The Cambridge History of Later Greek and Early Medieval Philosophy*, ed. A. H. Armstrong, Cambridge, 1967, p. 305.

p. 374 Dionysius in the Bible: Acts of the Apostles, 17.34.

p. 376 *denying or removing* . . . (etc.) Pseudo-Dionysius, *Mystical Theology*, 2 (trans. F. C. Copleston in his *History of Philosophy*, Doubleday, 1962, vol. 2, p. 95).

p. 377 *have said things which are true* . . . Augustine, *Confessions*, III, vi (p. 41).

p. 378 *distinguish the difference* . . . Augustine, *ibid.*, VII, xx (p. 130).

p. 378 *There are none* . . . Augustine, *City of God*, VIII, 5 (trans. H. Bettenson, Penguin, 1972, p. 304).

p. 378 *If these men* . . . Augustine, *De vera religione,* 7 (trans. H. Bettenson, *ibid.,* p. 304, n10).

p. 378 *Truth, truth* . . . Augustine, *Confessions,* III, vi (p. 40).

p. 378 *not to study* . . . Augustine, citing Cicero's *Hortensius* [now lost], *ibid.,* III, iv (p. 39).

p. 378 *unworthy in comparison* . . . Augustine, *ibid.,* III, v (p. 40).

p. 378 *men proud of their slick talk* . . . Augustine, *ibid.,* III, vi (p. 40).

p. 379 *one of being seduced* . . . Augustine, *ibid.,* IV, i (p. 52).

p. 380 *Away with* . . . Tertullian, *On Prescription against Heretics,* VII (trans. E. Gilson in his *Reason and Revelation in the Middle Ages,* Scribners, 1954, p. 9).

p. 381 *the Platonists* . . . Augustine, *City of God,* VIII, 11 (p. 313).

p. 382 *If I am deceived, I exist!.* Augustine, *ibid.,* XI, 26.

p. 383 *wanted to be as certain* . . . Augustine, *Confessions,* VI, iv (p. 95) p. 385

p. 385 *the lynching of Hypatia* . . . Bertrand Russell, *History of Western Philosophy,* p. 365.

p. 386 *But this is completely erroneous* . . . Philoponus, *Commentary on Aristotle's Physics,* 683 (trans. in *A Source Book in Greek Science,* ed. M. Cohen and I. Drabkin, Harvard, 1966, p. 220).

p. 388 *slippery Fortune.* Boethius, *The Consolation of Philosophy,* I, v (trans. V. E. Watts, Penguin, 1969, p. 47).

p. 388 *Grant, Father* . . . Boethius, *ibid.,* III, ix (p. 97).

p. 389 *my servant Plato.* Boethius, *ibid.,* I, iii (p. 39).

p. 392 *a single argument* . . . St Anselm, *Proslogion,* Preface (trans. in *Medieval Philosophy,* ed. J. Wippel and A. Wolter, Free Press, 1969, p. 154).

p. 392 *something than which* . . . St Anselm, *loc. cit.,* 2 (p. 155).

p. 393 *It is not your sublimity* . . . St Anselm, *loc. cit.,* 1 (p. 155).

p. 393 *Since I preferred* . . . Abelard, *Historia Calamitatum* (trans. J. T. Muckle, Pontifical Institute of Medieval Studies, 1954, p. 12).

p. 394 *success always puffs up fools* . . . (etc.) Abelard, *ibid.* (pp. 25–7).

p. 399 *Let it be added* . . . John of Jandun, quoted and trans. in *Reason and Revelation in the Middle Ages,* by Etienne Gilson, Scribners, 1954, p. 63.

p. 401 *for the sake of brevity* . . . William of Ockham, *Tractatus de successivis,* ed. P. Boehner, New York, 1944, p. 37.

p. 405 Luther on Copernicus: see T. S. Kuhn, *The Copernican Revolution,* Harvard, 1957, p. 191.

p. 406 *There is a* . . . *single vast immensity* . . . (etc) Giordano Bruno, *De l'infinito universo e mondi* (1584) (trans. D. W. Singer, cited in A. Koyre, *From the Closed World to the Infinite Universe,* Johns Hopkins, 1968, pp. 40 and 42).

p. 407 *new Philosophy calls* . . . John Donne, *An Anatomy of the World* (1611).

p. 409 *'No man is a stone . . .'* Lorenzo Valla (1405–87), *Opera Omnia,* II, 739, Turin, 1962 (trans. in *Renaissance Philosophy,* by B. P. Copenhaver and C. B. Schmitt, Oxford, 1992, p. 226).

p. 410 *it is safer* . . . *The Notebooks of Leonardo da Vinci* (trans. E. MacCurdy, cited in *Sources of the Western Tradition*, vol. 1, ed. M. Perry et al., Houghton Mifflin, 1987, p. 303).

p. 411 *unknown to the ancients* . . . (etc.). Amerigo Vespucci, *Mundus Novis* (trans. in *The Philosophy of the 16th and 17th Centuries*, ed. R. Popkin, Free Press, 1966, pp. 29–30).

p. 412 Christopher Marlowe: *The Massacre at Paris* (1592), 389.

p. 413 *Human knowledge* . . . Francis Bacon, *Novum Organum* (1620), I, 3 (trans. P. Urbach and J. Gibson, Open Court, 1994, p. 43).

p. 413 *the knowledge of Causes* . . . Francis Bacon, *New Atlantis* (c. 1623) (ed. A. Johnston, Oxford, 1974, p. 239).

p. 414 *many things . . . work upon the spirits of man* . . . Francis Bacon, *De Augmentis* (1623) (trans. B. Copenhaver in *The Cambridge History of Renaissance Philosophy*, ed. C. B. Schmidt and Q. Skinner, Cambridge, 1988, p. 296).

p. 414 Newton's alchemical manuscripts: see 'Isaac Newton: Alchemist and Fundamentalist', by Martin Gardner, *Skeptical Inquirer*, September/October 1996, pp. 13–16.

p. 414 *nature is* . . . Marsilio Ficino, *De vita coelitus comparanda* (1489) (adapted from translation in Copenhaver, *op. cit.*, p. 274).

p. 415 *there is no department* . . . Pico della Mirandola, *Conclusiones* (1486) (trans. Copenhaver, *op. cit.*, p. 270).

p. 415 *one scarcely knows* . . . B. Copenhaver and C. Schmidt, *Renaissance Philosophy*, Oxford, 1992, p. 289.

p. 415 *Was not Plato perfectly right* . . . Galileo, *Discorsi* (1638), II, 175 (trans. H. Crew and A. de Salvio, *Dialogues Concerning Two New Sciences*, Dover, 1954, p. 137).

p. 418 *Nothing reveals* . . . Ficino, *Liber de sole* (1576), trans. T. S. Kuhn in his *The Copernican Revolution*, Harvard, 1957, p. 130.

p. 418 *In the middle of all* . . . (etc.) Copernicus, *De revolutionibus* (1543), I, 10 (trans. J. F. Dobson and S. Brodetsky, cited in Kuhn, *op. cit.*, p. 131).

p. 420 *Are you married?* . . . François Rabelais, *Gargantua and Pantagruel*, III (1546), chapter 36 (trans. T. Urquhart and P. Le Motteux, Everyman, 1994, p. 442).

p. 421 *Since Ptolemy* . . . Michel de Montaigne, *Essais* (1580), II, 12 (trans. M. Screech, Penguin, 1991, p. 644).

p. 421 *the very pestilence* . . . Agrippa von Nettesheim, *De incertitude et vanitate scientarium* (English translation of 1569, quoted in *The History of Scepticism*, by R. Popkin, Berkeley, 1979, p. 24).

p. 421 *human affairs* . . . Erasmus, *In Praise of Folly* (1511), 45 (trans. B. Radice, Penguin, 1971, p. 135).

p. 422 *Nothing is more characteristic* . . . Martin Luther, *Selections from his Writings*, ed. J. Dillenberger, New York, 1961, pp. 168–9.

p. 422 *I put no trust* . . . Martin Luther, *Final answer at the Diet of Worms* (1521) (trans. H. Bettenson in *Documents of the Christian Church*, Oxford, 1963, p. 201).

p. 422 *conscious of the darkness* . . . Pierre Bayle, 'Pyrrho', *Historical and Critical Dictionary* (1697) (trans. R. Popkin, Hackett, 1991, p. 194).

p. 426 *it follows that in the Sacrament* . . . *Archive of the Sacred Congregation for the Doctrine of the Faith* (cited in *Galileo: Heretic*, by Pietro Redondi, Penguin, 1989, p. 334).

p. 426 *great automaton.* Robert Boyle, *Origin of Forms and Qualities* (1666), in *Selected Philosophical Papers of Robert Boyle*, ed. M. A. Stewart, Hackett, 1991, p. 71.

p. 427 *experience is the balance* . . . Pierre Gassendi, *The Selected Works of Pierre Gassendi*, ed. C. B. Brush, Johnson Reprint Corporation, 1972, p. 40.

p. 428 *no proposition* . . . Pierre Gassendi, *ibid.*, p. 102.

p. 429 *poor, nasty, brutish and short.* Thomas Hobbes, *Leviathan*, I. 13.

p. 431 *[Galileo's] building lacks a foundation.* Descartes, Letter to Mersenne, 11 September 1638 (PWD, vol. 3, p. 124).

p. 431 *If a man will begin* . . . Francis Bacon, *The Advancement of Learning*, I, v, 8.

# Index